C Programming
for UNIX®

C Programming
for UNIX®

John Valley

SAMS
PUBLISHING

A Division of Prentice Hall Computer Publishing
11711 North College, Carmel, Indiana 46032 USA

Copyright © 1992 by Sams Publishing

Trademarks

Dedication

The support and encouragement of friends and relatives is important to any large undertaking such as this book has been. My brothers, Jim and Clarence, both of whom share my fascination with computers, have provided an ever-ready companionship and understanding that is of great value to me. I present this book to each of you with pride and affection.

Overview

Contents

Contents

Acknowledgments

I would like to thank Joe Wikert at Prentice Hall Computer Publishing for originally suggesting the idea for this book. His idea seemed crazy at the time, considering the large number of books already published on the subject of C language programming, but he was persuasive, and now the book is done. I hope it was worth the effort.

Stacy Hiquet also deserves my thanks, at least as much for her patience during the long gaps between delivery of each chapter as for her helpfulness and support during the author review and production stages. Thanks, Stacy.

Tad Ringo edited the text. Authors and editors often have their disagreements, and the relationship is one that both parties approach with some trepidation. Tad, however, has done a very creditable job and I could not help but notice that his changes often improved the manuscript. I would be very pleased to have Tad as the editor for my next book.

About the Author

John Valley lives in Richmond, Virginia with his wife, Terri, and a labrador retriever named Brandon. As evidence of current employment he points to a small computer consulting and software development business operated out of his home, and a rather persistent tendency to write books about computer programming.

His programming experience includes machine-language coding for a variety of old computers, assembly language development of applications and operating-system software for IBM System/360 and System/370 mainframes, a period of several grueling years when he was repeatedly forced to write COBOL programs, and six years of C language programming for UNIX and DOS systems. He has spent a dozen years developing source-code management tools for mainframe and UNIX systems along the lines described in Chapter 16 of this book, and says that he most enjoys developing tools that help other programmers.

He enjoys classical music, plays the violin, goes to local theater productions as often as possible, reads lots of science fiction, makes terrible puns, and takes frequent breaks from writing to play with his dog.

Introduction

The C programming language, once used only at universities and research labs, has become a popular computer programming language for scientific, graphical, and business computing. With popularity also comes diversity, and C is no exception. There are C compilers for UNIX, C compilers for MS-DOS, and C compilers for OS/2. There is an old K&R version of the language, a newer ANSI standard version, and an unofficial C++ advanced version of the language.

C Programming for UNIX is intended to serve the needs of several different groups.

For the beginner, this book contains 18 chapters that teach the ANSI C programming language, starting at the beginning and covering the entire range of language features.

For the experienced C programmer, the second part of this book examines the tools and libraries specific to the UNIX environment for programming in C. These chapters should be of special interest to those who have prior experience with MS-DOS versions of the language, such as Turbo C or Microsoft C, and who now need to use their language skills in the UNIX environment.

For everyone, this book contains a comprehensive reference section summarizing the syntax of ANSI C, the functions in the UNIX standard libraries, and the many UNIX commands available to and specially designed for the C programmer.

How This Book Is Organized

C Programming for UNIX is divided into three parts:

- Part I, "The C Programming Language," teaches the syntax and usage of the ANSI standard C programming language. Read this part if you don't know C or need to brush up on the ANSI standard definition of the language.

- Part II, "The UNIX Programming Environment," discusses the function libraries customarily found in UNIX systems, and the commands and utilities used to create and edit source files, to compile source files into object form, to link object modules together, and to analyze and maintain programs. Read this part if you already know the ANSI C language but are unfamiliar with UNIX.

- Part III, "Reference," contains material of interest to all C programmers. The many tables in Part III describe the syntax of the language, the functions in the standard libraries, the differences between K&R and ANSI C, and the syntax of UNIX commands of special interest to programmers.

Conventions

This book uses a number of stylistic conventions to help you understand and interpret technical descriptions. Conventions are absolutely necessary when discussing C and UNIX, where command names often look like ordinary words (for example, `read` or `if`). If you take a minute to review these notes, you will find the text much easier to understand.

- Parts of a UNIX command or C language statement which you must type exactly as shown appear in a `computer` font similar to computer printing:

  The `-i` option of the `typeset` command...

- Command output and examples also appear in a `computer` font. In examples, the portion that you type appears in a **bold computer** font:

```
$ echo Hello
Hello
$
```

- The variable parts of a command's syntax appear in an *italic computer* font in the command description, and in the explanatory text that follows it:

```
cat -v filename
```

For *filename*, specify the filename or path of the file to be printed.

- Optional parts of a command are enclosed in brackets:

```
cd [ dirname ]
```

Notice that the brackets are not part of the command.

- *Italics* highlight technical terms when they first appear in the text, and are sometimes used to emphasize important points.

- The notation ^x indicates a control character that you enter by pressing the Control key and the x key at the same time:

Enter ^d when you finish typing your input.

Terminal Keys

Most computer books can refer to keyboard keys by their real names, so if the book mentions the Enter key you can look down at your keyboard and find a key labeled *Enter*. This is true because most software in the world today is written for one specific manufacturer's hardware. The situation is quite different with UNIX. UNIX in general, and the UNIX described in this book in particular, is purposely designed to run on a wide variety of computer systems.

Usually this portability is an advantage. It also implies, however, that no author of UNIX books can know how the keys are labeled on your terminal.

UNIX users have evolved a body of terminology to refer to terminal keys which often bear strikingly little relationship to any real keyboard. This way, nobody's products receive undue preference.

Table I.1 presents the most commonly used names for terminal keys. I use these key names throughout this book because they are already familiar to UNIX people.

Table I.1. UNIX terminal key names.

Key Name	Function of the Key
^	Often called *control*, *ctrl*, *Ctrl*, or *CTRL*, this key, when pressed while simultaneously pressing a letter key or opening bracket ([), generates an ASCII code from 0 to 37 octal.
EOF	The EOF key signals the end of input from the keyboard (analogous to the MS-DOS ^z key). Usually assigned to ^d.
INTR	Also called *cancel* or *interrupt*, this key terminates the currently executing command. Usually assigned to ^c.
Erase	Also called *backspace*, this key moves the cursor backward one character. Most keyboards generate the ASCII 08 code (^h) for the backspace key.
Kill	Discards everything you previously typed on the current line. Usually assigned to ^u.
Return	Generates a newline code (^j). Signals that you are finished typing and now wish the computer to observe and react to what you have typed.
Space	The spacebar. Generates the ASCII 20 code.
Tab	Usually labeled *tab*, *Tab*, or *TAB*, generates the ASCII 09 code.

To some extent, you can select which key on your keyboard is assigned to each of these functions. This is done using the `stty` command, which establishes a correspondence between a physical keyboard code and a logical keyboard function. For more information, refer to the description of the `stty` command in the manual for your system.

UNIX systems generally do not require or support the use of other keys, such as program function keys and cursor movement keys, primarily because terminals (as opposed to PCs) do not always have such keys. If you have these keys, you may be able to use them. Consult the documentation for your particular hardware and software for more information.

P A R T

I

The C Programming Language

Fundamentals

This chapter provides an overview of the C programming language. Its purpose is to introduce you to all the principal elements of the language before discussing any element in detail. Hopefully, this will give you an overall context for understanding the detailed information presented in later chapters.

To begin, you need to understand the basic building blocks of working programs. At the highest level these are source files, functions, and statements. This chapter briefly introduces each topic; later chapters discuss them in much greater detail.

Source Files

The most basic element of a C program is a *source file*. Every C program begins its life with the construction of at least one source file containing lines of C statements.

You can and should, for various reasons, consider breaking a large program into multiple source files. This is because people find very large, complex programs difficult to understand. When you divide the program into smaller pieces, each simple and straightforward in design, the whole program is easier to understand.

Only the smallest C programs are written as a single source file. More often, a C program is constructed from a suite of files of two general types. The first type, called a *header file,* contains definitions and data descriptions that are used by all the other files of the program. The second type contains mostly executable statements, as opposed to descriptive statements. Header files usually (but not necessarily) have filenames ending in *.h* and nonheader files usually have filenames ending in *.c.*

The C compiler compiles the source files of a program separately, each compilation yielding an *object file* (also called an *object module*). Object files, in contrast to source files, contain binary machine code; they are understandable by the computer, but generally are not understandable by human beings. Source files are input to a compiler, whereas object modules are its output. Hopefully the object module says the same thing as the source file, just in a different language (machine language).

A *compiler* is a sophisticated program that translates statements in a source language into executable machine instructions. Although computer programming languages are convenient for people to use, the computer cannot directly execute instructions in any language but its own binary machine code. In the early days of computers, people wrote programs directly in machine code. That process was so tedious and error prone, however, that people worked with great intensity to devise higher level languages and compilers to translate those languages into machine code. Now that we have a choice, virtually nobody programs in machine language.

The compilation process digests source files, converting them into the binary language of the computer. Figure 1.1 illustrates the general compilation process.

When a program is complete within one source file, the compilation process is almost as simple as Figure 1.1 suggests. When a program is written as several source files, however, the process is a bit more complicated, as shown in Figure 1.2.

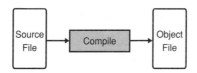

Figure 1.1. The compilation process.

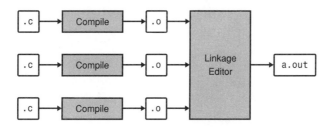

Figure 1.2. Compiling with multiple source files.

Figure 1.2 shows that each source file comprising a program must be compiled separately, and the outputs combined using a *linkage editor*. Linkage editors are an old technology with a very important and fundamental purpose: to resolve references in one source file to data and procedures defined in another source file. It is only because of the linkage editor that we have the capability of building a program from many small source files. The linkage editor enables us to define a data element in one source file and refer to it in another. This is important if the separate source files of a program are to operate in a coordinated fashion.

Here is a very small program that, nonetheless, is written as three source files (Listings 1.1, 1.2, and 1.3). The function of the program is not important at this point. What I want you to see is how a program's content can be split over multiple files.

Listing 1.1. A simple header file.

```
/* glob.h - Global Definitions for Program 1 */
#include <stdio.h>
#include <stdlib.h>
#include <string.h>

extern void sysfail(int rc, char *message);
extern void usrfail(int rc, char *message);
```

5

Listing 1.2. A source file of utility functions.

```c
/* error.c - error handling functions */
#include "glob.h"

void sysfail(int rc, char *message)
{
    perror(message);
    exit(rc);
}

void usrfail(int rc, char *message)
{
    fprintf(stderr, message);
    exit(rc);
}
```

Listing 1.3. The main program.

```c
/* main.c - count the number of lines in a file */
#include "glob.h"

int main(int argc, char *argv[])
{
    FILE *in;
    int   count = 0;
    int   ch;

    /* Check for filename on the command line */
    if (argc < 2)
        usrfail(1, "Command requires a filename");

    /* Open the input file */
    if ((in = fopen(argv[1], "r")) == NULL)
        sysfail(2, argv[1]);
```

```
    /* Read and count the lines */
    while ((ch = getc(in)) != EOF)
        if (ch == '\n') count++;

    /* Close the file */
    fclose(in);

    /* Print the number of lines and exit */
    printf("%d\n", count);
    return(0);
}
```

As the initial comment in Listing 1.1 suggests, the first file is named glob.h. (Text enclosed between /* and */ is called a *comment* and is ignored by the C compiler.) Both the second source file (shown in Listing 1.2) and the third file (shown in Listing 1.3) contain the statement #include "glob.h". This tells the C compiler to treat the file glob.h as if it physically replaced the line containing the include statement (more about include statements can be found in Chapter 10, "The Preprocessor"). Telling the compiler to embed one source file in another is one way to combine parts of a program that have been written in separate files.

You can easily combine Listings 1.1, 1.2, and 1.3 into one source file. The only change you need to make, other than combining the three files end to end, is to remove the two include "glob.h" lines. The resulting combined file is equivalent in every way to the three separate files.

You may notice that the first source file contains other include statements. These are for standard definition files that are provided with the C compiler. You may use them freely, and you do not have to write them yourself.

Functions

Looking at Listings 1.1 through 1.3 discloses another bit of order in C programs. After a hodgepodge of miscellaneous specifications at the front of the program, the remainder of the program is essentially just a series of functions.

A C function has the following general structure:

```
return-type name (arguments)
{
function body

}
```

A *function* is a set of instructions that performs a single task. If your program is complex, it probably performs many distinct tasks to achieve its overall objective. It is best to write each of these tasks as a separate function. When you need to execute the task of the function, you call or *invoke* the function by writing its name. You can define the function in the same source file in which it's invoked, or in another source file.

Because the structure of C programs is oriented around functions, C encourages you to think in terms of discrete processing steps. A function can represent each major step. You can then accomplish the overall task of the program by calling each of the functions one or several times in the appropriate order.

Functions are arranged linearly in the source file, each one following the other. When your program executes, however, the computer does not perform the functions in the order you list them; the order in which the functions appear in your source program is entirely immaterial.

One of the functions must be called `main`. This is the function that the operating system calls and is where execution of your program begins. The `main` function is the *only* function required to be in your program, and unless you make other provisions it will be the *only* function executed.

You invoke a function by writing its name followed by a (possibly empty) argument list. The compiler generates code that causes the computer to jump to the named function. When the invoked function completes its task, it returns to the point where it was called. The effect is the same as if the body of the named function were inserted in place of its name.

The net effect is that the functions in your program are executed like the branches of a tree. The `main` function calls another function a, which in turn calls another function x. Figure 1.3 shows a diagram of how the functions in a program might call one another.

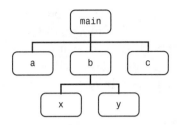

Figure 1.3. The hierarchical relationship of functions.

The vertical distance of a function from the top-level function main is called the *level* of the function. In Figure 1.3, function b is at level 2 and function y is at level 3. A function doesn't always need to be called from the same level. This is often the case for utility functions, such as those used to copy text or open a file. Such functions are sometimes called directly from within main, and sometimes from very low-level functions. Generally, the level on which a function is called is of no importance.

A special exception to this is when one function calls another function that is on a higher level than itself. For example, in Figure 1.3, if function x calls function b, and b then calls x, a special situation arises called *recursion*. In recursion, a function is called again before it completes a previous call. C supports recursive function calls, but you must take care when using functions recursively. Make sure you do not start an *infinite descent* in which the functions never stop calling each other. Chapter 8, "Pointers and Arrays," and Chapter 9, "Complex Declarations," contain examples of recursive functions.

Statements

There are many ways in which the C language is like the English language.

The source files that comprise a program play a similar role to the chapters in a book. Each chapter contributes a major theme or plot development to the story of the book. Similarly, each source file should deal with one major task of the program's overall job.

Functions are like the paragraphs of a chapter. A paragraph certainly is not a self-contained story, and a function (ordinarily) is not a self-contained program. But both present a single thought or topic. The function may perform any sort of task, but it usually performs only one task, well-defined and detailed in its scope. Thus a function may print a report heading, allocate a block of storage, or look up an entry in a table.

The units from which you build functions are called *statements*. In C, statements play a role similar to sentences in English. Studying C statements quickly becomes a discussion of grammar and syntax, just as if you were discussing valid English sentence structure. You must follow a set of very specific syntax rules when writing a statement in the C language.

Still, it is strangely difficult to specify exactly what a valid C statement *is*. You do not have to confine a statement to one line; you can spread it over as many lines as you like. Not all C statements require an ending semicolon, although most do. Statements usually begin with one of a set of reserved keywords that you can think of as the C counterpart to verbs in English, but some types of statements do not begin with a verb.

Perhaps the best way to get a feel for statements in C is to look at a sample program. Listing 1.4 shows a very simple program that prints the integers from 1 to 10. The lines of the program have prefix numbers for easy reference in the following text.

Listing 1.4. A program that prints the first ten integers.

```
1   #include <stdio.h>
2   int main()
3   {
4       int n;
5
6       for (n = 1; n <= 10; n++)
7           printf("%d\n", n);
8       return(0);
9   }
```

The first line that begins with a # is a preprocessor directive. Chapter 10 discusses preprocessor directives in detail; all you need to know now is that such directives are not part of the basic C language and that lines beginning with a # are not normally called *statements*. For now, ignore the first line except to note that it must be there.

Line 2 begins the first statement of the C program. It's a function definition for the main function that must be present in every program. The function definition statement here consists of four parts.

1. The int reserved word says the function returns a value to its caller, and the type of value is an *integer*. C supports a number of different kinds of data (called *types*) and it's important to note the type of each value. You learn more about types in Chapter 3, "Simple Declarations."

2. The word main stands in the position of the function name and identifies this as the main function.

3. The paired parentheses () note the list of arguments passed to the function by its caller. There are none, so the list is empty.

4. The { on the next line begins the function body. The function body continues until the next matching }, which occurs on line 9 of the program.

Ironically, the first statement in the program contains the whole program. The pair of braces ({}), however, delimits the definition of the function, which you must give as a list of C statements to be executed when the function is called, so there are still more statements to look at.

Line 4 is an example of a declarative statement. It tells the compiler to reserve a variable of type *integer* for the function to use. This statement ends with a semicolon (;). The semicolon serves as the standard statement delimiter in the C language.

Line 5 is left blank as a matter of style. This book does not attempt to teach you a C coding style except by example. Most C programmers follow the stylistic convention of leaving a blank line after the data descriptions at the beginning of a function and before the first executable statement of the function.

Lines 6 and 7 are a for loop. The statement consists of the initial for keyword, a parenthetical expression telling how many times to execute the loop, and the statement body—in this case, a call of the `printf` function. To be exact, the statement initializes a variable n to the value *1*, executes the loop as long as the value of n is less than or equal to 10, and increments the value of n each time through the loop (denoted in C by the ++ symbol).

Line 7, besides being the body of the `for` loop, is also a statement by itself. In this case, the statement is an invocation of the `printf` function and passes it two arguments: a character string enclosed in quotation marks, and the value of n. As you learn in more detail later, the `printf` function uses the first argument as a model of the line to be printed. Subsequent arguments are values to substitute into the model text. The model text here consists of just the substituted value of n. Conveniently, the `printf` function converts the binary value of n into the equivalent decimal number and then prints it. A typical output of this statement would be the character 7 followed by an end-of-line character. (End-of-line characters are a special feature of UNIX discussed in Chapter 2, "Tokens.")

Line 8 executes after the `for` loop finishes. This `return` statement returns control to the caller of the `main` function. But the operating system itself called `main`, so here the `return` statement effectively ends execution of the whole program.

The last line, line 9, contains only the closing brace (}) that marks the end of the `main` function. Although it must be present, it causes no special action to be performed.

Taking a broader look at the program, it should be evident that C uses a variety of statement formats. Chapters 2 through 9 of this book present the format of C statements in detail.

Summary

This chapter introduces a wealth of new terms and concepts. The purpose of this introductory chapter is to expose you to the flavor of C without adding too much detail. Later chapters study small parts of the C language in great detail. That study will be more meaningful if you have a framework to hold the details. This chapter is meant to provide such a framework.

The main concepts to remember from this chapter are the three top layers of organization to C programs. At the very highest level, programs consist of one or more *source files*. Source files, in turn, contain sequences of *functions*. Finally, functions are composed of one or more *statements*, each of which instructs the computer to perform a specified action.

To proceed with the real definition of the C programming language, start reading the next chapter.

Tokens

In the previous chapter, you looked at the C language from a high-level point of view, first noting the division of a program into source files, then into functions, and finally into statements. In this chapter, you look at C from the lowest level of detail.

The lowest level of detail in C is the *token*. Technically, a token is an indivisible group of characters that, together, have a unique meaning. Dividing a token into smaller parts destroys the meaning of the character group; it yields only meaningless characters.

In English, tokens are words and punctuation. You can group these elements into larger units, such as sentences and paragraphs, but words and punctuation marks are tokens because they are the smallest elements of English that have meaning.

C has a much greater variety of token types than does English. This is because programming languages need to be more terse than English and at the same time more precise. The kinds of tokens C allows are as follows:

- Identifiers are the names of variables, functions, structure types, and so on. You make up the names of objects as needed, but you must follow certain rules for forming names.

- Numeric literals are actual numbers that occur in the source program text. Examples are 0, 3.5, or 3.15E+06.

- Character literals have as their value the ASCII code of the character. A character literal is written as a single character between apostrophes: ´c´ has the value 99, the ASCII code for a lowercase c.

- String literals represent a sequence of characters to be treated as a unit. For example, the string literal "William of Orange" has a value that represents exactly those characters, including spaces. The quotation marks identify the text between them as a string literal to the C compiler, and are not part of the string.

- The C language defines some words as keywords. You cannot use these words as variable names; for example: if, for, and signed. Wherever these words are found, C assumes they have the meaning defined by the language (except when they occur within string literals).

- Operators are certain punctuation marks the C language uses to represent mathematical and logical operations. Included among these are +, -, *, /, and the less familiar &, |, ^, ++, and --. C defines more operator symbols than most languages do, and it may be a while before you are familiar with all of them.

- Delimiters are a few additional special characters C defines for use as punctuation. These are used to clarify the meaning of source code, and you must often use specific punctuation in order to achieve a desired result. Examples are the braces ({}) that surround a function body, and the parentheses that enclose the argument list of a function call.

The remainder of this chapter discusses all these token types. Unfortunately, a list of rules for forming valid tokens in the C language makes for very dry reading, and you might be tempted to skim this material. Be warned that these rules are very important, and by the time you are fluent in the C language you will know all these rules by heart.

Notation

This chapter uses a special notation to denote the formation rules for tokens. In this notation, most characters simply stand for themselves. Thus, the expression abc means the letter a followed by the letter b followed by the letter c. The following symbols, however, have special meanings:

[ ]   Square brackets are used to denote any single character chosen from a set of characters. For example, [0123456789] denotes a decimal digit. A special shorthand is allowed when the characters form a natural sequence. For example, the set of digits can be written as [0-9], and the set of uppercase letters can be written as [A-Z]. To form the token described by this expression, select one character from the set.

*   The asterisk means zero or more occurrences of the preceding expression. Thus, [0-9]* describes a token consisting of zero or more digits.

+   The plus sign means one or more occurrences of the preceding expression; that is, the expression preceding the plus sign must occur at least once in the token. For example, [0-9]* is not a valid integer; you must write at least one digit, symbolized by [0-9]+.

?   The question mark symbolizes zero or one occurrence of the preceding expression. In other words, when the question mark follows another expression, it indicates that the expression is optional.

¦   The vertical bar is used to indicate a choice. Thus, in the expression a¦b, you may choose either the letter a or the letter b, but not both, when forming a token.

( )   Parentheses are used to group a compound expression into a single unit, usually to apply another operator. For example, the expression (a¦b)+ means one or more occurrences of the letter a or b. Valid tokens derived from this expression would be a, b, aa, ab, babba, etc.

w   An italicized word is a previously defined name for a token expression. The use of naming allows an expression to refer to another expression.

This notation amounts to a restricted form of *regular expressions*. Regular expressions occur frequently in UNIX, and you may already be familiar with them. The remainder of this chapter contains many examples of how this notation is used.

Numeric Literals

A *numeric literal* is a sequence of digits and punctuation that represents a number. Depending on the exact way you write the number, the computer stores it in different ways. Once you gain experience, you will be able to write numeric literals that work efficiently in the context you use them.

In C, numbers have a *radix* attribute as well as attributes of sign, magnitude, and type. The radix attribute is the base notation—decimal, hexadecimal, or octal—you use to write the number. The notation you choose has no effect on the value stored in memory (*fourteen* is *fourteen* regardless of how you write the number). The most commonly used radix is base 10 (decimal). The base 16 (hexadecimal) and base 8 (octal) representations are used most frequently when the bits of the value are significant; these notations make it easier to visualize which bits are set in a value.

Octal Numbers

To write a number in octal, write a 0 followed by one or more of the digits from 0 to 7. Because octal is a base 8 representation, only the digits from 0 through 7 are defined in octal notation. More formally, an octal number is written as follows:

`octal_number: 0[0-7]+`

Each octal digit generates three bits in the stored numeric value, but the size of the stored value is rounded up to the size of an integer.

One of the side effects of this rule is that you must use a little care when writing numbers: never begin a number with 0 unless you mean to write the number in octal. If you write the number 012, for example, its actual value is 10 in decimal. To write *twelve* in decimal you must write just 12.

Here are some examples of octal numeric literals:

Octal	Decimal	Binary
012	10	1010
018	*Not a valid octal number*	
0177	127	1111111
0377	255	11111111

Hexadecimal Numbers

To write a number in hexadecimal, write 0x or 0X in front of the number followed by one or more hexadecimal digits. A hexadecimal digit is one of the characters *0* through *9*, *a* through *f*, or *A* through *F*:

```
hex_number: 0[xX]([0-9]¦[a-f]¦[A-F])+
```

The letters *a* through *f* (and *A* through *F*) represent the numbers *10* through *15*, respectively. Whether you use upper- or lowercase letters makes no difference to the compiler.

Each hexadecimal digit generates four bits in the stored binary value. The value is stored as an int unless long is larger than int and the literal value is too large to be contained in an int. In such a case, the literal is stored as a long int.

Here are some examples of hexadecimal numeric literals:

Hex	Decimal	Binary
0x12	18	10010
0x1h	*Not a valid hex number*	
0x177	127	101110111
0xff	255	11111111

Decimal Numeric Literals

Decimal numeric literals are any numbers that are not otherwise octal or hexadecimal literals. That is, a decimal numeric literal does not begin with *0* and contains only the digits from *0* through *9*.

C supports the use of floating-point values as well as integer values, but only for decimal numeric literals. You cannot express a floating-point value in octal or hexadecimal notation.

Also unlike octal and hexadecimal numbers, a decimal numeric literal may be signed; its value may be positive or negative. The following description identifies the formation rules for integer numeric literals (called *integer* in the description) and for floating-point numeric literals (called *real* in the description).

```
decimal_number: integer ¦ real
integer: (+¦-)?[1-9][0-9]*
real: (+¦-) mantissa ([eE](+¦-)?[0-9]+)?
mantissa: [0-9]*.[0-9]+ ¦ [0-9]+(.[0-9]*)?
```

The description of floating-point numbers is a little complicated because the C compiler allows either the part before the decimal point or the part after the decimal point (but not both) to be missing. The following are examples of valid decimal numeric literals and an indication of their type:

Literal	Type	Interpretation
37	integer	37
.37	real	0.37
–712	integer	–712
3.14159	real	+3.14159
–3.14159E05	real	–314159.0
–3e5	real	–300000.0
3.14E–8	real	+0.0000000314
–3.14e–01	real	–0.314

An integer numeric literal is stored as signed int unless it is too large to be represented by signed int and signed long is larger than signed int. In such a case, the literal is stored as signed long. A real literal is stored as a double regardless of its size.

Suffixes

You can append a suffix to any of the numeric literal types (octal, hexadecimal, and decimal) to modify the way the literal is represented in memory.

Append an l or L to the literal to expand the literal to a long integer. A numeric literal having a value greater than 32,767 or less than –32,768 is automatically stored as a long integer.

Append a u or U to the literal to force interpretation of the literal as an unsigned number. By default, all numeric literals are considered to be signed integers.

To signify an unsigned long integer, append LU or UL. The order of the suffix letters is immaterial.

Character Literals

A *character literal* is the numeric value corresponding to a printable character. In all UNIX implementations, the internal representation of characters uses the ASCII code. A character literal has as its value the ASCII code for the character you specify.

A character literal is as much a numeric value as is a decimal literal. Writing ´A´ and writing 97 have exactly the same effect and meaning. To write a character literal, enclose the character in apostrophes:

```
character_literal: ´x´
```

For example, the value of ´a´ is 97; the value of ´A´ is 65; and the value of ´?´ is 63.

Only one character is allowed between the apostrophes. Although you can imagine that the value of ´XY´ would be 22,617 (numerically, 0x5859 = 22,617), the C language considers such a token to be an error.

String Literals

String literals are almost indispensable in writing useful programs. Using them you can easily print report headings, search files for known text values, and write error messages. Without them you must denote each character as a numeric value or as a character literal—a tedious process indeed.

To write a string literal, enclose the desired characters between quotation marks. To write a quotation mark in a string literal, place a backslash (\) in front of the embedded quotation mark.

Here are some valid and invalid string literals:

`"ITEM DESCRIPTION"`	valid
`"John´s"`	stored as `John´s`
`"the \"big\" book"`	stored as `the "big" book`
`"January`	ending quote missing

You can continue a string literal onto additional lines by writing a backslash (\) after the last character of the current line and continuing the literal at the beginning of the next line. Any whitespace you enter at the beginning of the continuation line is considered part of the string literal.

Here is an example of continuing a string literal:

```
static char ruler[] = "....:....1....:....2....:....3\
....:....4....:....5....:....6....:....7....:....8";
```

ANSI C also enables you to define a long string literal by writing two or more shorter string literals one after the other; adjacent string literals are glued together by the C compiler into one long string literal. You may insert any amount of whitespace between the adjacent string literals, including newline characters.

Here's the previous example rewritten to use adjacent string literals:

```
static char ruler[] =
           "....:....1....:....2....:....3....:....4"
           "....:....5....:....6....:....7....:....8";
```

All compilers conforming to the ANSI C standard store one character per 8-bit byte. The length of a string literal in bytes is always one greater than the number of characters in the literal value. This is because C always stores a zero byte at the end of the string. This byte of zeros, called a *trailing null*, is useful for handling strings of varying lengths, because it serves as a unique marker for the end of the string.

The value of a string literal is not the string itself; rather, it is a *pointer* to the first character of the string. Pointers are discussed in much greater detail in Chapter 8, "Pointers and Arrays." For now, suffice it to say that character strings, including string literals, cannot normally be manipulated as a single unit. In fact, learning the proper methods for string handling is a major part of learning the C language.

Escape Sequences

If you are familiar with UNIX or with other small systems such as MS-DOS, then you probably know that peripheral devices such as printers and terminals are often controlled with special characters embedded in the data stream. Such characters, called *control codes*, have values distinct from the printable graphics so that the device can readily identify them.

Control codes perform useful functions such as causing a printer to start a new line or to skip to a new page, or causing a terminal to clear its screen. As the programmer, you must tell the device when to take such actions by embedding the appropriate control characters in the data stream you send to the device.

C simplifies this task by providing you with the ability to specify a control code anywhere in a string literal. To enter a control code in a string literal, write one of the backslash sequences (listed in Table 2.1) at the desired position in the string literal.

Table 2.1. ANSI C escape sequences.

Sequence	Meaning and Effect
\a	Bell. Causes the device to ring a bell, sound a beep, or otherwise generate an audible alarm if the device is capable. Devices which do not support the bell character may treat it as a data character.
\b	Backspace. Causes the print element to back up one position. This control code is often used to overprint characters on printer output. Terminals usually erase the character backspaced over since video displays cannot overprint.
\f	Form feed. The device skips to the start of the next "page." For printers, the length of a page is defined either with other special control characters or by controls on the front of the device. For terminals, the length of a "page" is usually the height of the display.
\n	Newline. The device returns the print element to the start of the next line and resumes printing.

continues

Table 2.1. continued

Sequence	Meaning and Effect
\t	Tab. The device skips horizontally to the next tab position, leaving whitespace in the skipped columns of the line. For terminals, the tab positions can be set with a UNIX command.
\r	Carriage Return. Causes the print element to return to the start of the current line. Although most printers and terminals require the use of this character, UNIX can be instructed to output a carriage-return character automatically after each newline character.
\v	Vertical Tab. Causes the device to skip to the next vertical tab position. Most printers are capable of vertical tabbing for applications such as printing on preprinted forms. Terminals do not usually support vertical tabbing and may try to print a vertical tab character as a graphic.
\0	Denotes the ASCII null character. Used in character and string literals to mark the end of a string.
\\	A double backslash prints as a single backslash. Use two backslashes to generate a single backslash in a string literal.
\"	Use a backslashed quotation mark to include a quotation mark in a string literal without ending the literal.
\´	Use a backslashed apostrophe inside a character literal to get the ASCII value of the apostrophe; written ´\´´.

Identifiers

An *identifier* is the name of something. You assign names to objects when you declare them. Chapter 3, "Simple Declarations," describes the kinds of objects to which you can assign names; this chapter is principally concerned with the rules for writing names.

An identifier may contain only letters, digits, and the underscore (_), and must begin with a letter or underscore. An identifier can be as long as you wish, but some compilers use only the first 31 characters of the identifier. If you write identifiers longer than 31 characters, make sure all your identifiers are unique in the first 31 positions to ensure that your program works properly when compiled with other C compilers.

Sometimes an identifier needs to be known outside of the source file in which it is defined. This might be the case, for example, if you define a function in one source file, but wish to call it from another source file. The name of the function is *external* in the sense that it must be known outside the source file where it is defined.

The length restriction on external identifiers may be more stringent than that on internal identifiers. Some systems (but not UNIX) limit an external identifier to as few as six characters, and treat lowercase letters as uppercase. Both UNIX System V Release 4 and BSD Release 3.2 allow unlimited identifier lengths for both internal and external identifiers.

Here are some identifiers, both valid and invalid:

Identifier	*Notes*
`$SYS_Term`	Invalid. The $ is illegal in identifiers.
`1st_file`	Invalid. The first character must be a letter.
`FirstRecord`	OK.
`_ctr`	Also OK, but see caution.
`time-of-day`	Invalid. Use underscore, not dash, to separate words.
`H23615`	OK. Only the first character has to be a letter.

Although C allows the first character of an identifier to be any letter or the underscore, in practice, the code supplied with the system often uses identifiers beginning with an underscore. For this reason, you should not write identifiers beginning with the underscore.

Operators

Operators are sequences of special characters that denote actions. For example, the addition (+) and subtraction (-) signs of arithmetic are operators that manipulate numeric values. C supports the arithmetic operators +, -, * (multiplication), and / (division), as well as many others. Actually, there are more C operators than there are special characters to represent them. To get around this limitation, C uses a pair of characters (sometimes even a triplet) to represent some of the operators.

Character groups representing operators must always be written immediately adjacent, without any whitespace between them. For example, you must write the && operator (defined in Chapter 4, "Expressions") as shown. If you write & & (with a blank between the two ampersands), you receive an error message from the compiler.

As a matter of good form, you generally should place whitespace before and after operators to set them off from the operands on which they operate. The primary operators ([ ], (), ->, and .) and the unary operators (!, ~, ++, --, +, -, *, and &) generally are written without surrounding whitespace, adjacent to the name or expression they operate on.

Table 2.2 lists the C operators. They are defined in Chapter 3.

Table 2.2. ANSI C Operators.

Operator	Priority	Meaning
()	1	Function call when following an identifier
[ ]	1	Array reference (subscripting)
->	1	Reference by pointer (dereference)
.	1	Member reference
!	2	NOT. Logical inverse
~	2	One's complement of a binary value
++	2	Increment

Operator	Priority	Meaning
- -	2	Decrement
+	2	Unary plus
-	2	Unary minus (negate a value)
*	2	Reference by pointer
&	2	Address of
(type)	2	Cast a value to type
sizeof	2	Return length of operand
*	3	Multiplication
/	3	Division
%	3	Remainder
+	4	Addition
-	4	Subtraction
<<	5	Left shift
>>	5	Right shift
<	6	Less than
<=	6	Less than or equal
>	6	Greater than
>=	6	Greater than or equal
==	7	Equal
!=	7	Unequal
&	8	Bitwise AND
^	9	Bitwise exclusive OR
¦	10	Bitwise OR
&&	11	Logical AND

continues

Table 2.2. continued

Operator	Priority	Meaning
¦ ¦	12	Logical OR
? :	13	Conditional expression
=	14	Assignment
+=	14	Additive assignment
-=	14	Subtractive assignment
*=	14	Multiplicative assignment
/=	14	Quotient assignment
%=	14	Remainder assignment
&=	14	Bitwise AND assignment
^=	14	Bitwise exclusive OR assignment
¦=	14	Bitwise OR assignment
<<=	14	Assign left-shifted
>>=	14	Assign right-shifted

Punctuation

The C language, like other languages, uses some special characters just for the purpose of setting off the meaningful text. These characters, called *punctuation* in English, are often called *delimiters* in programming languages.

The most important delimiter in C is whitespace, which is actually four characters instead of just one: the *newline* character at the end of each line of source text; the *form feed* character that forces a skip to a new page when printing the source file; the *blank* character; and the *tab* character.

Wherever one whitespace character is permitted, you can write any number of whitespace characters. You cannot insert whitespace between the characters of an operator, an identifier, a keyword, or a numeric constant.

Whenever two or more identifiers or keywords occur in succession, you must use whitespace to separate the words; otherwise, the compiler can't tell where one word ends and another begins.

In addition to whitespace, other important delimiters are the semicolon (;), the colon (:), the comma (,), and braces ({}). Each of these delimiters is required for certain C statement types and disallowed in other contexts. These delimiters are discussed together with the statements that require their use.

A useful rule is that whenever you use a delimiter to separate words or tokens, you do not also need to use whitespace for separation.

Summary

This chapter introduces the concept of tokens and describes the tokens of the C programming language. The tokens of a programming language are, like the words and punctuation of the English language, a basic vocabulary that you assemble in structured ways to make meaningful statements.

The tokens of the C language consist of identifiers, literal values, reserved words, operators, and punctuation.

An identifier is the name of something such as a function or a variable. You invent identifiers as you need them, using strict rules prescribed by the C language. An identifier must begin with an upper- or lowercase letter or an underscore, and be followed by any number of letters, digits, or underscores. The ANSI standard guarantees that the compiler will keep at least the first 31 characters of the identifier; some compilers may treat identifiers longer than that as identical when they begin with the same sequence of 31 characters.

A literal value is a character literal, an integer or floating-point number, or a string literal. A character literal is one ASCII character surrounded by apostrophes (for example, 'a'); it denotes the numerical ASCII code for the character. A string literal is a sequence of ASCII characters enclosed in quotation marks (for example, "string"); it denotes a pointer to the first character. An integer number is a sequence of decimal, octal, or hexadecimal digits and denotes a numerical value that is stored in computer memory in a format suitable for arithmetic operations. A floating-point number is written in standard scientific notation and denotes a numerical value suitable for use in floating-point calculations.

Reserved words are words with a special meaning in the C language. You must not use a reserved word as an identifier. Examples of reserved words are *if*, *else*, *do*, *while*, *static*, and *register*. The C language dictates the meaning of a reserved word.

Operators are special characters or groups of special characters that denote an arithmetic or logical operation such as addition, bit shifting, or testing for the equality of two values. Some operators consist of two or three characters, such as && and <<=; you must not interpose blanks or other characters between the characters of such operators. You use operators to form expressions. Chapter 4 describes expressions.

Punctuation in the C language consists of characters such as the semicolon (;), used to mark the end of a statement, and braces ({ and }), used to mark the beginning and end of a group of executable statements. Blanks, tabs, and newline characters, collectively called whitespace, are also punctuation characters and mark the beginning and end of consecutive identifiers or reserved words.

Armed with a basic understanding of the vocabulary of the C language, you should now be ready to tackle the subject of the next chapter, which discusses C declarations, or how to designate the variables, arrays, and structures your program manipulates.

3

Simple Declarations

The instructions of a program are often thought of as its most essential feature; the variables and constants the program contains are relegated to a secondary role. The kind of data structures you choose to use, however, largely determines the program's instructions. A wise choice of data structures leads to a straightforward efficient program, whereas a poor choice produces an awkward, inefficient program. This book discusses data declarations before statement types because it's almost impossible to write a statement without referring to one or more data items.

C is a strongly typed programming language, which means you must always describe data in a manner consistent with the way you intend to use it. This sometimes causes problems when you want to manipulate a data item in a way that C doesn't allow. In compensation, the C compiler can check your programs thoroughly and bring to your attention not only errors, but also any suspicious operations it finds.

Some languages offer only two or three data types; C has many basic data types, all of which are explained in this chapter. C also allows data definitions that combine two or more basic declarative elements, leading to so-called *complex* data declarations. Complex data declarations are covered in a later chapter.

The basic data types in C are the following:

- *Integer.* An integer is a simple numeric item that can contain a positive or negative whole number.

- *Floating-point.* A floating-point is a class of numeric variables that allows fractions and exponents for very precise arithmetic.

- *Character.* A character is a single byte containing a printable or control character in ASCII code.

Each of these basic types can be further qualified by one of the following attributes:

- *Signed* or *unsigned.* Unsigned data items always appear to have a positive value, whereas signed items can range from a maximum negative value to a maximum positive value.

- *Short* or *long.* Short types are half the length of long types. A short data item saves computer memory at the cost of a smaller value range.

- *Constant.* A constant data item is considered read-only; you can use its value, but you cannot change it. There are ways to assign an initial value to a constant data item. Also, a data item can be considered constant for some functions and not for others.

- *Volatile.* A volatile data item can change while the compiler isn't looking. For example, the value might be changed by an interrupt-handling routine so that, from the point of view of some other function, the value changed at an unpredictable time.

These basic or qualified data types can be further augmented in the following ways:

- *Pointer to type.* In C, a pointer is not a unique type as it is in some languages. Rather, you must declare a pointer as a pointer to something else. Thus, one kind of pointer is a *pointer to int*, and a *pointer to char* is another kind of pointer. Because the combination type *pointer to int* is itself a legal type, it is also legal to have a pointer to it. This yields a data item of type *pointer to pointer to int*. Because pointers may form long chains of reference, handling pointers can be confusing.

- *Array of type.* An array is a data aggregate consisting of repeated occurrences of the same type of data item. C does not place a limit on the number of dimensions in an array; two- and three-dimensional arrays occur commonly, but arrays of 200 or 300 dimensions are also legal (if impractical).

- *Structures.* A structure is a collection of data items of (possibly) dissimilar type. (In COBOL and Pascal, structures are called *records*.) The data items in a structure are called *members* of the structure. Some C operators can treat a structure as a unit, lending the appearance of a new data type to your structure declarations.

- *Unions.* A union is like a structure, except that all its members occupy the same area of memory. The length of a union is the length of its largest member. Unions often are used to convert data from one type to another, or to store varying information in a structure.

- *Enumerations.* An enumeration is a data type that has only a few distinct values; the enumeration declaration enables you to associate a symbolic name with each possible value of the data type. For example, a structure containing personnel information about an employee might contain an enumeration called *sex* that can have only one of two values: *male* or *female*.

- *Storage class.* A storage class can be static, automatic, external, or unspecified. The storage class of a variable determines when and for how long physical memory is allocated to a variable. It also affects the *scope* of a variable—that portion of the program where a reference to the variable is legal.

Although there are only three basic data types, the many ways in which you can qualify or group a basic data type provide an incredible variety of actual data types. This richness makes programming in C both a challenge and a joy, because it provides the opportunity to tailor data representations to the form best suited for each program.

The remainder of this chapter examines each elementary data type and type qualifier the C language permits, starting with the basic types: `int`, `float` or `double`, and `char`. Later chapters examine arrays, structures, unions, enumerations, and pointers.

Integer Data

In mathematics, an *integer* is a signed whole number ranging from negative infinity to positive infinity. An example of an integer is –32,768, as is 2,147,365,299. However, 3.14159 is not an integer because the number has a fractional part.

In C, you declare an integer variable with a statement similar to the following:

```
int area;
```

As with all declarations, the initial word is the C keyword designating the variable type (in this case, `int`). The type name is followed by the name of the variable. Variable names are identifiers, as described in Chapter 2, "Tokens," and must therefore comply with the rules for writing identifiers. The end of the declaration is noted by a final semicolon. Whitespace *must* appear following `int` and *may* appear before and after the semicolon.

You can declare several integers with one `int` statement by listing their names:

```
int area, volume, height, width;
```

By default, integers are 32 bits long in the UNIX environment. This contrasts with MS-DOS usage, where integers are usually 16 bits long. Because the size of an integer can differ depending on the machine and operating system, you should specify long integers whenever you require a 32-bit integer and short integers whenever you prefer 16-bit integers.

To allocate a 32-bit integer, use the qualifier `long int`, or just `long`; the compiler assumes `long int` if it sees `long` without a basic data type following it. The following declaration allocates long integers:

```
long seconds, yawns;
```

To allocate 16-bit integers, use the qualifier `short int`, or just `short`. As with `long`, the compiler assumes `short int` unless you specify another kind of short. Here are declarations of some short integers and some long integers:

```
long fuel, distance;
short hours;
int i, j, k;
```

Notice that you cannot declare long, short, and default-length integers all in the same statement; a given statement declares all named variables as being of the same type.

By default, all integer variables are *signed* integers. You can explicitly specify this by prefacing the declaration with the keyword `signed`. Integers can also be *unsigned*. An unsigned integer cannot be negative; instead, its maximum positive value is roughly twice as large as the maximum positive value of the corresponding signed integer. To declare an unsigned integer, include the keyword `unsigned` in front of the declaration. For convenience, C enables you to shorten `unsigned int` to `unsigned`.

Table 3.1 summarizes the length and magnitude range for each of the possible integer types.

Table 3.1. Characteristics of integers.

Declared	Length in Bytes	Signed	Value Range
int	2 or 4	Yes	At least −32,768 to 32,767
long int	4	Yes	−2,147,483,647 to 2,147,483,648
short int	2	Yes	−32,768 to 32,767
unsigned int	2 or 4	No	At least 0 to 65,535
unsigned short	2	No	0 to 65,535
unsigned long	4	No	0 to 4,294,967,295

Floating-Point Data

All C compilers support floating-point arithmetic, even when the machine on which the compiled program will run does not provide floating-point arithmetic hardware. Systems without floating-point hardware provide a software emulation of the hardware. For this reason, C has gained some popularity as a scientific and engineering language.

Floating-point numbers differ from integers by having a fractional part and an exponent. A fully explicit floating-point number has a sign, an integer part, a fractional part, and an exponent, as in this example: +5.186755E+04. If you're not familiar with floating-point numbers, the confusing part of the number probably is the exponent—*E+04* in this example. An exponent indicates how many positions left or right to move the decimal point to find the true number. In the example, the exponent says to move the decimal point four positions to the right to get the true number, 51,867.55. Similarly, the true value of –5.186755E–04 is –0.0005186755 because a negative exponent moves the decimal point left instead of right.

You might wonder why bother with exponents. The reason is that not all numbers are as easy to write as 51,867.55. Consider another number, such as 3,150,000,000,000. Because it has only three significant figures, it's more natural to write *3.15E+12*. It's also easier to read because the exponent tells you how many zeros follow; you don't have to count them. In science and engineering, very small numbers occur as well, such as 2.83E–22. The floating-point form is much easier to write and read than 0.000000000000000000000283.

The overpowering reason for using floating-point numbers in programs, however, is to represent fractional parts of quantities, or very large or very small values.

Floating-point variables come in two or three varieties, depending on the implementation of your compiler. Short floating-point numbers are 32 bits long (four bytes) and declared with the `float` type. Variables of type `float` can represent values with a magnitude (ignoring the sign) of 8.43E–37 to 3.37E+38. Short floating-point values can maintain about six significant digits of precision.

Long floating-point values are declared with the `double` type. Variables of type `double` are 64 bits long (eight bytes) and can represent values in the range of 2.225074E–308 to 1.797693E+308. Variables of type `double` can maintain 10 to 12 significant digits of precision.

The ANSI standard defines a third floating-point variable type called `long double` using ten bytes of memory, two more than `double`. The two extra bytes are used for additional significant digits, thus allowing greater precision but not greater magnitude with long doubles.

Table 3.2 summarizes the characteristics of floating-point types.

Table 3.2. Characteristics of floating-point numbers

Declared	Length in Bytes	Smallest Positive Value	Largest Positive Value
float	4	8.43E–37	3.37E+38
double	8	2.225074E–308	1.797693E+308
long double	10	2.225074E–308	1.797693E+308

Floating-point numbers are always signed. The qualifier `signed` is permitted, but it is ignored in front of a floating-point type; the qualifier `unsigned` causes a compiler error message.

Character Data

Data items declared as `char` occupy one byte each. All compilers conforming to the ANSI C standard store a character in a byte of 8 bits.

Characters are represented in the ASCII code, which defines printable graphics and control characters for the first 128 code positions, hex values 00 through 7F. Any meaning attached to character values from 128 through 255 (hex values 80 through FF) is application or system dependent and undefined by the C language.

A variable of type `char` is considered a numeric variable because it has a numeric value. By default, a `char` variable is signed and has a numeric value range of –128 to 127. You can make this explicit by writing `signed char` as the type in a declaration statement:

```
signed char c1, c2;
```

37

This statement declares both variables c1 and c2 as signed character variables each occupying one byte.

Because all ASCII codes have the values from 0 through 127, they have a positive value when assigned to a signed character variable. Codes in the range from 128 through 255 appear to have a negative value (–128 to –1 respectively) when assigned to a character variable.

Character variables can also be unsigned, specified by writing the type as unsigned char, as in the following example declaration:

```
unsigned char uc1, uc2;
```

This example declares the uc1 and uc2 variables as unsigned character variables. Unsigned character variables have values in the range from 0 through 255.

When used in input/output and string operations, it makes little difference whether you declare a character variable as signed or unsigned. When you use character variables in arithmetic or when you convert them to integer values, the result depends on whether the value is considered signed or unsigned. Thus, a character value of hex 85 (decimal 133) converts to an integer value of –123 if signed, or +133 if unsigned.

Character Arrays

So far this chapter has made no mention of character strings. (A *string* is a sequence of adjacent characters in which the order is important.) You're probably wondering how to declare a string variable, such as a word, a report title, or a line of input, in the C language.

You must declare character strings as an *array* of characters using C array notation. For example,

```
char city[30];
```

sets aside an array of 30 characters called city, presumably to hold a city name such as in an address. You can declare any number of character arrays in a single statement, as in the following example:

```
char name[35],
     address[40],
     city[30],
     state[2],
     phone[12];
```

This statement declares five arrays, each containing a different number of characters.

A character array differs from a character variable in fundamental ways. For one thing, a character variable is a single data item and can be manipulated as a unit (assigned a value, copied, incremented or decremented, and so on), whereas a character array is not a unit. You must individually manipulate each element of the array. The only method C provides for copying one array to another array is to copy each element individually.

A second important difference is that the value of a character variable is the byte it contains, whereas the value of an array is a pointer to the first element. Thus, passing the name of an array to a function passes a pointer to the first character rather than the bytes in the array. Although this book hasn't formally discussed pointers yet, you should at least recognize that a pointer is a very different kind of object than a character value.

The third important difference is that the identifier naming the array, besides being of type `pointer to char`, is also a constant value and not a variable. That is, you cannot change the pointer value of the array name, although in general, you can manipulate pointer values in various ways. The reason for this is that the character array is assigned a definite and specific location in memory; the array identifier has as its value the address of that location. That address is constant because, once allocated, the location of the array doesn't change.

You will frequently encounter occasions to use character arrays in C programming. Techniques for handling arrays and pointers are very important for that reason. The following chapters contain many examples of manipulating character arrays.

The *void* Type

In addition to the `int`, `float`, `double`, and `char` basic data types, C also supports a data type called `void`. Unlike the other types, which describe data in memory, the `void` type denotes a nonexistent value.

The `void` type is useful in two contexts: to indicate that a function returns no value, and to describe a generic pointer. Other than these uses, `void` has little application, because you cannot describe a data item as being of type `void`; by definition, the `void` type occupies no memory.

You may recall that a function declaration has the following general form: `int name(args)`. The `int` at the beginning of the declaration describes the data type of the value returned by the function. When a function returns no value, the appropriate declaration is then `void name(args)`.

If a function returns a pointer to an arbitrary area of memory, you can describe that pointer with the following declaration:

```
 void *alloc();
```

You must cast the pointer to the actual data type of the allocated area before using it. (For more information about casts, see Chapter 4, "Expressions.")

Storage Class

All program variables must be assigned a location in computer memory. The most straightforward method is to ask the compiler to assign a location at compile time; such a location assignment is permanent, and the character variable occupies the assigned memory location throughout the execution of the program. A program variable assigned space in memory in this way is called *static* because its memory address never changes.

There are two other methods for allocating memory to variables: the *automatic* and *dynamic* methods of allocation. The discussion of dynamic allocation is deferred until Chapter 8, "Pointers and Arrays."

Static Allocation

All variables declared outside of functions are assigned the *static* storage class. They are also automatically defined as external symbols, which means that such symbols are passed to the linkage editor and can be referenced from other source files.

If you explicitly specify the static storage class when you declare a variable, it will *not* be tagged as an external symbol and will be private to the source file where it is defined.

Both static and external variables can be referenced from the point where they are declared through the end of the file. You cannot reference a variable before its first declaration. For this reason, static and external variables are often called *global*, although the C language does not formally use the term.

Automatic Allocation

Variables declared inside functions are declared as *automatic* variables by default. You can explicitly declare a variable to have the automatic storage class by prefixing the declaration with the keyword auto. Only variables declared inside functions can have the automatic storage class; variables declared outside functions must be either static or external. The auto keyword is rarely used by programmers because the default is always correct, and auto is valid only where it is also the default storage class.

The compiler allocates space on the *stack* for automatic variables when a function is entered, and automatically relinquishes the space when a function exits.

The program stack is a region of memory managed exclusively by the compiler; when program execution begins, the compiler sets aside an amount of memory for the stack. Throughout program execution, a pointer to the top of the stack moves up and down as functions are called and then return. The amount by which the pointer moves is equal to the amount of temporary memory needed to execute the function, which includes space for automatic variables among other things.

Automatic variables are known only within the function that declares them. If two functions declare automatic variables with the same name, no conflict occurs because each function gets its own copy of the variable when it begins execution. The variables may have different types or differ in other ways, because to the compiler they are different variables even though they have the same name. In effect, automatic variables are automatically undeclared when a function exits.

If the name of an automatic variable duplicates that of a previously defined global static or external variable, the compiler treats uses of the name as references to the automatic variable within that function. The automatic variable is said to "hide" the global declaration.

Examples of Storage Classes

Listing 3.1 presents a small program excerpt containing examples of each kind of storage class.

Listing 3.1. Examples of storage classes.

```
#include <stdio.h>
#include <stdlib.h>
int exit_code;
char heading[50];

static char line[120];
static long line_count;

int main(int argc, char *argv[])
{
    FILE *input;
    static char workarea [64];

    if ((input = fopen("employee.db", "r")) == NULL) {
        perror("employee");
        exit(5);
    }
    /*
     *  Input file processing would go here
```

```
    */
    fclose(input);
    return(0);
}
```

The program in Listing 3.1 declares variables with all three storage classes: static, external, and automatic.

The variables exit_code and heading are both static and external. The compiler assigns them memory space when it compiles the program, and the variables remain in memory at the assigned location throughout the execution of the program. Because these variables are declared before the first function, all functions can reference them; they are global variables.

The variables line and line_count are also static, but because they are declared with an explicit static storage class, they are not also external—they can be referenced only by functions in this source file. As with the previous two variables, line and line_count are accessible to the main function and to any other functions that might follow in the same source file.

The variable input in main is an automatic variable. This is true even though auto is not explicitly specified, because the input variable is declared inside the boundaries of a function. (You might notice that input is declared as a new variable type you haven't seen before, namely FILE. FILE is a system-defined data type, representing a file, used for input and output operations.)

The variable workarea is defined inside the main function, but because its storage class is explicitly specified to be static, the variable is static and not automatic. Unlike static variables declared outside functions, the workarea variable is private to the main function; other functions cannot reference it.

The compiler does not allocate space on the stack for the workarea variable; only automatic variables are assigned to stack memory. Because the variable is static, the compiler assigns it to permanent storage in memory. As a result, any values the main function stores in the variable are retained from one call to the next. Values assigned to automatic variables are lost when a function exits because the stack space holding the variable is deallocated. This is not so with static variables. This use of static variables within a function is not unusual; it provides a method for saving data between calls of a function. However, it has disadvantages as well.

External Variables

Earlier, this chapter mentioned external variables, describing them as data items accessible to functions in source files other than the one declaring the external variable. You've also seen how to declare an external variable—namely, by declaring the variable outside the boundaries of any function (typically at the start of a program source file) and omitting the `static` storage class specifier. What you haven't seen yet is how to use an external item in files that do *not* declare it.

Actually, data items must be declared in all source files that reference them, because C must always know the characteristics of a data item. The distinction is between items *defined* in one source file and *referenced* in others. In C, a defining declaration is one that reserves memory for the data item; a reference declaration informs C of the existence and characteristics of a variable, but does not reserve space for it.

To reference a data item defined in another source file, you must declare the item again in the source file making the reference, and also specify the `extern` storage class for the declaration. The `extern` qualifier tells the compiler that the data item has static allocation, external scope, and is defined in another source module. The compiler makes all necessary arrangements to reference the item, but does not reserve memory for it. The allocation of memory must be performed in some other module that defines the object as static external *without* the `extern` qualifier.

You can reference the `heading` variable shown in Listing 3.1 using the following declaration:

```
extern char heading[50];
```

Notice that you do not write `extern static`; the `extern` keyword implies `static` because automatic variables can never be external.

The *const* Type Qualifier

This chapter talks about many ways to qualify the basic data types. You might wonder if any more are truly necessary. The `const` and `volatile` qualifiers, however, provide a useful ANSI extension to the original C language. They aid in both checking programs and enabling the compiler to make some desirable optimizations of the generated code. It takes a little work to fully explain their use because the explanation involves some concepts I haven't discussed before.

Early implementations of the C language made little distinction between memory used to store computer instructions and memory used to store data. As computer hardware became more sophisticated, it became advantageous to store program instructions and program data in separate areas of memory. The purpose of this strategy was to permit several copies of the program to execute simultaneously, with each executing copy sharing the same instructions but keeping a separate copy of the data areas. This kind of design was particularly effective in multiuser systems such as UNIX, where several users might be executing the same program at once.

To share program instructions (called *code*) between users, it was necessary to protect the instruction (also called *code*) portion of the program from modification by itself and other programs. Intentional changes by self-modifying programs were not permitted because such changes were valid for only one of the copies of the currently running program, and accidental changes would destroy the program.

Programmers came to see the protection of program instructions from modification as an advantage, because some kinds of program errors, normally difficult to identify, are automatically diagnosed by the protection facility. It was apparent that program data also falls into two categories: data that changes throughout the execution of the program (called *variables*), and data that remains constant throughout execution. Eventually it was recognized as desirable to also protect program constant data from modification, if for no other reason than to ease the programmer's debugging task.

Until the introduction of the const qualifier, there was no practical way for the C compiler to distinguish between constant and variable data; after all, every variable must be set to a value at some point in the program.

The const qualifier does not, however, have to be permanently associated with a variable. Through the use of *casting* (discussed in Chapter 4, "Expressions"), you can convert a program variable from one type to another. Implicit casting takes place when values are passed to a function; the values are converted from the type supplied by the programmer to the type required by the called function.

When a function requires a data value but has no need to modify it, it is convenient to describe the passed value (called an *argument*) as constant. The compiler then flags any attempt to modify the data value within the function as an error, and the programmer can either correct the data description (concluding that the data value must be modified by the function after all), or correct the errant instruction in the function that would modify the data.

The implicit casting that occurs in the case of values passed to functions affects only the value passed; the original data variable remains unmodified. Because of this, the const attribute associated with the function argument has no effect on the variable that supplies the value of the function argument. Perhaps a short example will make this clearer.

Suppose a function (call it first) calls another function and passes a pointer to an array of characters. The called function should inspect the characters in the array and return the number of characters it finds. (This is the strlen function provided with the system.) During the inspection, the called function has no need to modify the contents of the array. Hence, the declaration of the called strlen function looks like this:

```
int strlen(const char *string);
```

The presence of the const qualifier specifies that the characters which string points to are considered constant values; any instruction in the function that attempts to change one of the characters will result in a compiler error message. (Function declarations are fully explained in Chapter 6, "Functions."

The position of the const qualifier in the declaration is important. If, for example, the declaration had been written instead as

```
int strlen(char const *string);
```

then the pointer (signified by the * symbol) would have been characterized as constant. In the first example, the strlen function can freely modify the pointer to inspect each of the characters in the array, but cannot modify the characters themselves. In the second example, the strlen function is free to modify the first character pointed to by string, but cannot change the pointer itself, making it difficult to inspect any other characters of the array.

The *volatile* Type Qualifier

Like the const qualifier, the volatile qualifier introduced by the ANSI standard is a recent addition to the C language. Its purpose is to solve a technical problem, and as many years of programming in C have shown, the volatile qualifier is rarely needed.

C compilers generally assume that at any given point in time one and only one function in the program is executing. If this is true, the compiler can assume that the only time a variable changes is when an instruction in the current function changes it. By making this assumption, the compiler can optimize the code generated for a function by carrying some of the values in registers, storing any changed values into the real variables only when the function exits.

Some operating systems (UNIX is one of them) are capable of calling a function during the execution of another function. When such an event occurs, the current state of the executing function is saved on the stack, and the new function is entered as if called in the normal fashion. When the new function exits, control is returned to the interrupted function as if nothing happened. The signal standard library function is an example; it can be called when a condition external to the program arises, such as when a timer expires.

Functions called out-of-line with the main program flow of execution are called *interrupt handlers*. An interrupt handler can reference any static global variable that a normal function can reference. A problem can arise, however, when the interrupted function happens to be carrying the value of a static global variable in a hardware register.

If the interrupt handler changes the value of the static global variable, the interrupted function will be unaware of the change. It will destroy the change when it saves the register-cached value before exiting. An equally undesirable result could occur if the interrupt handler behaves incorrectly because it does not have access to the current value of the static global variable.

The volatile qualifier modifies the way the C compiler generates code, avoiding the side effects of register caching variables. Although register caching is usually desirable when improving program performance, it is not desirable when a global variable may be referenced or changed by an interrupt handling function.

To use the `volatile` qualifier, prefix the basic variable type with the keyword `volatile`, as in the following example:

```
static volatile char terminating;
```

The declaration of `terminating` defines it to be a one-byte character variable, global to the source file, allocated in permanent memory (in other words, static) but not external, and volatile. The compiler does not cache the value of `terminating` in a register because the `volatile` keyword specifies that the value of `terminating` can change unpredictably, including when the compiler does not normally expect it to change.

Initializing Variables

The C language provides a way to initialize a variable with a starting value at the time you declare it. When you initialize a variable with an *initializer* as part of the declaration, you do not need to expend execution-time effort initializing the variable.

The general syntactic form for initializing a variable as part of the declaration is

```
declaration = initial_value ;
```

The way you write *initial_value* depends on the type of variable you are initializing. For integer, floating-point, and character variables, the syntax is straightforward:

```
int max_lines = 56;
float pi = 3.14159;
char end_of_file = 'N';
```

Notice that the character variable is initialized using a character literal. This is more readable than using the integer value *78*, but either method works just fine. Remember, the C language considers character variables as numeric data.

To initialize a character array with a string of characters, write the string in quotation marks:

```
static char title[] = "Gone With The Wind";
```

The quotation marks, although necessary to delimit the start and end of the string initializer, are not stored as part of the string. The square brackets after the variable name identify title as an array. Normally you write the number of elements in the array inside the brackets. (In this case, the elements are characters). However, if you omit the element count, the compiler automatically counts the number of characters between the quotes, adds one for the ending null character (remember the null?) and allocates that number of characters to the array.

To write an initializer for any other array type, as well as the char type, specify each element value individually. Here are some examples:

```
int months[3] = { 5, 10, 12};
float rates[3] = { 0.051, 0.062, 0.085 };
char greeting[] = { 'H', 'i', '\0' };
unsigned int tabs[] = { 8, 16, 32, 48, 60, 68, 76, 80 };
```

Notice that the list of initializers for an array is enclosed within braces, and the individual values are separated by a comma. The last value in an initializer list may also be followed by a comma. (Experienced programmers often write a final comma after the last element to simplify program maintenance later when adding new values to the end of the list.)

Summary

This chapter examines the basic data types of the C language and the type qualifiers that can be combined with the basic data types to control the representation of data.

You learned that the basic data types are the following:

- int, which describes integer numeric data 16 or 32 bits in length

- float, which describes 32-bit floating-point numeric data

- double, which specifies a 64-bit floating-point numeric variable

- `char`, which designates a variable as 8-bit character data

- `void`, which describes nonexistent data

These basic types can be qualified by a number of *type qualifiers* that modify the type as follows:

- `long` requests the long form of an item, either `long int` (32-bit integer) or `long double` (80-bit floating point).

- `short` requests the short form of an item, valid only in combination with `int` (`short int` data is 16 bits long).

- `signed` describes a variable ranging in value from a maximum negative to a maximum positive value (used in the form `signed short int`, for example).

- `unsigned` describes a variable ranging in value from 0 to a maximum positive value. Valid only with the `int` and `char` basic types.

- *Storage class*, one of `static`, `extern`, or `auto`, describes the manner in which memory is allocated to a variable.

- `const` describes a value as unmodifiable within a specific context, such as a function.

- `volatile` describes a variable as subject to unpredictable modification.

These modified types can in turn be extended by declaring a variable to be one of the following:

- A pointer to one of the basic or qualified types

- An array of a basic or qualified type

Finally, you can declare a function that returns a value of any of the above types, pointers, or arrays.

In the following chapters, you study the action verbs of the C language: statements that inspect or modify the variables you declare.

Expressions

Although expressions are an important part of the C language, an expression is not usually a complete statement, nor is it a token like those described in the preceding chapter. An *expression* is a computed value that you can use in most places that allow a literal value. For example, you can use the expression 3 + 4 in place of the numeric literal 7 with the same meaning and effect.

Expressions fall into two main categories: those that the compiler can compute, and which therefore require no execution-time evaluation; and those for which the value is unknown at compile time and must be computed during program execution. The expression 3 + 4 is an expression of the first kind and is called a *constant expression*. You can use a constant expression wherever a literal value is legal.

The expression x + 3 is also legal, but the value of the expression depends on the value of x, which may change from time to time during program execution. The compiler cannot predict in advance what the value of x + 3 will be during program execution; in fact, the expression may have a different value every time it is evaluated. An expression of this type cannot be used where the language syntax requires a constant value.

Now that expressions have been characterized by usage and example, take a more precise look at them.

Expression Syntax

An expression is composed of terms and operators combined according to a few simple rules.

A *term* is a literal value, a variable, or another expression. An *operator* is a special character, combination of special characters, or word defined by the C language that modifies or combines the values of one or more terms. For example, the special character + (the plus sign) requires two terms and operates on them by adding the terms together.

The C language provides unary operators as well as binary and ternary operators. A *unary* operator requires only one term; a *binary* operator requires two terms; and a *ternary* operator requires three terms. The + operator is usually a binary operator, whereas the - (minus) symbol can be used as either a unary operator (to create a negative value, such as -7 or -x) or as a binary operator (to subtract one value from another, such as x-3). C has only one ternary operator (comprised of the two symbols ? and :) which is discussed later in this chapter.

You can use expressions as terms, which enables you to build complex expressions from simpler expressions. You probably recognize the expression x+y-2 from algebra. This is a valid expression in C and is interpreted to mean what you would expect: "subtract 2 from the sum of x and y." You may also write x+y*2, but it doesn't mean to multiply the sum of x and y by 2; rather, it means to add x to the product of y and 2. If you suppose that the value of x is *3* and the value of y is *4*, the expression x+y*2 has a value of *11*, not *14*.

The expression x+y*2 involves a built-in trap: it's an ambiguous expression that can be interpreted in either of two different ways. You can eliminate the ambiguity by using parentheses to show your intent: (x+y)*2 means *14*, whereas x+(y*2) means *11*. Alternatively, you can let C determine the order in which to evaluate the operators, which is to assign a relative *priority* to each type of operator. C then evaluates the operators in priority order. In the expression x+y*2, the * (multiplication) operator has higher priority than the + (addition) operator, so the multiplication is performed before the addition.

Table 4.1 lists the operators of the C language, defines their meaning, and gives the priority of each operator. Afterward, the rules for using these operators are reviewed. (Notice that Table 4.1 uses a convention common in computing but somewhat counterintuitive: low numbers indicate a high priority. This makes sense if you think of *1* as meaning first priority, *2* as meaning second priority, and so on.)

Table 4.1. C Operators.

Operator	Priority	Example	Meaning
()	1	fn()	Function call; the value returned by fn
[]	1	x[3]	Subscript; element 3 of array x
->	1	p->x	Pointer; the x pointed to by p
.	1	x.a	Member; the member a in structure x
!	2	!x	Not; the inverse logical value of x
~	2	~x	One's Complement; invert bits of x
++	2	++x	Increment; add 1 to x
- -	2	- -x	Decrement; subtract 1 from x
+	2	+x	Unary plus; the value of x
-	2	-x	Unary minus; the negative of x
*	2	*x	Points to; the value pointed to by x
&	2	&x	Address of; the address of x
(*type*)	2	(int)x	Cast; convert x to data type *type*
sizeof	2	sizeof(x)	Size of; the length of x in bytes
*	3	x * 3	Multiplication; the product of x and 3
/	3	x / y	Division; the quotient of x divided by y

continues

53

Table 4.1. continued

Operator	Priority	Example	Meaning
%	3	x % y	Remainder; the remainder of x divided by y
+	4	x + y	Addition; the sum of x and y
-	4	x - y	Subtraction; y subtracted from x
<<	5	x << 2	Left shift; x shifted left two bits
>>	5	x >> 1	Right shift; x shifted right one bit
<	6	x < 4	Less than; x is less than 4
<=	6	x <= 4	Less than or equal; x is less than or equal to 4
>	6	x > 4	Greater than; x is greater than 4
>=	6	x >= 4	Greater than or equal; x is greater than or equal to 4
==	7	x == 4	Equal; x is equal to 4
!=	7	x != 4	Not equal; x is not equal to 4
&	8	x & 15	Bitwise AND; the AND of x and 15
^	9	x ^ 7	Exclusive OR; the exclusive OR of x and 7
¦	10	x ¦ y	Inclusive OR; the OR of x and y
&&	11	x && y	Logical AND; x is true and y is true
¦¦	12	x ¦¦ y	Logical OR; x is true, y is true, or both x and y are true
?:	13	x?a:b	Conditional; if x is true then a else b
=	14	x = 5	Assignment; set x to the value 5
+=	14	x += 5	Addition; add 5 to x
-=	14	x -= y	Subtraction; subtract y from x
*=	14	x *= y	Multiplication; multiply x by y
/=	14	x /= y	Division; set x to the quotient of x/y

Operator	Priority	Example	Meaning
%=	14	x %= y	Modulus; set x to the remainder of x/y
&=	14	x &= y	Bitwise AND; set x to x&y
^=	14	x ^= y	Exclusive OR; set x to x^y
¦=	14	x ¦= y	Inclusive OR; set x to x¦y
<<=	14	x <<= y	Left shift; shift x left y bits
>>=	14	x >>= y	Right shift; shift x right y bits
,	15	x=(a,b)	Comma; evaluate a, discard the value, then evaluate b, assign the result to x

Binary Expressions

By far the most familiar and the most frequently used operators are the *binary* operators—those requiring two values to perform the operation. All these operators use the *infix* format, where the operator is written between the two values. For example, x + 3 (using the addition operator) and x - y (using the subtraction operator) are both in the infix format.

Arithmetic Operators

The C language supports the familiar operators of arithmetic including + (addition), - (subtraction), * (multiplication), and / (division). C also provides the % operator, called *modulus*, which returns the remainder of a division instead of the quotient.

A few examples should clarify the usage of these operators. In the following examples, assume that the value of y is 5:

```
x = y + 4;              /* 5 + 4 equals 9  */
x = y - 4;              /* 5 - 4 equals 1  */
x = y * 4;              /* 5 * 4 equals 20 */
```

55

```
x = y / 3;              /* 5 / 4 equals 1  */
x = y % 3;              /* 5 % 3 equals 2  */
```

These examples assume that y is an integer variable, which causes the division operator (/) to perform integer division. When you divide *5* by *3*, you get a quotient of *1* with a remainder of *2*. The expression y/3 returns the quotient, and the expression y%3 returns the remainder.

If you declare the variable y to be of type `float` or `double`, a floating-point division is performed. Floating-point division yields a different kind of result:

```
double x, y;
y = 5;
x = y / 4;      /* value is 1.25  */
x = y % 4;      /* Illegal operation! */
```

The modulus operator (%) is not defined for floating-point values because floating-point division does not generate a remainder.

Floating-point addition, subtraction, multiplication, and division work like conventional arithmetic with decimal-point numbers. Keep in mind, though, that a computer representation of a number is not mathematically precise. Variables, even floating-point variables, have maximum and minimum values. Floating-point variables also have a minimum *resolution*, specified in the number of digits of precision maintained for a number. If you try to add a very small number to a very large number, the sum may be no different than the very large number.

Both rounding and truncation errors can occur in floating-point arithmetic. Truncation errors occur when a value cannot be precisely represented. For example, the expression 1.0 / 3.0 is not precisely one third, because the fraction ⅓ cannot be represented in a finite number of bits (0.3333333...). For more information about the limitations of floating-point arithmetic, refer to one of the many books on numerical calculations.

Relational Operators

The operators <, >, <=, >=, ==, !=, &&, and || are commonly called *relational* operators because the result of one of these operations indicates the type of relationship between two values. In C, every expression must have a value.

The value of a relational expression is `true` if the two values have the relationship described by the operator, and `false` if not.

The C language represents *false* by the integer value 0, and *true* by any non-zero integer value. The result of a relational operation is always either 0 (*false*) or 1 (*true*). The two values compared by a relational operator must be of the same type or promotable to the same type. (Promotion of types is discussed later in this chapter.)

The < (less than) operator determines whether the left term is less than the right term. For example, in C, `4 < 3` has a zero value because 4 is not less than 3 (it is *false* that 4 is less than 3). You can use the < operator with any numeric variable. The value of a relational expression such as `4 < 3` is considered to be of type `unsigned int`.

Similarly, the <= (less than or equal) operator tests whether the left value is less than or equal to the right value. The value of the expression is 0 if the relation is false; 1 if it is true.

The > (greater than) operator is the opposite of <=, and the >= (greater than or equal) operator is the opposite of <, in the sense that if `x < y` is true, `x >= y` is always false. Do not use > to mean the opposite of <, because they treat the equal condition differently. For example, if both x and y equal 4, both the expressions `x < y` and `x > y` are false.

The == symbol is the C operator for *equal to*. Do not confuse = and ==; the = symbol is an assignment operator that changes the value of the left term, whereas == is a relational operator that has no side effects. If both x and y equal 4, the value of the expression `x == y` is true (1).

The != symbol is the way you test for *not equal* in the C language. If both x and y equal 4, the value of the expression `x != y` is false (0).

Throughout this section, I talk about the numerical value of relation expressions. The C language considers these expressions to have a numerical value, and enables you to use such expressions in all places where you can use a numerical value. This can lead to some unusual expressions, such as

```
x[y > 3]
```

which references either element 0 or 1 of array x, depending on whether or not y is greater than 3. If y is greater than 3, the expression is the same as `x[1]`; if y is not greater than 3, the expression is the same as `x[0]`.

You can also combine relation expressions, as in

```
0 < y < 4
```

but beware—it may not have the value you think.

All relational operators have the same priority, so an expression such as `0 < y < 4` is evaluated left-to-right, as if written as `(0 < y) < 4`. This expression always has the value *1* (true), because regardless of the value of y, the expression `(0 < y)` can only have the value *0* or *1*. The expression `0 < 4` is true, and the expression `1 < 4` is true, therefore `(0 < y) < 4` is always true.

Relational operators have a lower priority than the arithmetic operators, so the expression `x < y + 4` is evaluated as `x < (y + 4)`. This is reasonable, because programmers are more likely to mean something such as `x > (y+1)` than `(x > y) + 1`. Until you know the operator priorities off the top of your head, however, you should use parentheses to make your meaning explicit.

Logical Operators

The `&&` operator forms an expression that is true only if two subordinate expressions are true. For example, to execute a statement only when an integer value is in the range from 0 to 4, use the following `if` statement to form a logical AND of two relation tests:

```
if ((x >= 0) && (x <= 4))
    /* statement to be executed */ ;
```

Because the `&&` and `¦¦` operators have lesser priority than the relational operators, you can also write the `if` statement as follows:

```
if (x >= 0 && x <= 4)
    /* statement to be executed */ ;
```

The `¦¦` operator enables you to form a logical expression that is true if either of two conditions are true:

```
if (x < 0 ¦¦ x > 4)
    /* x is not in the expected range */ ;
```

A special feature of the `¦¦` operator is that, if the left term of `¦¦` is true, the value of the right term is not calculated. The following code uses this rule to advantage by combining two tests in one `if` statement:

```
if (str == NULL || *str != 'a')
    /* str doesn't exist or doesn't start with 'a' */
    ;
```

If the left term (str == NULL) is true, the right term (*str != 'a') could cause a program crash by attempting to use an invalid pointer. This if statement is safe to execute only because the || operator doesn't evaluate both of its terms before forming its result when the left term is true. If no such rule existed, the if statement would have to be written like this:

```
if (str == NULL)
    /* Error: null pointer */
else if (*str != 'a')
    /* Error: string doesn't start with 'a' */
    ;
```

As you can see, the early termination rule saves effort and makes C programs easier to write.

Bitwise Operators

The C language provides a number of operators that manipulate the bits of a value. These operators are modeled on facilities provided by most computers, and are intended to enable you to take advantage of those facilities. You can usually achieve the effect of a bitwise operator using arithmetic and logical operators, but judicious use of the bitwise operators can save coding effort and execution time.

The bitwise operators C provides are & (AND), | (OR, also called inclusive OR), and ^ (exclusive OR), and also the unary bitwise operator ~ (complementation). See the section "Unary Expressions" later in this chapter for information about the complementation operator.

The & operator (AND) sets a result bit to *1* if and only if the corresponding bit position of the two source values are *1*s. For example, the AND of the two integers *4* and *5* is *4*. This may be clearer if you calculate the result by hand, writing down the two numbers to be ANDed together as follows:

```
0100        Bit representation of 4
0101        Bit representation of 5
____
0100        Result of AND: bit representation of 4
```

The result is *4* because only the 4-bit is *1* in both values. The bitwise AND operator is sometimes called bitwise multiplication, because the result is calculated as if multiplying corresponding bits.

The ¦ operator (OR) sets a result bit to *1* if either of the two corresponding bit positions of the two source values are *1*s. Here is an example using the values *5* and *6*:

```
0101        Bit representation of 5
0110        Bit representation of 6
____
0111        Result of OR: bit representation of 7
```

The ^ operator (exclusive OR) sets a result bit to *1* if the corresponding bit positions of the two source values are different; if they are the same, the result bit is *0*. Here is an example once again using the two source values *5* and *6*:

```
0101        Bit representation of 5
0110        Bit representation of 6
____
0011        Result of exclusive OR: bit representation of 3
```

You can use the exclusive OR operator to invert the setting of a bit in a value by exclusive-ORing the bit position to be changed with *1* and all other bit positions with *0*.

You can use the three bitwise operators &, ¦, and ^ to manage the bits of an integer as a set of flags (yes/no indicators), using each bit position of the integer (up to 32 bits for each integer) as a different indicator. Use the OR operator to set a bit on, use the AND operator to set a bit off, and use the exclusive OR operator to switch a bit.

Listing 4.1 shows the use of bit switches to remember, and later act on, command-line options.

Listing 4.1. Using command-line toggle switches.

```c
/* toggle.c - Using command-line toggles */

#include <stdio.h>
#include <stdlib.h>

#define FLAG_C 0x01
#define FLAG_F 0x02
#define FLAG_L 0x04

int main(int argc, char *argv[])
{
    int key, flags;

    flags = 0;  /* Initialize flags to all off */

    /* Check command line for -c, -f, and -l switches */
    while ((key = getopt(argc, argv, "cfl")) != EOF)
        switch (key) {
        case 'c':
            flags = flags | FLAG_C;
            break;
        case 'f':
            flags = flags | FLAG_F;
            break;
        case 'l':
            flags = flags | FLAG_L;
            break;
        }

    if (flags & FLAG_C) {
        printf("Option -c specified\n");
        /* code for option -c */
    }

    if (flags & FLAG_F) {
        printf("Option -f specified\n");
```

continues

61

Listing 4.1. continued

```
        /* code for option -f */
    }

    if (flags & FLAG_L) {
        printf("Option -l specified\n");
        /* code for option -l */
    }

    /* Finished, exit the program */
    return(0);
}
```

The toggle.c program in Listing 4.1 uses the getopt library function to scan the command line for the options -c, -f, or -l. For more information about getopt, see my book, *UNIX Programmer's Reference* (Que, 1991), which explains the getopt library function in detail, as well as all the other functions in the standard C function library.

You should enter this source program using a text editor such as vi (see Chapter 12, "Using the vi Editor"), and then compile and execute the program with the following command-line options:

```
$ cc toggle.c -o toggle
$ toggle -c -l
Option -c specified
Option -l specified
$ toggle -lc
Option -c specified
Option -l specified
$ toggle -mfc
toggle: illegal option -- m
Option -c specified
Option -l specified
$
```

Notice that the program output always identifies the options in the same order, regardless of the order in which you specify them on the command line.

This is because the toggle.c program first collects the options in the `flags` variable, then tests them in a set order.

Shift Operators

The shift operators << (left shift) and >> (right shift) change their operands by moving the bits of an integer value to the left or right, filling vacated positions with the sign bit. A left shift of one moves all the bits of a value one position to the left; it is equivalent to multiplying the value by two. A right shift of one moves all the bits of a value one position to the right; it is the equivalent of dividing by two.

The expression x<<2 shifts the value of x two bits to the left, which is the same as multiplying by four. The expression x<<y shifts the value of x left by the number of bit positions specified by the integer value of y—in other words, by a variable amount. The left term of the shift operators specifies the value to be shifted; the right term specifies the number of bit positions left or right to move the value.

A left shift discards bits shifted off the left (most significant bits) and fills positions on the right with 0. A right shift discards bits shifted off the right (least significant bits) and fills positions on the left with the sign bit (if the value is signed) or with 0 (if the value is unsigned). The loss of significant bits does not generate an abnormal condition.

Figure 4.1 diagrams a right shift of one bit position. Notice that the rightmost bit of the value is discarded, and that the leftmost bit is used to fill new positions on the left. The figure assumes that the shifted value is of type signed int. If the value were of type unsigned int, then a zero would have been placed in the leftmost position.

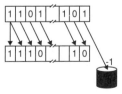

Figure 4.1. A right shift of one bit position.

Left and right shifts most often are used as a quick way to multiply or divide integers by powers of two. Shifting left by three positions effectively multiplies by 8, whereas shifting right by four positions effectively divides by 16.

Assignment Operators

In C, the assignment operator is = (the equal sign). In some other languages, the = symbol does double duty as both the assignment operator and the equality relation. This is not so in the C language. The = and == operators are quite different, and you must be careful to use them appropriately.

The usage of the assignment operator = in C differs from its usage in other languages in a second important way: it is merely an operator, not a statement type. In fact, an assignment expression can be a subordinate expression in a larger, more complex expression.

The value of an assignment expression is the value assigned.

The priority of the assignment operator is lower than that of most other operators, so to use an assignment expression within a larger expression, you usually must enclose the entire assignment expression in parentheses.

The left term of an assignment expression must be an *lvalue*. The term *lvalue* was introduced by the original authors of the C language to describe an expression that references a memory location. The term is intended to suggest an expression that you can write to the left of an assignment; in other words, an lvalue is an expression with a changeable value.

Many kinds of expressions are not lvalues. For example, (x+3) is not an lvalue because its value does not reside in memory; it is a calculated value.

On the other hand, all variable names, all primary expressions of the form x[y], x->y, or x.y, and pointer references of the form *x are lvalues because they refer to a specific memory location. (The section "Primary Expressions" later in this chapter presents the [], ->, and . operators; the * unary pointer operator is presented in the section "Pointer Operators" also appearing later in this chapter.)

The right term of an assignment expression can be any expression that results in a value you can store in the left term, or that can be converted to such a type. Generally, you can store any numeric value in a variable of any of the numeric types, whereas you can store pointer values only in pointer variables of the same type. This is because the C language knows how to convert an unsigned short integer to a signed long integer (or to floating-point), but makes no assumptions about how to convert a pointer to character to a pointer to integer. The section "Automatic Type Conversions" later in this chapter discusses the kind of data type conversions the C language makes automatically in the course of computing an expression.

Although the idea of using an assignment as a subordinate term in a larger expression may be novel, C programmers actually use the technique rather freely. For example, the following code shows how the technique simplifies the process of opening a file for input.

```c
#include <stdio.h>
int main()
{
    FILE *input;

    /*
     * Open a file called "data" for reading
     */
    if ((input = fopen("data", "r")) == NULL) {
        perror("data");
        exit(2);
    }

    /* Insert code here to process the file */

    /* Close the file and exit. */
    fclose(input);
    return(0);
}
```

The function call that actually opens the file is fopen, which takes as its arguments the name of the file and a code to indicate whether the file will be read or written. If it successfully opens the file, fopen returns a value (of type FILE *) which can be used in other function calls to refer to the file. But if it fails to open the file, fopen returns a NULL (zero) value. The if statement therefore both opens the file and tests for failure all at once; if the open fails, the program prints a warning message with perror and then exits.

You can achieve the same effect by separating the assignment expression and the `if` statement as follows:

```
input = fopen("data", "r");    /* Open the file */
if (input == NULL) {           /* Unable to open it? */
    perror("data");            /* Then write a message */
    exit(2);                   /* and halt. */
}
```

The C language provides a number of special assignment operators, of the general form *op=*, to help you write shorter, more expressive programs. These operators are all equivalent to writing x = x *op exp*. In other words, writing x *op= exp* (where *op* is any of several simple operators such as + or =) is equivalent to writing x = x *op exp*. For example, to add 10 to a value, you could write

```
x = x + 10;
```

or you could write the shorter form

```
x += 10;
```

The *op=* operators are especially helpful when manipulating an lvalue represented by a complex expression. Suppose a pointer gives the location of a structure that contains an array, and you want to add a constant to some element of that array, where the expression i/2+1 specifies which element.

You can write the assignment like this:

```
p->items[i/2+1] = p->items[i/2+1] + 8;
```

Or you can add 8 to the element using this assignment:

```
p->items[i/2+1] += 8;
```

The second form is not only easier to write, it is also easier to read and understand. Furthermore, there is less danger of mistyping the expression p->items[i/2]+1, which must be the same on both sides of the equal sign.

Table 4.1, at the beginning of this chapter, lists the *op=* operators. In general, these include all the binary operators except the relational operators, the assignment itself, and the comma operator.

The Comma Operator

The *comma* operator (written x,y) discards the value of its left term and sets the value of the expression to the value of its right term. Successive comma expressions are evaluated in a left-to-right order.

In an expression of the form (x = a, b), the value assigned to x is the value of the expression b. The value of a is computed, but not used, and can be useful only if its computation has side effects.

Use of the comma operator is never necessary; you can safely ignore it until you discover an occasion to use it. The comma operator is used most often with the for statement.

The following code fragment illustrates one way you might use the comma operator:

```
n = 10;
while (n = n - 2, n >= 0) {
    /* body of loop */
}
```

The first statement assigns the value *10* to the integer variable n. The while statement decrements n on every iteration, stopping when the value of n becomes negative. The reason for using the comma operator here is that the while statement syntax allows only one expression inside the parentheses. By using the comma operator, you can write one expression that first decrements n by two and then tests whether the new value is positive.

In all fairness, I should also point out that the while statement could have been written in the form while ((n = n - 2) >= 0), which directly tests the result of the assignment. In C programming, there are often many ways to write the same thing.

Unlike most binary operators, the value of a comma expression is not computed all at once. Rather, the value of the left term is completely computed, and then the right term is computed. This synchronization assures that, in the while example above, the decremented value of n is used in the >= expression. Without this guarantee, the n in n >= 10 might be evaluated using the initial value of n before the subtraction, which gives a different result.

To use a comma expression where a comma also has syntactic significance, you must enclose the comma expression in parentheses. For example, to write the comma expression x,y as an argument in a function call, write fun((x,y), z).

Unary Expressions

Unary expressions use one operator and one term; the operator changes the value of the term in some way. The unary operators are unusual in that multiple unary operators in succession are evaluated in right-to-left order instead of the more common left-to-right order. Understanding this order of evaluation is essential to correctly interpret expressions such as *++x or *x++ that are not unusual in the C language.

Unary operators always come *before* the value they modify, except in the case of ++ or --, which can come either before or after the value. When determining the order of evaluation, ignore the variable in a sequence of operators. For example, in both of the expressions *++x and *x++, the ++ operator is applied first; the expressions are equivalent to *(++x) and *(x++).

Unary Plus and Minus

The unary plus and minus operators control the sign of a numeric constant or variable. You must prefix the operator to the constant, variable, or expression it modifies, as in -x or -(x*y+2).

The unary minus (-) inverts the sign of the following expression. If the expression has a negative value, it changes to a positive value; if the expression has a positive value, it becomes negative.

The unary plus (+) leaves the sign of the following expression unchanged. In other words, +x has the same value as x. The C language supports the unary plus operator merely as a decoration to the language, enabling you to write a constant in the form +1 to emphasize that the constant has a positive value. Be careful not to think that the unary plus forces an expression to have a positive value; this is not the case.

You can prefix an expression with more than one unary operator. Remember that the operators are evaluated from right to left, instead of from left to right. In the expression -!x, for example, the logical NOT operator ! executes before the unary minus.

Because C also provides the ++ and -- operators (see the following section), you cannot write two unary sign operators in succession. To write *minus minus x*, you must code it either as -(-x), using parentheses, or as - -x, leaving a space between the first and second minus sign.

Increment and Decrement

The ++ operator increments a variable by adding one to it, and the -- operator decrements a variable by subtracting one. The ++ or -- operator may either precede or follow the expression it modifies. That is, both ++x and x++ are valid C expressions. In either case, the value of x is incremented by one. The difference is in the value of the two expressions taken as a whole.

The value of a prefix expression such as ++x is that of x after incrementation; first x is incremented, and then the result is taken as the value of the expression.

The value of a postfix expression such as x++ is that of x before incrementation. The value of x is taken as the value of the expression, and then x is incremented.

If you intend only to increment or decrement a value, you can write either ++x or x++; either order has the same effect on x. If you plan to use the result in a larger expression, however, it makes a difference where you place the operator. If you place the operator before the variable, the variable is incremented before the expression is evaluated. If you place the operator after the variable, the variable is incremented after the expression is evaluated.

As an example, consider the following statement:

```
y = x++ + 3;
```

Assuming that the value of x is *10*, the value *13* is assigned to y. After the value of x is used in the expression, though, it is incremented to *11*. The ++ operator is coded in the postfix position, meaning that x is not incremented until after the value of x is used in the expression.

The operators ++ and -- must be applied to lvalues. lvalues are explained in the section titled "Assignment Operators."

When combined with primary expressions, the ++ and -- operators are often difficult to interpret. For example, the array expression ++x[1] increments the second element of array x, not x itself. The array operator [] takes priority over ++, so the subscript is resolved to an element of the array before ++ is applied.

Similarly, the expressions ++p->x and ++p.x both increment the member x, not p. The expressions p->x++ and p.x++ are also valid, and specify postfix incrementation of member x. The notations p->++x and p.++x are invalid because, by definition, a structure member name must follow the -> and . operators.

The combination of incrementation and decrementation operators with the * pointer operator, in expressions such as *x++, occurs so frequently in C that this book defers interpreting such expressions until pointers are formally introduced in Chapter 8, "Pointers and Arrays."

Logical Negation

The ! (read as NOT) inverts the logical value of the subsequent expression. As a logical operator, ! can return only the value 0 (signifying *false*), or 1 (signifying *true*). If the expression following ! has a true value (nonzero), then ! returns *false* (0); otherwise it returns *true* (1).

You can apply logical negation only to integer-valued expressions, although a subject expression may contain other kinds of variables. For example, in the following code fragment

```
float x, y;
int same;

same = !(x > y);
```

the expression (x > y) has an integer value, because the > operator itself returns an integer value—namely the result of comparing the two variables x and y. If x is greater than y, the value of the expression (x > y) is *1* (meaning *it is true that x is greater than y*). The value of !(x > y) is then *0* and set into the variable same.

The expression !!x is valid. It has the value *1* if x is nonzero, or *0* if x is zero.

One's Complement

The ~ (tilde) operator returns the one's complement of the expression that follows the operator. The one's complement is formed by inverting the bits of the value. Thus, the complement of the short integer *0* is *–1*, because when you invert the bits 0000000000000000, you get the bit pattern 1111111111111111, which is –1.

The complement of a value is not the same as its negation. For example, if x has the value *4*, then -x has the value *– 4*, whereas ~x has the value *–5*. In bit patterns, this is shown by inverting 0100 (the value *4*) to get 1011. Because the leftmost bit of 1011 is 1, the value is interpreted as a negative number. It works out that the binary representation of *–5* is 1111...1011. To verify this, notice that you have to add binary *5* (0101) to 1011 to get 0000, which implies that 1011 is equal to *–5*.

Pointer Operators

The * and & operators, when used as unary operators, perform pointer operations. The * and & symbols are also binary operators, and have different meanings when used as unary or binary operators. The compiler determines the meaning of the symbol from the context in which it is used.

The * operator returns the value pointed to by a pointer variable. You will often see the * operator used in expressions such as *s or *ptr. To understand its meaning, first consider the meaning of the simpler expression x. When used in a larger expression such as x + 3, you understand the symbol x to mean "take the value of x." The pointer operator * can be used in a similar expression such as *x + 3 to mean "take the value pointed to by x." In other words, x is not the value to be used in the addition problem; it is only a pointer, and the value to be used is the integer to which it points.

A pointer variable is a separate entity from the value to which it points. It occupies separate memory and can be manipulated in ways that are meaningful to pointers. For that reason, if variable x is a pointer to an integer, you must have a way to refer to the pointer itself or to the object to which it points. Used by itself, the symbol x refers to the pointer. You must apply the * operator with x to access the value to which x points.

The & operator returns the address of a variable. Once again, let x be the name of a variable. Whereas the expression x means the value of x, the expression &x means the *address* of x. The value of the expression &x is a pointer value that you can use in any way that you can use a pointer value. In particular, you can use it to initialize a pointer variable, as in the following code fragment:

```
int *ip, sum;

ip = &sum;
*ip = *ip + 3;
```

The declaration creates a pointer variable ip and an integer variable sum. The first executable statement sets ip to the address of sum. The second executable statement adds three to whatever ip points to, which in this example is the variable named sum. The expression *ip denotes the memory variable pointed to by ip. You could write this program fragment more simply as sum = sum + 3 without the use of pointers; I used it here to show that the pointer reference *ip is equivalent in every way to the simple value reference sum.

Note that the * and & unary operators are essentially the inverse of each other. The expression *&x is equivalent to just x, because & first takes the address of x, and then * resolves that address to the value it points to. The expression &*x is nonsensical, because *x first references the value to which x points, and then & takes the address of the value, which is just the value of x. Writing &*x is therefore also equivalent to writing just x.

The *sizeof* Operator

The sizeof operator returns the size of its operand as an unsigned integer number of bytes. You use the sizeof operator in an expression by writing it in one of two forms: sizeof *term* or sizeof(*term*). In the parenthetical form, sizeof(*something*), you may replace *something* with either an lvalue or a typename. In the nonparenthesized form, sizeof *something*, *something* may only be an lvalue. Because the parenthesized syntax is more general, many programmers use only that format.

If *term* is an lvalue, sizeof returns the actual size of the memory object. The sample program in Listing 4.2 prints out the size of several variables.

Listing 4.2. Using the sizeof operator.

```
/* samp.c - print size of integer variable types */
#include <stdio.h>
int main()
{
    int    i;
    short  si;
    long   li;

    printf("sizeof i  = %d\n", sizeof i);
    printf("sizeof si = %d\n", sizeof si);
    printf("sizeof li = %d\n", sizeof li);
    return (0);
}
```

You can compile and run this program using the following two commands (shown in bold in the output):

```
$ cc samp.c
$ a.out
sizeof i  = 4
sizeof si = 2
sizeof li = 4
$
```

The output from this program shows the size of integer, short, and long variables. These sizes are defined by the ANSI standard for the C language, which requires a short integer to be 16 bits (two bytes) long and a long integer to be 32 bits (four bytes) long. An integer type without the short or long modifiers turns out to be the same length as a long integer.

The sizeof operator can also take the name of a data type as its operand. Using typenames is convenient when you want to know the size of a generic data type instead of any specific variable. To use a typename, you must enclose the typename in parentheses:

sizeof(*type*)

Listing 4.3 shows the program from Listing 4.2 written using typenames. Notice that the program in Listing 4.3 does not require the definition of any variables, as does Listing 4.2, which doesn't actually use them anyway.

Listing 4.3. Using typenames with `sizeof`.

```
/* samp2.c - print the size of integers */
#include <stdio.h>
int main()
{
    printf("sizeof int = %d\n", sizeof(int));
    printf("sizeof short int = %d\n", sizeof(short int));
    printf("sizeof long int  = %d\n", sizeof(long int));
    return(0);
}
```

As before, you can key in this program using any text editor, and then compile and execute it using the following commands:

```
$ cc samp2.c
$ a.out
sizeof int = 4
sizeof short int = 2
sizeof long int  = 4
$
```

For more information about typenames, see the section "Writing Typenames" later in this chapter.

The Cast Operator

The *cast* operator changes the type of an expression to another data type. To use the cast operator, write the typename of the resulting data type inside parentheses in front of the value to be cast. The C compiler already knows the type from which to convert, and arranges to perform any conversion of representation that may be needed.

C programmers often use the cast operator to convert a pointer from one type to another, or to change the size or representation of a number.

For example, to increment a floating-point number by two-thirds, you might use the following computation:

```
float x, third;
third = x + 2 / 3;
```

According to operator priorities, the compiler must first evaluate 2/3 before performing the addition, because division has a higher priority than addition. Both the constants 2 and 3 are integers, so the division is performed using integer arithmetic, yielding a result of 0. This result is then converted to floating-point to perform the addition, yielding the erroneous result that third is equal to x+0. One way to get around this difficulty is to explicitly promote either 2 or 3 or both to floating-point before performing the division:

```
third = x + (float)2 / 3;
```

This latter expression works correctly because the cast operator (float) has a higher priority than either + or /. Also, if either operand of an arithmetic operator is floating-point, then floating-point arithmetic is used. Thus, the value of (float)2 / 3 is approximately *0.6666666...*, which yields the expected result.

Notice that floating-point division can also be forced using the expedient of specifying one or both of the constants as floating-point constants in the first place. All you need to do is write 2.0 and 3.0 in the statement.

As another example of using casts, suppose you have a pointer to void and you want a pointer to char. This often occurs when allocating memory using the malloc library function, which returns a pointer to void. To allocate ten bytes of memory, you might use the following code fragment:

```
char *string;
string = (char *) malloc(10);
```

Here, the value returned by malloc() is cast to type char * (pointer to character) before being assigned to the string variable.

Casts sometimes convert the internal representation of data, but not always. In general, a cast from one type of pointer to another does not require any change of representation. Casting an integer to a floating-point variable, or floating-point to integer, however, does require a change of representation and runtime instructions to execute.

As a beginner to the C language, you will usually be unsure when a cast is necessary. If you use the lint utility to check your source programs for correctness (lint is discussed in Chapter 14), lint tells you where you need casts. Often, the C compiler automatically performs data conversions for you. The section "Automatic Type Conversions" later in this chapter describes the type conversions that the C language automatically performs for you.

For more information about writing the typenames that appear inside the parentheses of a cast, see the section "Writing Typenames" also appearing later in this chapter.

Primary Expressions

A *primary expression* is an expression formed using one of the primary operators (), [], ->, or . (pronounced *dot*). A primary operator has higher priority than all other operators; in a compound expression, a primary expression is evaluated before any other subexpressions. Two or more primary expressions in a row are evaluated in left-to-right order.

Using Parentheses

Parentheses have two syntactic uses: to denote a subexpression, as in (x+y)*2; or to invoke a function, such as sqrt(x+y). Parentheses used for bracketing an expression cause the bracketed expression to be treated as a unit, and to be evaluated before other parts of the expression. For example, in the expression (x+y)*2, the addition operator normally has lower priority than the multiplication operator, but by enclosing x+y in parentheses, the addition is performed before the multiplication.

When parentheses occur after an identifier, they indicate that the identifier is the name of a function. After the named function executes, the function call then is logically replaced by the value returned by the function, and evaluation of the expression continues. The parentheses may contain a list of arguments to pass to the function or, if the function requires no arguments, the parentheses may not contain anything.

The square root function sqrt requires one argument: the value for which the square root is to be extracted. To take the square root of a value, write the value as an argument to the sqrt function, like this: sqrt(x+3). The expression x+3 is evaluated and then the result is passed to the sqrt function. The entire expression sqrt(x+3) is then replaced by the value returned by sqrt. In the assignment

```
y = sqrt(x+3)
```

the term x is first replaced by the value of x, say 6. The expression 6+3 is then evaluated, giving 9. Next, the sqrt function is invoked with the value 9 as its argument, as if sqrt(9) had been written. The square root of 9 is 3, so the entire function call is replaced by 3, reducing the original expression to y = 3. Finally, the value 3 is assigned to y.

To pass several arguments to a function, list the arguments inside parentheses and separate the arguments with commas. Such a function call might look like this:

```
dist = hypot(x+3,y-2)
```

Notice how the comma improves the clarity of the expression (both for humans and for the C compiler). In this example, both of the arguments to hypot are themselves expressions. Each of the two arguments is evaluated before hypot is called. The C language standard does not guarantee that function arguments will be evaluated in left-to-right order; some compilers might evaluate y-2 before evaluating x+3. For that reason, you should avoid the use of expressions having side effects in argument lists.

Side effects are a very important consideration in writing clear, bug-free code in C. A *side effect* is any expression that permanently changes the value of one or more variables. The ++ and -- operators, as well as all the assignment operators (+, +=, and so on), cause side effects. Although these operators enhance the convenience of writing in C, the fact that an operator hidden deep inside a complex expression can change the value of a variable can also make C programs hard to understand and debug.

Subscripting with []

In Chapter 3, "Simple Declarations," you saw that you can use square brackets in a declaration to specify an array of variables. For example,

```
int x[3];
```

declares an array called x with three elements of type int. You use the same symbols, [], to reference one of the elements of the array. (You must reference and manipulate arrays one element at a time. There are no C operators that operate on an array as a unit.)

In C, the elements of an array are numbered from 0 to $n-1$ where n is the number of elements in the array. You can access the first element (element 0) by writing the expression x[0], the second by writing x[1], and the third by writing x[2]. The expression x[3] is invalid because it refers to the fourth element of array x.

An array of two dimensions requires two subscripts to uniquely identify an element; an array of three dimensions requires three subscripts. If you're already familiar with some other programming languages, you might want to write x[1,3] to access the element in row 1, column 3 of an array, but this would be wrong in C. In C, you must learn to think of higher-dimensional arrays as arrays of arrays. Thus, a two-dimensional array is an array of one-dimensional arrays, a three-dimensional array is an array of two-dimensional arrays, and so on.

Thinking of multidimensional arrays as arrays of arrays helps you remember the syntax for accessing an element. To access the element in row 1, column 3, you must write the expression x[1][3]. This is actually a compound expression consisting of two operators. The first operator, [1], selects the second element of x (itself a one-dimensional array). For clarity, I'll call the result of this first operation x1. The second operator, [3], is interpreted as x1[3], which finally selects the fourth element from the previously selected row.

Figure 4.2 depicts a two-dimensional array consisting of four rows of ten columns each, as you obtain from the declaration int x[4][10];. The C language considers the array x to consist of four elements, named x[0], x[1], x[2], and x[3]. Each of these "elements," however, is also an array. To access an individual element—say, in the second row—you have to perform an additional subscripting operation. To do that, you need to append a subscript operator to the expression x[1], which obtains the expression x[1][3] to access the fourth element.

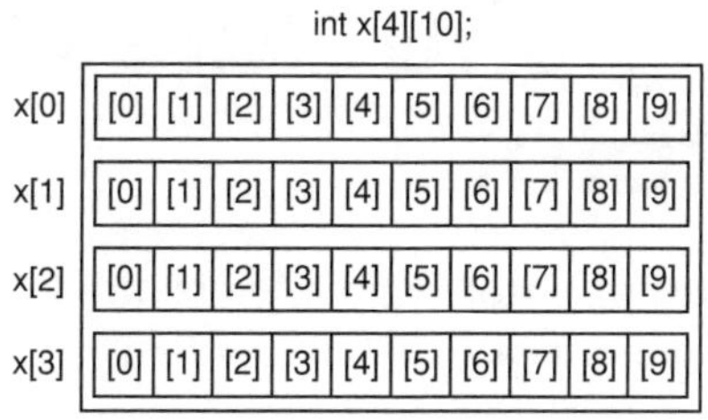

int x[4][10];

Figure 4.2. The two-dimensional array x[4][10].

In the C language, subscripting definitely is considered an operation and not merely a syntactic device. For that reason, you can use parentheses to indicate the order of subscripting. The expression (x[1])[3] is entirely legal, emphasizing that the fourth element is to be extracted from the array (x[1]).

As I have shown, a subscript index can be a literal number. In addition, it can be any valid numeric expression. If another integer variable y has the value 3, the expression x[1][y] obtains the fourth element of the second row just as the expression x[1][3] does.

More interestingly, you can apply the subscript operator to any expression that resolves to an array. In Chapter 3, the section "Initializing Variables" points out that a literal character string can be denoted by enclosing the string in quotation marks, as in "string of chars". It also notes that a character string is actually an array of characters, so the declaration of a character string must be in the general form char name[size]. Because it is valid to reference a character of the array using an expression such as name[8], it is also valid to reference a literal character string in the same form, because it is also an array. This leads to the strange looking expression "string of chars"[8], which references the character f in of.

The meaning and usage of arrays in the C language may seem a little out of the ordinary, but they are even stranger than you think. You must wait until the subject of pointers is discussed, however, for the gory details.

Accessing Structures with the Dot Operator

You must use the . (dot) operator in an expression of the form *p.m*, where *p* is any expression that represents a structure, and *m* is a member name occurring in the structure. The value of the expression *p.m* is the value of member *m* in structure *p*.

Difficulties using the dot operator arise from failing to understand the significance of *p* in the expression and from failing to combine unary operators such as ++ or * with the expression. To clarify some of these fine points, take a look at a few examples.

Consider the following structure declaration:

```
struct employee {
    char    emp_no [5];         /* Employee number      */
    char    name [30];          /* Last, First, MI      */
    int     dept;               /* Department nbr       */
    int     mo, da, yr;         /* Date of hire         */
    int     salary;             /* Regular salary       */
    char    period;             /* Pay period           */
    char    exempt;             /* 'E' if exempt        */
};
struct employee new;            /* Build area for new emp */
struct employee *list;          /* List of employees */
```

As Chapter 7, "Structures and Unions," explains, the first struct statement only describes a data structure; it does not allocate memory to hold any data. The second statement allocates storage to hold one occurrence of the structure and names it new. The third struct statement also allocates memory, but for a pointer to an employee structure, not the structure itself.

To store the value *25* in the department number member of structure new, use a statement like this:

```
new.dept = 25;
```

The value of.new is the whole structure; new.dept selects just the member dept from the structure.

To store the value *25* in the structure pointed to by list, use a statement like the following:

```
(*list).dept = 25;
```

In this case, (*list) represents the *p* in *p.m*. You need the unary * operator to tell C to use the structure *pointed to* by list. You need the parentheses because the . operator has a higher priority than *. If you write

```
*list.dept = 25;    /* Wrong! */
```

instead, the statement does not work properly because C sees it as the expression

```
*(list.dept) = 25;
```

This expression says to take the member dept from the structure list, use the value of the member as a pointer, and store the value *25* where the pointer points. But list is not a structure, and dept is an integer, not a pointer. The compiler would flag this statement with two, three, or even more errors before going on to the next line in your program.

Accessing Structures with ->

This section on the -> primary expressions is presented now along with the other primary expressions, but requires a knowledge of structures and pointers. On a first reading, you may want to defer this section until you read about structures and pointers in Chapter 7, "Structures and Unions," and Chapter 8, "Pointers and Arrays."

You may recall from Chapter 3 that the C language supports a type of object called a *pointer*. A pointer is a variable just like any other variable, except that its value ordinarily is not of any direct interest. In a certain sense, the value of a pointer is the name of another variable. To access the variable pointed to by the pointer, you must *dereference* it. This action causes the pointer to be used to locate the variable.

When a pointer points to a simple object like an integer or a character, the pointer can be used directly—for example, by writing the expression *p (where p is some pointer). The value of the expression *p is not the value of p, but rather the value of the object to which p points.

81

When a pointer points to a structure containing many individual data items, however, a simple dereference is often not satisfactory because its value is the entire structure. To access an individual member of a structure, you need to use the -> operator.

The -> operator is a binary operator (it requires two values to perform its function). Written in the form *p*->*m*, where *p* is a pointer variable or pointer expression and *m* is a member name in some structure, the operation of -> is to return the value of member *m* in the structure pointed to by *p*.

The right-hand side of the expression (m) is not a value in the ordinary sense; in particular, you cannot write an expression for m, because m must be a member name occurring in the structure declaration. The value of m is the offset of the member in the structure, which, when added to the pointer value p, yields a pointer to the member itself. The value of the member is retrieved from the structure and becomes the value of the expression p->m.

Listing 4.4 is a program that looks up an airport code in a table and prints out the name of the airport. The task is simplified by the use of a pointer variable to point to successive entries in the table, which shows the use of the p->m expression to examine each member of an entry.

Listing 4.4. Converting an airport code to a name.

```
#include <stdio.h>
#include <string.h>

/* Declare the structure of a table entry */

struct airport {
    char    *code;    /* String giving the airport code */
    char    *name;    /* String giving the airport name */
};

/* Define the search table */

struct airport codes[] = {
    { "ATL", "Atlanta Hartfield Intl" },
    { "BOS", "Boston/Logan Intl" },
```

```
        { "CLE", "Cleveland Hopkins Intl" },
        { "DTW", "Detroit Metro Intl" },
        { "IAD", "Washington Dulles Intl" },
        { "IAG", "Niagara Falls Intl" },
        { "LAX", "Los Angeles Intl" },
        { "SFO", "San Francisco Intl" },
        { NULL, NULL },
};

/* Program to match the first command-line argument
 * to an airport code in the table
 */
int main(int argc, char *argv[])
{
    struct airport *p;

    if (argc != 2) {
        fprintf(stderr, "Usage: apc <code>\n");
        exit(1);
    }
    for (p = codes; ;p++)
        if (p->code == NULL) {
            printf("%s: Unknown airport code\n", argv[1]);
            exit(2);
        }
        else if (strcmp(p->code, argv[1]) == 0) {
            printf("%s: %s\n", p->code, p->name);
            break;
        }
    return (0);
}
```

This program arranges its parts in an order fairly typical of C programming style: the preprocessor directives #include and #define (if any) are first, followed by structure declarations, then global data definitions, and finally the executable functions of the program.

There is only one function in the program: main, which must be present in all C programs. This function first checks that the command line contains two words (argc != 2). The first word is the command name itself; the second is the airport code to look up.

The main body of the function consists of a for loop that iteratively searches the table for the command-line argument argv[1]. The loop begins by setting p to point to the first table entry (p = codes), and increments the pointer p by one entry on each iteration (p++). On each iteration, the code first checks for a NULL code in the table entry, which signals the end of the table and means that the user's airport code was not found in the table. If the code is not NULL, it is compared to the character string specified on the command line using the strcmp library function. If a match is found, the printf statement prints out the code and the corresponding airport name.

The syntax of much of the code in Listing 4.4 is not covered until later chapters, so don't be concerned if the code looks like a meaningless jumble. The main thing to notice in this listing is the use of the expressions p->code and p->name. Because p is declared as a pointer to an airport structure, the C compiler concludes that code and name must be members of the airport structure. They are, and instances of p->code and p->name are resolved at runtime to reference the corresponding members of the table entry.

The Conditional Operator

A conditional expression takes the following general form:

```
logical-exp ? expt : expf
```

First, logical-exp is evaluated. If the resulting value is true (nonzero), the expression expt is evaluated and the result is taken as the value of the entire expression. But if the value of logical-exp is false (zero), the expression expf is evaluated and the result is the value of the entire expression.

The priority of the assignment operators is even lower than that of the conditional operators, so it is not unusual to see a conditional expression in the form x = (*cond*) ? a : b. The conditional expression is read as "if *condition* then *a* else *b*." In other words, the conditional expression is an expression form of an if statement, with the ? standing for then and : standing for else.

Sometimes you see the conditional expression used as an argument in the printf function to handle the case where a string pointer might have a null value:

```
printf("Airport name is %s\n",
    (p == NULL) ? "unknown" : p->name
    );
```

(For clarity, I isolated the conditional expression on the second line, although you can just as easily run all three lines together.)

Without the conditional expression, this printf statement must instead be written in the following way:

```
if (p == NULL)
    printf("Airport name is unknown\n");
else
    printf("Airport name is %s\n", p->name);
```

By using the conditional statement, you make the program more efficient, because it only needs to generate the code for one calling sequence to printf.

The C language provides the conditional expression as a way to improve your code; its use is never necessary. You can always rewrite any conditional expression as an if statement, although doing so may be considerably more verbose than the conditional statement form. Your use of the conditional expression will increase as your level of comfort with the language improves.

Typenames

There are a number of instances in the C language syntax that require the use of typenames. These include the sizeof operator, the cast operator (*typename*), and data declarations. A typename specifies an abstract data type without giving a variable name for the type to which it is attached. All the basic C data types are accepted as typenames, so you can use the expression sizeof(int) to determine the size in bytes of an integer, or sizeof(unsigned long int) to determine the size of an unsigned long integer.

Typenames become more complex whenever the type of a value involves arrays, functions, and pointers. For example, it is perfectly valid in C to define a variable which will be set during program execution to point to a function. The function to which the variable points can then be invoked by calling the variable name as if it were a function. However, the proper definition of such a variable must not only specify that the variable is a pointer to a function, but also describe the type of value the function returns and the type of all its arguments.

The following list shows typenames of increasing complexity and their messages:

`int`	Integer
`int *`	Pointer to integer
`int *()`	Function returning pointer to integer
`int (*)()`	Pointer to function returning integer
`int ()[]`	Function returning array of integers
`int (*)()[]`	Pointer to function returning array of integers
`int (*[])()`	Array of pointers to functions returning integers

You form typenames by writing the declaration for an example variable of the type, and then deleting the variable name from the declaration. If deleting the variable name would leave an ambiguous or invalid expression, you write `()` to stand for the missing name. The preceding list of typenames can be recast into the form of a series of declarations, each for a variable of the corresponding type. Such a set of declarations looks like this:

`int x;`	Integer x
`int *x;`	Pointer to integer
`char *strcpy();`	Function strcpy returning pointer to char
`int (*comp)();`	Pointer to function returning integer
`int sort()[];`	Function returning array of integer
`int (*sort)()[];`	Pointer to function returning array of integer
`int (*table[5])();`	Array of five pointers to functions returning int

You rarely have to write declarations or typenames of particularly great complexity. You should, however, be able to recognize and write typenames such as sizeof(char *), determine the size of a pointer that points to characters, or define an array of pointers to strings (defined as char *strings[8] for an array of eight pointer elements).

Automatic Type Conversions

The C language allows expressions to contain arithmetic and logical operations on variables of different types. There is a strict hierarchy governing the conversion of variables of differing types to the same type in order to execute an operation. (The operation to be performed has no effect on the conversion rules.) Obviously, type conversions occur only for binary arithmetic and logical operations; unary operations involve only one data value and thus need no conversion.

In general, signed values convert to unsigned, shorter types convert to longer types, and integer types convert to floating-point types. The purpose of these rules is to minimize the possibility of losing significance in the conversion, leading to inexact or incorrect results.

The rules imply a hierarchy of numeric data types, with each type ranked according to the range and precision of values it can represent. Any floating-point type is of a higher order than an integer type, because a floating-point variable can represent a wider range of values than an integer variable. Signed and unsigned integer types both support the same range of values, but an unsigned integer can be larger than a signed integer; part of the range of a signed integer is allocated to the representation of negative values.

The following lists show the relative priorities of numeric data types. The hierarchy of types is given in descending order of priority. To determine which if any conversion is performed in the evaluation of an expression, determine the first data type in the list that applies to either operand in a binary expression. The lower-order operand is converted to this type, and the result is of this type. If the expression contains multiple operators, the subexpressions are processed in order of operator priority and conversions are performed according to the type of intermediate results.

Floating-point types:

```
long double
double
float
```

Integer types:

```
unsigned long int
unsigned int/long int
long int
unsigned int
int
```

The `unsigned int` type appears in two places in the list because the ANSI C definition is ambiguous on the conversion rules for long integers. For the entry `unsigned int/long int`, read whichever form can contain all the values of the other type. On machines with a 32-bit integer, the `unsigned int` type has a higher order than `long int`; on machines with a 16-bit integer, `long int` is the preferred type.

If either operand of a binary expression is of type `char` or `short`, or is an enumeration or a bit field, it is first converted to type `int`, and then the normal conversions are applied if necessary. This implies that all calculations involving `char`, `short`, enumerated, or bit field values are performed as if the values are of type `int`, and thus generate an `int` result. If the computed result is stored in a variable of one of these types—by an assignment, for example—truncation of the result may occur. Some compilers warn of possible truncation; you can eliminate the warning by explicitly casting the expression result to the desired type.

Summary

Expressions are the core, the very heart, of the C programming language. Nearly all languages earlier than C incorporate a statement type called the assignment statement: a statement having the form *variable=value*. In C, there is no assignment statement as such; there is an assignment *expression*, and an expression *statement*. This permits you to assign values in ways never before possible in a computer language, and to write statements having very unusual forms.

You create an expression by writing an operator and one, two, or three terms. The operator describes an action to perform, and the terms are the values acted upon. The compiler doesn't evaluate an expression you write; rather, it generates machine-executable instructions that evaluate the expression when you run your compiled program.

Expressions come in three main varieties: unary, binary, and ternary. A unary expression combines an operator with one term; the operator manipulates the value of the term in a specified way to yield a new value that becomes the value of the expression. A binary expression combines one operator with two terms, and yields a new value that depends on the value of both terms. A ternary expression uses a two-part operator to derive one value from three terms.

You can build up complex expressions by using smaller expressions as the terms of larger expressions. For example, the expression (x+5) * (y+3) multiples the value yielded by the two smaller expressions x+5 and y+3.

Because the order of evaluation of the smaller expressions in a complex expression affects the final calculated result, C enables you to indicate an order of evaluation using parentheses. When you don't use enough parentheses, C chooses an order of evaluation by associating a priority with each kind of operator; operators with greater priority are then evaluated before operators with lesser priority. If you learn the relative priorities of the C operators, you can use that knowledge to reduce the number of parentheses in an expression, or conversely to ensure that the order of evaluation matches your needs.

The C language does not dicate that the final calculated value of an expression be used in any way; in fact, the expression statement (which you meet in Chapter 5) is specifically defined to throw away the final computed value. For this reason, many expressions you write are for the purpose of achieving a *side effect*, an effect not directly reflected in the evaluated result of the expression. For example, the assignment expression a=b+3 stores the result of adding b and 3 in variable a, even though you may not use the value of the assignment expression itself. The expression x[a=b+3] uses the value of the assignment expression as a subscript; the statement a=b+3; discards the value. In both cases, though, a side effect of the assignment expression is to store the value of one term (the right side of the assignment) in the left term.

Expressions are the basic objects on which statements of the C language act. In the next chapter, you meet all the statement forms of the C language. As you'll see, there aren't many.

Statements

This chapter examines the syntax and usage of the major statement types of the C language. There are four main types of statements in the C language: *expression, conditional, looping,* and *control.* It is noteworthy that there is no statement type in this list for input/output operations; the C language provides no built-in input/output facilities.

As you become familiar with C—discovering which tasks it performs well and which it supports awkwardly if at all—it will gradually become apparent that the language was planned according to a definite philosophy. To save you the effort of guessing about the design philosophy of C, I summarize it here.

The authors of the C language originally intended to use C to build operating systems for computers. Although the authors also wanted their language to be general-purpose enough for any task, the design of C was heavily influenced by its use as a system programming language. Chief among the considerations were the following:

● *The size of the resulting object program should be predictable and manageable.*

Whereas some languages permit statement forms with a high level of abstraction and generate a lot of machine code when you use such a statement, the C language tries to be close to the actual machine architecture. As a result, C programs tend to generate small object modules. Furthermore, you can intentionally adjust your coding techniques to economize your program's use of memory.

● *Programs written in C should be portable from one machine environment to another with minimum effort.*

This implies that the language must not make overt use of facilities specific to any one computer. It also implies that C must avoid areas where machine architectures differ widely. It so happens that input/output architecture varies considerably between computer types, which is why C supplies no built-in language support for input/output and does not offer operators for multibyte character fields.

● *C should strongly support modern structured programming techniques.*

By 1972, when the C language was being designed, it had been clearly demonstrated that structured program organization and strong modularization enhances the reliability of the program, and the use of such techniques increases programmer productivity. Most programmers use structured programming techniques exclusively when writing in C, avoiding the use of goto whenever possible. C encourages the organization of programs into functions and the collection of related functions into source files, and C programmers commonly practice this.

● *C should be terse.*

This objective derives mainly from the fact that operating systems are very large programs, and writing one is a big job that shouldn't be made any worse by encumbering the programmer with clumsy or wordy programming constructs. C programs tend to be cryptic because the language relies heavily on special symbols as syntactic markers rather than on English keywords.

● *C should support strong data typing.*

Compared to assembly language, C makes extensive use of data typing. In theory, strong data typing enables you to make more rigorous syntax checks and reduces the likelihood of errors. Because of this objective, C syntax insists on knowing the data type of every operand in an expression. This objective is also responsible for the complex type declarations that can occur in a C program.

● *Strong data typing should not be carried to the extreme of preventing a programmer from doing reasonable things.*

The C language tries to strike a balance between enabling comprehensive error checking and making the language unduly restrictive. The cast operator was introduced into the language expressly to get around the restrictions of strong type checking, and is why C compilers have a reputation for being weak on error checking.

The design objectives result in a language syntax that is powerful, flexible, and convenient to use, but that also omits some facilities programmers normally expect in a modern program language. Altogether, C seems to be a strange mixture of strengths and weaknesses that nonetheless appeals to many programmers.

I hope this introduction better prepares you for the oddities you encounter in the remainder of this chapter and this book.

The Expression Statement

The most commonly occurring statement in a C program is the expression statement. Its syntax is as follows:

```
exp ;
```

The value of the expression *exp* is computed and discarded.

Of course, the degree to which the expression value is discarded varies depending on the type of expression. For example, the assignment

```
pay = rate * hours;
```

stores a computed value in pay even though it discards the value of the expression as a whole. In a more subtle case, the expression may have a side effect. For example,

```
line_count++;
```

increments the line_count variable with the ++ operator.

If the concept of the expression statement seems odd, it's probably because you forget that all expressions in C have a value—even the assignment expression. Although the statement pay = rate * hours assigns a computed result to the variable pay, C also associates a value with the expression as a whole—namely, the assigned value. This is why the statement

```
pay_temp = pay = rate * hours;
```

is meaningful and has the effect of assigning rate * hours to both the variables pay_temp and pay. To C, the expression appears as though you wrote

```
pay_temp = (pay = rate * hours);
```

where the value assigned to pay_temp is the value of an assignment expression.

The fact that C considers any expression followed by a semicolon (;) to be a valid statement leads to a potential pitfall: pay_temp == pay; is a valid statement, but it has no effect. The equality is evaluated, but the result is thrown away. If you write such a statement accidentally, meaning to use = instead of ==, C finds no error.

As another example, consider the following statement:

```
sqrt(x);
```

The function call computes the square root of the value of x, but then throws the value away. You should probably write the statement as

```
root = sqrt(x);
```

but the C language finds no fault with the omission of the assignment.

Some of the more modern C compilers generate a warning for an expression statement that has no effect. The ANSI C compiler, supplied with System V Release 4 by default, provides no such warning, but the lint syntax checker utility does.

The Null Statement

A *null statement* does nothing. You may use it in a conditional statement to indicate that nothing should be done, or as the target statement of a `for` or `while` loop when no action in the body of the loop is required. The syntax of the null statement is as follows:

```
;
```

Because a semicolon by itself is a valid statement in C, excess semicolons never cause an error. The statement x=y;; is valid, and looks to C like two statements: an expression statement followed by a null statement.

The Block Statement

Many of the statement types examined in the remainder of this chapter require you to specify a subordinate statement as one of its parameters. In all such cases, you may provide only *one* statement in the allowed position. However, C does provide a way for you to write a group of statements where only one statement is allowed: by using the block statement.

The *block statement* collects several statements together into a unified group, which the compiler can then handle as if the group were a single statement. The syntactic form of a block statement is as follows:

```
{ [ declarations ] stmt ... }
```

where stmt represents a statement, and the ellipsis (. . .) means there can be one or more statements. In other words, a block statement is a group of initial declarations (that you may omit—the brackets indicate they are optional) followed by one or more statements, all enclosed within paired braces. Any statement within

95

the block may itself be a block statement, leading to the concept of *nesting*—blocks within blocks. C does not impose a limit on the level of nesting you can use.

The block statement also affects the scope of variable declarations, because you may place data declarations at the start of the block to define data used by statements that come later in the block.

Data declared within a block is known only within the block. Any declarations declared within the block are deleted at the end of the block. A declaration may define a variable with the same name as a previously defined variable. In such a case, the declaration within the more deeply nested block overrides the "outer" declaration. Consider the following example:

```
int main()
{
    int a, b;
    a = 5;
    {
        int a, x;
        /* now have variables a, b, and x */
        a = 3;
        {
            int x, y;
            /* now have variables a, b, x, and y */
            printf("a = %d\n", a);
        }
    }
    /* back to the original a and b */
    printf("a = %d\n", a);
}
```

The first declaration of variable a is known throughout the main function, but inside the first block and all inner blocks, the variable a is overridden. The first printf prints a = 3, whereas the second printf prints a = 5. Assigning 3 to a in the inner block does not change the value of the outer definition of a, because the two are actually different variables and occupy different memory. In C parlance, the second declaration of a *hides* the first declaration.

In general, a variable is declared and accessible only within the block where it is defined and all lower-level included blocks. Because all functions are also statement blocks, there are only two ways to pass information between functions:

using arguments and return values, or using global variables. Chapter 3, "Simple Declarations," explains how to use `static` and `extern` qualifiers to declare global variables. Chapter 6, "Functions," explains how to pass information between functions using arguments and return values.

The *if* Conditional Statement

The `if` statement provides a way to choose between two alternative paths a program can take, based on the outcome of a test. Its syntax is as follows:

```
if ( exp ) stmt1 [ else stmt2 ]
```

where *stmnt1* and *stmnt2* are statements, and *exp* is any expression that has a numeric or pointer value.

If the value of *exp* is nonzero (logical *true*), the single statement *stmt1* is executed. If the value of *exp* is zero (null in the case of a pointer expression), *stmt1* is skipped.

The optional `else` clause provides an action to be taken when the conditional expression *exp* has a *false* value (zero or null); *stmt2* is skipped when the conditional expression has a *true* value. In other words, either *stmt1* or *stmt2* is executed, but not both.

The range of conditions you may test with the conditional expression *exp* is broad because C supports a wide variety of expression types. You are not restricted to comparison tests using == (equality), != (inequality), <, >, <=, or >=. An expression can be a term by itself. Consider the following program excerpt:

```
int switch;
...
switch = 1; /* Set the switch on */
...
```

```
if (switch)
    x = x + 1;
...
```

The `switch` variable may be set to 1 or 0 for any convenient reason—for example, to indicate that an option was found on the command line. The `if` statement tests the switch by using the value of the switch as the value of the conditional expression. If the switch value is *1*, the value of the conditional expression is *1* and the condition is *true*. The `if` statement then executes the statement x=x+1.

The statements *stmt1* and *stmt2* must be single statements, not groups of statements. You may, however, write a group of statements to be executed by collecting them into a block statement (see the section "The Block Statement" earlier in this chapter). The following example uses the { and } delimiters to group several statements into one compound block statement:

```
if (option1)
    x = x + 1;
else
    {
    printf("Error occurred\n");
    exit(3);
    }
```

The *switch* Conditional Statement

Use the `switch` statement instead of `if` when more than two actions can be taken depending on the value of an expression, and each action depends on a constant value of the expression. The `switch` statement has the following syntax:

```
switch ( expt ) { case_list }
```

The `case` statement has the following syntax:

```
case expc : stmt ...
```

The `default` statement has the following syntax:

```
default : stmt ...
```

In each of these, *expt* and *expc* are expressions, and *stmt* is a statement.

A *case_list* is a series of one or more `case` statements. I describe the `case` and `default` statements together with the `switch` statement syntax because they are valid only within the range of a `switch` statement.

The `switch` statement evaluates the expression *expt* and uses the resulting value to determine where to resume execution in the list of cases. If the value of *expt* matches the *expc* of one of the `case` statements in *case_list*, execution resumes with the first *stmt* following that case. However, if the value of *expc* does not match any of the *expc* expressions and a `default` statement is provided, the first *stmt* following the `default` keyword is executed; otherwise, if no `default` case is present, no statements are executed.

The *expt* expression can be any valid C expression that has a numeric value; pointer values and structure values are not allowed. An enumeration is promoted to `int` before examining the list of cases for a matching `expc`.

The *expc* expressions must all be constant expressions; the compiler evaluates their values at compile time when it compiles the `switch` statement. You cannot reference the runtime value of a variable in an *expc* expression. Often, *expc* expressions are simple numeric or character literals.

Each `case` or `default` may be followed by zero or more statements. Once the `switch` statement begins executing a statement following a matching `case` or `default`, all remaining statements in the body of the `switch` statement execute sequentially unless a `break` statement is found:

```
break ;
```

The `break` statement causes the flow of execution to escape from the `switch` statement, leaving any remaining statements between `break` and the closing brace (}) unexecuted.

Typically each `case` or `default` statement group ends with a `break` statement. Sometimes, however, the processing one case needs includes some of the same processing another case needs. If you can place all the common processing under one of the cases and the special processing under another case, you can omit the `break` statement from the first case by placing the special case in front of the common case. This is called *fallthrough*. Fallthrough is usually an error, and some C compilers, as well as the `lint` syntax checker, warn of fallthrough from one case to the next.

The sample program in Listing 5.1 reads characters from the standard input file (normally the user's terminal) and counts the number of newlines, tabs, spaces, and nulls in the input file.

Listing 5.1. An example of the `switch` statement.

```
/* count.c - count special characters in a file */
#include <stdio.h>

int newlines;
int tabs;
int blanks;
int nulls;
int specials;

int main()
{
    int c; /* current input character */

    while ((c = getchar()) != EOF)
        switch (c) {
        case '\n': /* newline found */
            newlines++;
            break;
```

```
        case '\t': /* tab character found */
        case '\f': /* form feed counts as a tab */
        case '\v': /* vertical tab counts as a tab */
            tabs++;
            break;
        case '\0': /* null character found */
            nulls++;
            break;
        case ' ': /* blank character found */
            blanks++;
            break;
        default:
            if (c < 32) /* is it any other special char? */
                specials++;
            break;
        }

    /* print results */
    printf("newlines: %d  ", newlines);
    printf("tabs: %d  ", tabs);
    printf("nulls: %d  ", nulls);
    printf("blanks: %d  ", blanks);
    printf("other: %d\n", specials);

    /* finished, exit */
    return(0);
}
```

Notice that the cases for the tab (´\t´), vertical tab (´\v´), and form feed (´\f´) characters are combined to share one statement group. This is entirely legal, because case and default clauses are treated like statement labels, and a statement may have more than one label (statement labels are discussed in the "The goto Statement" section later in this chapter).

Notice that all the case expressions in Listing 5.1 are simple character constants, which C considers to be numeric.

Writing Loops with *while*

Almost all programs contain at least one *loop*: a series of computations performed repetitively until some condition occurs to indicate that the loop repetition should stop. Listing 5.1 contained one loop that repetitively fetched and examined characters from the input file.

Typically, the condition that terminates a loop must be determined dynamically while the program is running. Once again, Listing 5.1 provides an example: you cannot predict when you write the program how many times the main loop will repeat. Instead, the loop must continue until reaching the end of the input file, regardless of the number of characters in the file and the number of iterations that implies.

The while statement provides an easy and natural way to describe repetitive processing. Its syntax is as follows:

```
while ( exp ) stmt
```

where *exp* is an expression that has a true (nonzero) value as long as the execution of the *stmt* statement should be repeated. When the evaluation of *exp* yields a false (zero) value, the while statement performs no action; it stops. If *exp* has a false value when the execution of while begins, *stmt* does not execute at all; otherwise, *stmt* will be repeatedly executed until the value of *exp* is false.

Only one statement may be coded as the target of while, but it may be a block statement.

Listing 5.2 demonstrates several interesting points about the use of while.

Listing 5.2. Scanning a line of words with while.

```
/*
 * words.c - break an argument string into words
 */
#include <stdio.h>
```

```
static char string[] = " This  is   a   line   of   words.";

int main()
{
    char *p, *sp;

    p = string;
    while (1) {
        while (*p == ' ') p++;
        if (*p == '\0')
            break;
        sp = p;
        while (*p != ' ' && *p != '\0') p++;
        /* Found the end of the word */
        if (*p != '\0')
            *p++ = '\0';
        printf("'%s'\n", sp);
    }
    /* Finished, return to UNIX */
    return(0);
}
```

The program in Listing 5.2 scans the characters of string, locating each word in turn. As it identifies each word, the program uses printf to print the word. The program really has three tasks:

1. Skip over any initial blanks at the beginning of the word.

2. Find the end of the word.

3. Mark the end of the word with a null character and print the word.

The program uses a while statement to perform each of the first two tasks.

First, you should recognize the use of pointer variables in Listing 5.2. The declaration

char *p, *sp;

says that *p and *sp are pointers; what p and sp point to are characters. By implication, p and sp are themselves pointers. Throughout the remainder of the program, the expression *p examines the character to which p points, whereas expressions such as p++ manipulate the pointer itself.

The first while uses a numeric literal as the *exp* of the statement. Because the value *1* (and therefore the expression) is always nonzero, the outermost while always loops. Also notice that the *stmt* part is a statement block bracketed by { and }. All the statements between { and } repeat with each iteration of the loop.

The second while statement skips over any blanks that may precede the next word in the line. This instance of the while statement uses only one target statement to be iterated: the expression statement p++, which only increments p to point to the next character in the string. (The increment operator ++ is described in Chapter 4, "Expressions.")

The third and last while statement skips over the characters of the word, stopping when it finds a blank or null character. The remainder of the outer loop then finishes the job by changing the delimiter following the word to a null, making the word a proper string. It then prints the string with printf.

Writing Loops with *do ... while*

The while statement tests for the loop termination condition at the *start* of each loop. The do statement, on the other hand, tests for loop termination at the *end* of each loop; it is essentially the reverse of while. Because do defers its test until the end of each iteration, it always executes the body of the loop at least once. The syntax of the do statement is as follows:

```
do stmt while ( exp ) ;
```

As a matter of style, experienced programmers almost always write the *stmt* part as a block statement. This highlights the distinction between the do statement itself and the block of code to be iterated.

Listing 5.3 performs the same task as the sample program in Listing 5.2, but uses do...while instead. Notice that the program has been restructured somewhat to account for the fact that do...while always loops at least once.

Listing 5.3. Scanning a line of words with do...while.

```
/*
 * words.c - break an argument string into words
 */
#include <stdio.h>

static char string[] = " This  is   a   line   of   words.";

int main()
{
    char *p, *sp;
    char word[80];

    p = string;
    /* Skip any blanks at the start of the line */
    while (*p == ' ') p++;
    /*
     * Main loop
     */
    while (*p != '\0') {
        sp = word;
        do {
            *sp++ = *p++;
        } while (*p != ' ' && *p != '\0');
        *sp = '\0'; /* Mark the end of the word */
        /* Found the end of the word */
        printf("'%s'\n", word);
        while (*p == ' ') p++;
    }
    /* Finished, return to UNIX */
    return(0);
}
```

In this example, the program scans for leading blanks twice: before the main loop, and at the bottom of the main loop. The code as written guarantees that p always points to a nonblank character when the loop begins, or else to the end of the string. Also notice that the main loop no longer needs to use break to terminate the loop; the outer while can perform the test, because now p can only be positioned at the beginning of a word or at the end of the string.

The do...while loop copies characters of the input into a working character array called word. This technique eliminates the need to modify the input data in string and provides for an overall cleaner program design.

Writing Loops with *for*

Nearly all loops consist of three housekeeping operations in addition to the main work of the loop. These operations are *initialization*, *completion testing*, and setup for the next iteration (often called *incrementation*). The for statement provides for the specification of all three housekeeping steps in one statement, clarifying the basic structure of the loop and reducing the programmer's effort. The syntax of the for statement is shown as follows:

```
for ( [ exp1 ] ; [ exp2 ] ; [ exp3 ] ) stmt
```

The flowchart in Figure 5.1 diagrams the processing the for statement performs.

First, the for statement evaluates *exp1*. It evaluates the expression only once—at the start of processing. You may omit the expression, or perform any desired computation with it. Usually *exp1* is an assignment expression that sets a variable to an initial value. If you omit expression *exp1*, the for statement skips the initialization step.

Second, and at the beginning of each successive iteration of the loop, the for statement evaluates expression *exp2*. If the expression is false, the loop is abandoned and execution of the for statement ends. If expression *exp2* is true, *stmt* is executed. If you omit expression *exp2*, the for statement assumes it should always execute the loop. This is the same result as if you write `for (exp; 1; exp)`. In fact, many programmers write a simple nonterminating loop by writing `for (;;)`.

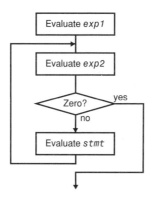

Figure 5.1. Flowchart of the `for` statement.

The expression `exp3` is evaluated after the execution of `stmt`, but before the loop restarts. The `for` statement does not use the result of the evaluation in any way. The `exp3` expression is often used to increment or adjust a control variable for each iteration of the loop.

Expression `exp1` is evaluated only once, at the beginning of the `for` loop. However, expressions `exp2` and `exp3` are evaluated every time around the loop. Any change in the body of the loop to variables used in `exp2` or `exp3` affects the result when the expressions are next evaluated around the loop.

The following trivial program uses the `for` statement to print the integers from 1 to 10.

Listing 5.4. Using `for` to print the first ten integers.

```
#include <stdio.h>

int main()
{
```

continues

Listing 5.4. continued

```
    int i;

    for (i = 1; i <= 10; i++)
        printf("%d\n", i);
    return(0);
}
```

The for statement really does all the work. The *exp1* expression (i=1) initializes a counter to 1. On each iteration of the loop, the expression i <= 10 confirms that the value of i lies within the stipulated range of 1 to 10; when i has a value of *11*, for terminates the loop. The expression i++ increments the loop counter after the body of the loop executes.

The body of the loop is just one statement, a printf that prints out the current value of i. If you compile and run this program, you should see the following on your terminal:

```
$ cc ten.c -o ten
$ ten
1
2
3
4
5
6
7
8
9
10
$
```

Using *break* and *continue*

You can use the break and continue statements with all of the looping statements (while, do, and for) to modify the looping action. The syntax of the break statement is

```
break ;
```

The syntax for the continue statement is

```
continue ;
```

When the break statement is encountered in the flow of execution, the current loop immediately terminates and control skips to the next full statement following the while, do, or for. Any remaining statements in the body of the loop are skipped.

The continue statement acts much like the break statement, causing the remaining statements in the body of the loop to be skipped. Instead of terminating the loop, however, continue causes the next iteration of the loop to start immediately.

If a break or continue statement appears inside an if statement, it only affects the execution of the loop if the if conditional expression is true. The following code fragment shows how this works:

```
while ( (nc = read(fd, buffer, size)) != 0) {
    if (nc < 0) {
        fprintf(stderr, "I/O reading file");
        break;
    }
    buffer[nc] = '\0';
```

109

```
        puts(buffer);
    }
    close(fd);
```

In this example, the return code from `read` is stored in the variable `nc`, and then it is checked for zero. The loop continues to repeat as long as the value in `nc` is not zero. The body of the loop that repeatedly executes consists of an `if` statement, an assignment expression to the variable `buffer`, and a call to the function `puts` to write out the input line.

The `if` statement tests the `nc` variable for a value less than zero, which the `read` function returns only when an error occurs. As long as no error occurs, the loop inserts a terminating null character at the end of the buffer and prints out the line just read. But if the `read` function returns an error indication (probably the value *–1*), the `if` statement succeeds and causes the execution of the `fprintf` and `break` statements. The `fprintf` function call prints an error message, and the `break` causes the loop to terminate at once. The next statement that executes after `break` is the `close` function call.

Here's the example modified a little by adding a `continue` statement:

```
while ( (nc = read(fd, buffer, size)) != 0) {
    if (nc < 0) {
        fprintf(stderr, "I/O reading file");
        break;
    }
    if (buffer[0] == '#')
        continue;
    buffer[nc] = '\0';
    puts(buffer);
}
close(fd);
```

In this version, if the first position of the input line (as contained in the 0th element of the array `buffer`) contains a hash sign (#), the `continue` statement executes, causing the assignment expression and `puts` call to be skipped. The next statement that executes after `continue` is the `while` statement itself as it begins the next iteration of the loop. The effect of the `if...continue` statement is to add support for comment lines in the input file.

The `break` and `continue` statements affect only the current (innermost) loop within which they appear; any outer loops remain active and unaffected. That is, in the skeleton example

```
for (...) {
    while (...) {
        if (...) break;
        ...
    }
}
```

the `break` statement can only terminate the `while` loop; the `for` loop continues to repeat until its normal stopping point. The `break` statement shown has no affect on the `for` statement, not because the outer loop is a `for` loop, but because the `break` can only affect the innermost loop within which it appears. In fact, it is difficult to break more than one level of looping. Making use of the `goto` statement discussed in the next section is often the only way to achieve a multiple-level break.

The `continue` statement is illegal outside the range of a `while`, `do`, or `for` statement. The `break` statement is also illegal outside of loops, except that it is legal inside a `switch` statement.

The *goto* Statement

The `goto` statement changes the sequence of execution so that the next statement that executes is the one designated by the operand of `goto`. The syntax of `goto` is as follows:

```
goto label ;
```

Replace *label* with the name of a statement label appearing within the same statement block that contains the `goto`, or any outer statement block. Because you cannot nest functions, you cannot jump out of one function into another.

To attach a label to a statement, write the name of the label followed by a colon in front of the statement:

```
[ identifier : ] ... stmt
```

The rules for writing a valid label identifier are the same as those for any other identifier: it must begin with a letter or underscore (_), and subsequent characters must be letters, the digits 0–9, or underscores. A statement may have any number of labels.

A statement label becomes undefined at the end of the block within which it is defined. Statement labels do not conflict with structure tags or variable names. In effect, the C compiler remembers statement labels separately from other names.

The use of goto has become unpopular in recent years because its use tends to obscure the structure of a program. There are situations, however, where it is easier and more natural to use goto than any other coding technique. The discussion of the break and continue statements shows one such case. You can use the goto statement to exit from any depth of nested loops, as the following example shows:

```
while (read(fd, buffer, size) != 0) {
    for (n = 0; n < size; n++) {
        if (buffer[n] == '}')
            goto done;
        ...
    }
}
done:
    close(fd);
```

This example uses two loops nested one inside the other to read lines from a file and examine each character of each line. When it finds the } character anywhere in any of the lines, reading stops and control jumps directly to the close function call. The same effect can be achieved without using goto, but is not as clear or straightforward as the solution with goto.

When you are thoroughly familiar with the C language, you will know when you must use goto. Until then, try to eliminate goto instructions from your programs; they are rarely necessary and almost always obscure the clarity of your program's code.

Summary

This relatively short chapter introduces you to every one of the statement types the C language supports. Here's a brief review of them:

- *Conditional*

  The if statement provides a way to execute a statement or statement block only under certain conditions. It also enables you to choose which of two alternative statement groups to execute.

  The switch statement provides a way to use the value of an expression as a selector for the statement that executes next.

- *Iterative*

  The while statement provides a straightforward way to repetitively execute a group of statements as long as a condition is true. If the conditional expression of the while statement is false when the while begins, the loop does not execute at all.

  The do...while statement provides an iterative facility similar to while that, unlike while, always executes its body at least once.

  The for statement also repetitively executes a group of statements. It requires three expressions: an *initialization* expression, a *test* expression, and a *post* expression. The initializer-expression describes any setup that should be performed prior to the first iteration. The test expression describes the conditions that must exist at the start of each iteration; when the test expression is false, the loop terminates. The post expression specifies an expression to be evaluated after each iteration of the loop. You can use the three expressions of a for statement for something as simple as a counter that increments on each iteration, or as complex as a series of assignments and conditional tests to manage the loop.

- *Control*

  The block statement (beginning with { and ending with }) is treated like a single statement, even though it contains many statements. The braces ({}) are grouping operators that bracket a list of statements and cause the list to be treated as a unit. Declarations given inside a statement block are known only to statements within the block and any included lower-level blocks.

  The break statement terminates a while, do...while, or for loop. It specifies the end of a case or default statement group in a switch statement.

  The continue statement interrupts a while, do...while, or for loop iteration and starts the loop again from the top without finishing the remainder of the statements in the loop.

  You can use the goto statement to transfer control arbitrarily from one point to another within the same statement block or any higher-level statement block containing the goto.

- *Miscellaneous*

  The null statement does nothing. It is sometimes used as the body of a while, do...while, or for loop, and sometimes as the *true* clause of an if statement.

  If you feel that some important operations are missing from the preceding list, you're right. Most of the missing operations are provided by system interface functions in the C function library.

  You've already seen some examples of the C library functions for input/output operations; the printf, fprintf, and getchar functions have been shown in examples without explanation. These are only a few of the many functions provided by the C programming environment to perform system-related tasks. For a detailed description of the functions in the C programming library, consult your system's documentation, or refer to my book *UNIX Programmer's Reference* (Que, 1991).

Functions

The *function* is the basic programming unit of a C program. Every program must contain at least one function, called main. A program may contain dozens or hundreds of other functions at your discretion.

In this chapter you learn how to write function declarations, called *prototypes*; how to write a function definition; and how to invoke functions. Also, the main function provides a special interface that enables you to examine the text of the command issued by the user to invoke your C program; this chapter explains that special interface.

A C function can be callable from all source files of a program, or known only within the source file that contains its definition. You determine the *scope* of a function by the way you declare it. This chapter also explains how to specify and how to use function scope.

Function Syntax

You can declare functions just as you can other C objects. You do not need to declare a function, however, if you *define* it before you reference it. A function definition differs from a declaration by providing a function body—the statements that implement the function—whereas a declaration merely describes attributes of the function. You can declare a function many times, but you can define it only once.

By common usage, a function declaration is called a *prototype*. Early versions of the C language supported only a minimal prototype that omitted function parameters. The term *prototype* refers to the complete modern form of the function declaration.

Syntactically, a function prototype and a function definition look very similar. A function prototype looks like this:

```
type name ( parameters ) ;
```

A function definition looks like this:

```
type name ( parameters ) { statements }
```

The C concept of a function is very similar to the mathematical concept, and C uses a similar notation. In mathematics, you write f(x) to denote a function named f having one independent variable x, and g(x,y) to denote a function named g taking two variables x and y. In the C language, you also describe a function by giving its name followed by a list of values the function requires as input to compute a result value.

Unlike mathematics, the C programming language requires all values to have an associated type. A function parameter could be a simple type such as int or double, but could also be a more complex type such as a pointer or a structure. The function prototype expands on the mathematical notation by enabling you to specify the type of value the function returns and the type of each of its parameters.

In the preceding syntax description, *type* must be a typename describing the kind of value returned by the function. If the function returns no value, specify void; otherwise specify int, double, or any other typename that accurately describes the kind of value the function returns.

For *name*, write the name of the function in the same form as any C identifier: it must begin with a letter or underscore, and be followed by any number of letters, digits, or underscores. The case of letters is significant; the function name Sqrt is different from sqrt.

Inside the parentheses you must list a declaration for each value to be passed to the function. If the function takes more than one parameter, you must separate the declarations by commas. To declare the parameters to a function, list the parameter names and provide a type for each. If the function takes more than one parameter of the same type, you must give a full declaration for each parameter. You cannot list variable names after a common type, as you can with a conventional declaration. Within the body of the function definition, you can reference a parameter name in the same manner as a variable. Parameter names declared in a function prototype are purely formal; they are not used in any way.

The purpose of a parameter is to provide a value to the function that the code of the function will use in some way to compute a result. Most functions require at least one formal parameter, but some functions don't need any. If the function does not require a parameter, write void as the entire parameter list.

Suppose you want to write a function that returns the product of two numbers. To compute its result, the function must receive the two numbers. An appropriate function prototype would look like this:

```
int product(int n1, int n2);
```

The corresponding function definition would have the following general format:

```
int product(int n1, int n2)
{
    /* statements to implement the function */
}
```

Notice that the parameter list provides a separate declaration for each of the two parameters. When writing a normal declaration, you would probably write int n1, n2. When declaring a parameter, however, you must provide a separate type declaration with each parameter name.

117

Calling a Function

You can call any function for which you provide the definition, or any function the standard C function library provides, by writing a *function call*. (Part II of this book contains a list of the functions in the standard C function library together with a brief description of each.) A function call has the following general format:

```
name( [ arglist ] )
```

The basic form of a function call is just `name()`. The parentheses following the function name tell C that `name` is the name of a function. The C compiler arranges to call the function and substitute the value the function returns for the function call.

If the function requires one or more values when called, you provide them inside the parentheses as an argument list. Each argument must be an expression that yields a value of the type the function expects for that argument, or that can be converted to the expected type. An argument can be a numeric literal. If the literal is an integer, then it is treated as type `int`; if it is a floating-point value, it is treated as type `double`. If the called function requires an argument of a different type, the literal or expression argument is forced to the expected type, if possible, using the standard promotion and conversion rules described in Chapter 4, "Expressions."

When providing an argument list of more than one argument, separate each argument expression with a comma from the preceding expression. For example, if you call the `product` function mentioned earlier with the expression `product(x,3)`, within the `product` function the parameter `n1` has the value of `x`, and the parameter `n2` has the value of `3`.

Each argument you provide in a function call is supplied to the called function by setting the corresponding formal parameter in the function definition to the value of the supplied argument.

The C language implements a *call by value*. Call by value means that the values provided to a called function are *copies* of the values supplied by the calling argument list. In the function call `product(x,3)`, the called function `product` can freely assign new values to n1 and n2; the assignments have no effect on the value of x or the literal 3, because n1 and n2 are separate variables, initialized with the appropriate values, existing only during the execution of the product function. In general, a C function cannot alter the value of an argument in a function call because the function does not have direct access to the arguments; it only has copies of the values of those arguments.

A function call is a term usable in an expression just like a variable or a literal. Instead of writing y = x + 1 you can just as easily write the expression as y = x + sqrt(3). To compute the value of the expression, C calls the sqrt function at the appropriate time, passing it the value *3*, and uses the value returned by the function as the value of sqrt(3). The value of the expression is then computed in the normal way, adding the value of x to the returned value, and assigning the sum to the variable y.

The following is an example of a valid expression statement:

```
ok = putpixel(x+1, y-sqrt(w + 0.5), "red");
```

The value returned by the putpixel function is stored in the variable ok. The putpixel function is passed three arguments: x+1, y-sqrt(w+0.5), and "red". The second argument requires the evaluation of a square root function before putpixel can be called; C fully supports nested function calls to any depth. The third argument is an example of a string literal; its value is a pointer to an array of characters. The use of a pointer as the third argument depends entirely on the expectations of the putpixel function. If it expects a pointer to a character string as the third argument, "red" is an example of a valid argument; otherwise, putpixel may produce incorrect results or fail entirely.

The C compiler uses a function prototype to ensure that the type of arguments you provide in a function call match the type of arguments the function expects. If the prototype does not match the function definition, or if you do not provide a prototype, the C compiler assumes you have provided legal values. The compiler does, however, remember the type of arguments you pass on a first call to a function, and it checks to see if you pass the same type of arguments on subsequent calls.

Because the C compiler is basically willing to pass argument values of incompatible type to a called function, experienced C programmers are careful to provide a function prototype at the start of a source file for all functions called in the source file. The C compiler and support package provide a set of *header files* that contain a declaration for each library function you can call. C programmers usually provide their own header files for function packages they write. (Chapter 10, "The Preprocessor," explains all about header files.)

The *return* Statement

This chapter has already made several references to "the value returned by a function." It is appropriate at this point to explain how a function returns a value.

The body of a function definition contains the statements that implement the function. For example, the function product might contain an expression statement that multiplies its two parameters together. Having computed the result, you indicate that the function has completed its work, and provide the value to be returned as the value of the function, by writing a return statement. The syntax of the return statement is as follows:

```
return [ expression ] ;
```

If your function does not need to return a value, the return statement causes the function to exit. A function that does not return a value must be declared as type void.

If the function type is anything other than void, the return statement must provide an expression that produces a value of the appropriate type. The compiler arranges to substitute the value of *expression* for the function call.

Using the return statement, I can now show an example implementation of the product function mentioned previously:

```
int product(int n1, int n2)
{
    int r;

    /* Compute the product of the two parameters */
    r = n1 * n2;
```

```
    /* Return the result and exit */
    return r;
}
```

You can implement the product function more directly by doing all the work on the return statement itself:

```
int product(int n1, int n2)
{
    return n1 * n2;
}
```

The closing brace (}) of a function always acts as an automatic return. For a void function, you can omit the return statement altogether and let the end of the function act as an automatic return. If you declare a function to return a type other than void, however, you must provide a return statement within the body of the function to supply a return value.

Function Scope

Within a source file, a function is known from the point where it is first declared (with a prototype) or defined (with a function body) through the end of the source file. After the point of first declaration or definition, the function can be freely called from other functions in the same source file.

If you define a function with the type qualifier static, the function is known only within the source file where its definition occurs, and it can be called only from within that source file.

If you define a function without the type qualifier static, however, its name is treated as an external symbol and the function can be called from other source files as well.

Function declarations (prototypes) can use the type qualifier extern to indicate that a function is defined in some other source file. However, because a function has external scope by default, it is not necessary to use extern. If a source file contains both declarations and a definition of the function (typically to allow a function to be called before its definition), the declaration must include the type qualifier static if the definition specifies static.

When writing large programs, C programmers often collect functions handling a common data structure, or functions with a similar purpose, into a separate source file. Grouping related functions together like this makes program maintenance easier, because it tends to reduce the size of source files and makes it easier to find a specific function.

Any source file needing to use one of the functions in a separate source file must include a declaration of the function, so that the C compiler knows the value type the function returns and the type of its arguments. For convenience, you can use a separate header file for each function package to simplify the inclusion of these declarations. (For more information, see Chapter 10, "The Preprocessor.")

Functions with Variable Parameter Lists

The C language definition does not require you to always call a function with the same number of arguments. The printf library function is a prime example, because it is called with a widely varying number of arguments, often in the same program.

On the other hand, C provides very little explicit support for variable-length parameter lists. The only concession in the language definition is a special type of parameter you can specify to indicate that the function accepts an indefinite number of parameters. This is the *ellipsis* (. . .), which, if present, must be the last parameter in a prototype or function definition. You can write the prototype for the printf function using the ellipsis:

```
int printf(const char *pattern, ...);
```

C does not provide a way for you to inquire within a function about how many arguments were passed, nor by scanning the arguments one by one can you definitely identify the last one. For this reason, all functions that accept a varying number of parameters require that one of the values specifies or implies the number of arguments that were passed.

The printf function in the standard C function library gets around this problem by analyzing the number of %x strings in the pattern (first) argument. The number of arguments following the first must match the number of %x strings in the format string.

The C programming libraries provide a tool called *varargs* to assist with writing a function that uses a variable parameter list. The tool consists of four macros: va_list, va_start, va_end, and va_arg. The C function library documents these macros; Part II of this book also mentions them briefly.

There is no rule in the C language that dictates the use of the varargs package for handling variable numbers of parameters on a function call. If you want to write a function that can be called with varying numbers of parameters, you're free to use any method you wish, provided you don't depend on C to provide a mechanism for identifying the number of arguments actually passed by any specific call.

The *main* Function

Every C program you write will contain one function called main; its presence is required. When execution of your program begins, it begins with the first statement in main; when your main function exits, your program terminates.

The main function must be external; you cannot declare it static (private to the source file) because the system must be able to locate the entry point to your main function.

You write the main function, but you will never call it under ordinary circumstances. Normally, UNIX calls main. As such, the definition of the parameters passed to main is made by the system, not by you; the call to main has already been written by the operating system programmers.

The operating system presumes that your main function has the following declaration:

```
int main(int argc, char *argv[], char *envp[]);
```

The function has a return type of int, meaning that main must normally return an integer value to its caller. The returned value is called the *exit code*, and is used by the shell. Only the low-order eight bits of the return code are considered significant. The exit code that `main` returns, therefore, has a value from 0 to 255. Usually you return a value of zero from `main` to indicate that your program performed its task without notable error. You can use a nonzero value to indicate that your program was unable to complete normally because of errors discovered in the course of execution. The shell makes your exit code available to the user, who can then decide how to deal with the error. It is generally good practice to write an error message before terminating with a nonzero exit code to inform the user what problem caused the abnormal termination. In any event, you decide the significance of a nonzero exit code when you design your program to return such a value from `main`.

The `main` function is called with three parameters: `argc`, `argv`, and `envp`. Because parameter names are known only to the code within a function, you can choose any names you like for these parameters.

As a refresher in case you are new to UNIX, here's a review of how a user invokes a program.

The *shell* is a program provided by UNIX to read terminal input and to execute the commands the user types. A command (a line of text ending with a return) always begins with a word that signifies the action for the shell to perform. If the first word is the name of your program, the shell loads and runs your program for the user. Any additional words the user types on the same line, called *arguments*, are passed to your program without inspection or analysis by the shell; your program can ignore the additional words, or make use of them in any way you choose.

The purpose of the three parameters to `main` is to pass these arguments to your program.

The `argc` parameter is initialized with the number of words appearing on the command line that invokes your program. The count includes the first word, which is always the name of your program. The `argc` count therefore is always at least one. If the count is exactly one, you can assume that the user typed the command line without additional words. In general, the number of argument words on the command line is one less than the value of `argc`.

The `argv` parameter is a pointer to an array of pointers to strings. In other words, `argv[0]` is a string containing the name of your program; `argv[1]` is the first word the user typed following the program name; `argv[2]` is the second word, and so on.

The argc and argv parameters together completely describe the command line typed by the user, omitting blanks, tabs, and other whitespace the user may have typed between words. As an example of how this works, Listing 6.1 shows a program that reports its command-line arguments.

Listing 6.1. A program to list its command-line arguments.

```
/* show.c - a program to list its command-line arguments */
#include <stdio.h>

int main(int argc, char *argv[])
{
    int j;

    for (j = 0; j < argc; j++)
        printf("argv[%d] = ´%s´\n", j, argv[j]);

    return 0; /* Return with normal exit code */
}
```

To experiment with the program shown in Listing 6.1, you must first type the text of the program into a file using a text editor. (You can use the vi text editor described in Part II of this book.) Name the file show.c.

After saving the file and exiting from the text editor, you must compile the source program. Do so by typing the following command:

```
cc show.c -o show
```

If you make any typing errors, the cc command displays a list of errors on your terminal screen. You must correct the errors by using the text editor to modify the C program statements in the source. Then repeat the cc command. When the cc command completes without displaying any error messages, you may execute the show.c program to see what it does, like this:

```
$ show my name
argv[0] = ´show´
argv[1] = ´my´
```

125

```
argv[2] = 'name'
$ show "Christopher Columbus"
argv[0] = 'show'
argv[1] = 'Christopher Columbus'
$
```

Notice that the successive strings `argv` points to are the words of the command line. Enclosing a group of words in quotation marks makes the group appear as a single word. The shell defines the rules for typing commands, which is outside the scope of this book. For more information about the shell, you might like to get a copy of my book, *UNIX Desktop Guide to the Korn Shell* (Hayden Books, 1992).

It should be apparent that it is a relatively easy matter to write your program so that the user can provide useful information with command-line arguments. There is even a tool in the standard C function library to assist you in analyzing command arguments: the `getopt` function, which scans the words and automatically identifies UNIX-style command options.

The `envp` parameter is similar in nature to the `argv` parameter, but where the `argv` parameter points to command-line strings, the `envp` parameter points to a list of environment variables. (Environment variables are text strings created by the shell. If you are not familiar with environment variables, refer to my book, *UNIX Desktop Guide to the Korn Shell*.)

The value of `envp` itself is a pointer to an array of string pointers. The array terminates with a null pointer so you can easily recognize the end of the list. Each element in the array is itself a string pointer. Thus, `envp[0]` is the first environment string, `envp[1]` is the second environment string, and so on. The program in Listing 6.2 lists all the environment variables. The `getopt` function in the standard C function library simplifies searching the environment list for a specific variable.

Listing 6.2. A program to list environment variables.

```
/* listenv.c - list all environment variables */
#include <stdio.h>
```

```
int main(int argc, char *argv[], char *envp[])
{
    for (; *envp != NULL; envp++)
        puts(*envp);
    return 0;
}
```

When I compile and execute the listenv program on my system, I receive the following output:

```
$ cc listenv.c -o listenv
$ listenv
_=listenv
HZ=100
XWINFONTPATH=/usr/X/lib/fonts/Xol
PATH=/usr/bin:/usr/sbin:/usr/ccs/bin:/usr/X/bin
CDPATH=.:/home/jjv
WINDOWID=4194314
LOGNAME=jjv
MAIL=/usr/mail/jjv
TERMCAP=/etc/termcap
DISPLAY=unix:0
SHELL1=/usr/bin/ksh
HOME=/home/jjv
TERM=xterm
PWD=/home/jjv/tmp
TZ=EST5EDT
ENV=/home/jjv/.sh_init
$
```

Don't worry what each of these strings mean; there are a great many environment variables defined in a typical UNIX environment. Each consists of a keyword (usually in all capital letters), followed by an equal sign, followed by a string value to be associated with the keyword.

If your program does not need to examine the array of environment variables, you can omit the envp parameter from the declaration of main as follows: int main(int argc, char *argv[]). The missing parameter has no unfavorable side effects, it just means you can't reference the envp variable in this program.

Similarly, if your program has no use for argument strings or environment variables, you can simplify the declaration of `main` to just `int main()`. Once again, this does not cause any problems unless you decide later to use argument strings in your program—in which case you'll need to go back and add the missing parameters to your `main` declaration.

Summary

This chapter focuses on the rules for writing and using functions. In a certain sense, this is the most important chapter of the book, because you cannot write a C program without writing at least one function.

Good programming style dictates that you should provide a complete set of function declarations at the start of your C program for all the functions appearing in a source file; this lets you order the functions in the source any way you want. A function declaration has the following general format:

```
type name ( type arg1, type arg2 ... ) ;
```

A function declaration, called a *prototype*, informs the C compiler of the calling interface to a function before the compiler sees the function definition. When a function is defined in another source file, prototypes are essential to permit effective error checking.

A function definition is similar to a prototype except that the definition also provides a *function body*. The function body contains the executable statements that implement the function. The general form of a function definition is:

```
type name ( type arg1, type arg2 ... )
{
    /* statements */
}
```

Both the function declaration and the function definition provide the two essential sets of information about a function (besides its name): the type of value the function returns, and the number and type of arguments that the function expects when called.

You call a function by writing the function name followed by parentheses in an expression. Some programming languages differentiate between functions that return a value and those that do not, calling the former *functions* and the latter *subroutines* or *subprograms*. The C language makes no such distinction; because you can make an expression a complete statement simply by appending a semicolon, you can invoke a function very tersely by writing `fn();` (where `fn` is the name of the function) as a complete statement.

Structures and Unions

In addition to the basic data types discussed in Chapter 3, "Simple Declarations," the C language also supports four types of data aggregates. A *data aggregate* is, as the name implies, a unit of data that is itself composed of subordinate elements. The four kinds of aggregates are *structures*, *unions*, *enumerations*, and *bit fields*. This chapter explains the syntax and use of all four aggregate types.

Structures

A *structure* is a collection of data elements arranged in a specific order. The term *structure* often refers to two different things: the abstract layout of the structure, and a particular instance of the structure in memory. According to Kernighan and Ritchie, the layout of the structure is called the *template*, and the term *structure* is reserved for a particular instance.

Before you can use a structure in your code, you must first tell the C compiler what the structure looks like. You do this with a structure declaration, using the following syntax:

```
struct [ tag ] [ { declarations } ] [ initializers ] ;
```

A structure declaration begins with the reserved keyword `struct`. Because the word is reserved, you cannot use the word `struct` as a variable name or other identifier anywhere in your program.

You may give a structure template a unique name, called a *tag*. The tag is a name for the particular pattern or organization of data elements, and is used to distinguish structures having different compositions. Structure tags do not conflict with variable names; you can give a variable the same name as a structure template. The compiler doesn't get confused because it only recognizes a name as a structure tag when `struct` precedes the name.

The body of the structure declaration starts with an opening brace ({) and ends with a closing brace (}). Between the braces you can write any sort of data declarations you wish. Each declaration you write describes one *member* of the structure. A structure template usually has several members, but must have at least one.

A structure declaration may conclude with one or more *initializers*. The initializers portion of the declaration allocates storage for instances of the structure. The simplest form of initializer is just a variable name. You can assign an initial value to a structure variable just like it was any other variable: follow the variable name with an equal sign and a brace-enclosed list of values for each of its members.

You can omit the body of a structure declaration when a previous `struct` statement already describes the structure. In fact, for a given tag, you should only specify the structure template once in the program. When subsequently declaring instances of the structure, omit the body; the type name `struct tag` tells the compiler everything it needs to know about the variables.

A structure variable declared to be `static` has an initial value of binary zeroes unless you provide an initializer for it. A structure variable defined outside the scope of a function (that is, between functions) has static allocation and external scope, and also defaults to a binary zero initial value.

An automatic structure, such as a structure variable declared inside a function, cannot have initializers; only statically allocated structures can be given an initial value. You can assign a value to an automatic structure only by using executable statements inside the function.

Take a look at some examples of structure declarations.

Example 1: An Airport Structure

```
struct airport {
    char    ident[4];       /* Airport code "LAX"  */
    long    latitude;       /* Latitude in dms     */
    long    longitude;      /* Longitude in dms    */
    short   variation;      /* Compass variation   */
    short   altitude;       /* Airport altitude    */
    short   ATIS;           /* ATIS frequency      */
    short   ground;         /* Ground Control freq */
    short   clearance;      /* Clearance delivery  */
    short   tower;          /* Tower frequency     */
    short   runway_ct;      /* Number of runways   */
    short   longest;        /* Longest runway      */
};
```

Example 1 is a structure template an airline scheduling program might use to describe an airport. The program also needs other structures to describe other kinds of objects—for example, booked airline flights. This particular structure template is named `airport` to distinguish it from other structures that might be used in the same program.

The `airport` structure consists of eleven member data elements. Members of the structure give the airport code, its location and geography, the various radio frequencies in use at the airport, and what kind of runways are available. Notice that the members of the structure are described with simple declarations as if they were variables. The only difference between declaring a variable and declaring a structure member is that the latter is enclosed inside the braces of a struct statement.

Example 2: A Flight Record

```
struct flight {
    int    flight;        /* Flight number      */
    char   airline[2];    /* Airline code       */
    char   org[4];        /* Origin airport     */
    char   dst[4];        /* Destination airport */
    short depart;         /* Departure time     */
    short arrive;         /* Arrival time       */
    float coach_fare;     /* Price of coach seat */
    int    coach_seats;   /* Num of coach seats  */
    int    coach_booked;  /* Num of seats booked */
    float cl1_fare;       /* First-class fare    */
    int    cl1_seats;     /* Num of 1c seats     */
    int    cl1_booked;    /* Num of 1c seats booked */
};
```

An airline scheduling program also has to keep track of airline flights available for consumer booking. The program organizes the information about a flight into a structure, but uses a different template for flights than for airports. Example 2 shows the template that describes a single flight. The flight structure contains most of the information a booking agent needs, but provides no way to reserve a specific seat for a customer. Later in this chapter you will see how to extend the data structure to provide for seat reservations.

Structures as Data Types

Examples 1 and 2 show two different structures intended for use by the same program, each distinguished by a unique tag. Each structure template, in effect, defines a new data type; a variable of type struct airport certainly has very different contents and usage than a variable of type struct flight.

Structure declarations provide a way to arbitrarily extend the number of data types available. Structures act like new data types in many different ways. For example, you can have arrays of structures, structure variables, and pointers to structures; you can even assign the value of one structure variable to another structure variable of the same type.

The simplest way to use a structure declaration is to declare a variable of that type. Here are some examples:

```
struct airport from, to;
struct airport airports[200];
struct flight f, *fp;
```

The variables from and to are declared as type struct airport. The declaration takes the same form as if they were being declared as integers, except that the type name is struct airport instead of int, and the two variables each require 28 bytes of memory instead of the four an int requires.

The declaration of airports instructs the compiler to allocate memory for an array of two hundred airport structures. Each element of the array airports is therefore a structure of type struct airport, and each array element has space for all of the members specified by the structure template shown in Example 1. The sizeof operator returns the value *28* for the expression sizeof(airports[0]), and the value *5600* for the expression sizeof(airports).

The third declaration allocates a variable f of type struct flight, and a pointer fp of type pointer to struct flight. The expression sizeof(f) has the value *42*, because a flight structure requires 42 bytes to store in memory. The expression sizeof(fp) has the value *4*, because all pointers are four bytes long (in UNIX implementations of the C language).

Unnamed Structures

So far, all our structure declarations include a tag to name the structure format. C syntax does not require a tag, though, and you can omit it whenever you do not need to make later reference to the structure format. This situation occurs when you declare all the variables you need as part of the template definition.

Example 3: An Unnamed Structure

```
struct {
    char  type[4];    /* Type of aircraft */
    short first;      /* Num of first-class seats */
    short coach;      /* Num of coach seats */
} B727, B737, B767, B747;
```

The declaration in Example 3 provides a template for a description of types of aircraft. This hypothetical airline scheduling program supports only four aircraft types, so the program not only describes the structure but also declares all the variables it needs of that type in one statement.

The declaration in Example 3 declares four variables named B727, B737, B767, and B747. Each of the variables is eight bytes long and contains three members. The struct statement contains both a structure body enclosed in braces, and an initializer list consisting of the variable names separated by commas. Only the tag portion of the struct statement syntax is omitted.

The program cannot declare additional variables of the same type as B737 because the structure template has no tag. Even if a later structure declaration describes the same members in the same order and with the same names, the C compiler considers the two unnamed structures to be different. Whereas you can easily copy the contents of the B727 variable into the B737 variable with the statement B737 = B727; you cannot perform a similar assignment to any other structure because the structure types are incompatible.

Unnamed structures are a convenience when you don't need to declare many variables of the same structure type. Many programmers avoid unnamed structures, however, because future program maintenance may require the declaration of more variables, and that requires adding a tag to the structure declaration. In a large program that uses many tag names, selecting a unique name might be difficult. It costs little to invent a tag when you declare a structure, and it saves trouble later.

Nested Structures

You may wonder whether a structure declaration can appear within another structure declaration. The answer is *YES*. A structure declaration is merely one more kind of declaration, and you can use it anywhere a declaration is permitted. Therefore, it can also appear inside a structure declaration. The ability to nest structures arises rather naturally in the C language definition, and is quite useful.

Example 2 earlier in this chapter gives the description for a flight structure to use for airline reservations. The structure description is incomplete, however, in that it makes no provision for seat reservation. By using nested structure declarations, you can easily add a seat reservation capability. The amended structure might look like the following:

```
struct flight {
    int   flight;        /* Flight number       */
    char  airline[2];    /* Airline code        */
    char  org[4];        /* Origin airport      */
    char  dst[4];        /* Destination airport */
    short depart;        /* Departure time      */
    short arrive;        /* Arrival time        */
    float fare_first;    /* First-class fare    */
    float fare_coach;    /* Coach fare          */
    struct seat {
        char  avail;     /* 'A'vailable or 'B'ooked */
        char  type;      /* Type: Y or C            */
        char  name[30];/* Passenger name            */
    }     seat[300];     /* Array of seats          */
};
```

This new description of the `flight` structure contains an array of `struct seat` for each seat on the aircraft. To save space, the fare for each seat class is recorded just once in the `flight` structure and does not appear in each seat. Each seat structure is coded with a `type` member to indicate whether the coach or first-class fare applies.

Unfortunately, the C language provides no way to say that the number of seat structures in a `flight` structure varies, so the rewritten example allocates enough seats even for the very big 747 flights. This results in considerable wasted space for smaller aircraft. Avoiding this waste of space requires using pointers and dynamic memory allocation, techniques that I don't discuss until the next chapter.

Initializing Structures

It is possible to initialize a structure variable when you define it, using syntax similar to that used to initialize elementary variables. In general, the value of a structure is a list of values, one for each member of the structure; the entire list of values must be enclosed in braces. If the list contains fewer values than the structure contains elements, the remaining elements are set to zero.

You can extend the declaration in Example 3 to provide an initial value for each of the four variables, as shown in the following example:

Example 4: Initializing the `aircraft` Structure

```
struct {
    char   type [4];    /* Type of aircraft */
    int    first;       /* Num of first-class seats */
    int    coach;       /* Num of coach seats */
}
B727 = { "727",  12, 125 },
B737 = { "737",   8,  98 },
B767 = { "767",  24, 198 },
B747 = { "747",  24, 320 };
```

For clarity, each initializer appears on a separate line. Remember that C ignores whitespace between tokens; how you arrange the parts of the statement over a series of lines is up to you. Notice, however, that each initializer is still separated from the next by a comma.

In addition to the variable name, each initializer in Example 4 follows the variable name with an equal sign followed by a brace-enclosed list of values for each of the structure members. Thus the value of structure variable B737 specifies that the aircraft type is the string 737, and that it has eight first-class seats and 98 coach-class seats available.

When a structure contains subordinate structures, an initial value list, in turn, contains an initial value list for each subordinate structure member. This implies that you can nest brace-enclosed value lists. The following is an example of an initialized nested structure:

```
static struct flight sample = {
    541,       /* Flight number */
    "UA",      /* Airline code */
    "LAX",     /* Departure airport */
    "JFK",     /* Destination airport */
    0530,      /* Departure time */
    1145,      /* Arrival time */
    225.48,    /* first-class fare */
    109.60,    /* coach fare */
    {
      { 'B', '1', "John Jones" }, /* Seat #1 */
      { 'B', 'Y', "Mary Smith" }, /* Seat #2 */
      { 'A' },                    /* Seat #3 */
    }
};
```

For ease of reading, the example shows each member of the structure on a separate line with a comment to remind you of the significance of each field. Actual C programs often use this style for initializing structures because it is so much easier to understand than a bare list of undescribed values.

The seat array is enclosed in an outer pair of braces because it is one member of the structure. It in turn contains a list of values, one for each array element. Each element of the seats array is itself a structure, so each array element is also shown as a brace-enclosed list giving the value of each struct seat member. Because the example gives an initial value for only the first three elements of the seat array, the remaining 297 are initialized to zero by default.

Accessing Structure Members

There are several ways you can use a structure as a unit. You can assign the value of a structure variable to another variable of the same structure type with the assignment operator (=). You can pass a structure value to a function as an argument, or a function can return it. You can also determine the size of a structure in bytes with the sizeof operator.

Programming for UNIX

Of all the C expression operators, only the assignment operator can legally be applied to structures. Structures cannot be added together, logically ORed, compared with the relation operators, or manipulated in any other way.

You can manipulate each member of a structure individually in any manner appropriate to the data type of the member. To do so, you must be able to reference individual members of a structure. The C language provides two methods of reference, both involving the use of an expression operator.

The *dot* operator (.) selects a member from a structure. The general syntax for selecting a member from a structure is *exp*.*name*, where *exp* must be an expression that evaluates to the structure itself, and *name* is the name of a member defined within the structure referenced by *exp*.

Referring back to the unnamed structure in Example 3, you can reference the value of the `first` member of the B737 structure using the expression `B737.first`. The `first` member of the B747 structure is referenced in the same way, using the expression `B747.first`.

The *pointer* operator (->) selects a member from a structure when you have a pointer to the structure rather than the structure itself. The reference expression is similar to that for the dot operator: *exp*->*name*, except that *exp* must be a pointer expression rather than a structure value.

The expression used with the dot operator is very often the name of a structure variable, but it can also be a complicated expression. Using the declaration `struct airport airports[300]` shown earlier in this chapter, you reference the airport code for the 20th element in the `airports` array using the expression `airports[19].ident`.

The pointer `fp` mentioned earlier (having the declaration `struct flight *fp`) gives rise to an even more complicated expression if you want to reference one of the seat elements in the flight pointed to by `fp`. For example, the expression `fp->seats[50].avail` has as its value a character, either *A* or *B*, from the `avail` member of the 51st element of the `seats` array in the structure pointed to by `fp`.

The expression `fp->seats[50].avail` can be difficult to understand, yet is a commonly occurring type of expression in C programs. It might help to break the expression down in the following way:

140

- `fp` is a pointer to a structure of type `flight`.

- `fp->seats`, therefore, is an array in the structure.

- `(fp->seats)[50]` is the 51st element of that array.

- `((fp->seats)[50]).avail` is the value of member `avail` in that element.

Notice that although I use parentheses to emphasize the grouping of subexpressions in `fp->seats[50].avail`, the parentheses are not needed. The array operator (`[ ]`), the dot operator (`.`), and the pointer operator (`->`) are all primary expression operators having the same priority; the C language scans and applies them in natural left-to-right order. This explains why the subscript `[50]` applies to the expression `fp->seats` (which is an array), rather than to `seats`, which immediately precedes it (which is just a member name).

You should be able to see that the expression `ptr->name` is merely a convenient shorthand for the expression `(*ptr).name`. The expression `*ptr` dereferences the pointer `ptr`, yielding as its value the structure itself. The dot operator then extracts the value of `name`, a member in that structure.

Undefined Structures

Normally, you must declare the template for a structure before declaring any instances of the structure. For example, many compilers will reject the following code sequence:

```
struct date Today, Tomorrow;
struct date {
    int day;
    int month;
    int year;
};
```

The problem with this code is that the variables `Today` and `Tomorrow` are declared before the content of the `date` structure is defined. When it encounters the first `struct` statement, the compiler has no idea how much memory to allocate to the `Today` and `Tomorrow` variables, so it cannot fully process the declaration. (Some modern compilers require only that the template be declared somewhere in the source file and do not insist that it be declared before its first use.)

The following code sequence, however, is always valid:

```
struct date *date;
struct date {
    int day;
    int month;
    int year;
};
```

The first declaration creates a pointer variable called date, whereas the second provides a description of the structure. A pointer requires four bytes of memory regardless of the kind of object it points to, so the C compiler can process the code sequence without difficulty, and does so.

In general, you can define pointers to structures before you declare the structure template, even though you cannot define structure instances until afterward. The ability to declare a pointer to a structure without defining the structure content is well suited to the development of code modules using the concept of information hiding.

Information hiding, as a software design principle, refers to the isolation of code that manipulates a particular set of data, and to hiding the data from the code that uses it. The isolation of code has two implications. First, it implies that any program error in handling the data can be easily tracked to the code responsible. Second, it implies that the critical data must be hidden from view by other portions of the program.

Undefined structures, when combined with other features of C, support information hiding by allowing only the privileged code to access the contents of structures. Other portions of the program can use structure pointers to designate the data on which the privileged code operates. Normally, the privileged code resides in a separate source file, and only that source file contains the declarations for the contents of the controlled structures. In such implementations, the controlled structures become abstract data objects, and the privileged code acts as a function package to manipulate the abstract objects.

The standard I/O package, consisting of the functions fopen, getc, and putc, among others, is almost an information-hiding construction, because most C programs can use FILE structures without any awareness of their contents. The standard I/O package just misses a full implementation because the stdio.h header file contains a full declaration of the FILE structure. The X Window

System, on the other hand, explicitly uses undefined structures to implement abstract data objects, which the user program manipulates by receiving and passing pointers to the library functions.

Unions

A union is almost identical to a structure syntactically and operationally; the only difference is the way space is allocated to its members. The members of a structure are allocated space consecutively, and the size of a structure is equal to the sum of the sizes of its members. The members of a union all overlap, and the size of a union is equal to the size of its largest member.

When the C compiler processes a source program text, it encodes the information in a struct or union declaration into an internal table that describes each of the members. One of the elements the compiler computes for each member is the *offset* of that member from the beginning of the structure or union. The offset tells where each member begins in the structure, whether five bytes past the beginning, a hundred bytes, or whatever. For a structure, the offset of a member is generally equal to the offset of the previous member plus the length of the previous member. For a union, however, the offset of every member is zero.

You can think of the members of a union as alternative descriptions of a memory area, where at any given time the union contains one and only one of its members. The member that properly describes the contents of the union is the one you last stored a value into. The size of the union then is the smallest size that will contain any one of the members.

Unions are often used for the same purpose as a REDEFINES clause in the COBOL language, a defined attribute in PL/1, or an EQUIVALENCE statement in Fortran; it provides a way to specify multiple uses (or, if you like, alternate images) of a memory area.

Keep in mind that the union provides the capability of storing different types of values in the same area, but at any given time only one member of the union properly describes the contents of the union. As the programmer, you actually write the code that assigns a value to a member of the union; you must also take responsibility for determining which member of the union can be reasonably referenced later for retrieving a value.

Normally, the content of a union provides no clue as to which member is currently the correct view of the union's contents. Often a union is an element of a larger structure, and the containing structure provides a clue as to the current proper member to reference within the union. In some applications, the program context implies which member of a union is currently valid.

The following union contains two members that have different, conflicting formats:

```
union amount {
    int    integer;
    float real;
} value;
```

If at some point in your program you assign a value to value.integer, the content of the union is integer numeric. If you later reference the member value.real, your program retrieves the original integer value, but interprets the value as a floating-point number. The representation of *10* in integer and floating-point formats is quite different and not at all compatible. The floating-point interpretation of the bit pattern comprising integer *10* is likely a very small number. By writing a small program to print out the two members, I found that the value of value.real is 0.00000000000000000000000000000000000000014013, or 1.4013E-44 in scientific notation.

Clearly, the ability to store either an integer or a floating-point value in the union is an advantage only when you can correctly interpret the contents of the union. The following structure describes a component of a financial portfolio, and can describe a stock, bond, or real estate property. It uses a union to collect the information that is unique to each type of asset:

```
struct asset {
    long    purchased;    /* Date purchased         */
    double  basis;        /* Amount invested        */
    double  value;        /* Current value of asset */
    char    *name;        /* Name of asset          */
    char    *broker;      /* Broker or fiduciary agt */
    char    type;         /* Type: Stock/Bond/Real  */
    char    account[22];  /* Identifying number     */
    union   {  /* Particulars of asset */
        struct stock {
```

```
            int    shares;      /* Num of shares owned */
            int    price;       /* Eighths at purchase */
            char   exchange;    /* Exchange whr traded */
            char   ticker[5];   /* Ticker code         */
        }   stock;
        struct bond {
            int    issues;      /* Num of bonds owned   */
            int    rate;        /* Interest rate 1/32nds */
            int    maturity;    /* Life in months       */
            char   ticker[8];   /* Ticker code          */
        }   bond;
        struct property {
            char   *mortgagee;  /* Mortgage holder name */
            char   *address;    /* Address of property  */
            char   state[2];    /* State where located  */
            char   exempt;      /* Tax exemption status */
            char   type;        /* Property type code   */
        }   property;
    }   d; /* Description of asset */
} asset;
```

The asset structure might appear in a file used by an investments program. The key things to note in this structure are the asset type code asset.type, and the fact that each of the three members of the union are structures. The length of the union d is that of the longest structure: bond, which requires 22 bytes to store. The stock structure is 14 bytes long, and the property structure is 12 bytes long.

Any one instance of the asset structure contains only one of the three members of the union, depending on whether the asset is a stock, a bond, or a real estate property. The type code asset.type contains the letter S if it is a stock, B if it is a bond, or R if it is a real estate property.

A program can easily print the contents of an asset structure. For example, the following code fragment prints the structure by choosing one of three print strategies based on the asset type code:

```
/* Print info common to all asset types */
printf("%s ACCT:%s  AGENT:%s\n",
       asset.name, asset.account, asset.broker);
printf("TYPE:%s  PURCHASED: %06d\n",
```

```
        (asset.type == 'S' ? "Stock" :
         asset.type == 'B' ? "Bond" :
                             "Property"),
        asset.purchased);
printf("Basis: %8.2f  Price: %8.2f  Profit: %8.2f\n",
        asset.basis, asset.value,
        asset.value - asset.basis);

/* Print unique asset info */
switch (asset.type) {
    case 'S': /* Print stock */
        printf("%d Shares at %8.3f\n", asset.d.stock.shares,
                asset.d.stock.price * 0.125);
        printf("Exchange:%c  Ticker:%%s\n",
                asset.d.stock.exchange, asset.d.stock.ticker);
        break;
    case 'B': /* Print bond  */
        printf("%d Bonds at %8.3f%%\n", asset.d.bond.issues,
                asset.d.bond.price / 32.0 );
        printf("Maturity:%d mths  Ticker:%s\n",
                asset.d.bond.maturity, asset.d.bond.ticker);
        break;
    case 'R': /* Print real estate property */
        printf("ADDRESS:   %s\n", asset.d.property.address);
        printf("STATE:     %.2s\n", asset.d.property.state);
        printf("MORTGAGEE: %s\n", asset.d.property.mortgagee);
        printf("CLASS: %c   EXEMPT: %c\n",
                asset.d.property.type, asset.d.property.exempt);
        break;
}
```

The whole design of this code is predicated on the assumption that the union d contains a stock structure, a bond structure, or a property structure, but not more than one, and that only one such structure is a valid view of the contents of asset.

Notice that to reference a member of the stock, bond, or property structure, a fully qualified expression is required that names the asset structure, the d union within asset, the proper structure within d, and finally the member itself.

Enumerations

The original definition of the C programming language did not include enumerations as one of the legal data types. Enumerations were added later to enhance the convenience of writing programs in C, and became an official part of the language definition with the adoption of the ANSI standard.

Strictly speaking, an *enumeration value* is nothing more than an integer. The value in declaring an enumeration is that, in addition to specifying the type of a variable, the enumeration also enables you to assign names to specific values of the variable. This has two advantages. First, you can use the value name in assignments and equality tests instead of the explicit value, thus increasing the readability of your programs. Second, only those named values specified in the enumeration can be explicitly assigned to the variable. This prevents the variable from having any but the enumerated values.

The C language designers expect you to use enumerations to define variables that have restricted or coded values. For example, in the previous example of an asset type code, the type member can be declared as an enumeration with the allowed values of STOCK, BOND, or PROPERTY.

Syntactically, an enumeration declaration is written in the following manner:

```
enum tag [ { value_list } ] [ initializers ] ;
```

In this declaration, *value_list* is one or more of

identifier [= integer]

The tag of an enumeration serves the same purpose as the tag of a structure or union; it distinguishes one enumeration from another. An enumeration tag may not duplicate the tag of any other enumeration, or of any structure or union. Structure, union, and enumeration tags constitute one name set, and each name in the set must uniquely identify a structure, union, or enumeration.

The *value_list* portion of an enumeration statement specifies the list of values that instances of the enumeration may assume. If the value list is previously declared and named with *tag*, you can omit the value list and its enclosing braces.

The value list is basically just a list of identifiers. The C compiler assigns a unique integer value to each identifier, beginning with zero and adding one for each name. Optionally, you can choose to explicitly specify the numeric value associated with an identifier by writing an equal sign after the identifier, and then writing the value of the identifier. This becomes the new current value, and any subsequent identifiers in the list without an explicit value are assigned the next consecutive value.

An initializer list, if present, creates instances of the enumeration, with or without an initial value. An initializer list consists of one or more variable names separated by commas. A variable name may optionally be followed by an equal sign, and then by an initial value. Of course, the initial value must be one of the identifiers declared in the value list.

Take a look at some examples of enumerations. To begin with, you can declare the asset.type member as an enumeration, as follows:

```
enum assetType {
    Stock,           /* Public stock certificates */
    Bond,            /* Corporate bonds */
    Property         /* Real estate parcel */
    } type;
```

This declaration creates three new symbols, Stock, Bond, and Property, with values of *0*, *1*, and *2*, in addition to a new data type (enum assetType) and a new variable called type. The compiler assigns the values of Stock, Bond, and Property, but they could have been explicitly specified in the declaration. The following declaration explicitly assigns the codes S, B, and R to the value names:

```
enum assetType {
    Stock = 'S',     /* Public stock certificates */
    Bond = 'B',      /* Corporate bonds */
    Property = 'R'   /* Real estate parcel */
    } type;
```

Subsequent code that references the asset.type field must use one of the Stock, Bond, or Property identifiers when setting or testing its value. The switch statement is rewritten as shown here:

```
/* Print unique asset info
switch (asset.type) {
```

```
    case Stock: /* Print stock */
        ...
        break;
    case Bond: /* Print bond   */
        ...
        break;
    case Property: /* Print real estate property */
        ...
        break;
}
```

Another illustrative use of enumerations is to create a new data type called boolean that indicates a simple truth value (TRUE or FALSE). You can create and use a boolean enumeration as in the following example:

```
#include <string.h>
enum boolean { FALSE, TRUE };
...
enum boolean
okdate(int m, int d, int y)
{
    enum boolean leapyear = (y % 4 == 0);
    static int days[12] = {
        31, 28, 31, 30, 31, 30, 31, 31, 30, 31, 30, 31 };

    if (y < 99) y += 1900;
    if (y < 1900 || y > 2099
            || m < 1 || m > 12
            || d < 1 || d > 31)
        return FALSE;
    if (d > days[m-1] + (m == 2 && leapyear))
        return FALSE;
    return TRUE;
}
```

The routine shown above tests whether a month, day, and year represents a valid date. For example, January 31 is valid, whereas April 31 is not. The function returns a boolean value indicating TRUE if the date is valid, and FALSE otherwise. The function also internally uses a boolean value to note whether the year indicates a leap year.

The compiler assigns a numerical value of 0 to FALSE, because it appears first in the list of value names, and a value of 1 to TRUE. The order in which FALSE and TRUE are listed was chosen specifically to match the values C uses internally to represent *true* and *false*. Considering that the actual values assigned to the value names are important to the program, it is not inappropriate to write the declaration as

```
enum boolean { FALSE = 0, TRUE = 1 };
```

although most C programmers consider the explicit values superfluous.

The function okdate is declared as type enum boolean, meaning that it returns a value of that type. Having a return type of enum boolean is not really much different from a return type of int, and you can use a function call of okdate virtually anywhere an integer value is required.

The first statement in the function declares a variable called leapyear that is of type enum boolean; it receives an initial value that is the expression (year % 4 == 0). The program calculates the value of this expression every time the function is called, and then assigns the result to the variable leapyear.

The second statement declares a static variable called days that is an integer array giving the number of days in each month of the year. The array is used later to determine whether the day value is valid.

The logic of the function is straightforward, except for the statement if (d > days[m-1] + (m == 2 && leapyear)). The conditional expression in this if statement calculates the number of days in a month by taking the table value days[m-1] and adding the value of the expression (m == 2 && leapyear). This expression is true only for February in leap years. In that one case its value is 1; in all other cases its value is 0. In other words, when m is 2, the number of days is the number given in the table (28), plus one if the year is a leap year.

The okdate function can be written without the enum boolean type by substituting int for each occurrence of enum boolean in the code. However, many experienced programmers would prefer the version using enumerations because it more clearly documents the use of integers as logical variables.

Fields

Fields, or more specifically *bit fields*, are data items comprising a group of contiguous bits, often as a portion of a machine word. With other elementary data types, the type implies the size of the item: a short is always 16 bits long, a long is always 32 bits long, and so on. The size of a bit field, however, can vary from one bit to the number of bits in a machine word. The size of a machine word (in most C implementations) is the same as the size of an int.

The C language includes bit fields to allow easy access to multiple data items that are packed into a single machine word. Such data sometimes arises when programming a peripheral device interface at the hardware level, and when processing data created on a different computer system.

A bit field must be a member of a structure. The structure may contain other data types as well as bit fields, or may contain bit fields exclusively. The structure may comprise one or several machine words, but a single bit field cannot be longer than one word. Some C compilers permit a bit field to overlap word boundaries; others require a bit field to fit completely within one word. As many adjacent bit fields are packed into a word as can fit; subsequent bit fields are stored in the following word.

The presence of bit fields in a structure cannot offset any other data type within a word; members other than bit fields always begin at the next byte or word boundary, as appropriate for the data type.

The declaration of a bit field uses the following syntax:

```
type [ identifier ] : bits ;
```

A bit field must always be an integer numeric type such as char or short; you may qualify the type with signed or unsigned as desired. Whether a bit field is signed or unsigned by default is compiler dependent.

For *identifier*, specify any desired member name using the standard C rules for forming an identifier. The identifier may be omitted from a bit field declaration, in which case the field reserves unused space within a word.

151

For *bits*, specify the number of bits in the field, from one to the size of a word. Notice that the size of a word is compiler-dependent, but for most systems a word is 32 bits. If *bits* is 0, the next bit field is forced to begin in a new word.

The order of bits within a bit field, and the order of bit fields within a word, is compiler dependent, except that bit fields that are declared adjacent are stored adjacent.

As the authors of the C language noted, most of the characteristics of bit fields are determined by the specific compiler you use. The only things about which you can be certain are that the size of the field in bits is at least as large as you state, and that the representation of bit fields is consistent within your own compiler and hardware environment. Programs intended to be portable do not use bit fields.

The following structure defines a number of bit fields within a single word:

```
struct {
    int motor     : 1;    /* Start-motor signal */
    int direction : 1;    /* 0=Forward, 1=Reverse */
    int power     : 4;    /* Power level 0-15   */
    int           : 1;    /* unused */
    int overload  : 1;    /* 1= disable overload protect */
};
```

Because structure declares only eight bits, you can be assured that all the bits are placed in the same word for any modern computer and compiler implementation. On some implementations, however, the overload bit may be the leftmost bit in the word, whereas motor may be leftmost on other implementations.

Bit fields are numeric data, and you can use a bit field in an expression just like any integer numeric item. For example, in the preceding example, you can increment the power value with the expression power++. Most systems interpret the power value as a number in the range from –8 to 7; if you desire the range from 0 to 15 as the comment notes, declare the member as unsigned int.

Summary

This chapter presents the aggregate data types supported by the C language, including structures, unions, enumerations, and bit fields.

The *structure* is the vehicle in C for grouping data elements into larger units. Its members may be the elementary data types examined in Chapter 3, but may also be other structures, unions, enumerations, or bit fields. You can assign the value of a structure to another structure of the same type, and you can pass structures to a function as arguments or have them returned as the value of a function; other types of operations are not permitted on structures. The most common operations performed on structures are *dot* (.), which references a member of a structure, and *pointer* (->), which references a member of the structure pointed to by a pointer variable.

A *union* contains a list of members like a structure. Unlike the members of a structure, however, the members of a union overlay each other and, therefore, the size of the union is the size of its largest member. Unions are usually used to provide alternative formats for an area, but can also be used to change the representation of a value.

An *enumeration* is not really a composite data item as are structures and unions. Treated like an integer in most respects, an enumeration lists the possible values an instance can assume and associates a name with each value. Enumerations are used primarily to increase the clarity of program code by replacing an obscure statement such as `marital_status = 1;` with the more explicit `marital_status = SINGLE`.

The bit field is an integer variable where you specify the size of the integer in bits. Bit fields are used to subdivide an `int` into groups of bits, each group having a particular meaning or usage. Bit fields are used primarily in programs dealing with hardware interfaces.

Pointers and Arrays

The previous chapters of this book present the basics of the C language. This chapter discusses the heart and soul of the language: pointers. Almost all C programs use pointers. The primary distinction between an experienced, fluent C programmer and a beginning C programmer is the ease with which the former manipulates pointers, and the constant confusion or timidity the beginner experiences when confronted by them.

The basic concept of a *pointer* is simple; it is a special kind of integer containing the address of some other data element. In hardware terms, an *address* specifies the location in memory where a data item can be found. For nonpointer variables, the compiler keeps track of the address of each data item and generates the correct address when accessing an item. When you use pointer variables, you supply the address that designates the data item you want to access and the compiler generates the appropriate instructions to perform the access.

Because a pointer is nothing more than a designator for some other data item, pointers in the C language have no specific data type of their own; rather, they take on the data type of the object they point to. Thus you cannot (easily) use a pointer to an integer as a pointer to a character. In C, *pointer to integer* and *pointer to character* are different data types.

C introduces the term *dereferencing* to denote the operation of using a pointer to reference the item it points to. When a pointer is dereferenced, the result is the value of the data item designated by the pointer. There are several different syntax forms for dereferencing a pointer, depending on the context. All involve the use of an operator; the . and -> operators use a pointer to locate a structure or union member, and the * operator (used as a unary operator) dereferences a pointer to an elementary object.

The C language recognizes an intimate relationship between pointers and arrays, though the nature of the connection may not be immediately apparent to you. The relationship lies in the name of an array. An array is not a single object, but rather a set of objects, so to what does its name refer? In C, the name of an array is treated in every way as a pointer to the first element of the array. Subscripting an array and dereferencing a pointer are identical and synonymous operations, so much so that the language allows you to use the two forms interchangeably. In other words, you can subscript a pointer and you can use an array name in pointer expressions.

In this chapter, I look first at declaring pointers and arrays, and then at the kinds of operations you can perform with them. The interchangeability of pointer and array expressions is emphasized throughout. The chapter finishes with a discussion of arrays of pointers, and the Medusa that slays most beginners: pointers to pointers.

Pointer Declarations

Because pointers take on the data type of the object to which they point, it is awkward to give a formal syntax description for pointer declarations. (A formal description appears in Part III, "Reference," at the end of this book.) Previous chapters show how to declare integers of various kinds, floating-point variables, character variables, functions, structures, unions, and enumerations. You declare pointers to these objects by writing the same kind of declaration you write for the object itself, and then prefixing the object name with *. The asterisk in front of an identifier in a declaration changes the object declared from the specified data type to a *pointer* to the specified data type.

The following examples show the declaration of several kinds of pointers:

```
int *sum;
```

```
unsigned long *total;
```

```
char *string;
```

```
static struct employee {
    char   name[30];
    short  age;
    long   date_of_hire;
    double salary;
} *emp;
```

```
enum boolean {FALSE, TRUE} *truth;
```

The declarations of sum and total show sum to be a pointer to an integer, and total to be a pointer to an unsigned long integer. Because these variables are pointers, beware of using them directly; sum+3 does not mean what you might expect. In fact, sum does not point to any one specific integer; at any given point in your program, sum can point to any one of a dozen different integers or to none at all. You must assign a pointer value to a pointer before it points to anything specific. Also, you can change the value of a pointer variable freely during your program's execution, making it point first to one integer and then another, as is convenient for you. (If you're not clear why you might want to do this, you have to wait until the section "Using Pointers" later in this chapter for an explanation.)

The declaration char *string creates a variable called string that is used as a pointer to a character. Usually when you see a declaration such as this, you assume that string points to an array of characters terminated by the null character, which is a commonly occurring type of data in C called a *string*. Often you think of a variable like string as if it is the string itself, although this is a dangerous way of thinking. Actually, string is a pointer to a single character. That character can be the first character of a string, or one character of a character array, or just an isolated character; you can't tell from the declaration.

The struct declaration is an example of declaring the template for a structure and allocating instances of the structure all in one statement. The portion enclosed between braces describes the content of any instance of struct employee (see Chapter 7, "Structures and Unions," for more information). If you subtract the brace-enclosed description, you obtain the declaration of a pointer to the structure:

```
static struct employee *emp;
```

The structure declaration creates one variable, called emp, of type *pointer to structure*. The qualifier static stipulates that the pointer variable is permanently allocated in memory, accessible by all functions in this source file, and invisible to functions in any other source file.

Notice that, as with the previous declarations, the declaration of a pointer to a struct employee does not in any way create any instances of the employee structure itself. Declaring a pointer is not the same thing as declaring the object, but declaring the pointer does sort of promise that somewhere, somehow, the program will create instances of struct employee to which the pointer emp can point.

The enum statement declares an enumeration and creates a pointer variable called truth that can point to an instance of the enumeration. As before, this declaration does not create any instances of the enumeration to which truth can point.

You can declare objects and pointers in the same statement. If you combine pointers and nonpointers in the same declaration, be careful to prefix all the pointer names with *; the asterisk goes with the identifier, not with the type name. For example, the statement

```
int planes, flights, airports, *total;
```

declares four variables: three integers named planes, flights, and airports, and one pointer to an integer named total. In this case, the statement declares something to which total can point: any one of the three integer variables.

In general, you can declare a pointer to any object in memory. This includes not only the standard data types, but also other pointers and functions. The following example shows the declaration of an integer, a pointer to an integer, and a pointer to such a pointer:

```
int count;
int *counter;
int **ct;
```

The number of asterisks in front of an identifier indicate the number of times you must dereference a pointer to obtain the nonpointer object. Once again, notice that the asterisks go with the identifier. Therefore, when declaring multiple items in one statement, identifiers of pointers require one or more asterisks in front of the name, and nonpointer objects require none, as in the following rewrite of the previous example:

```
int count, *counter, **ct;
```

To declare a pointer to a function, you must enclose the variable name and asterisk prefix inside parentheses. Without the parentheses, the asterisk can be confused with the data type of the function's return value. For example,

```
ch1ar *search(void);
```

declares a function returning a pointer to a character, whereas

```
char (*search)(void);
```

declares a pointer named search that points to a function returning a character, and

```
char *(*search)(void);
```

declares a pointer to a function that returns a pointer to a character. In the first case, search is the name of the function declared; in the second and third cases, search is the name of the pointer variable. Declarations of pointers, arrays, and functions can be complicated when mixed together. This is the subject of Chapter 9, "Complex Declarations."

You can initialize a pointer variable when you declare it, just as you can with other kinds of declarations. The syntax takes the usual form:

```
type *name = pointer-expression
```

159

For *pointer-expression*, write any expression that yields a pointer value. Typical examples use the & operator to yield the address of an object, or use an array name, and possibly employ pointer arithmetic to modify the address. (Chapter 4, "Expressions," explains the & operator. The section "Pointer Arithmetic" later in this chapter further discusses the & operator along with pointer arithmetic.)

The C language defines the value *0* for pointers to mean the pointer has no value; *0* is never a valid address in the UNIX environment and so cannot be mistaken for a valid pointer value. The standard header file stdio.h defines the symbolic value NULL as the null pointer, and usually you should use NULL in preference to 0 to initialize a null pointer. Using these conventions, you often see pointer declarations of the form

```
char *string = NULL;
```

to create a pointer that does not yet point to anything specific.

Array Declarations

This section presents a more detailed and precise definition of arrays than the casual introduction in Chapter 3, "Simple Declarations."

An array is a list of objects all of the same type. The objects comprising an array are called *elements*. The *dimensions* of an array describe how many elements an array contains and how its elements are arranged in memory. An array of one dimension arranges its elements in a linear list like a row of mailboxes beside a country road. Each element is identified by an *index* giving the relative position of the element within the list, with the first element having an index of 0 and the last element having an index equal to $n-1$ where n is the number of elements in the array.

The elements of a two-dimensional array are arranged like the squares on a sheet of graph paper. Each element is identified by a row and column index. For an array having m rows and n columns, the row indexes run from 0 through $m-1$ and the column indexes run from 0 through $n-1$. The number of elements in the array is $m \times n$.

The C language supports arrays of any number of dimensions; C does not limit you to three dimensions as do some programming languages. For arrays of dimension greater than two, the array is characterized by the number of indexes required to uniquely specify an element; three-dimensional arrays require three, four-dimensional arrays require four, and so on.

The elements of an array are arranged contiguously in memory—there are no gaps between them. The elements for a one-dimensional array are laid out from low to high address, with element 0 first in the list. The elements of an array of two dimensions or more are laid out in row-major order, meaning that element Xi,j,k of an array X is followed by element Xi,j,k+1.

The C language does not incorporate a data type specific to arrays—as is the case with pointers. Rather, an array takes on the data type of its component elements. To declare an array, write the declaration for any one of its elements, and then append the size of the array in each dimension. The syntax of an array declaration is as follows:

```
type identifier [ size ] ... ;
```

Within a declaration, an identifier followed by an expression of the form `[n]` indicates that the identifier names an array of *n* elements of the specified type. A two-dimensional array is defined as an array of one-dimensional arrays using the form `identifier[m][n]` where *m* is the number of rows and *n* is the number of columns.

A key to understanding arrays in the C language is to realize that C treats an array of two or more dimensions as an array of arrays. Thus, a two-dimensional array is an array of one-dimensional arrays, a three-dimensional array is an array of two-dimensional arrays, and so on. Arrays are declared according to that view, and elements are referenced according to that view. C is very consistent about this. If you subscript a three-dimensional array, you get a two-dimensional array; if you subscript a two-dimensional array, you get a one-dimensional array; and if you subscript a one-dimensional array, you get an element. This is why an array of three dimensions requires three subscript indexes to yield an element. Unlike other less consistent languages, C has no trouble interpreting a reference to an array with fewer subscripts than the array has dimensions: you get a subarray of the original array.

An array can be comprised of elements of any desired data type, including structures, unions, enumerations, pointers to these or any other data type, and other arrays. The only restrictions are that all elements of an array must be of the same type and size, and you cannot form an array of functions (although you can have an array of *pointers* to functions).

To specify an initial value for the array, follow the identifier and dimensions with an equal sign (=) and a brace-enclosed list of elements. If the array has more than one dimension, you should enclose the initializers for each subarray in braces as well. However, you can omit inner braces when you provide a value for all elements of a subarray. Notice that an initializer list is allowed only for static arrays; arrays declared automatic (whether explicitly or implicitly) at the beginning of a function cannot be initialized. Because all initializer values are computed at compile time, they must be symbolic or literal constants.

The following declaration shows how to declare a static array of two dimensions with initial values:

```
static int table[3][4] =
    {
        { 0, 1, 2, 3 },
        { 2, 4, 6, 8 },
        { 4, 3, 9, 6 },
    };
```

To understand the geometry of the array declaration table[3][4], read the declaration as (table[3])[4] even though the parentheses are invalid if you actually write them. If you then mentally substitute x for the expression table[3], you obtain the declaration int x[4]. This means x is an array of four integers. However, x represents table[3], so when table is subscripted once, the result is an array of four integers; the first subscript selects one of three subarrays, and the second subscript selects one of four elements from the subarray. This is equivalent to the row-column organization where each of three rows contains four integers.

Each row of the array is enclosed in braces because each row constitutes one element of the array table[3]. Then the list of three elements (rows) is enclosed in braces to complete the initializer list.

You can omit the *size* value from within the brackets of the last or only array dimension when you include an initializer for the array; the C compiler chooses *size* equal to the number of elements in the initializer list. You can write the previous declaration this way:

```
static int table[3][] =
    {
        { 0, 1, 2, 3 },
        { 2, 4, 6, 8 },
        { 4, 3, 9, 6 },
    };
```

Using Pointers

Once you declare a pointer, the question becomes how to use it. The underlying purpose of a pointer is to enable reference to the item it points to; the main reason for using a pointer is to be able to easily reference different but similar objects during program execution. From these two purposes arise the principal operations performed with pointers: dereferencing them, and setting their value.

If p is a pointer, *p is the object to which p points; the value of the expression *p is the value of the object pointed to by p. Suppose the value of p is a pointer to the integer variable sum. Using the expression *p is then equivalent in every way to using the variable sum. In particular, you can add 1 to the value of sum by writing *p + 1, and you can set sum to zero by writing *p = 0.

The dereferencing operator * has the same effect when you apply it to a pointer, a structure, or a union: the value of the expression *p is the structure or union pointed to by p. Notice that the value is the *entire* structure or union. You can do anything with the structure or union value that you can do with the structure or union itself, including assigning it to another structure variable or passing it to a function as one of the arguments of the call. To reference a member of the structure pointed to by p, you can use the dot operator—(*p).mem for example. You must enclose the expression *p in parentheses because the dereferencing operator * is a unary operator and has lower priority than the . operator. Without the parentheses, the compiler sees the expression *p.mem as equivalent to *(p.mem), which is invalid; p is a pointer, not a structure, and as such contains no member named mem nor any other member.

163

An easier way to access a member of a structure when you have a pointer to the structure is to use the `->` operator. The value of the expression `p->mem` is the value of the member named `mem` in the structure pointed to by `p`. The value to the left of `->` must be a pointer or a pointer expression. Writing `p->` is identical to writing `(*p).`, except that the form `p->` requires two fewer key strokes to write than `(*p).` and that `p->` is clearer in meaning than the `(*p).` form.

You cannot dereference a pointer variable until it contains a valid pointer value. As with other variables, a pointer contains only meaningless garbage until you initialize it. Any attempt to use an uninitialized pointer yields a meaningless result, and may cause abnormal termination of your program.

Pointer variables receive their values from assignment expressions, as do other variables. The value assigned to a pointer must be of the same type as the pointer. For example, the type *pointer to character* (typename `(char*)`) is considered different from the type *pointer to integer* (typename `(int*)`), although you can convert a pointer of one type to a pointer of another type by using a cast. The following example shows the use of a cast to convert from one type of pointer to another:

```
char *string;
unsigned char *data;
...
string = (char *)data;
```

To assign the address of a variable to a pointer, use the `&` operator to get the address of the variable and the `=` operator to make the assignment, like this:

```
p = &sum;
```

To obtain the address of a structure member, you must apply the `&` operator to an expression that yields the member as its value. Either of the following types of expressions do the trick: `p = &s->mem` if `s` is a pointer to the structure, or `p = &s.mem` if `s` is an instance of the structure.

As I discuss in greater detail in the next section, the C language considers an array name to be a pointer constant. Pointer variables are often initialized by assigning the name of an array to the pointer, thus setting the pointer to the address of the first element of the array. Function names are also pointer constants, and you can use them (without parentheses after the name) to initialize a variable of type *pointer to function*.

Pointer Arithmetic

The C language supports three kinds of operations on pointers in addition to the dereferencing and assignment operations already discussed: adding an integer to a pointer, subtracting an integer from a pointer, and taking the difference of two pointers. To understand the meaning of these operations, we must return to the topic of arrays.

The C language does not support operations on arrays. An assignment such as A = B doesn't work when A is the name of an array, because array names behave like *constants*. Although the name of an array has a value, you can't change that value. The name of an array is actually a symbol for the address of its first element; an array name is a pointer or, to be more specific, a pointer constant.

Consider the following array:

```
int table[] = { 5, 10, 15, 20 };
```

The name of the array is table. It consists of four elements, each of type int. If table is the address of the first element, or table[0], the value 5, the pointer expression table+1 is a pointer to the second element, or table[1], which contains the value 10. Herein lies the basis of all pointer arithmetic.

Associated with every pointer is the size of the object to which it points. Adding an integer c to the pointer increases the pointer's value by the amount c x sizeof(*p). This advances the pointer c elements if the original value pointed to an element of an array.

Returning to the declaration of table, it is possible to interpret the following statements:

```
t1 = *table;
t2 = *(table + 2);
```

The value assigned to integer t1 is 5, which is the value of the first element in the array. The second statement assigns the value 15 to t2 because it is two elements beyond the element designated by table.

You can also write the same two statements in the following form using subscript notation:

```
t1 = table[0];
t2 = table[2];
```

When encountering a subscript expression, the C compiler first converts it into the equivalent pointer expression. The final generated code always uses pointer values to access array elements because most computers do not really implement subscript operations at the hardware level. Virtually all computers, however, have instruction sets that support pointer arithmetic and pointer dereferencing.

The following example shows the use of subscript notation to search an array—in this case, to find the first element with a value that falls between the two limits min and max. If the function finds such an element, it returns the element's value; otherwise it returns 0.

```
int search(int min, int max)
{
    int i;
    for (i = 0; i < 4; i++)
        if (table[i] >= min && table[i] <= max)
            return table[i];
    return 0;
}
```

You can write the same function using pointer expressions instead of subscript expressions, as follows:

```
int search(int min, int max)
{
    int *item;
    for (item = table; item < table + 4; item++)
        if (*item >= min && *item <= max)
            return *item;
    return 0;
}
```

The version using pointer expressions is more efficient. Both versions reference the table element twice on each iteration: the subscript version uses the expression table[i], and the pointer version uses the expression *item. However, to resolve the expression table[i] the system must actually compute the expression *(table + i * sizeof(int)), which involves a multiplication, an addition, and a pointer dereference. The expression *item requires only the dereference of a pointer value already available, and therefore executes much quicker. The advantage arises from the fact that the pointer version maintains a pointer to the current item, which needs merely to be incremented on each iteration of the loop, whereas the subscript version increments an integer from which a pointer value must be computed on each iteration.

Subtracting an integer from a pointer is equivalent to adding a negative integer, the net effect of which is to back up a pointer to a preceding element of the array.

Subtracting two pointers is legal when both point to elements of the same array; the result is the difference between the indexes of the two elements. For example, if two pointers pa and pb both point to elements of the same array A, the value of the expression pa - pb is *2* when pa points to element A[4] and pb points to element A[2]. To put it a different way, the pointer difference operation is consistent with the definition of pointer addition: the subtraction of pb from pa (pa - pb) yields the integer i such that pb + i is equal to pa.

You can use the comparison operators (==, !=, >, >=, <, and <=) to compare two pointer expressions when both expressions designate locations within the same array. This restriction is necessary because the comparison operators are based on the difference operation; p < q essentially entails testing the difference p - q for a positive, negative, or zero integer result.

Some qualifications and limitations concerning the use of pointer arithmetic are necessary.

Pointer arithmetic is only valid within the bounds of a contiguously allocated area of memory. This requirement is automatically fulfilled when a pointer expression selects elements of a single array, because all elements of an array are contiguously allocated in memory. You can also use pointer arithmetic within the bounds of a memory area you dynamically allocate with the malloc library function, because malloc only allocates memory in contiguous chunks. C does not check that you obey the restriction, so it is your responsibility to ensure that a pointer calculation spans a valid memory range. Depending on the memory architecture of your system, not all address ranges are valid, and pointer arithmetic need not obey the rules of addition and subtraction when the pointer would stray outside the range of a known, contiguous area of memory. Only an array, and the memory allocated by malloc, are guaranteed to span a contiguous range of memory. In particular, variables themselves can be stored in any order in memory, and may have gaps of possibly illegal addresses between them, so you cannot be sure that two variables declared one after another occur consecutively in memory.

The ANSI standard allows a pointer to increment to the position immediately following the end of an array; in other words, to the element that would follow the last in the array. It is not legal to reference the resulting pointer value; it is only guaranteed that such an address will be properly formed and can be used in comparisons such as p < q, where q points to the element beyond the end of the array, to determine whether p is actually within the bounds of the array. If, however, p and q are pointers to different arrays, the expression p < q (or any comparison of p to q) gives a meaningless result.

Pointer Arrays

Pointer arrays, or, to be more precise, arrays of pointers, occur frequently in C programming, mainly because it is often useful to have lists of things, and often those things to list are dynamically allocated with malloc and occupy unpredictable areas of memory. The next section discusses the subject of dynamic memory allocation; this section provides some examples of statically allocated pointer arrays and their use. The techniques remain the same, however, regardless of how the memory is allocated.

To begin with, study an example of processing strings, an application where pointer arrays often arise. A review of the concept of a *string* might be helpful to you here.

Text must be stored in an array of characters because the C data type char is only large enough to hold one character. By convention, you allocate enough elements in the array to hold the longest string of text you want to process, and follow the last character with an ASCII null character (binary zero, represented '\0') to mark the end of the text. This allows the array to contain text shorter than the array, and makes it easy for all sorts of text processing utility functions to determine the actual length of text stored in the array. A character array following this convention is called a *string*.

To define a character array (which from now on I'll call a string), you can write a statement such as

```
char month[12];
```

This allocates twelve bytes of memory to hold a string and its trailing null, for a maximum of eleven characters of text. The declaration leaves the array uninitialized. If this statement appears outside a function, such as at the beginning of the program and before the first function, the array is automatically initialized with twelve elements of binary zero. Conveniently, the binary zeros are null characters, so the string called month appears empty. Programmers say it contains the null string, or a string of zero length.

You can give the character array an initial value by writing an initializer. As you learned earlier in this chapter, you can initialize an array by writing its elements enclosed in braces after the declaration, like this:

```
char month[12] = { 'J', 'a', 'n', 'u', 'a', 'r', 'y', 0 };
```

The example shows an explicit null character at the end of the string, although it's really not necessary; when fewer initializer values are present than the array requires, C automatically fills out the array with zeros. As a time-saving convenience, C supports a special notation for a list of character values: just write the string of text enclosed in quotation marks. A string of characters enclosed in quotation marks is identical in meaning to an array of characters shown previously, thus you can shorten the above declaration to the following:

```
char month[12] = "January";
```

You can simplify this declaration even further by recalling that C automatically calculates the number of elements required for an array when you omit the size between the [] brackets. Using the C default, the declaration becomes

```
char month[] = "January";
```

Once you define and initialize the array, you can print or display its contents on the terminal using the putc function, which writes one character at a time, as shown in the following code:

```
int i;
for (i = 0; month[i] != '\0'; i++)
    putc(month[i]);
```

Recalling that using subscripts is less efficient than pointers, you can better write the output loop using pointers:

```
char *c;
for (c = month; *c != 0; c++)
    putc(*month);
```

Notice that the version using pointers is somewhat shorter to write than the array version. Using pointers is very natural for string processing, and most experienced programmers automatically resort to pointer techniques when doing such processing.

The statement `char *c;` is an example of declaring a pointer variable: c takes on different values as the loop executes, pointing first to one character and then the next as it steps across the string. You can easily initialize the loop by setting c to the value of `month`, because the C language defines the name of an array as a pointer constant to the first element of the array.

To extend the example to pointer arrays, redefine the program task to printing out the month name corresponding to an integer in the range from 1 to 12, and write a function to do so.

The function requires a list supplying the name of each month. The data organization that readily springs to mind for such a list is to create an array where each element is a month name. The following declaration might be a first attempt at creating such an array:

```
char month[12][] = {
    "January", "February", "March", "April", "May",
    "June", "July", "August", "September", "October",
    "November", "December"
    };
```

The C compiler does not like this declaration and rejects the program containing it, because the size is omitted from the second dimension of `month`. Although C is willing to determine the size of an array automatically, in this declaration the compiler is confronted with an array of arrays. As noted earlier in the section "Declaring Arrays," all elements of an array must be the same size. The declaration as written, however, asks that `month` contain first an array of eight characters, and then an array of nine characters, and then an array of six characters, and so on. It refuses to do this.

As an alternative, you can force each word in the list to the same length by allocating 15 characters for each word. The following declaration uses this strategy:

```
char month[12][15] = {
    "January", "February", "March", "April", "May",
```

```
"June", "July", "August", "September", "October",
"November", "December"
};
```

A weakness of this approach is that the array contains wasted space. A better approach is to use an array of 12 pointers, each of which points to the name of the corresponding month. Because each pointer is the same length, you can list the pointers in an array without difficulty. The following shows one way to create such a pointer array:

```
char month1[] = "January";
char month2[] = "February";
char month3[] = "March";
char month4[] = "April";
char month5[] = "May";
char month6[] = "June";
char month7[] = "July";
char month8[] = "August";
char month9[] = "September";
char month10[] = "October";
char month11[] = "November";
char month12[] = "December";

char *months[12] = {
    month1, month2, month3, month4, month5, month6,
    month7, month8, month9, month10, month11, month12
    };
```

The declaration of months hinges on the fact that the name of an array is a pointer to the array, and therefore the names of the arrays for each month serve as pointers to initialize the months array. For this to work, it is essential that you define the arrays month1 through month12 before months; otherwise the identifiers month1 through month12 are unknown to the compiler when it processes the initializer list.

This declaration is much longer and clumsier than it needs to be. Programmers write the above set of declarations only if they fail to completely understand that an array is equivalent to a pointer, and that the compiled program replaces the string constant `"January"` with a pointer wherever such a string constant appears. Using this fact, you can more easily write the declaration like this:

```c
char *months[12] = {
    "January", "February", "March", "April", "May",
    "June", "July", "August", "September", "October",
    "November", "December"
    };
```

This form of the declaration capitalizes on the fact that the C compiler replaces any occurrence of an array name with a pointer to the array. In the declaration, the string literals `"January"` through `"December"` are treated as array names. The C compiler takes on the task of allocating memory for string literals by supporting the string literal in the first place, and as a general rule the literal is not stored where it appears in the program. In fact, the code generated for the declaration of `months` consists only of 12 pointers. The strings themselves are stored elsewhere in memory (only the compiler knows their exact locations) and through the pointers in the `months` array.

Because the array declaration now consists of equal-sized members, the compiler agrees to fill in the count of elements. In its final form, the declaration of the `months` array looks like this:

```c
char *months[] = {
    "January", "February", "March", "April", "May",
    "June", "July", "August", "September", "October",
    "November", "December"
    };
```

Now you only have to write the function to use the `months` array. Here is the way I would write it:

```c
void
printMonth(int month)
{
    puts(months[month - 1]);
}
```

The function `puts` appears in the standard C function library. Like `putc`, it prints its argument. However, `puts` prints an entire string and requires a string pointer as its argument instead of a single character.

You might object that the function uses array subscripting rather than point-ers, when pointers are presumably more efficient than subscripts. The pointer version looks like this:

```
void
printMonth(int month)
{
    puts(months + (month - 1));
}
```

The pointer version uses pointer arithmetic to locate the array element. The value of months is a pointer to the first element of the array; by adding the integer month to it you obtain a pointer to the desired pointer element. However, the compiled program must multiply the integer (month - 1) by the size of a pointer to locate the pointer, so both versions of the function require the same effort to execute. The meaning of the array version is somewhat more apparent than the pointer version, so I chose it over the pointer version.

The task of printing out the name of a month corresponding to an integer turned out to be pretty simple. A more complicated task is to print out the long-est and shortest month names. The best implementation of such a function uses a new kind of object: a *pointer to a pointer*. The following code performs this task:

```
static char *months[] = {
    "January", "February", "March", "April", "May",
    "June", "July", "August", "September", "October",
    "November", "December",
    NULL
    };

void
printNames(void)
{
    char **name, *longname, *shortname;
    int  longest = 0, shortest = 99;

    for (name = months; *name != NULL; name++)
    {
        if (strlen(*name) < shortest)
            shortname = *name;
```

```
        if (strlen(*name) > longest)
            longname = *name;
    }
    puts(shortname);
    puts(longname);
}
```

The solution begins with a slightly modified version of the months array in which an extra element is added at the end. The extra element is a NULL pointer that marks the end of the list. Its presence makes it easy for the printNames function to check for the end of the list, and eliminates the need to know exactly how many elements the list contains. Pointer lists often end with a NULL pointer to simplify the task of checking for the end of the list.

The printNames function itself uses three pointer variables: name, longname, and shortname. The name variable points to the current name as the function works its way through the list. It is an example of a pointer to a pointer, and is necessary because the elements of the months list are themselves pointers. Use the longname and shortname variables to remember which strings contain the longest and shortest month names respectively.

The integers shortest and longest keep track of the shortest and longest *lengths* encountered. Choose an initial value of shortest greater than the length of the longest name, and an initial value of longest less than the length of the shortest name; this is because shortest must be adjusted downward during the for loop, and longest must be adjusted upward. If shortest starts out too low, or longest too high, shorter words or longer words aren't found.

The main purpose of the printNames example is to illustrate the use of a double pointer (a pointer to a pointer). When initialized, the value used to initialize it must also be a pointer to a pointer, but because months is an array of pointers, and the name of the array is a pointer to its first element, it is just such a pointer to a pointer. The two statements shortname = *name and longname = *name show that you must dereference the value of name once to obtain a normal string pointer.

The usage of double pointers can be even more complicated than the printNames function demonstrates. In some applications, for example, you might need to reference a character of the string array pointed to by the pointer to which name points; in such a case, the proper expression to reference the *i*th character is (*name)[i]. The expression first dereferences name with the expression (*name) to obtain a direct string pointer, and then subscripts this with [i] to obtain a character of the string. The more natural expression *name[i] yields an entirely different result. Because the dereference operator * has a lower priority than the subscript operator [], the compiler treats the expression *name[i] as if it is enclosed in parentheses *(name[i]), first fetching the ith element (pointer) beyond name, and then dereferencing it to fetch the first character of that string.

Dynamic Memory Allocation

The need to allocate memory on demand arises with surprising frequency in programming tasks of all kinds. Dynamic allocation can cope with the need to create arrays of unforeseeable dimensions, and to create tables of linked structures where the number of elements depends on the program's input. Programs that use static allocation tend to have fixed capacity limits, whereas programs that use dynamic allocation can process data of arbitrary complexity or volume.

Dynamic memory allocation is so commonly needed that the standard C function library includes a set of functions intended specifically for that purpose. Although I properly should defer the description of the malloc function package to Part II of this book, the use of dynamic memory allocation is intimately tied to the C language facilities for manipulating objects with pointers, and demands treatment in this chapter.

The malloc function package consists of the functions malloc, free, calloc, and realloc (and the infrequently used mallopt, which I don't discuss here). These functions are remarkably easy to use.

The call malloc(n) returns a generic pointer to a memory area n bytes in length; its declaration is void *malloc(unsigned int size). If enough memory is not available to satisfy the request, it returns the NULL pointer. You must cast the pointer returned by malloc to the type of pointer your application requires.

The call free(ptr) releases the storage area to which ptr points, which is presumably a pointer value malloc previously returned. If you call free with a pointer value other than one you obtained from malloc, the memory management tables used by the malloc function package will likely become corrupted; future calls to malloc may return garbage, an event your program probably can't survive. In particular, don't call free with a NULL pointer. The declaration of free is void free(void *area).

The call calloc(*size*,*count*) allocates space for an array of *count* elements each *size* bytes long. For your convenience, the elements of the array are initialized to binary zeroes. The return value is a generic pointer to the first element of the array; you must cast it to the appropriate type. The declaration of calloc is void *calloc(unsigned int size, unsigned int count).

The call realloc(*ptr*,*size*) is equivalent to a call to free with *ptr*, followed by a call to malloc with *size*; the memory area designated by *ptr* is enlarged or shrunk to *size* bytes, or reallocated from scratch if there isn't room to enlarge it. If you must reallocate the area and the reallocation attempt fails, realloc returns a NULL pointer and the original area is discarded and its contents lost. If realloc succeeds, any data in the *ptr* area is copied to the new area if necessary. (The realloc operation is somewhat risky, so beware.) The declaration of realloc is void *realloc(void *ptr, unsigned int size).

To demonstrate the use of these functions, I use a bill-of-materials application.

Bill of Materials is a standard term in the manufacturing industry that describes a way of organizing and processing a file of records, each of which describes one part required to manufacture a product. Together, the records describe the contents of the manufacturer's warehouse of raw parts and partially assembled components, from which he builds finished products. The organization of the file also shows which parts you need to build a component of the product, and in turn which components are assembled together to build the final merchandisable item. In other words, the file not only contains detailed information about each stock item, but also shows the "explosion" of a finished product into its subassemblies, the subcomponents of a subassembly, and finally the individual parts.

In a UNIX system, you can reasonably store the parts file in ASCII form as a series of text lines, each of which describes one part or one subassembly. Assume that each line of the file looks like this:

```
part-no part-no cost usage unit description
```

An individual line might read as follows:

```
1015A6,1015A,3.08,5,EA,1-1/2" slotted machine screw
```

This line identifies part number 1015A6 as a component of an assembly, which in turn has a part number of 1015A. Each part number 1015A6 costs $3.08, and you use five of them to build 1015A. The part is counted in units of EA, a common abbreviation for *each*. The description of the part is 1-1/2" slotted machine screw.

Because each part in the file can have an associated subassembly part number, it is easy to build up a complex hierarchy of structures from basic parts. Such a hierarchy might show that a table-top rotating fan consists of a stand, a motor housing, a three-bladed fan, a wire cage to enclose the fan, a drive shaft, a rotor assembly, a motor, a power cord, and an on/off switch. The motor housing might consist in turn of two pieces of molded plastic—an upper housing shell and a bottom housing shell—which must be fastened together with screws and nuts to keep it closed (after placing the motor inside, of course). Even the power cord is an assembly, consisting of an 8 ft. cord, three amp, with brown or white plastic insulation (two different part numbers, one for white and one for brown), and a three-prong 115-volt plug that someone on the assembly line must attach to the cord.

One application for such a bill-of-materials file is to compute the cost of an assembly, given the cost of the parts from which it is built. The sample program prints out the cost of subassemblies.

The main loop of the program must read the entire bill-of-materials file and store it as a set of linked structures in memory. After reading the file, the structure lists must be scanned from the lowest-detail basic parts to the highest level components, accumulating the cost of each assembly until the cost of the final product is known. Then the program must traverse the data structure again, printing out the cost of assembled parts.

The sample program begins with a fairly standard prologue, shown in Listing 8.1.

Listing 8.1. Bill-of-materials processing, program prologue.

```
/*************************************************************

bomp.c - sample program to process a bill-of-materials file

This program reads lines in the following format:

    1011A  1011  1  1.38  Drive shaft

where
    1011A        part number
    1011         part containing this part
    1            number of times this part is used in 1011
    1.38         the cost of this part
    Drive shaft  description, up to 30 characters

The output is a listing showing the computed cost to
manufacture assemblies and the final products.

*************************************************************/

#include <stdio.h>
#include <stdlib.h>
#include <string.h>
```

The program prologue starts with a long comment that describes the program. It should mention the program's name, give a short description, and then describe the program's principal inputs, outputs, and processing performed.

The #include lines copy header files into the source program from system libraries. These header files contain standard definitions for the stream input/output functions (stdio.h), other commonly used library functions (stdlib.h), and the string-handling functions (string.h). The #include statement itself is a preprocessor directive; Chapter 10, "The Preprocessor," explains them. Most C programs need these three #include lines at the beginning of each source file.

As with most programs, the bomp.c sample program requires some sections to perform basic support tasks that have little or nothing to do with the main purpose of the program. One of these basic tasks is the reading and analysis of the program's input. To the extent possible, the details of file reading should be hidden from the program's main logic. The bomp.c program accomplishes this by packaging all the input processing in a function called GetInput, which returns the contents of an input line in a structure. The declaration for struct input appears next in the program so that it is available to all functions; Listing 8.2 shows the declaration of struct input.

Listing 8.2. Bill-of-materials processing, input structure.

```
/* Input Structure - generated by GetInput function */
struct input {
    char    *part_no;           /* Part number */
    char    *parent_no;         /* Part containing this part */
    char    *description;       /* Part description */
    int     usage;              /* Count of times used */
    double  cost;               /* Cost of the part */
};
```

The program also requires a structure template to describe each part record preserved in dynamic memory. Listing 8.3 shows the declaration for the part structure. Remember, the program must begin by reading the entire parts file into memory; each part record is saved in a structure so the information can be processed later. This structure, called struct part, differs from struct input not only in its detailed contents, but also in that only one instance of struct input exists at any given time, even though many instances of struct part are created.

Listing 8.3. Bill-of-materials processing, parts structure.

```
/* Parts Structure - describes one inventory part */
struct part {
    struct part *next;      /* Next part in same assembly */
    struct part *parent;    /* Part containing this one   */
    struct part *children;  /* List of parts in this one  */
    char    number[9];      /* Part number */
```

continues

179

Listing 8.3. continued

```
    char   description[31];   /* Description of part */
    int    usage;             /* Times used in parent assembly */
    double cost;              /* Cost of this part */
};
```

Note that `struct part` contains three pointers, all of type *pointer to struct part*. At first this might look like a recursive definition of the structure, which C does not allow (the recursion causes the structure to have an infinite length). However, no difficulty arises because `next`, `parent`, and `children` are pointers rather than structures; they just happen to point to other instances of `struct part`. The pointers are used to organize the `part` structures into nested lists of parts, modelling the real-world hierarchical relationship of component parts to the subassemblies they build. Figure 8.1 shows how you might organize a group of `part` structures for a table lamp:

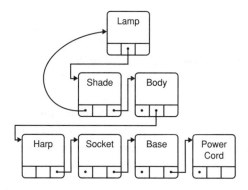

Figure 8.1. Hierarchical structure of parts for a table lamp.

The three boxes at the bottom of each box represent the `parent`, `children`, and `next` pointers, respectively. An empty box indicates a null pointer. The structure for *Lamp* has null parent and next pointers because it is the only structure on the product level. Its `children` pointer points to *Shade*, the first subassembly of *Lamp*, which in turn has a `next` pointer to *Body*. The subassemblies *Shade* and

Body comprise the only two major subassemblies of the lamp. The *Body* sub-assembly is further broken down into four parts: *Harp*, the bow-like piece of wire that holds the shade; *Socket*, the bulb socket with switch that is inserted into the top of *Base*; and *Power Cord*.

The pointers make it easy (at least in principle) to examine parts, subassemblies, or products on the same level, or to look at the composition of any item in terms of its component parts.

The front part of the program needs two more sections: the set of function prototypes, and any static global variables the program's functions use. These are shown in Listing 8.4.

Listing 8.4. Bill-of-materials processing, global declarations.

```
/* Function Declarations */
static struct input *  GetInput(void);
static void            ComputeCost(struct part *);
static void            MakePart(struct input *);
static struct part *   FindPart(char *name, struct part *list);

/* Global Variables */

static struct part *products; /* List of top-level assemblies */
```

The GetInput function reads one line from the input file and converts its data into a struct input; it then returns a pointer to that structure to its caller. The ComputeCost function is intended to perform the main action of the program: computing the cost of an assembly by adding the cost of each of its component parts. The MakePart and FindPart functions are support routines that create a struct part from a struct input, and find a part structure given its part number.

Because all the principal processing tasks of the program are allocated to internal functions, the job of the main function is straightforward: calling GetInput and MakePart until all the input lines have been read, and then calling ComputeCost for all the top-level assembles. The text of the main function is shown in Listing 8.5.

Listing 8.5. Bill-of-materials processing, main function.

```
/* main : program main driver code */
int main(void)
{
    struct part *part;
    struct input *in;

    /* Read the parts file into memory */
    while ((in = GetInput()) != NULL)
        MakePart(in);

    /* Compute the cost of all composite parts */
    for (part = products; part != NULL; part = part->next)
        ComputeCost(part);

    /* Finished, return to operating system */
    return(0);
}
```

Notice how the GetInput and MakePart functions are paired: the one reads an input record, the other converts the input record into a struct part and stores it in memory. Because these are support routines that are necessary but incidental to the main objective of the program, I show them a little later, in Listings 8.7 and 8.8.

The for loop scans the list of top-level part structures, calling ComputeCost for each one. The pointer called part is initialized to the value of products, which should point to the first top-level part; it is the job of MakePart to ensure that it does. For each part it finds, the ComputeCost function is called to compute the cost of the product using the cost of the product's component parts. Notice that ComputeCost is called here only for the top-level products, because the for loop only follows the horizontal list of next pointers. How is the cost of subordinate subassemblies computed? Listing 8.6, the ComputeCost function, gives the answer.

Listing 8.6. Bill-of-materials processing, ComputeCost function.

```
/* ComputeCost: determine the cost of a part.
 *  If the part has no subcomponents, its cost is given
 *  by the cost member of struct part, otherwise its cost
 *  must be computed as the sum of the cost of its
 *  component parts.
 */
static void
ComputeCost(struct part *part)
{
    struct part *child;

    if (part->children == NULL)
        return;  /* part->cost already contains the value */

    /* Sum the cost of each component part */

    part->cost = 0.00;
    for (child = part->children; child; child = child->next) {
        ComputeCost(child);
        part->cost += child->cost * child->usage;
    }

    printf("%-8s %8.2f %s\n", part->number, part->cost,
            part->description);
}
```

The ComputeCost function is recursive—it calls itself. The use of recursion in ComputeCost is suggested by the fact that the organization of the parts file is itself recursive: a part may in turn comprise other parts, each of which can in turn comprise still more subordinate parts. Because the ComputeCost function is designed to figure the cost of a part (whether a basic part or a composite assembly), by its definition it can be called to figure the cost of each of the components of an assembly. Note that ComputeCost does not get into an unending loop of calling itself, because every composite assembly must at some level be constructed of basic unit parts.

The `printf` statement prints out the calculated cost of a subassembly. Because the `ComputeCost` function returns immediately for any basic part, the `printf` function is reached only for composite parts. By placing the `printf` function here, the program assures that a cost report is generated for every composite part, whether top-level product or subassembly.

Listing 8.7 shows the `GetInput` function. This function performs all file management services, including opening the file, reading its lines, and closing it. The use of `static` variables inside the function provides the means by which `GetInput` can remember its status from call to call, while hiding the details of file processing from other functions. (To fully understand the `GetInput` function, you may have to review the stream file functions `fopen`, `fgets`, and `fclose`, as well as the `strtok` function from the string-handling package. These functions are fully described in the C manuals for your system. Part III, "Reference," gives the syntax of these functions.)

Listing 8.7. Bill-of-materials processing, GetInput function.

```c
static struct input *
GetInput(void)
{
    static FILE *fp;            /* Input file pointer */
    static struct input rec;    /* Input record area */
    static int eof_flag = 0;    /* Received EOF indication? */
    static char *seps = "\t\n"; /* Field separators in line */
    static char line[100];      /* Space for input line */
    char *word[5], *w;          /* Words in the line */
    int nw;                     /* Num of words found */

    /* If file already at end, return NULL */
    if (eof_flag)
        return (NULL);

    /* If file not already opened, open it */
    if (fp == NULL) {
        fp = fopen("parts.db", "r");
        if (fp == NULL) { /* Did fopen fail? */
            perror("parts.db");
```

```
            exit(2);
        }
    }


    /* Read the next record */
again:
    if ( fgets(line, sizeof(line), fp) == NULL) {
        /* got end of file, tell caller */
        eof_flag = 1;
        fclose(fp);
        return (NULL);
    }


    /* Break out the fields */
    nw = 0;
    w = strtok(line, seps);
    while (w != NULL) { /* while still have fields ... */
        if (nw < 5)
            word[nw++] = w;
        w = strtok(NULL, seps);
    }
    if (nw == 0) /* line was empty, ignore it */
        goto again;
    if (nw != 5) { /* wrong number of fields */
        fprintf(stderr, "%s: bad format\n", *word);
        goto again; /* skip to next line */
    }


    /* store info in struct input */
    rec.part_no     = word[0];
    rec.parent_no   = word[1];
    rec.usage       = atoi(word[2]);
    rec.cost        = atof(word[3]);
    rec.description = word[4];


    return (&rec);
}
```

There are a couple of points worth mentioning in the GetInput routine. Notice first that the struct input variable called rec is declared static; this is necessary so the pointer returned by GetInput to its caller remains valid after GetInput returns. The value &rec is not valid if rec is an automatic variable, because automatic variables are discarded when a function exits. Also, because the area is static and is reused on each call to GetInput, the values in the struct input are lost when GetInput is next called. In other words, there is only one instance of struct input in the entire program; information in it must be copied elsewhere if you are going to save it.

Also notice that struct input contains pointers to strings such as the part number, the parent part number, and the description, rather than the strings themselves. Because of this, you don't need to copy the strings from the line area to the struct input structure. Each of the string pointers in struct input is actually a pointer into line where strtok originally finds the string.

The MakePart function, shown in Listing 8.8, converts the values in an input structure into a part structure. Besides the basic tasks of allocating a part structure from dynamic memory and filling it in with information from the input structure, the MakePart function must also insert the new part structure into the correct position in the product tree. To do this, it must locate the point to insert the new part (*underneath* which part, and *after* which part on the same level). It may have to adjust the pointers of adjacent structures to keep the tree structure intact.

Listing 8.8. Bill-of-materials processing, MakePart function.

```
/* MakePart: convert an input line into a part structure */
static void
MakePart(struct input *rec)
{
    struct part *new, *p, **pv;

    /* Allocate a new part structure */
    new = malloc(sizeof(struct part));
    if (new == NULL) {
        fprintf(stderr, "Not enough memory!\n");
        exit(8);
```

```
    }
    new->next = NULL;
    new->parent = NULL;
    new->children = NULL;

    /* Copy data to new part structure */
    new->usage = rec->usage;
    new->cost  = rec->cost;
    strncpy(new->number, rec->part_no, sizeof(new->number) - 1);
    strncpy(new->description, rec->description,
            sizeof(new->description) - 1);

    /* Insert part structure into tree, underneath its
     * parent part, and alphabetically in the list of
     * children.
     */
    if (*rec->parent_no == '-') /* top-level part? */
        pv = &products; /* start at product list */
    else { /* find parent, insert in parent's child list */
        if ((p = FindPart(rec->parent_no, products)) == NULL) {
            fprintf(stderr, "%s: unknown part-no\n", rec->parent_no);
            return; /* ignore the part if parent unknown */
        }
        new->parent = p;
        pv = &p->children; /* start at parent's child list */
    }

    /* Add to end of children list */
    for (; (p = *pv) != NULL; pv = &p->next)
        if (strcmp(rec->part_no, p->number) < 0) break;
    new->next = *pv;
    *pv = new;
}
```

This is a fairly large chunk of code. Nevertheless, MakePart is straightforward up to the point where it inserts the new part structure into the tree. Then you encounter a large if statement that sets a double pointer variable: **pv. What is this all about?

187

The insertion process consists of two principal steps: finding the parent part under which the new part is inserted, and then inserting the new part in the list of subordinate parts following the part whose number sorts alphabetically prior to the new part number. In most cases, the first step can be accomplished by calling FindPart to search the list of parts already known for the parent part number. Top-level parts (products) have no parent, however; they are a complete construction and not part of any other part. Keep top-level parts in a list anchored by the products static global variable, so that main can find them.

The if statement begins by checking whether the part is a top-level part. If it is, its parent part number is a dash—a code chosen to mean "no part number" and therefore "no parent." If you are the program designer, it is your responsibility to inform whoever prepares the parts file to enter a dash as the parent part number for top-level items. Of course, use of the dash to mean "no part number" is an arbitrary decision; any code will do that cannot be mistaken for a real part number (such as the word NONE, or the number 0). The point is that you must choose some arbitrary way to fill the parent part-number field of input lines for those items that are not components of anything else; the sample program uses a single dash.

Continuing to follow the logic of the if statement, when the parent part number is a dash, indicate the list in which the new part goes as the products list by setting the pointer pv to point to that variable. Otherwise, when a parent part number is available, you must find the part structure corresponding to that part number so you can enter the new part underneath it; the FindPart function is called to perform this service. But FindPart returns NULL when it cannot find the given part number; in this case the program must write an error message and skip the new part because its position in the parts hierarchy is unknown.

When a new part is not a top-level product, and its parent part number is valid, the list of parts in which to insert the new part is anchored by the children member of the parent's part structure. The statement pv = &p->children sets pv to point to that value.

The for statement searches the list of parts for the part *before* which you should insert the new part. Designate the starting point with the pv variable, which, because it points to a pointer, is a double pointer. As long as the for statement finds parts with a lower part number, it repeatedly sets pv to point to the next member of the part structure it just checked. Thus, when the insertion point is found, pv points to that pointer which must be adjusted to point to the new part structure; the original value of *pv is copied into new->next before it is changed to the value of new. The two pointer operations have the effect of inserting the new part structure in between the two parts that precede and follow it in the list.

The insertion of a structure into a linked list, of which the final statements of the MakePart function are an example, is an operation that occurs frequently in C programming—much more frequently than you might expect, judging by the complexity of the operation. The code shown in the preceding example is a somewhat shorter, faster version of list insertion than most inexperienced programmers write. If you use the technique shown—that of keeping track of the *pointer* to be changed rather than the structure containing the pointer—you'll find that the technique eliminates some awkward complications such as insertion before the first item in the list, or insertion in an empty list. These are complications that bedevil most other list insertion techniques.

The following code listing shows the FindPart function. Like ComputeCost, FindPart is a recursive function. It is based on the idea that, if a part is not in a given list of parts, it must be a component of one of them. The function proceeds by scanning a given list of parts. For each part, it checks whether it is the desired part, or if not, whether any of the part's children is the desired part. However, because the children of a part is a list, and FindPart searches a list for a given part number, the best way to examine each of the subparts of a part is to call FindPart again, this time using the list of children. The FindPart function is called only in one other place: MakePart, which calls it with the list pointed to by products. The FindPart function was expressly designed to search using a given starting list so you can use recursively.

Listing 8.9. Bill-of-materials processing, FindPart function.

```
/* Find the part structure for a given part number */
static struct part *
FindPart(char *name, struct part *list)
{
    struct part *child;

    for (; list; list = list->next) {
        if (strcmp(name, list->number) == 0)
            return (list); /* *list is the desired part */
        if ((child = FindPart(name, list->children)) != NULL)
            return (child);
    }
    return (NULL);
}
```

If you run together all the code listings in this section, you get a working program that you can use, with some extensions, as part of a pricing system for a manufacturing concern. A real-life implementation would try to deal effectively with off-the-shelf parts that are components in many different products; ideally, the cost and description of such a component would appear in the parts file only once, even though the part itself might be a subcomponent of many different parts.

The file I used to test the program looked like this (using a Tab character between each field):

```
101                 1       0       Fan,19" Rotating
1011      101        1       0       Drive Assembly
1011A     1011       1       1.38    Drive Shaft
1011B     1011       2       0.06    C Clip, 1/2"
1011C     1011       1       0.71    Hub
1012      101        1       2.48    Fan, 3-Blade 19"
1013      101        1       0       Rotor
1013A     1013       1       0.62    Rotor shaft
1013B     1013       1       0.55    Rotor lever
1013C     1013       1       1.89    Hinge
1013D     1013       1       0.42    Shaft Nut, 3/8"
1015      101        1       0       Motor Housing
1015A     1015       1       1.04    Upper Housing Shell
1015B     1015       1       1.07    Bottom Housing Shell
1018      101        1       3.65    Stand
1019      101        1       1.58    Power Cord, 8' 3-Prong 5A
562       101        1       8.15    Motor 1/2 HP Electric
781       1015       2       0.18    Screw, Machine, 5/8" Slotted
782       1015       2       0.13    Nut, 3/4" OD
```

If you compile and execute the sample program using this sample data, you get the following result:

```
1011      2.21 Drive Assembly
1013      3.48 Rotor
1015      2.73 Motor Housing
101       24.28 Fan,19" Rotating
```

The bottom line is that, for this particular 19-inch rotating electric fan, it costs $24.28 to build the product. If the manufacturing company wants a 7-percent margin on sales, they must sell it to wholesalers for $26.11 (ignoring the cost of shipping, advertising, etc.), who would probably sell it to you for $34.95 plus tax. (Who says manufacturing isn't an interesting application?)

A Note about Coding Style

In the course of reviewing the code examples in the previous section, you may have noticed some odd coding conventions. Rather than leave you guessing, let me explain them now.

I always show the heading of a function definition on two lines: the first gives the function return type, and the second begins with the name of the function. The reason for this technique is to make it easy to skip to any function in a source file from within the `vi` text editor: just search for the function name at the beginning of the line. All uses of the function appear offset in a line, so a search such as `/^FindPart` can only find the function definition itself. This technique also makes it easy to get a list of the functions in a source file; although the command `grep ´^[a-zA-Z_][a-zA-Z0-9_]*(´` is awkward, it nonetheless finds all lines, and only those lines, that contain the function heading.

Some `for` statements contain only a variable name in the second position; for example, `for (; list; list = list->next)`. The termination condition of the loop is more properly written `list != NULL`, but because a nonzero pointer means *true* and a zero pointer means *false*, the tokens `!=` and `NULL` are redundant and can be omitted.

Many programmers prefer to write the expression of `return` in parentheses, even though the parentheses are rarely necessary. The parentheses tend to lend an appearance of unity to what may be a long expression, but in cases such as `return 0` or `return NULL` the parentheses add little to the clarity of the code. Whether to use the extra parentheses is largely a matter of personal preference.

191

Many programmers like to embed a function call in the `if` statement that tests the return value, such as

```
if ((ptr = malloc(size)) == NULL) {
    fprintf(stderr, "Not enough memory\n");
    exit(8);
}
```

You can write the same code in the form

```
ptr = malloc(size);
if (ptr == NULL) {
    fprintf(stderr, "Not enough memory\n");
    exit(8);
}
```

The second format makes the call of `malloc` more visible; the first format is more succinct and shows the close relationship between the function call and the `if` test. You'll find yourself in plenty of company if you use the first format in preference to the second, but once again there are no strong arguments either way.

Lastly, you may have noticed that most of the functions and variables in the sample program are declared `static`. For a program complete in one source file, the use of `static` is not necessary, and for programs comprising multiple source files the use of `static` is governed by the desired scope of the function. So why the scrupulous use of `static` in a single-file program? The reason is that the `lint` program in UNIX System V Release 4 complains about functions and variables not declared `static` that could have been. I make everything `static` that can be, mainly to reduce the volume of output from `lint`.

Summary

This chapter examines the closely related subjects of pointers and arrays. Because these are topics of central importance to using the C language, this chapter attempts to present more than the syntax and usage rules for pointers and arrays by delving into typical techniques for using these data types. I must unfortunately admit that the explanations are not as clear as I wish—a failing shared by many

C programs. The difficulty in dealing with pointers and arrays arises from the high degree of abstraction involved in such objects, particularly in objects like pointers to arrays of pointers to arrays of characters (such as the argv argument to the main function).

The potential complexity of pointer and array objects arises because the C language provides a few simple rules for creating pointers to things and arrays of things, and then places no limitation on the degree to which you can compound them. In fact, it is typical of the C language that, if you understand the rules and how to apply them, any implication you can draw from the rules is supported by the compiler. The C language exhibits very few rough edges, inconsistencies, or arbitrary limitations when compared to some of the older, more traditional programming languages.

The ability to work fluently with pointers, arrays, pointers to arrays, arrays of pointers, and combinations of these with other objects, comes only with practice and many mistakes. Unfortunately, the cost of errors is high. The effects of invalid or incorrect pointer values can be more difficult to diagnose than any other coding error, and errors made with pointers occur more frequently than any other kind of coding error. You need to use the lint program religiously to eliminate the more glaring errors from your code, and then the sdb debugging aid to detect the more subtle errors. But by far your sharpest weapon is a full understanding of the nature of pointers and an unshakable faith in their essential simplicity.

Complex Declarations

The syntax of the declaration statement is by far the most complicated of any statement in the C language. Basic data types such as integers and characters are easy to declare. Structure declarations are a bit more involved, and simple pointers aren't too bad. The declaration, however, of an object such as an *array of pointers to functions returning pointer to function returning pointer to array of character*—well, that's another story.

You can use any simple object (int, long int, short int, float, double, char, struct, union, or enum) as the basis for a new data type by augmenting its definition in one of three ways: by declaring a pointer to the object, by declaring an array of the object, or by declaring a function that returns the object. Furthermore, you can recursively apply any of these three augmentations in any combination, yielding an array of pointers, a function returning an array of pointers, a pointer to a function returning an array of pointers, and so on ad infinitum.

In fact, people have developed rules of thumb for figuring out what a declaration means. Others have developed programs that actually read a declaration and tell you what it means. To emphasize the severity of the problem, consider the declaration of the C library function `signal`, a function that takes two arguments (an integer and a pointer to a function), and that returns a pointer to a function that in turn returns `void`. The proper declaration of `signal` is

```
void (*signal(int, int (*handler)(int)))(int);
```

However, several versions of the UNIX operating system were released with an incorrect declaration for `signal`, proving how difficult and confusing declarations can be. (Fortunately, currently used releases of UNIX contain the correct declaration.)

The declaration of `signal` is an example of a complex declaration. This chapter is intended to help you easily and accurately read and write complex declarations.

Operator Priorities in Declarations

An important step in understanding complex declarations is realizing that declarations, even though they are not expressions, nonetheless can contain operators and must be analyzed using operator priorities, just like an expression.

The operators that can appear in a declaration are the two primary operators `[]` and `()`, signifying array and function respectively, and the unary `*` operator signifying pointer. The `[]` and `()` operators have equal priority, whereas the `*` operator has a lesser priority. The parts of a declaration that are not operators are identifiers, type qualifiers, and the formal parameters of functions.

As an example of the way priorities work, consider the rather simple declaration `void *alloc(size_t size)`. The object being declared is `alloc`. Notice that the word `alloc` is surrounded by two operators, the unary `*` on the left and the primary `()` on the right. For good or ill, you must ignore the position of the identifier in the declarator expression (everything coming after the initial type name is called the *declarator*). This leaves the operator pair `*()`, but `()` has higher priority so you read it first; `alloc` is a function returning a pointer, not a pointer to a function.

Now comes the tricky part. You can use parentheses to alter the interpretation of operator priorities, just as you can with expressions. For example, the declaration `void (*alloc)(size_t size)` describes an entirely different kind of object, one in which `alloc` is a pointer, not a function. To what does `alloc` point? Substituting the symbol x for `(*alloc)` in the declaration, you obtain `void x(size_t size)`, which is a straightforward declaration of a function returning `void`. In other words, `alloc` is a pointer to a function returning `void`.

Similar observations apply to the array operator `[]` that you can combine with pointer and function operators to yield complex declarations. For example, `char string[8]` defines an array of eight characters, `char *string` defines a pointer to a string, `char *string[8]` defines an array of eight pointers to character, and `char (*string)[8]` defines a pointer to an array of eight characters. (I have more to say about pointers to arrays in a moment.)

The trick to reading such declarations is to start at the identifier and then read `()` or `[]` operators to the right of it before reading any `*` operators to the left of it, and resolve the inside of parentheses before reading any operators outside the parentheses. For example, `*name[]` is an array of pointers (array operator before pointer operator), but `(*name)[]` is a pointer to an array. Because of the parentheses, the `[]` operator does not come immediately after `name`, and the pointer symbol is resolved first.

Now try to write a complex declaration—for example, an array of five pointers to functions returning integer. To begin with, the object to be declared must have a name—call it `handlers`. Next, indicate that `handlers` is an array: `handlers[5]`. Then specify that each element is a pointer: `*handlers[5]`. Now show that the pointer points to a function: `(*handlers[5])(int)`. Finally, specify the type of value returned by the function: `int (*handlers[5])(int)`.

To specify that the pointer `*handlers[5]` points to a function, you use the same syntax as to specify that the identifier `sqrt` is a function: you place the function operator `()` after the function name giving `sqrt()`. The same is true for the `handlers` example, except that `*handlers[5]()` would indicate that `handlers` is an array of five functions returning a pointer—not the intended result. To force the pointer operator to take precedence over (), the expression `*handlers[5]` must be enclosed in parentheses: `(*handlers[5])()`. This declarator has the same format as `x()`, where x stands for `(*handlers[5])`.

You may notice from the previous example that complex declarations tend to be written from the inside out. Complex declarations should be read in the same fashion, from the inside out, beginning with the identifier naming the object.

There is an algorithm to convert a declaration to an English-language description, which appears in the following list. You might step through the algorithm using the declaration of `handlers` just developed. To execute the algorithm, keep two lists: one showing the current state of the declaration as you eliminate identified parts, and the second showing the English-language description as you build it.

1. Locate the first identifier in the declaration, write it down and replace it with x, and then repeat steps 2 through 5 until all of the declaration has been identified.

2. If the current token is `(x)`, replace it with x.

3. If the current token is `x[]`, replace it with x and write *array of* at the end of the English description.

4. If the current token is `x()`, replace it with x and write *function returning* at the end of the English description.

5. If the current token is `*x`, replace it with x and write *pointer to* at the end of the English description.

6. Write the typename of the declaration and you're done.

Using the `handlers` example, you go through the following steps:

1. Using rule 1, replace the identifier with x.
   English: ***handlers***
   Simplified declaration: `int (*x[5])()`

2. Using rule 3, replace `x[]`.
   English: *handlers [is an]* ***array of***
   Simplified declaration: `int (*x)()`

3. Using rule 5, replace `*x`.
   English: *handlers [is an] array of* ***pointer to***
   Simplified declaration: `int (x)()`

4. Using rule 2, replace `(x)`.
   English: *handlers [is an] array of pointer to*
   Simplified declaration: `int x()`

5. Using rule 4, replace `x()`.
   English: *handlers [is an] array of pointer to **function returning***
   Simplified declaration: `int x`

6. Using rule 6, write the typename.
   English: *handlers [is an] array of pointer to function returning **int***

If you want to try a couple of examples yourself, try to follow the conversion of the following declarations:

● From: `void (*signal())();`
  To: *signal is a function returning pointer to function returning void*

● From: `char *(*select())[];`
  To: *select is a function returning pointer to array of pointer to char*

● From: `static int *(*lookup[])();`
  To: *lookup is a static array of pointer to function returning pointer to int*

In the last exercise, you should notice that `static` remains a descriptor of the declared object. Thus, it is the array `lookup` that is static, not the integer returned by the function. If your conversion result is *lookup is an array of pointer to function returning pointer to static int*, you have `static` in the wrong place. Type qualifiers such as `static` and `const` are always descriptors of the declared object, in both simple and complex declarations.

The *typedef* Statement

The C language includes one declarative statement type not yet covered: the `typedef` statement. It can assist with the declaration of complex data types, and is popular with experienced programmers because it enables you to define new typenames and use them like built-in data types.

The syntax of the `typedef` statement is the same as any declaration; the `typedef` keyword is treated syntactically in the same manner as `auto`, `static`, or `extern`. However, a typedef never allocates memory. Instead, the variable names you declare with `typedef` become new typenames representing the declared type. An identifier declared with `typedef` is defined in the same name space as variables; you cannot use an identifier as both a variable name and a typename.

The following examples may help to clarify the usage of `typedef`.

```
typedef char *string;
```

This looks like a declaration of a variable called `string` as a pointer to character. Because of `typedef`, `string` is not a variable; it is a new typename that is equivalent to the type `char *`. A subsequent declaration reading `string ptr;` means the same as `char *ptr`.

```
typedef int Table[8];
```

This declaration creates a new typename called `Table` representing an array of eight integers. You can use the new typename in a subsequent declaration such as `Table *division` to create a pointer to an array of eight integers. Without the typedef declaration, you must declare the `division` variable like this:

```
int (*division)[8];
```

The wrong way to think of typedefs is to imagine that the typedef is a template and that, when you use the typedef, a declared variable name is substituted into the typedef declaration. If you think of typedefs in this manner, you are inclined to think that the declaration

```
Table *division;
```

is equivalent to writing `int *division[8]`.

C uses a typedef declaration in a much more sophisticated manner: the typedef name becomes a symbolic representation of the kind of value the typedef declared. Subsequent use of the typedef name is treated as a reference to the object type defined by the typedef, not merely as a text replacement operation.

```
typedef void (*Trap)(int sig);
```

This `typedef` statement defines a new data type called `Trap`. A `Trap` object is a pointer. More specifically, it is a pointer to a function returning void that takes one argument, an integer. You can use the new type `Trap` to simplify the declaration of the `signal` library function as follows:

```
Trap signal(int, Trap);
```

The new declaration of signal says the same thing as the declaration at the beginning of this chapter: signal is a function taking an integer and a pointer to a function, and that it returns a pointer to a function returning void. Using the typedef name Trap as a shorthand for *pointer to function returning void* considerably simplifies the declaration of signal.

You can simplify the declaration of handlers in a similar manner, as the following example shows:

```
typedef int (*Handler)();
Handler handlers[5];
```

The typedef statement creates a typename representing a pointer to function returning int. The declaration of handlers says handlers is an array of five Handler objects.

```
typedef double Dollars;
typedef char * String;
typedef enum { Stock, Bond, Property } AssetType;
typedef enum { Trade, Hold, Trust }    AssetUse;
typedef struct Asset *AssetList;

typedef struct Asset {
    AssetList  next;
    AssetType  type;
    AssetUse   usage;
    String     name;
    Dollar     value;
    Dollar     basis;
} Asset;
```

This lengthy set of declarations creates a family of types for an application program. Subsequent code in the program may declare specific instances of these types. For example:

```
static AssetList portfolio[8];
static Dollars    totalAssets;
```

The portfolio variable is an array of eight pointers to struct Asset. The totalAssets variable is a double that you can use to accumulate the total value of an investment portfolio.

Notice the typedef of `AssetList`, which declares it as a pointer to a `struct Asset`. This kind of declaration is legal even though the declaration of `struct Asset` itself does not yet appear in the program. It is a great convenience to be able to declare a typename for the pointer to the structure before the structure itself, because it enables you to avoid the awkwardness explicitly writing `struct Asset *next`:

```
typedef struct Asset {
    struct Asset *next;
    ...
} Asset;
```

The typedef for `Dollars` is fluff in one sense; you can just as easily write `double totalAssets` as you can `Dollars totalAssets`. The difference is that you can easily change the representation for dollar amounts from `double` to some other type in the program that uses the `Dollars` typedef, whereas the program that explicitly writes `double` is more difficult to change; the programmer must track down each declaration that uses `double` to represent a dollar amount. Programmers often use a special typename for a standard type used in a limited sense. The point is that the investment program needs a way to represent dollars and cents amounts; `double` may be a good representation, and it may not. By using the typedef name `Dollars` whenever the program needs a dollar value, you can change the choice of a good representation later without disturbing most of the program.

Typedefs are a great convenience. Sophisticated C programs, often consisting of many source files and hundreds of functions, use typedefs heavily. The judicious use of `typedef` can improve program readability, facilitate program porting to other systems, simplify program maintenance, and reduce coding errors.

Pointers to Functions

The previous section of this chapter mentions pointers to functions a number of times. If the C syntax did not support function pointers, complex declarations would not be very complex. There are a few things about pointers to functions that you should know.

A pointer to function is a variable just like any other pointer variable, except that a function pointer points to a function rather than to a data item. You use function pointers, just as you use other types of pointers, to be able to reference one function or another, depending on the current state of the program. Function pointers are also passed as arguments to some functions.

For example, the qsort library function is a function you can call from within your own program to sort the elements of an array. One of the things qsort needs to know is how to compare two elements of the array. The elements can be integers, structures, or any other type of data object. You tell qsort how to compare two array elements by providing your own function to do the comparison. qsort uses the result your function returns to tell whether any two elements are in order or out of order. The prototype of the qsort function shows that one of its arguments must be a function pointer:

```
extern void qsort(void *, size_t, size_t,
        int (*)(const void *, const void *));
```

This declaration says that qsort requires four arguments: a pointer to the array, two size values, and a pointer to an unnamed function taking two arguments and returning int. If you write a function to perform the comparison, you pass a pointer to the function to qsort by writing the function name in the call argument list—for example, qsort(strings, 10, 35, compar), where 10 is the size of an element, 35 is the number of elements, and compar is the name of your comparison function.

The C language treats function names in a manner similar to array names. Like an array name, a function name is a pointer constant to the function. If you use the function name in an expression but without a parenthesis following the name, the C compiler substitutes the address of the function for the function name. Thus, it is redundant and unnecessary to write &compar to get a pointer to the compar function; compar as a name by itself is already a pointer.

You can manipulate function pointers in the same way as other pointers: passed as arguments to functions, stored as elements of an array, and so on. You cannot, however, assign a value to the dereferenced pointer. The function itself is treated as if declared const, and cannot be modified.

To call the function pointed to by a function pointer, write the pointer name as if it were a function. You may legally write the call as (*ptr)(args) to show that ptr must be dereferenced to find the function, but the syntax is redundant. It is sufficient to write ptr(args), because C always requires a function pointer in front of an argument list; it's just that most programmers usually use pointer constants instead of pointer variables.

The following code shows an example of using function pointers. The purpose of the code is to look up a math symbol in a table and, depending on the symbol, add, subtract, multiply, or divide two numbers. The code uses a function pointer in each table entry to tell the search routine what it should do for each operator. Notice that each function name appearing in the operator table must be declared before it is used, so that C recognizes the name as a function pointer of the correct type.

```c
int add(int num1, int num2);
int subtract(int num1, int num2);
int multiply(int num1, int num2);
int divide(int num1, int num2);
int error(int num1, int num2);

static struct optab {
    char operator;
    int  (*handler)(int,int);
} operators[] = {
    '+' , add,
    '-' , subtract,
    '*' , multiply,
    '/', divide,
    0,   error
};

int exec(char opcode, int val1, int val2)
{
    struct optab *op;
    int (*compute)(int, int);
    int result;

    for (op = operators; op->operator != 0; op++)
        if (opcode == op->operator) {
            compute = op->handler;
            break;
        }
    result = compute(val1, val2);
    return result;
}
```

The statement `compute = op->handler` assigns the function pointer to a function pointer variable of the same type. The assignment looks ordinary, but shows that you can manipulate function pointers in an ordinary way. The critical statement is `result = compute(val1, val2)`, which uses the name of the pointer variable `compute` as if it were a function. There is, of course, no function in the program called `compute`. Instead, the compiler takes the current value of the `compute` variable and calls whatever function the variable points to, which (if everything works properly) is one of the functions `add`, `subtract`, `multiply`, or `divide`.

C programmers don't use function pointers too often, but in some situations they greatly simplify the code you would otherwise need to write.

dcl—A Program to Decode Complex Declarations

At the beginning of this chapter I mention that programs exist to convert a C declaration to an English-like description. Two program listings follow: the first converts a C declaration to English, the second compiles an English-type description to C declaration syntax.

To use these programs, you must type the text of each into source files using a text editor. Each program must be a separate file. Compile the programs using the `cc` command, as in the following examples:

```
cc -O dcl.c -o dcl
cc -O undcl.c -o undcl
```

To execute the programs, just type the program name, then enter the C-language declaration (`dcl`) or English description (`undcl`) that you want to convert. The following shows a sample dialog:

```
$ dcl
char *string
string: pointer to char
void (*signal())()
```

```
signal: function returning pointer to function returning void
[Ctrl-d]
$

$ undcl
string is pointer to char
char *string
signal is function returning pointer to function returning void
void (*signal())()
handlers is array of pointer to function returning int
int (*handlers[])()
[Ctrl-d]
$
```

If you're interested, you might try to figure out how the two programs work. The `dcl` program recursively calls the `dcl` and `dirdcl` functions because of parenthesized nesting. It begins working from the left to right, and when it finds a parenthesized expression it delves deeper until it finds the identifier in the declaration. Then it generates output as it works its way back up the levels of parentheses.

The programs in Listings 9.1 and 9.2 use a number of library functions, primarily the string-handling group such as `strcpy` and `strcat`. If you're not familiar with these, you need to review their definition in your system's manuals, or in the book *UNIX Programmer's Reference* (Que, 1992).

Listing 9.1. Converting a C declaration to English.

```
/************************************************************

NAME
    dcl.c - Translate C declaration to English description

SYNOPSIS
    dcl
```

DESCRIPTION

Dcl is based on the grammar that specifies a declarator;
this is a simplified form:

```
dcl:         optional *'s direct-dcl
direct-dcl: name
            (dcl)
            direct-dcl()
            direct-dcl[optional size]
```

The heart of the dcl program is a pair of functions, dcl
and dirdcl, that parse a declaration according to its
grammar. Because the grammar is recursively defined, the
functions call each other recursively as they recognize
pieces of a declaration; the program is called a
recursive-descent parser.

```
**************************************************************/

#include <stdio.h>        /* Standard system definitions */
#include <string.h>       /* String handling functions   */
#include <ctype.h>        /* Classification functions     */

#define MAXTOKEN 100

enum { NAME, PARENS, BRACKETS };


/**************************************************************
 FUNCTION PROTOTYPES
 **************************************************************/

void    dcl(void);
void    dirdcl(void);
int     gettoken(void);
```

continues

Listing 9.1. continued

```
/**************************************************************
 GLOBAL DATA DEFINITIONS
 **************************************************************/

int     tokentype;         /* Type of last token */
char    token[MAXTOKEN];   /* Last token string */
char    name[MAXTOKEN];    /* Identifier name */
char    datatype[MAXTOKEN]; /* Data type = char, int, etc. */
char    out[1000];         /* Output string */




/**************************************************************
 MAIN : Program main driver
 **************************************************************/

main()
{
    int error = 0;

    while ( gettoken() != EOF ) {
        /* First token on the line is the datatype... */

        if (error) {
            if (tokentype == '\n')
                error = 0;
            continue;
        }

        strcpy(datatype, token);
        out[0] = 0;

        dcl(); /* Parse the rest of the line */

        /* Print result */
```

```
        if (tokentype != '\n') {
            printf("syntax error\n");
            error = 1;
            continue;
        }
        printf("%s: %s %s\n", name, out, datatype);
    }
    return(0);
}



/************************************************************
 DCL: Parse a declarator
 ************************************************************/

void dcl(void)
{
    int stars;

    for (stars = 0; gettoken() == '*'; ++stars)
        /* Count *'s */
        ;
    dirdcl();
    while (stars-- > 0)
        strcat(out, " pointer to");
}



/************************************************************
 DIRDCL: Parse a direct declarator
 ************************************************************/

void dirdcl(void)
{
    int type;

    if (tokentype == '(') {
        /* We have a () declaration */
```

continues

Listing 9.1. continued

```
        dcl();
        if (tokentype != ')') {
            printf("error: missing )\n");
            return;
        }
    } else if (tokentype == NAME)
        /* Variable name found */
        strcpy(name, token);
    else {
        printf("error: expected name or (dcl)\n");
        return;
     }

    while ((type = gettoken()) == PARENS || type == BRACKETS)
        if (type == PARENS)
            strcat(out, " function returning");
        else {
            strcat(out, " array");
            strcat(out, token);
            strcat(out, " of ");
        }
}


/****************************************************************
 GETTOKEN: Identify next token in input
 ****************************************************************/

int gettoken( void )
{
    int c;
    char    *p = token;

    while ( (c = getc(stdin)) == ' ' || c == '\t' ) ;
```

```
        if (c == '(') {
            if ( (c = getc(stdin)) == ')') {
                strcpy(token, "()");
                return tokentype = PARENS;
            } else {
                ungetc(c, stdin);
                return tokentype = '(';
            }
        } else if (c == '[') {
            for (*p++ = c; (*p++ = getc(stdin)) != ']'; )         ;
            *p = 0;
            return tokentype = BRACKETS;
        } else if (isalpha(c)) {
            for (*p++ = c; isalnum(c = getc(stdin)); )
                *p++ = c;
            *p = 0;
            ungetc(c, stdin);
            return tokentype = NAME;
        } else
            return tokentype = c;
}
```

Listing 9.2. Converting English to a C declaration.

```
/*************************************************************

NAME
    undcl.c - K&R Chapter 5.12, convert words to declaration

SYNOPSIS
    undcl

DESCRIPTION
    Undcl converts a word description like "x is a function
    returning a pointer to an array of pointers to functions
    returning char" to an equivalent C declaration.
```

continues

Listing 9.2. continued

```
**************************************************************/


#include <stdio.h>           /* Standard system definitions  */
#include <string.h>          /* String handling functions    */
#include <ctype.h>           /* Classification functions      */

#define MAXTOKEN 100

enum { NAME, PARENS, BRACKETS, DUMMY };


/**************************************************************
 FUNCTION PROTOTYPES
 **************************************************************/


int gettoken(void);


/**************************************************************
 GLOBAL DATA DEFINITIONS
 **************************************************************/


int     tokentype;          /* Type of last token */
char    token[MAXTOKEN];     /* Last token string */
char    name[MAXTOKEN];      /* Identifier name */
char    datatype[MAXTOKEN]; /* Data type = char, int, etc. */
char    temp[MAXTOKEN];
char    out[1000];          /* Output string */



/**************************************************************
 MAIN : Program main driver
 **************************************************************/


main()
```

```
{
    int type;
    int error;

    while (gettoken() != EOF )
    {
        error = 0;
        strcpy(out, token);
        while ((type = gettoken()) != '\n')
            if (error || type == DUMMY)
                ;
            else if (type == PARENS || type == BRACKETS) {
                if ( out[0] == '*' ) {
                    sprintf(temp, "(%s)%s", out, token);
                    strcpy(out, temp);
                }
                else
                    strcat(out, token);
            }
            else if (type == '*') {
                sprintf(temp, "*%s", out);
                strcpy(out, temp);
            }
            else if (type == NAME) {
                sprintf(temp, "%s %s", token, out);
                strcpy(out, temp);
            }
            else {
                printf("invalid input at %s\n", token);
                ++error;
            }
        if (!error)
            printf("%s\n", out);
    }

    return 0;
}
```

continues

213

Listing 9.2. continued

```
/*************************************************************
 GETTOKEN: Identify next token in input
 *************************************************************/

static char *words[] = {
    "function",
    "array",
    "pointer",
    "int", "char",
    "is", "a", "an", "returns", "returning", "to", "of",
    ""
    };

int gettoken(void)
{
    int c, i;
    char *p;

    *(p = token) = 0;
    while ( (c = getc(stdin)) == ' ' || c == '\t' )
        ;

    if (!isalpha(c))
        return tokentype = c;

    for (*p++ = c; isalnum(c = getc(stdin)); )
        *p++ = c;
    *p = 0;
    ungetc(c, stdin);

    for (i = 0; *words[i]; i++)
        if (strcmp(token, words[i]) == 0)
            switch(i) {
```

```
            case 0: /* Function */
                strcpy(token, "()");
                return tokentype = PARENS;

            case 1: /* Array */
                strcpy(token, "[]");
                return tokentype = BRACKETS;

            case 2: /* Pointer */
                strcpy(token, "*");
                return tokentype = ´*´;

            case 3: case 4:
                return tokentype = NAME;

             default: /* Dummy word, try again */
                return tokentype = DUMMY;
            }
        /* The word is not in the table */
        return tokentype = NAME;
}
```

Summary

This chapter does not introduce much new material: the typedef statement (really a form of the declaration statement), and the interpretation of function parentheses (), array brackets [], and the pointer symbol * as operators with operator priorities.

The principle purpose of this chapter is to present some of the techniques people use to interpret complex declarations, and to show the extent to which the C language permits nesting and recursive use of its declaration syntax.

All complex declarations arise from three definitions in the C language:

- A *pointer* is any object declaration prefixed with `*`.

- An *array* is any object declaration suffixed with `[ ]`.

- A *function* is any pointer suffixed with `( )`.

With the two suffixing rules and the one prefixing rule, you can build progressively more complex objects:

`int x;`	An integer named x
`int *x;`	A pointer named x to an integer
`int *x()`	A function named x returning a pointer to an integer
`int (*x)()`	A pointer named x to a function returning an integer
`int (*x[])()`	An array named x of pointer to function returning integer
`int *(*x[])()`	An array named x of pointer to function returning pointer to integer

The list of complex declarations could go on much further. As you might imagine, the recursive character of the C declaration syntax makes it difficult to describe using conventional techniques. Part III, "Reference," gives a syntax description for the C language, but uses a method of syntax description that may be unfamiliar to you.

The implication you should draw from this chapter, and from the syntax description of the C language in the back of this book (from its form as much as its content), is that the C language definition is rather simple as computer languages go, but recursive in nature. The complexities and oddities you can build are almost unlimited. For example, would you guess that the expression `fun(x)->foo`, which uses a pointer value returned by a function directly in a pointer expression, is valid? Or that the expression `(c == 0) ¦¦ fun(c)` is one way to call the function `fun` when `c` is not zero?

This chapter on complex expressions ends the presentation of the C language as such. The next chapter, "The Preprocessor," discusses an adjunct to the language that, although many people think of it as inherent in the language, is

216

nonetheless discardable. At this point, therefore, you already know about as much of the C language as you will learn from this book. It would be a good idea for you to seriously entertain the thought of writing some real, if not necessarily useful, C programs. You will need plenty of hours at the terminal before you find C a comfortable, natural programming language. I hope you enjoy the exercise.

CHAPTER

10

The
Preprocessor

The C language includes a preprocessor as one of its features. The preprocessor is a macro processor providing file inclusion, text replacement, and some conditional statement capabilities. This chapter presents all the features and capabilities of the C preprocessor, and attempts to demonstrate how experienced programmers use these capabilities.

Just because the preprocessor is the last language feature I discuss in Part I doesn't mean the preprocessor is unimportant or infrequently used. Quite the contrary, most programs contain some preprocessor directives, and few programmers want to write in C without the facilities of the preprocessor.

Benefits of the preprocessor include reduced programmer effort, more readable programs, and a reduced incidence of certain kinds of programming errors. On the other hand, conditional code generation can introduce additional complexity into a program which can be difficult to test, diagnose, and debug.

All of the preprocessor commands (called *directives*) operate by adding to, deleting, or modifying the text of the source program. The changes are temporary, however, and do not affect the image of the source file as stored on disk. Instead, the preprocessor passes the edited text directly to the compiler.

All preprocessor statements are identified by a special symbol, the hash mark (#), written as the first nonblank character of the line. The remainder of the line is free-format, but the preprocessor does not recognize a directive unless the line begins with a #. Most programmers write the hash mark in column 1, but it may be preceded by any number of blanks or tabs.

If a line contains only a #, and nothing else, the preprocessor ignores the line and removes it from the text passed on to the compiler. Any other line beginning with a # must have one of the preprocessor directive keywords as the next token of the line. Some programmers like to leave one or more blanks or tabs after the #; others like to write the directive immediately following the #. The preprocessor allows either convention.

The C compiler itself does not understand preprocessor directives, so the preprocessor removes all such lines from the source text before passing it to the compiler. The preprocessor may remove a line by physically deleting it or by substituting a blank line for the preprocessor line. Replacement by a blank line is the usual method of removal because it helps the compiler maintain an accurate line count for its error messages.

The preprocessor is line oriented; a statement is terminated by the physical end of line. However, you can continue any line onto the next physical line by writing a \ at the end of the first line. The preprocessor immediately recognizes and deletes the sequence of a backslash followed by the newline character, effectively joining the two lines into one. Notice that the continuation of the first line begins with the first character of the next line; whitespace at the beginning of the next line is *not* skipped.

When using the preprocessor, it is important to remember that it does not understand the C language, it is merely a text processor and works by replacing or altering strings of text in the source program. The preprocessor does not know, for example, the size of structures, because a structure declaration must be parsed and analyzed before its size can be determined and these are compiler functions.

When you use constant expressions in preprocessor statements, the constants must be values evident from the source text itself; the sizeof operator in particular is not available in preprocessor expressions.

With these preliminaries out of the way, it's time to examine each of the preprocessor directives and their syntax, function, and usage.

The *#include* Directive

The preprocessor logically replaces the line containing the include directive with the contents of the file specified as the directive's operand. I say *logically* because the replacement only occurs in the text stream passed to the compiler; the original source file remains unaltered.

File inclusion can be nested. That is, a file included by #include can in turn contain an #include directive, and so on up to a fixed limit defined by the preprocessor implementation.

Syntax Rules

The operand of include specifies the file to read and insert into the source program, using one of the three following formats.

```
#include < pathname >
```

For *pathname*, specify any legal pathname recognized by the UNIX operating system. The pathname may be relative (beginning with ./ or ../), absolute (beginning with /), or implicit (beginning with a directory or filename). A simple filename (containing no / characters) is treated the same as an implicit pathname.

Relative pathnames are resolved by searching for the file in the directory containing the source file (which is not necessarily the current directory). Implicit pathnames are resolved first by searching the directories given by the -I compiler option, and then the default include directories for the compiler. The current directory is not searched.

The default directories for finding `include` files are built into the C compiler and cannot be changed, although you can add to the list by specifying the `-I` compiler option (see the "Comand-Line Options" section in Chapter 13, "Compiling Programs with `cc`"). Usually the directory `/usr/include` is the only directory searched by default, although the C language standard (and UNIX) do not specify the default directories.

```
#include "pathname"
```

When the pathname of the file to be included is enclosed in quotation marks, the preprocessor first searches for the file in the directory where the source file was found. If the preprocessor does not find the file there, it searches the directories specified by the `-I` compiler option, and finally the default directories. In other words, the `"pathname"` form works the same as the `<pathname>` form except that the directory containing the source file is searched first.

Notice that for relative and absolute pathnames, no search order can be used because the pathname is explicit. The file to be included must be found at the specified directory location, otherwise the preprocessor reports an error. For such pathnames, you may use either `< >` or `" "` to the same effect.

Programmers usually use the quoted form of `include` when referencing application-specific `include` files, because you usually cannot store your own files in any of the default directories. You should use the bracketed form of `include`, however, when retrieving system-provided `include` files, to avoid any possibility of retrieving a like-named application file instead.

Notice that it is possible to override a system-provided `include` file by providing a file with the same name in the directory containing the source, and using the quoted form of `include` to retrieve the file. However, it is generally considered bad form to give application `include` files the same filename as the system standard `include` files.

```
#include token-list
```

For *token-list*, specify one or more tokens that, when glued together, form a string in either the `"pathname"` or `<pathname>` form. The token list may contain symbols defined by the `define` directive, in which case the value of the symbol is used to form the pathname to be searched. The list may also contain literal words that have no special meaning to the preprocessor that therefore stand for themselves, and delimiter characters such as . and / that form normal parts of a pathname.

After any replacement and concatenation of the tokens in *token-list*, the resulting string must specify either a quoted or bracketed pathname as in the first two forms of `include`. The search for the file then occurs using the rules appropriate to the generated string.

How to Use *include* Files

The syntax of the `#include` statement doesn't tell you anything about good and reasonable ways to use the statement. However, a large body of practice has built up over the years and much can be said about how you can and should use `include` files.

To begin with, files copied by the `include` directive are normally called *header* files. You don't often hear the term *include files* spoken by experienced C programmers. They are called header files because the `include` statements most often appear at the beginning of a source program, and contain declarations, `define` directives, and other types of statements that most often occur before any functions.

Header files usually contain statements that define the environment of a program. They may contain preprocessor macros, structure declarations, `extern` declarations for global variables, `typedef` statements, and even other `include` directives. Header files almost never contain executable code, however, with the sole exception of macro functions (see the section "The `define` Directive" later in this chapter for a discussion of macro functions).

There are a number of reasons why the C programming community seems to have a tacit proscription on executable code in header files. For one thing, because most programmers don't create such header files, maintenance programmers rarely suspect a header file of causing an execution error, and programmers developing new code avoid the practice to avoid making trouble (sort of a feedback loop there).

Another (better) reason for the proscription is that any executable code appearing in a header file would be duplicated in every program that includes the header file. It is more efficient to store the executable code in its own source file, compile it separately, and link the compiled code with the programs that use it.

Header files are used most often with programs that are partitioned into several source files. The header files then contain declarations common to two or more source files. By putting the declaration of a shared object in a header file, you assure that all the program components that use the object also use the same declaration for the object.

You can say that header files fall into two main categories: application header files that group together all the global resources of an application; and package header files that contain the interface definition for a function package. The application header file may contain definitions of unrelated objects, grouped together only because two or more of the application source programs use them. A function package header, however, defines the interface to the function package.

The string.h or the malloc.h system header files provide good examples of the function package header. The string.h header contains a function prototype for each of the functions in the string header package, saving you the trouble of writing the prototypes yourself. The malloc.h header also contains function prototypes, but in addition declares a structure that can pass back and forth between the user program and package functions.

Listing 10.1 provides an example of an application header file. The header file could be used by a (fictitious) airline scheduling system, and you'll notice that it contains structure declarations likely to be used in any program in the system. The header file also contains some definitions that are not peculiar to the application, but are useful, so they are gathered into the header file for convenience and to assure a degree of consistency of style between the programs. Included in this category are the TRUE and FALSE symbols, the typedefs for String and Pointer, and the extern declarations for generic support functions.

Listing 10.1. A sample header file.

```
/* air.h - version 1.23 - last change 08/22/91
 *
 * This header file contains definitions common to the
 * modules of the airline scheduling system. Note that, in
```

```
 * addition to structure declarations used by the database
 * files, this header also contains prototypes for library
 * functions available to support the scheduling system.
 */
#include <stdio.h>            /* Most programs need this */
#include <stdlib.h>           /* and this */
#include <string.h>           /* and usually this */

/* STANDARD DEFINITIONS - USE THESE, DON'T MAKE UP OTHERS */

#define TRUE   (1)
#define FALSE  (0)
#define OK     (0)
#define ERROR  (-1)

typedef char *String;        /* Use for string pointers only */
typedef void *Pointer;       /* Generic pointer */
typedef long  offset;        /* disk/file address */

typedef struct Aircraft  Aircraft;
typedef struct Airport   Airport;

/* Aircraft structure - describes flight, seating capacity */

struct Aircraft {
    Aircraft    *next;       /* Next-in-list pointer */
    char        type [6];    /* Aircraft name & model */
    char        serial [6];  /* Inventory number */
    char        status;      /* Non-blank = out of service */
    char        crew;        /* Type of flight crew needed */
    char        stewards;    /* Num of stewardesses needed */
    char        class;       /* Runway class needed */
    short       first;       /* Num of first-class seats */
    short       business;    /* Num of business-class sts*/
    short       coach;       /* Num of coach seats */
    short       min_range;   /* Minimum practical flight */
    short       max_range;   /* Maximum safe distance */
};
```

continues

Listing 10.1. continued

```
/* Airport structure - describes location, runway capacity */

struct Airport {
    Airport     *next;          /* Next-in-list pointer */
    long        latitude;       /* Degrees.tenths * 36000 */
    long        longitude;      /* Degrees.tenths * 36000 */
    short       variation;      /* Magnetic compass variation*/
    short       start, stop;    /* Hours of runway operation */
    char        simul;          /* Num of simult. approaches */
    char        maxcat;         /* Highest category runway avail */
    char        ident [4];      /* Routing code */
    char        state [2];      /* State */
    char        city  [25];     /* City name */
    char        name  [31];     /* Airport name */
};


/*************************************************************
 *
 *    Global Declarations
 *
 *************************************************************/

/* Load the list of airports into memory ...*/
extern Airport *LoadAirports(void);

/* Load the list of available aircraft into memory */
extern Aircraft *LoadAircraft(void);

/* Calculate the distance between two airports */
extern int GCDistance(Airport*, Airport*);
```

The purpose of the code in Listing 10.1 is to give you a feel for the kind of statements typically appearing in a header file. You can also find more examples by browsing through the many system header files in the /usr/include and

/usr/include/sys directories. In particular, because you'll use it a lot, you might want to take a look at the stdio.h header file on your system (also found in the /usr/include directory), although keep in mind that you don't need to understand its contents in order to use it.

The *#define* Directive

You've already seen many examples of the define directive, because most programs—including the examples in this book—contain at least a few of them. In this section I try to give a precise definition of its syntax, describe what it does, and make some recommendations on how to use it.

The define directive is used to define a macro. A *macro* is a name that stands for a piece of text. Whenever the preprocessor discovers the macro name in your source code, it replaces the name with the macro's value, which is a simple text replacement operation. The resulting source text is passed on to the compiler. The preprocessor is not particular about the format or contents of the replacement text, and especially does not care whether the replacement generates good C syntax, so it is your responsibility to ensure that the text replacement makes sense.

Syntax Rules

There are two versions for the syntax of the define directive. The syntax for a simple macro is

```
# define name replacement-text
```

The syntax for a function macro is

```
# define name(arguments) replacement-text
```

A `define` statement consists of two parts: the name defined, and the text that is its value. You must form the name using the usual C syntax, beginning with an upper- or lowercase letter or the underscore, and containing any number of additional letters, digits, or underscores.

If a second `define` directive attempts to create a macro with the same name as a previous `define`, the new definition must be of the same type and specify the same replacement text as the previous definition. If the macro is a function macro, the new definition must have the same number of arguments. (See the section "The `#undef` Directive" later in this chapter for a way to change a macro definition.)

The replacement text may be any text whatsoever; you do not need to restrict it to the characters normally used in the C language or that constitute any part of a C language statement. The replacement text may be nothing at all; if the rest of the `define` statement after the macro name is blank, occurrences of the macro name in the program source are replaced with a zero-length string. At least one whitespace character (blank or tab) must follow *name* and precede the replacement text; it is discarded and not considered part of the replacement text. Any additional whitespace between *name* and the replacement text becomes part of the replacement text.

To be recognized, the macro name must appear as a token. That is, you must set it off from the surrounding source text with some form of delimiter (whitespace, parentheses, commas, etc.). This rule ensures that a macro named BAD, for example, does not cause replacement in a name such as BADLY or TOOBAD that might also appear in the source text.

If the replacement text contains an occurrence of the macro name, it is not replaced; therefore, you cannot use macros recursively because there is no way to halt the recursion. However, the replacement text is scanned for other macro names known at the time of replacement.

Notice that the preprocessor does not recognize occurrences of the macro name embedded in a quoted string and that no replacement of the name string will occur.

Function Macros

The function macro is distinguished by a parenthesized argument list written after the macro name. To be recognized as a function macro, no whitespace may appear between the macro name and the open parenthesis beginning the argument list. The argument list contains zero or more or identifiers separated by commas; extra whitespace around the identifiers or commas is ignored, both in the macro definition and in calls appearing in the subsequent source text.

A function macro call is recognized in the source text when the macro name is found followed immediately by paired parentheses. Values inside the parentheses in the call, separated by commas, are matched up in left-to-right order with the identifiers in the macro definition's argument list. The text value from the call becomes the value of each identifier. Then each occurrence of that identifier in the macro replacement text is replaced by the text value of the identifier. The text value of an argument in the macro call may contain quotation marks and parentheses, but such delimiters must be paired so that the end of the argument can be properly recognized.

In versions of the C language prior to the ANSI standard, substitution of argument identifiers in the replacement text occurred even when the identifier occurred inside a quoted string. ANSI standard C compilers do not expand argument identifiers that occur inside a quoted string in the macro replacement text. You can substitute call values into quoted strings, however, by using the # operator as described in the section "String Operations" later in this chapter.

Perhaps a couple of examples can clarify the operation of function macros. Assume that a program contains the following macro definition:

```
#define abs(x)   ((x) < 0 ? -(x) : (x))
```

Also assume that the program later contains the following text line:

```
time = abs(end - start + 8*60);
```

The preprocessor substitutes the macro call with the replacement text after changing all occurrences of x in the replacement text with end - start + 8*60 from the call. The line, as actually compiled, looks like this:

```
time = ((end - start + 8*60) < 0 ? -(end - start + 8*60)
        : (end - start + 8*60));
```

Notice that the replacement is a text replacement, not a value replacement. The preprocessor cannot evaluate C statements or expressions, and so cannot use the result of evaluating the expression end - start + 8*60. It is the actual text in the macro call that replaces the symbol x in the macro definition.

The macro definition for abs was carefully written to include extra parentheses; each occurrence of x in the replacement text is surrounded by parentheses, and the entire expression is enclosed in parentheses. There is a reason for this: the preprocessor replaces text literally, and the parentheses prevent confusion about operator priorities in the resulting text statement. Suppose the definition of abs had been written like this instead:

```
#define abs(x)  x < 0 ? -x : x
```

The replaced statement would now look like this:

```
time = end - start + 8*60 < 0 ? -end - start + 8*60
       : end - start + 8*60;
```

Without the extra parentheses, the compiler interprets the assignment using default priorities, as if parenthesized as follows:

```
time = ((end - start + 8*60) < 0)
       ? ((-end) - start + 8*60)
       : (end - start + 8*60);
```

Of course, the two statements are different and give different results. The latter expression uses the term -end, whereas the former version uses -(end - start + 8*60). Without the extra parentheses in the macro definition, the abs macro does not work properly for an x with two or more terms.

How to Use Macros

Experienced C programmers make frequent use of both simple macros and function macros.

You can use simple macros in two ways. The most direct way is to use the define directive to create a symbolic name for a literal or constant. Your source program is more readable and understandable when constants are represented by a meaningful name. This is especially true for buffer sizes, the number of elements in an array, and similar fixed limits in your program. For example, the following code uses the symbolic constant MAXLINE to represent the size of an input line buffer:

```
#define MAXLINE 120

char *GetLine()
{
    static char line[MAXLINE];

    if (fgets(line, MAXLINE, stdin) == NULL)
        return NULL;
    return line;
}
```

Not only does writing MAXLINE instead of 120 in your program improve clarity, but the symbolic constant also makes it easier to change the program. To increase the size of the line buffer from 120 to 256 characters, you only need to modify the define statement to specify 256 instead of 120. In a large program that might use a given constant in many different places, it can be very difficult to locate all the places where you need to change the constant.

Another way you can use macros is to specify the macro replacement text on the cc command with the -D option, omitting the define statement from your program. This enables you to customize your program when you compile it, without touching the source text at all, merely by specifying different values of the -D option on the cc command. For example, a program that uses an array to contain input data values might need a very large array for some executions, and a smaller array at other times. If the array is declared with the statement

```
int values[NUMVALUES];
```

you can set the array size when you compile the program using the following form of the cc command:

```
cc -DNUMVALUES=1000 prog.c
```

You can use externally specified macros for many different purposes. Using the if directive described in the next section, you can even test whether a macro is specified on the cc command, and if so what value is specified for it.

Function macros are usually used as inline functions. The abs function macro is an example of an inline function: the code for the function is generated in each place where the abs macro is used. This differs from a normal function, which is written in just one place and called when needed. An inline function usually increases the size of an executable program, but also improves the execution speed of the program. The improvement in execution speed comes from the fact that each function call requires extra instructions to get into the function and then return to the calling routine. These extra instructions are overhead that is usually justifiable, but an inline function may be more efficient for some frequently used yet simple operations. The getchar, getc, putchar, and putc standard library functions are usually implemented as macros because they are called many times in the course of a typical program execution, yet most programs call these input/output functions from only a few places. Thus the increase in program size is negligible while the improvement in speed is substantial.

You must use caution when writing and using function macros. If you provide as an argument to a function macro an expression that has a side effect, unexpected results can occur if the argument is used more than once in the replacement value of the macro.

For example, suppose the abs macro discussed earlier was called in the following manner:

```
nv = abs(*x++);
```

When expanded by the preprocessor, the C compiler actually sees the following statement:

```
nv = ((*x++) < 0 ? -(*x++) : (*x++));
```

The problem with this is that the x variable increments twice: once when tested in the (*x++) < 0 expression, and again when one of the two alternatives (? or :) executes. Someone using the abs macro in such a way would conclude that abs doesn't work right.

In general, you can't rely on proper results when you use the increment or decrement operators or the assignment operator as an argument value in a function macro. When you write function macros, try to write the replacement text in a way that works correctly for expressions with side effects. When you use a function macro, assume that such expressions don't work correctly unless you know for a fact that it does.

Because some system functions (such as the aforementioned `getchar`, `putchar`, `getc` and `putc`) are actually macros, you must learn to be wary of using expressions with side-effects in standard system functions.

You must be somewhat cautious in your use of string literals with the preprocessor. If you specify a string literal as the value of a macro using the `#define` directive, the replacement of the macro name includes the quotation marks; the preprocessor does not strip the quotes when saving the replacement text. You can use this to good effect by creating symbolic names for the names of files in your program. This enables you to easily change the filenames. The following example shows how you can use such macros:

```
#define ITEM_FILE    "items.db"
#define CUST_FILE    "customers.db"
#define INPUT        "r"
...
    item = fopen(ITEM_FILE, INPUT);
```

The preprocessor replaces the assignment statement with the following text:

```
item = fopen("items.db", "r");
```

Notice that the quotes are preserved from the `#define` and appear in the replacement text. The preservation of quotes proves to be a problem in other case, for example, if you want to use a macro to represent a directory name and another macro for each file you plan to open in the directory:

```
#define INVENTORY    "/usr/inventory"
#define PARTS_FILE   "parts.db"
#define PRICE_FILE   "price.db"
...
    item = fopen(INVENTORY/PARTS_FILE, "r");
```

This time the replaced text is incorrect because it looks like the division of two pointer values to the compiler:

```
item = fopen("/usr/inventory"/"items.db", "r");
```

You can get around this particular problem by including the final slash in the directory name and using string gluing (a feature of the compiler, not the preprocessor):

233

```
#define INVENTORY    "/usr/inventory/"
#define PARTS_FILE   "parts.db"
#define PRICE_FILE   "price.db"
...
    item = fopen(INVENTORY PARTS_FILE, "r");
```

This time the replaced text works correctly because the compiler glues adjacent strings together into one string literal:

```
item = fopen("/usr/inventory/" "parts.db", "r");
```

If you need the directory name without the trailing slash anywhere in your program, the definition of the INVENTORY macro is not usable. Probably the best coding strategy is the following:

```
#define INVENTORY    "/usr/inventory"
#define PARTS_FILE   INVENTORY "/parts.db"
#define PRICE_FILE   INVENTORY "/price.db"
...
    item = fopen(PARTS_FILE, "r");
```

If you try to define macros for file and directory names without using quotes in the #define statements, you encounter other difficulties. Consider the following example:

```
#define INVENTORY    /usr/inventory
#define PARTS_FILE   parts.db
#define PRICE_FILE   price.db
...
    item = fopen("INVENTORY/PARTS_FILE", "r");
```

The problem is that the generated assignment looks like this:

```
item = fopen("INVENTORY/PARTS_FILE", "r");
```

The preprocessor does not replace the macro names INVENTORY or PARTS_FILE, even though they are properly delimited, because the preprocessor does not examine or replace the contents of string literals in the program source text.

Predefined Macros

The ANSI standard requires the preprocessor to define certain macro symbols automatically before processing any source text. The standard also permits the preprocessor to define other macros that may describe the compiler's hardware and software environment.

The UNIX compiler defines the following macros before processing the first line of text:

__LINE__   The value of the __LINE__ macro is the line number of the source line where the macro appears. Lines are numbered relative to 1 and start over for each source file and included file.

__FILE__   The value of the __FILE__ macro is the filename of the current source or header file enclosed in quotes. For example, the macro would have the value "/usr/include/stdio.h" inside the standard stdio.h header file, and the value "myprog.c" inside an ordinary source file.

__DATE__   The value of the __DATE__ macro is the current date as returned by the operating system. The macro is replaced by a string literal of the form "Jan 02 1992".

__TIME__   The value of the __TIME__ macro is the current time as returned by the operating system. The macro is replaced by a string literal of the form "08:32:53". Time is reported using a 24-hour clock, where "16:32:05" would represent about 4:32 PM.

__STDC__   The value of the __STDC__ macro is 1 if the compiler and preprocessor support the full ANSI standard language definition, 0 otherwise. Generally this macro has a value of 0 even with advanced compilers unless you specify an appropriate command-line option, because the ANSI standard requires conforming compilers to exclude extensions that conflict with the standard. For information about your specific compiler, refer to the vendor manuals accompanying your UNIX system. Chapter 13 describes the -X compiler option that influences the value of the __STDC__ macro.

The UNIX C compiler also defines a macro named unix (note the lowercase spelling). The unix macro has a value of 1 to indicate that your program is being compiled in the UNIX environment. Many UNIX C compilers also define a symbol identifying the type of hardware in use; the names of such macros are obviously machine-dependent and depend on your specific hardware and software configuration.

If any of these predefined macros conflicts with your source code, you can disable the predefined macro using the -U (undefine) compiler option. For information about the -U option, see Chapter 13.

The *#undef* Directive

The undef directive removes a previously defined macro. Subsequent occurrences of the macro name in the program source text remain unchanged, as if no macro of that name was ever defined. The syntax of the undef directive is as follows:

```
#undef name
```

Specify only the name of the macro to be undefined, even for function macros.

Most often the undef directive is used to cancel a previous macro definition so you can redefine it with new replacement text.

The *#if* Directive

The if directive provides the ability to test the value of a macro and to include or omit lines from the source program text depending on the outcome of the test.

Syntax Rules

You must use the if directive in conjunction with the endif directive to define the range of lines included in the conditional code. The else directive can provide an alternative case when the test fails, and the elif directive combines the effect of the if and else directives into one statement.

The syntax of a complete preprocessor if statement, together with the else, elif, and endif directives that you can use together with if, is as follows:

```
# if constant-expression
lines
[
# elif constant-expression
lines
]
[
# else
lines
]
# endif
```

The brackets show which parts of the statement are optional, and must not be written in the actual program. The elif directive together with the text lines following it are optional. The else directive and its following text lines are also optional. Only the #if and #endif lines are required to form a complete preprocessor if statement.

The if directive requires a constant expression to specify the condition to be tested. You can form the expression using any of the standard C operators. The terms of the expression can be macro names previously defined in the source program, macros defined with the -D compiler option, or literal values. The value of a macro name is the replacement text defined for the macro; if it is not defined, its name is its value.

The expression must evaluate to an integer value. A nonzero integer result means *true* and lines following the if directive are processed. A zero integer result means *false* and lines following the if directive up to the next elif, else, or endif directive are deleted from the source text passed to the compiler.

The value of a macro is not restricted to numerical values; it can be text as well. In particular, any name appearing in a conditional expression that is not a defined macro stands for itself, and its value is the sequence of characters comprising the name. You can test the text value of a macro for equality.

Notice, however, that you cannot use a quoted string as a literal term in a conditional expression. Therefore, you can test a macro for equality to a text value only when you write the text value as a word obeying the rules for forming a macro name.

Unlike the C if statement, the preprocessor if declarative does not require the constant expression to be enclosed in parentheses. However, because an expression contained in parentheses is a valid expression, you can enclose the entire constant expression in parentheses if you wish.

The lines following #if, #elif, or #else may include preprocessor statements. Such preprocessor statements, if present, are acted upon only if the line group is included; if the line group is skipped, any preprocessor statements in the group are skipped as well.

You can use the special built-in preprocessor function defined(*name*) in the expression to test whether the macro *name* is defined. If it is, the value of the function is 1 (*true*), otherwise the value of the function is 0 (*false*).

Alternatively, you can use the directive #ifdef to test whether a macro is defined, and #ifndef to test if the macro is undefined:

```
# ifdef name
# ifndef name
```

The `#ifdef` directive is exactly equivalent to writing

```
#if defined(name)
```

and the `#ifndef` directive is equivalent to writing

```
#if !defined(name)
```

Of course, you can specify a more complex expression on the `if` directive. The `#ifdef` and `#ifndef` directives accept only a macro name by itself as the operand.

If the constant expression of `if` is true, any `elif` and `else` line groups remaining in the statement are deleted from the source program text, up to the final `endif`.

If the constant expression of `if` is false, the next `elif` or `else` directive is processed. Lines following `else` are always processed, whereas lines following `elif` are processed only if its constant expression is true.

You can nest the `if` statement, which means lines following `#if`, `#elif`, or `#else` can in turn contain one or more complete `#if`-`#endif` groups, possibly with nonpreprocessor text lines preceding or following them. When processing an `else` or `elif` directive, whether the directive is executed or skipped depends on the outcome of the preceding `if` directive of the same nesting level.

The `#elif` directive does not introduce nesting as would an `#else` directive followed by another `#if`. The `elif` directive, therefore, considerably simplifies the preprocessor code when testing for a number of alternative mutually exclusive conditions.

The constant expression of an `if` or `elif` directive is subject to macro replacement. This means you can use a macro function as part of a conditional expression. Use caution, though, because some values that you can assign to a macro with `define` are not accepted as terms of `if`. Quoted strings are a case in point.

Using Conditional Compilation

The `if` directive and its associated `else`, `elif`, and `endif` directives provide the ability to conditionally include or omit selected lines from the compilation. Often the decision is based on the setting of a macro symbol specified with the `-D` compiler option, but not necessarily.

The following example shows the conditional inclusion of a print statement in the program that depends on the setting of a DEBUG macro. You might intersperse many such print statements in your program, each conditioned on the DEBUG macro, and use the -D compiler option to compile the print statements during program testing and omit them when compiling the final production version of the program. The use of conditional compilation means you can leave the test aids in the source code to help with future maintenance to the program.

```
void
ComputeAverage(int array[])
{
#if DEBUG
    fprintf(stderr, "begin: ComputeAverage\n");
#endif
...
}
```

To enable debugging of the ComputeAverage function, use the following cc command when compiling the program:

```
cc -DDEBUG=1 myprog.c
```

Because the value of the DEBUG macro is set to 1, the expression on the #if directive evaluates to 1 and the code following #if up to the following #endif is included in the compilation. If you don't specify a macro value on the cc command, the compiler assumes you mean =1, so you can shorten the command a little bit to just

```
cc -DDEBUG myprog.c
```

To compile the program without debugging, omit the -DDEBUG operand entirely from the cc command. By default, the value of any undefined macro is 0.

You can use more sophisticated expressions when your purpose goes beyond testing whether a particular macro is defined. For example, the following preprocessor code checks the NUMVALUES macro presented in the section "The #define Directive" earlier in this chapter:

```
#ifndef NUMVALUES
#define NUMVALUES 20    /* Establish a default value */
```

```
#elif NUMVALUES < 10 ¦¦ NUMVALUES > 500
#error NUMVALUES range error
#define NUMVALUES 50
#endif
```

This sequence of conditional code first tests whether the NUMVALUES macro was defined on the cc command at all. If it was not, the #define directive is used to provide a value. If NUMVALUES has a value, however, the elif directive tests whether the value falls within an acceptable range. If it does not, the code provides an error message and another default value. The following version is more straightforward if you don't need to distinguish the undefined from the out-of-range cases:

```
#if !defined(NUMVALUES) ¦¦ NUMVALUES < 10 ¦¦ NUMVALUES > 500
#define NUMVALUES 50
#endif
```

You can test macro values for equality to strings, although this ability is somewhat limited because the terms of a constant expression must be either numeric literals or macro names. Because the value of an undefined macro name is equal to the text of its name, you can in effect test a macro value for equality to any word that can be used as a macro name. The following example shows how you can use a macro defined on the cc command to customize the code used to open a file:

```
#if SYSTEM == DOS
    file = fopen(filename, "rb"); /* Open binary */
#elif SYSTEM == UNIX
    file = fopen(filename, "r");
#endif
```

This code sequence accounts for the fact that MS-DOS versions of C differentiate between text and binary files, whereas UNIX does not. To compile a program containing this code, you must write -DSYSTEM=UNIX or -DSYSTEM=DOS on the cc command as appropriate.

Miscellaneous Directives: *#pragma* and *#error*

The ANSI standard for the C language introduced two new directives, #pragma and #error, which solve some problems and create some new ones.

The #pragma directive enables you to take advantage of special facilities of your C compiler, or to warn the compiler that your code contains syntactic constructs requiring special handling. To use the directive, write a code word as the operand that specifies the special compiler feature you want to invoke. For example, some C compilers allow embedded assembly-language statements in your program, but require a warning that such statements are present. You could issue that warning to certain C compilers using the following statement:

```
#pragma asm
```

The problem is that each compiler supports a different set of pragmas. If you include a #pragma directive in your code, you probably limit yourself to using one specific C compiler, making your code unportable.

The #error directive is a useful addition to the preprocessor introduced by the ANSI standard. Any sequence of tokens may appear as the operand of #error. Any macro names in the operand of #error are substituted with their replacement text. The final string is written to the same place as compiler error messages. You use the #error directive to issue a warning message, usually from within a preprocessor #if sequence. The following is an example of the #error directive:

```
#ifndef NUMVALUES
#error You must specify a value for -DNUMVALUES
#define NUMVALUES 20 /* default value */
#endif
```

String Operations: # and

The operators # and ## have use in the replacement text of a macro definition. They have no significance elsewhere and will likely result in a compiler error message.

Place the # operator in front of the name of a macro argument to indicate that, when the value of the argument replaces the name, the value should be placed within quotation marks. Older versions of the preprocessor would replace a macro name appearing in a quoted string; the ANSI standard preprocessor does not. To achieve the same effect, combine the # operator with string concatenation.

For example, assume a program contains the following definition:

```
#define printvalue(x)   printf(#x " = %d\n", x)
```

The following statement that may appear later in the program

```
if (t->size > 0)
    printvalue(t->size);
```

generates the following result after substitution:

```
if (t->size > 0)
    printf("t->size" " = %d\n", t->size);
```

Because the compiler glues together adjacent string literals, the message t->size = 35 would be written if the value of t->size were in fact 35.

Notice that #x appears in the replacement text of the #define macro. Its presence means that after the argument x is replaced with the calling value (in the example, this is the string t->size), the value is then surrounded with quotes. The macro definition then arranges to have another literal string follow immediately, in effect joining the two strings together. The second use of x in the macro definition substitutes the value of argument x without surrounding quotes. In the generated statement, the string t->size is generated twice: once inside quotes so that it appears in the output message, and once without quotes so that the actual value of t->size is passed to the printf function.

Take a look at another example. Here, you want to write a macro to verify that an expression is true, and if the expression is false then write a suitable error message. A sample use of the macro might look like this:

```
assume( t->size >= 0 && t->size < 32000 );
```

If the assumption is false, the error message should document the expression that failed. The macro that performs this service is the following:

```
#define assume(exp) ((exp) ¦¦ \
    fprintf(stderr, "assumption `" #exp "´ failed\n"))
```

The macro value is written as an expression so the assume macro can be used as part of a larger expression. The expression itself is true if exp is true; otherwise the value of the expression is the return value from the fprintf function. The fprintf function, in turn, prints an error message with the text of the expression embedded in the message. A sample output might look like this:

```
assumption `t->size >= 0 && t->size < 32000´ failed
```

Notice that the second argument of fprintf actually consists of three string literals glued together. The first string is "assumption `", the second string is "t->size >= 0 && t->size < 32000" after substitution of the #exp argument, and the third string is "´ failed\n".

Use the ## operator in the replacement text of a macro definition. If you write it in the form x ## y, it has the effect of pasting together the value of x and the value of y into a single string. The following is a trivial example of a macro definition using the ## operator:

```
#define join(a,b) a ## b
```

If the macro call join(name,1) then appears later in the program, the call is replaced with the text name1.

Summary

The C preprocessor is a "front end" to the C compiler in the sense that the preprocessor scans and edits the text of a source program before passing the text on to the compiler.

The facilities of the preprocessor are relatively few in number, but each is hedged with reservations and restrictions that make the facilities themselves rather complicated.

The `#include` directive is perhaps the simplest. You use it in the form `#include <stdio.h>` to read a system header file into your program. The angular brackets (<>) tell the compiler to look only in the standard directories for the file named stdio.h. You use the form `#include "myheader.h"` to copy a header file you wrote into your source program text; you should store the header file in the same directory as your source program when using the quoted version of the `include` directive. The tokenized version of `include` is rarely used, but is provided to enable macro replacement to generate the filename.

The `#define` directive is used almost as much as the `#include` directive, making an appearance in almost every C program. The `#define` directive creates a *macro*—a name or function call that, when found in the source program text, is substituted with replacement text. If you use it in the form

```
#define TRUE 1
```

the macro provides a symbolic name for a constant, enabling you to write TRUE in an expression instead of the literal value 1. If you use it in the form of a function definition, the macro

```
#define abs(x) ((x) < 0 ? -(x) : (x))
```

enables the programmer to create an inline function. The replacement text can be a simple expression, a single statement, or several statements, depending on the needs of the macro writer. If the definition is too long to fit on one line, you can split the replacement text over several lines by appending \ to the end of each line but the last:

```
#define terminate(code, mesg) {\
    fprintf(stderr, "fatal error: " #mesg "\n"); \
    exit(code); \
    }
```

Writers and users of function macros must use care when the argument of a function macro can be an expression with side effects; multiple occurrences of the argument in the macro's replacement text can cause duplication of the side effect.

The #undef directive removes a previous macro from the preprocessor's memory. You usually use #undef so you can redefine a macro.

The #if directive, together with #elif, #else, and #endif, provide a conditional compilation facility. You write an expression using only constant values on the if or elif directive, which evaluates to an integer value. If the result of evaluating the expression is nonzero, lines following the if or elif are processed; otherwise, the lines are skipped. You can use the else directive to provide an alternate set of lines to process in case the if or elif constant expression evaluates to a false (zero) value. Preprocessor statements can appear in the lines following if, elif, or else and are processed or skipped the same as any other text lines.

The #pragma directive provides access to special compiler features. The features you can use, and the way you write the pragma directive to activate the feature, depends on the particular C compiler you use. Consult your specific vendor's documentation for the details of the pragma directive.

The #error directive provides a way to generate an error message to the user. The message is generated as if it were a preprocessor error message, except that processing of the source program continues.

The newer ANSI standard C compilers do not recognize or replace macro names occurring inside a quoted string. The # and ## operators provide a means to construct strings containing variable text to achieve the same effect as substitution.

To have a macro name recognized in source program text, you must offset it from the surrounding text by whitespace or a delimiter. This rule ensures that a short macro name cannot replace a portion of a longer, different macro name. This does not mean you should introduce special delimiters or whitespace around a macro name, because they are not replaced or removed by the preprocessor. Rather, it means you should not expect the word UNTRUE to be changed by a macro called TRUE; the preprocessor considers UNTRUE to be a different identifier.

You cannot change a macro definition without first removing it with #undef. However, you can issue the same macro definition more than once if each repetition is truly the same as the first. This allows the same macro to be defined in several header files, even when a program might include more than one of them.

The replacement text of a macro can contain occurrences of the macro name. These are not replaced, but they remain unchanged in the replacement text.

However, the replacement text is scanned for the presence of other macro names. If found, these are also replaced just once.

The preprocessor automatically defines a number of macros that are available for your use. These are the `__FILE__`, `__LINE__`, `__DATE__`, `__TIME__`, and `__STDC__` macros. You are not supposed to issue your own `#define` statements for these macros; just use them when you want the information they provide. In addition, most UNIX preprocessors also define the `unix` macro to indicate that your program is being compiled in the UNIX environment, and may define additional macros to indicate the CPU type on which your program is being compiled.

As a final note, you should realize that although experienced programmers use the preprocessor facilities extensively, those who might have to maintain your program some day never appreciate excessive complexity. Here, as with all coding, brevity is the sole of wit.

II

The UNIX Programming Environment

The UNIX Environment

The purpose of this chapter is to briefly introduce the UNIX environment to those who have never before encountered it, and to compare and contrast its features with those of the MS-DOS environment with which you may already be familiar. The discussion emphasizes the programmer's perspective, as is appropriate to a book about programming. Many books already exist describing UNIX from the terminal user's perspective, and if you are completely new to UNIX you may want to consult one of them, such as *Exploring the UNIX System*, Revised Edition (Hayden Books, 1992).

By anyone's reckoning, the UNIX operating system is not new. The system is over 12 years old as of this writing, having seen its first light of day in 1972. One of the consequences of its age is that, just as a piece of furniture can build up layers of wax and grime over the years, so too has the UNIX operating system, originally simple in plan and outline, added many complications to its user interface.

One of these complications has to do with the marketing and packaging of UNIX. Originally, the vendors of UNIX provided the operating system in one complete package that included even the operating system source code. When UNIX became commercially important, the vendors dropped the source code from the package to protect their rights. As UNIX became more complicated, its vendors began to split the package into several components so that users could select and pay for only those parts they needed. One of the parts that in recent years has become optional is the C programming support, which includes the compiler itself. As a result, your system may or may not have the facilities you need to support C language programming.

If you intend to do C language programming for UNIX, you must work with a UNIX system that includes the compiler facilities. Without it, you cannot compile the C programs that you write, and therefore you cannot execute them. If your system has the compiler facilities installed, you will find an executable file called cc somewhere in the system. If you cannot find it, you cannot do any C language programming. In addition to the compiler itself, you want access to a number of additional, essential tools. These include at a minimum a decent text editor and an interactive source-level debugger.

An Overview of UNIX

At the most basic level, UNIX consists of a kernel and a number of command programs.

The *kernel* is that portion of UNIX that automatically loads into memory when you turn on the computer. It remains resident in memory throughout the life of the system. Although the UNIX kernel is a complex piece of software, you will be aware of it primarily through its implementation of the following features:

● *Files and Directories*. The UNIX kernel is responsible for managing all accesses to disk files and devices. The UNIX file system is much like the DOS file system, but there are some differences that are apparent at the programming level.

● *Access Permissions.* UNIX is a multitasking, multiuser operating system. As such, it needs to provide means to protect the work of one user from destruction or misuse by others. UNIX uses two principal kinds of protection: login passwords, and file access permissions. File access permissions enable you to decide who can use your files, and in what manner. UNIX security measures can be unobtrusive or stringent according to the needs of the system's users.

● *Operating System Services.* This heterogeneous group of functions includes such basics as getting the date and time, allocating memory, and more advanced functions such as interprocess communication.

Over and above the kernel, the UNIX environment includes a number of components that also affect you as a programmer:

● *Function Libraries.* The C language is incomplete without a library of operating system interface functions. These functions are usually grouped together into a so-called standard library. It is no coincidence, but rather due to a unified effort on the part of compiler developers for the DOS environment, that both the DOS and UNIX standard libraries contain similar functions. Differences between the DOS and UNIX libraries occur primarily in the set of functions available: functions common to both environments generally have the same operation and usage.

● *Shells.* The DOS command shell (called COMMAND.COM) and the UNIX command shells (sh, csh, and ksh being important examples) are quite different. You use the shell to issue commands from the keyboard, and to execute commands from within a program. Most interactions with the shell are different in the UNIX environment from their DOS counterpart.

● *Commands and Utilities.* The UNIX system provides an extensive set of commands to assist the programmer and the general user. The DOS system provides very few of these commands, and in most cases the DOS user must separately purchase and install many of the tools that come bundled with the UNIX system.

● *Subsystems.* Modern UNIX systems contain a number of free-running tasks to perform system housekeeping chores, such as print spooling. The closest DOS equivalent is terminate-and-stay-resident (*TSR*) utilities, but the UNIX facilities are more complete and more powerful because UNIX was designed from the beginning to be a multitasking operating system. You may need to interact with some of these subsystems, and you may need to know how your program works in such an environment.

The MS-DOS system is newer than UNIX, and its design is based partly on features of UNIX. The developers of MS-DOS, however, never intended it to duplicate the functionality of UNIX. Remember, at the time MS-DOS was implemented, UNIX ran on more powerful machines, whereas MS-DOS was intended for the PC. For that reason, MS-DOS omits many of the features viewed as unnecessary or unaffordable on the PC. This accounts for the fact that you can find many similarities between UNIX and MS-DOS, but the UNIX environment is richer and more complex than its DOS counterpart.

The differences between DOS and UNIX appear less marked to a C programmer than to the user at the keyboard. This is because the C language uses a standard function library to communicate with the operating system, and developers of C compilers for the DOS environment have (fortunately!) gone to great lengths to duplicate the UNIX function set in the DOS environment. The standard libraries the two systems offer mask many of the differences that otherwise make programs difficult to port between DOS and UNIX.

This also helps you if you have previous experience writing C programs for either DOS or UNIX; your experience transfers very well to the other environment.

With this introduction in mind, take a look now at the more glaring differences between the DOS and UNIX environments as seen by a C programmer.

Files and Directories

The UNIX kernel is responsible for managing all accesses to disk files. The kernel treats regular files as an undifferentiated stream of 8-bit bytes, just as in the DOS world.

Both UNIX and DOS rely on the ASCII character set for alphanumeric representation. Although DOS uniformly recognizes a standard set of graphics corresponding to the hex character codes 80 through FF, UNIX does not have any such standard. If you use character codes greater than 7F (decimal 127) in your program, the graphic represented depends entirely on the kind of device to which you write the character. In particular, UNIX terminals differ greatly in the character graphics they can display, unlike PC displays that are uniform in their character support.

Unlike DOS, UNIX text files do not end with the ^Z character (read "Control-Z") and lines end with a single newline character instead of line feed and carriage return. These differences amount to saying that UNIX stores text files on disk in the same form your program sees them, whereas in DOS extraneous characters appear in the disk file that the standard I/O functions hide from your program. These differences do not generally affect your program (because the standard library functions hide them), but they do imply that a stored text file looks different in the UNIX and DOS environments.

As in DOS, in UNIX you can put files in directories, and you can put those directories in higher-level directories. Where DOS uses the backslash character (\) to separate directory names in a path, UNIX uses the regular slash character (/). This difference affects your program when you use literal pathnames in the fopen function call, but are generally transparent to you if you open pathnames provided on the command line. If your program makes any attempt to search for the separator between directory names, however, you must remember to use \ in the DOS environment, and / in the UNIX environment.

DOS requires the user to be constantly aware of which disk volume contains a particular directory structure. In DOS, you need to know whether a file or directory is on the current drive; if not, you must prefix the file or pathname with a drive designator such as A: or C:. The UNIX system treats all mounted disk volumes as a contiguous disk space, and keeps track internally of which disk volume contains which set of directories. Thus, in UNIX, path /usr/include might be on one drive, and path /usr/lib might be on another. The significance of this is that the UNIX user never specifies drive prefixes, and doesn't ever need to know which physical disk contains a particular directory or file; the pathname alone is sufficient to find it. UNIX, however, does not consider a drive designator to be an error if your program mistakenly uses it. To UNIX, the designator looks like part of the pathname. Thus, if your program tries to open a file named A:INFO.TXT, UNIX considers A: to be the first two characters of the filename.

255

UNIX filenames differ from DOS filenames in several important respects:

- UNIX filenames can include any character except the slash (/) and the NUL character (ASCII 0). Lowercase letters in particular are valid and yield a filename that differs from one that uses uppercase letters.

- UNIX filenames can be at least 14 characters long; some versions of UNIX allow filenames up to 255 characters long. The maximum length of a pathname, including the / separators, is 2,048 characters. A program written for DOS that assumes a maximum filename length of 12 characters, and a maximum path length of 64 characters, could overflow internal character arrays when given a long UNIX pathname.

- UNIX does not attach any special significance to the sequence *.XXX* (the DOS three-letter file extension) appearing at the end of a filename. The name jones.a is valid, as is jones.text, as is .info, as is 1.2.3.4.5. Obviously, you can use virtually any DOS filename in the UNIX environment, but many UNIX filenames cannot be used in the DOS environment.

If you've written C programs for the DOS environment, you've probably used library functions such as `getc` and `putc`, `fopen` and `fclose` to access disk files. You use the same library functions in the UNIX world. The chief differences are that, in UNIX, the pathnames you provide to `fopen` must contain regular slashes instead of backslashes (for example `/usr/include` rather than `\usr\include`), and UNIX does not recognize the `b` option in the second argument of `fopen` for opening binary files.

UNIX does not support the `b` option because in UNIX you always read and write files as UNIX stores them. The DOS system changes a newline character to a carriage return and line feed when writing a text file, and changes a carriage return and line feed to a newline when reading a text file; the `b` flag causes DOS to bypass these translations when you want to process a file containing arbitrary binary data. UNIX makes no such changes because it stores the newline in the text file verbatim. There are no distinctions between a text and a binary file in the UNIX world.

For example, the following statement is valid in the DOS environment:

```
in = fopen("C:\\PAYROLL\\TODAY.DAT", "rb")
```

The `fopen` call attempts to open the file C:\PAYROLL\TODAY.DAT in binary mode. You can write the same open request for UNIX in the following manner:

```
in = fopen("/PAYROLL/TODAY.DAT", "r");
```

In UNIX, filenames are usually lowercase, so the open statement would more likely look like this:

```
in = fopen("/payroll/todays.data", "r");
```

Because C programs usually get pathnames from the command line, most of these differences do not affect your C programming. To move a program written for UNIX to DOS, it may be necessary only to add the b option to the fopen statement, or to remove the b when transferring a DOS program to UNIX.

Access Permissions

The DOS environment is intended to be used only by a single user. Nothing prevents several users from consecutively using the same machine (other than physical security measures you might take), but DOS doesn't recognize the transition from one user to the next, makes no attempt to verify that a user is permitted to access the system, and provides no means to protect one user's files from disturbance by another user.

The situation is much different in UNIX. To gain access to UNIX you must first log in at a terminal, presenting a password to confirm your identity. Once you log in, UNIX stamps every file you create to identify you as the owner, and it associates a set of *permissions* with the file to control the set of users that can read, modify, or delete the file. You can set up a default set of permission flags that UNIX associates with every file you create, and you can individually modify the permissions flags for any specific file.

Access permissions do not usually affect the internal implementation of C programs, except for those programs that are specifically intended to manipulate file access permissions. As a UNIX user, however, you might occasionally find that a program fails because it cannot access an input file or create an output file, and that the reason for the program failure is that you do not have the appropriate permissions. You can usually resolve these situations by noting the error message the program issues, and either adjusting the permission flags of your files and directories to allow the access, or asking another user to grant you access to the file or directory.

The ls command is helpful for identifying the ownership and access permissions of files and directories, and the chmod command is useful for setting and changing access permissions. The chown command can change the user identified as the owner of a file or directory. The documentation for these commands also provides some useful information on the details of the permissions scheme.

If you are unfamiliar with the UNIX permissions facility, you can get the details from a number of books including my *UNIX Programmer's Reference* (Que, 1991).

Standard I/O Devices

C programming systems for DOS typically provide five standard devices: stdin, stdout, stderr, stdprn, and stdaux. UNIX only provides three: stdin, stdout, and stderr.

UNIX provides many alternatives for sending output to a printer. First, you may write your print file to stdout and pipe that, in turn, to the lp utility. The lp utility forwards its input to the UNIX print spooler that arranges the subsequent printing of the file. Alternatively, you can open a special output file, using a filename built into your program or specified on the command line, to which UNIX writes printer output. You can then print the disk file later using the lp command. Finally, you can open the printer device itself if you know its name (usually /dev/lp). If you have write access, your program can write directly to the printer.

The main purpose of the stdprn standard device in DOS is to provide programs with a default printer to use when one is not specified in the program. There is no equivalent facility in UNIX; either the program or the program's user must specify the device or file to receive output.

Inasmuch as stdprn in DOS systems corresponds to logical device 4, you can achieve a similar effect in UNIX by pre-opening logical device 4 before invoking your C program. The UNIX shell provides the ability to associate logical devices 0 through 9 with any file. As an example, consider the C program in Listing 11.1.

Listing 11.1. Using a pre-opened file.

```
#include <stdio.h>
#include <stdlib.h>

int main()
{
    FILE *stdprn;

    stdprn = fdopen(4, "w");
    fprintf(stdprn, "Output to device 4.\n");
    return(0);
}
```

If you compile the program in Listing 11.1 and then execute the program using the following commands, you obtain the output of the `fprintf` statement in whatever file you specify on the `demo` command.

```
$ cc demo.c -o demo
$ demo 4>demo.out
$ cat demo.out
Output to device 4
$
```

The sample assumes that you typed the program in Listing 11.1 into a file called demo.c. The `cc` command compiles the demo.c source and stores the executable program in a file called demo. When you execute demo, the I/O redirection `4>demo.out` tells the shell to open logical device 4 for output to a file called demo.out. The `cat` statement displays the contents of the file demo.out.

The advantage to using pre-opened files is that the program—in this case demo.c—need not concern itself with the name of the output file. The shell handles these details automatically, just as with the standard files `stdin`, `stdout`, and `stderr`.

259

Library Functions

The UNIX standard function library shares many of the functions that appear in the DOS standard function library.

The following input/output functions are common to both the UNIX and DOS environments and have similar definitions:

clearerr	fgets	fseek	getw	remove	sscanf
fclose	fopen	fsetpos	perror	rename	tmpfile
fdopen	fprintf	ftell	printf	rewind	tmpnam
feof	fputc	fwrite	putc	scanf	ungetc
ferror	fputs	getc	putchar	setbuf	vfprintf
fflush	fread	getchar	puts	setvuf	vprintf
fgetc	freopen	gets	putw	sprintf	vsprintf
fgetpos	fscanf				

The DOS compiler libraries may provide additional functions not available in the UNIX libraries, notably fcloseall, fgetchar, flushall, fputchar, vfscanf, vscanf, and vsscanf. When converting programs from DOS to UNIX, you must provide your own equivalent of these functions; when writing new programs, you should avoid using them.

The UNIX environment provides a few additional input/output functions not available in DOS: ctermid, cuserid, popen, pclose, system, and tempnam. Of these, all but tempnam are concerned with the multiuser, multitasking nature of UNIX and have no equivalent in the DOS environment, which is essentially a single-user, nonmultitasking operating system.

In both the DOS and UNIX environments you must include the stdio.h header at the front of your program when using any of these standard input/output functions.

The C standard library also provides a number of functions for handling strings and character arrays; DOS and UNIX both define these functions in the string.h header file. At a minimum, you should find the following functions available with similar definitions in both environments:

memccpy	strcat	strcspn	strncmp	strspn
memcmp	strchr	strdup	strncpy	strstr
memcpy	strcmp	strlen	strpbrk	strtok
memmove	strcoll	strncat	strrchr	strxfrm
memset	strcpy			

Notice that the `strcoll` and `strxfrm` functions are relatively new to both the UNIX and DOS environments, and may not be available with some C compiler systems for MS-DOS. They are standard with UNIX System V Release 4 and compatible UNIX operating systems.

Functions for testing and classifying characters, common to both DOS and UNIX environments, are: `isalnum`, `isalpha`, `isascii`, `iscntrl`, `isdigit`, `isgraph`, `islower`, `isprint`, `ispunct`, `isspace`, `isupper`, and `isxdigit`, as well as the case conversion functions `_toupper`, `_tolower`, `toupper`, `tolower`, and `toascii`. These functions require you to include the ctype.h header file in your program. As noted earlier, the ASCII character set is common to both systems; the extended graphics for character codes 0x00 through 0x1f and 0x80 through 0xff are unique to DOS.

Some C compiler systems for DOS support the following low-level functions borrowed from UNIX: `access`, `chmod`, `close`, `creat`, `dup`, `dup2`, `ioctl`, `isatty`, `lock`, `lseek`, `open`, `read`, `remove`, `rename`, `unlink`, and `write`.

Other functions available in both systems include: `atof`, `atoi`, `atol`, `exit`, `getenv`, `putenv`, `rand`, `strtod`, and `strtol`.

Functions available in DOS that are not available in UNIX are too numerous to permit a complete listing. Noteworthy, however, are the following:

- Any functions beginning with _ (an underscore). Although similarly named in DOS and UNIX, they are operating system dependent and cannot be considered equivalent.

- All dynamic memory allocation functions beginning with `far`, such as `farmalloc`.

- All functions intended to provide direct access to BIOS services, such as `int86`.

- The DOS string-handling functions `strlwr`, `strupr`, `strtoul`, `ultoa`, and `itoa`. Although they are sometimes useful, they are not generally available in UNIX.

- Most functions that provide display, keyboard, or graphics capabilities, including `getch` and `kbhit`.

261

- The DOS functions for reading and searching directories, particularly `findfirst` and `findnext`. These functions are unique to DOS, but can be converted into the UNIX functions `opendir`, `closedir`, and `readdir`.

- The DOS functions for determining the size of a file or its creation date, such as `filelength` or `getftime`. In the UNIX environment, you can use the `stat` function to determine file characteristics.

In general, you can transport programs that are primarily file oriented or computation intensive between the DOS and UNIX environments. Programs that depend on device interfaces, particularly the display and keyboard graphics interfaces, differ significantly in the DOS and UNIX versions.

Memory Models and Word Size

The DOS environment typically is based on a 16-bit machine architecture that employs either 16-bit or 32-bit pointers. The UNIX operating system is almost exclusively implemented on 32-bit machine architectures. This difference has some impact on your programming techniques between the two systems.

C programming systems for DOS frequently offer several memory models, each offering a different strategy for using machine addresses (pointers). Small, Medium, Compact, Large, and Huge are the typical model choices. Without delving into the significance of each of these models, suffice it to say that UNIX almost universally employs just one memory model, roughly equivalent to the Huge memory model in DOS.

In UNIX, the program address space is contiguous and usually consists solely of virtual memory as opposed to real memory. Because your program can only address virtual memory, you cannot directly access hardware-significant portions of the machine's memory or operating system tables. Programming techniques common in DOS—such as referencing hardware DMA registers, the video display buffers, or the BIOS memory tables—are not possible under UNIX. Today, several vendors provide UNIX for the IBM-compatible PC; even these versions of UNIX do not allow such access.

Because the program address space is essentially contiguous, you do not need to concern yourself with the size of data objects when programming for UNIX: 64K does not represent a boundary in any sense, either as the size of an array or as the size of a memory segment. Many systems running UNIX do not use segmented memory. All this adds up to a considerably easier memory environment for which to program.

The fact that words are 32 bits long, and pointers are always 32 bits long, may result in some different programming techniques between DOS and UNIX. When writing for DOS, a programmer commonly assumes that an `int` is 16 bits long and is equivalent to `short`. When writing for UNIX, `int` and `long` are equivalent instead. You will have the least difficulty moving from one environment to the other if you always write `long` when you need 32-bit representation, `short` when 16-bit representation is desired or adequate, and `int` only when you do not care which representation is used and your program will work properly with either a 16-bit or a 32-bit representation.

Program code that dynamically allocates arrays using calculations such as `150 * 2`, where the `2` represents the size of an integer or a pointer, is bad code. When calculating the size of an array, use expressions such as `sizeof(int)` or `sizeof(char*)` to determine the number of bytes needed.

The most subtle type of program error involving word size is code that expects bits to be truncated or discarded when shifting an `int`. In the DOS environment, an `int` has a value of zero after a left shift of 16 bits. In UNIX, the `int` may still contain a nonzero value. When your program is manipulating the bits of a value using left or right shifts, be careful to specify `long` or `short` (and `unsigned` if appropriate) to guarantee that you get the result you expect. Even on a 32-bit machine, a left shift of a 16-bit `short` results in bits discarded on the high-order (left) end of the value.

Shells

The DOS operating system provides a rather simple shell that provides only rudimentary facilities for entering and executing commands. The UNIX shells `sh`, `csh`, and `ksh` are much more powerful and flexible, and correspondingly more difficult to learn.

The difference between DOS and UNIX shells affects you in two ways. As a user, you must enter commands through the shell, so you must learn at least a minimum about one of the UNIX shells. As a programmer, you'll find that the features of the shell make some programs you might think to write unnecessary, while providing some capabilities that you might want to take advantage of in your UNIX programs.

Perhaps the most significant difference between the shells, from the programmer's perspective, is that all UNIX shells recognize and expand wildcard filenames, whereas the DOS shell does not. This implies that programs for DOS often include code to recognize filenames such as *.TXT. The C compiler systems for DOS often include a special object module you can link with your programs that automatically recognizes and expands wildcard filenames occurring on the command line.

Such code is unnecessary and wasteful in programs for UNIX, because the shell facilities for wildcard expansion are extensive and more complicated than any you might write in an application program. All the UNIX shells expand a wildcard filename to a list of filenames on the command line before invoking your program. Programs written for UNIX, therefore, always use a filename exactly as it appears on the command line.

The implementation of pipes (symbolized by ¦ on the command line) is more sophisticated in UNIX than in DOS, making pipes more useful. The primary difference in implementation is that in UNIX all the commands in a pipeline execute simultaneously. This eliminates the need for temporary files to buffer output between stages of the pipe, and greatly speeds the execution of the pipeline. As a result, UNIX includes many more programs designed for use in pipelines, having stdin and stdout as their primary or exclusive data files. Such programs are called *filters*. You may find that some programs you want to write are best implemented as filters.

In UNIX, you can pass to the shell for execution a character string having the form of a command. The system and popen functions are the primary tools for doing this. UNIX does not need to load an additional copy of the shell into memory to process the command, nor does it suspend your program while the command executes. UNIX simultaneously executes both your program and the command you passed. This facility makes it practical for you to implement some functionality by issuing a command rather than coding the function yourself.

With popen, you can arrange to receive or pass data to another program without involving the user in constructing pipes. You might, for example, find this the easiest way to sort a data collection.

The UNIX shells are sufficiently sophisticated to make them useful as programming languages. It's not unusual for an application to be partially implemented in a shell script that calls on a C program to perform only those functions that are difficult or impossible to accomplish any other way. Implementing applications this way saves time and makes the application easier to change in the future because you can make changes without recourse to C language programming.

Suppose you want to write a program that processes all the files in a directory and in any subdirectories. You could write the code you need to open directories and read their entries, or you could simplify your program by calling it from a shell script containing the following line:

```
find $1 -type f -print ¦ myprog
```

The find command locates every file in the directory named by shell argument $1, and in every subdirectory, passing a list of filenames, one per line, to your program. Your program then only needs to read stdin to get the name of each file you should process; open the file, process it, close it, and go on to the next name.

Of course, in this particular example, the simplification results not just from the capabilities of the shell, but also from the existence of the find command as a standard UNIX component. Because UNIX includes such a great many general-purpose commands like find, you can implement a lot of chores using a handy command that in the DOS world you must implement using C code. In the case of this example, and in many real-life situations, the usefulness of the shell derives mainly from its ability to hide the complexities of the find command from the terminal user.

Commands and Utilities

Over and above the general-purpose commands such as find, mentioned in the previous section, UNIX provides many commands of special usefulness to the C language programmer. Together they constitute a "programmer's workbench,"

265

and as such you may find that the commands are available only when the C development system is installed. This section reviews the major programming tools.

The C Compiler

The cc command is of primary importance to the C programmer because it is the C compiler. You can use the cc command to expand preprocessor statements in your source code, in case you have a question about how a particular macro expands. Or you can ask the cc command to compile your program to assembler source statements and then stop. You can then either submit the resulting text to the assembler, or discard it after inspecting the assembler source. Normally, the cc command compiles source code all the way to object form, producing a file with a name ending in .o containing the machine instructions corresponding to your program. The cc command can compile any number of source files with one command invocation. With the appropriate options, the cc command can link together the compiled objects, yielding a final executable program.

Syntax Checker

The lint command is often the second most important command to a C programmer. It scans a C source file without compiling it, issuing error messages for invalid syntax, warnings for unusual or suspicious but legal constructions, and recommendations for improvement of the code. Often the lint command helps you find errors that the cc compiler would never diagnose. Many programmers make it a habit to run lint before attempting an execution test of their program.

Programmers experienced with other computer languages but unfamiliar with C are often suspicious of the lint command and feel that the C compiler itself should provide all the syntax checking needed. They understandably feel that if the compiler cannot detect program errors, the compiler must be inadequate, poorly designed, and improperly programmed.

The C language is somewhat unique among computer languages in being *regular,* by which I mean that expressions and syntax that C permits in one context are permitted in all contexts. The syntax of the C expression statement implies that the following statement, for example, is valid:

```
x + 5;
```

The statement, however, is useless because the result of the calculation is not used or retained and the expression has no side effects. Removal of the statement from the program would have no effect on the program's operation. The `lint` program suggests that this statement be removed with the diagnostic message `has no effect`. The C compiler, on the other hand, permits it without complaint because the statement is unquestionably legal.

As another example, consider the following statement:

```
while (*words++ = strtok(NULL," \t\n")) ;
```

The `while` loop fills an array with pointers to the successive words of a text line. On each iteration, the `strtok` library function returns a pointer to the next whitespace-delimited word in the line, which the C compiler then assigns to the next element of an array.

The C compiler processes the `while` statement without complaint, which is reasonable because the statement is not only syntactically valid but also useful. Most versions of the `lint` program complain about the statement. Why? Because it contains the = operator in the condition expression. Usually a condition expression as found in a `while` or `if` statement contains a relational operator such as ==. A common programming error is to type the assignment operator (=) when you mean the equality operator (==) instead. Hence, nine times out of ten a statement of the form `if (a = b)` is an error and you should write `if (a == b)`. The authors of the `lint` program consider it worthwhile to draw your attention to such statements and ask you to reconsider whether you mean = or ==. The C compiler itself should not complain, however, because it should compile all syntactically valid statements.

Thus, the quandary facing compiler writers is that the C compiler should process all syntactically valid statements, yet not all valid syntax is reasonable. The UNIX development system solves the problem well by providing a compiler that diagnoses only true syntax errors, while also providing a syntax checker that can apply more stringent tests without limiting your freedom to use unusual constructions.

Interactive Debugger

Most C programmers consider an interactive source-level debugger essential. Most compiler systems for DOS provide a windows-oriented, menu-driven debugger that supports breakpoints, instruction stepping, stack traces, and the viewing and modification of registers and variables.

The UNIX development system also provides these facilities, but does not offer a graphics-oriented, menu-driven interface, in part because many UNIX systems are not equipped with graphics terminals. The sdb utility uses a command language to control the debugging process, and displays output in Teletype fashion. Although you may find the different user interface of sdb more difficult to learn, it's quite likely that with experience you'll find yourself at least as productive with sdb as with a graphical interface.

When you first initiate sdb, it loads the program to debug into memory and then waits for your instructions with a prompt. This enables you to set breakpoints and inspect or modify the program before beginning execution.

Each sdb subcommand consists of a single letter that might be preceded or followed (or both) by modifiers. For example, the command 235w asks sdb to display a "window" of source text around line 235; the sdb command displays lines 230 through 240 of the source program. The command 235b asks sdb to set a breakpoint at line 235. The command e main tells sdb to locate the source file containing the function main and to interpret commands with respect to the main function. After e main, the command x/ displays the contents of variable x in function main; if variable x is automatic and declared in several functions, the compiler ignores variables called x in other functions and sdb understands by x the variable of that name in function main. Chapter 17, "The Symbolic Debugger: sdb," discusses the details of using sdb.

Execution Profiler

The C compiler and libraries, together with the prof command, provide a tool for locating bottlenecks in the execution of your C programs. Using the measurements provided by prof, you can optimize your program for execution speed by concentrating your recoding and redesign effort on just those portions of your program that execute most frequently.

To use the execution profiler, you must first compile your program for profiling by specifying the -p option on the cc command together with any other options you would normally use for the compilation. The -p option causes the compiler to insert special code in the generated object that counts the number of times a function executes, and the amount of time spent in each function. You must link the generated object file with a special version of the C standard library that was also generated with the -p option. The cc command automatically arranges the link step to use the proper library.

When you subsequently execute the compiled and linked program, it creates a binary data file named mon.out in the current directory. Because of the extra code present in your program to obtain frequency counts and execution times, the program as a whole runs slightly slower than if compiled without the -p option.

You run the prof command after executing your program. The command reads the mon.out file and generates a printed report showing each function in your program, the number of times your program executed the function, the average time in milliseconds required for one execution of the function, and the total number of seconds spent executing the function. The report accumulates the total execution time for the program by function, and calculates the percentage of the total that the program spent in each function.

To optimize your program for execution speed, you use the report from prof to determine which function or functions are responsible for the majority of your program's execution time. You must then redesign and recode that function to reduce the amount of time required to execute it. You might, for example, change the representation of some data so the compiler performs fewer type conversions, or redesign a loop so that fewer instructions are performed inside the loop.

After recoding the functions you selected for optimization, compile the program once again with the -p option and run it again with the same test data as before. If you succeed in reducing the execution time for those functions, you reduce the total time required to execute the test run. It's also likely that some other function or group of functions now require the majority of your program's execution time.

If the improvement in execution speed is sufficient, you can stop your optimization process, recompile the program without the -p option, and place the program in production status. Or, if you need still more speed improvements, you can attack the functions that prof shows are now the bottleneck functions. You can iterate the cycle as often as you like until either the execution speed meets your requirements or you can't think of any more ways to improve your code.

Unfortunately, there is no sure-fire formula for improving the runtime performance of a piece of code. You need both ingenuity and experience to guess at ways to restructure your algorithms to achieve speed improvements. The computer can't show you how to improve program performance, but the profiling facility can tell you where the program needs improvement and where your efforts will give the greatest gain.

Without a profiler, you must guess which portions of your program need improvement. In days of old the common approach to performance enhancement was to discard the entire program and recode from scratch. Experience has shown that usually only a small portion of a program is responsible for the majority of its execution time. Logic suggests, therefore, that a small effort to recode just the offending portion will result in a disproportionate improvement in runtime. Experience usually bears this out. The profiler provides just the tool you need to achieve the greatest improvement with the least effort.

Archive Maintenance

The standard C library (libc.a), the math library (libm.a), and the curses function library (libcurses.a) are just a few of the object libraries provided by the UNIX C development system. They are indispensable tools that save you time and effort.

Each of the object libraries provided with the C language was originally constructed using the ar command. You can use the ar command to create object libraries of your own. For example, you might want to collect general-purpose functions you write into your own object library and link them with new programs you write. Programmers working with applications having multiple programs often like to store the program's object modules in an object library, especially when they use some modules in two or more of the application's programs.

Because the C language lends itself especially well to modularized programming techniques, systems are often designed in a combination of top-down and bottom-up methods. When top-down analysis identifies the general functionality of the application, bottom-up methods can suggest some common functions that the application needs. If you code and test the low-level common functions and then place them in object libraries, the higher-level routines can use the application libraries as if they were extensions to the C libraries.

To build an object library, you first write each function as a separate source file. When several functions share a common data object or have a related purpose, it makes sense to combine then into a single source file. When you compile the resulting source files with option -c, the compiler converts each source file named foo.c to a corresponding object file foo.o. You then use the ar command to collect the object files into a single file called an *archive* using a command like ar r libapp.a *.o. The command creates an archive file named libapp.a by writing all the *.o files into a new file along with enough directory information to allow the linkage editor to find an individual object module.

To use the archive, add the -lapp option to the cc command. The compiler automatically adds the prefix *lib* and the suffix *.a* to the name you give with -l to derive the filename of the archive, in this case libapp.a.

Ordinarily the ar command places files into the archive in the same order as you specify them on the ar command. The linkage editor, however, usually needs to have files ordered in the archive in the order of reference. For example, if program main.c calls object file integrate.o, and integrate.o calls chebyshev.o, the objects should appear in the archive in the order integrate.o–chebyshev.o even though alphabetically they would be stored chebyshev.o–integrate.o.

You can use the lorder and tsort commands to determine the optimal ordering of object files in an object library. The lorder and tsort commands are so peculiar that they are rarely used for any other purpose, and it's not worthwhile to explain their individual operation and use. Chapter 13, "Compiling Programs with cc," explains in detail how to use the ar, lorder, and tsort commands to build object libraries.

Automatic Program Building

You can build a simple piece of software consisting of one source file, no headers, no object libraries, and no documentation files with just the cc command. You cannot, however, generate more complex applications composed of several executable programs so easily.

For example, consider a flight planning tool for private aviation. The tool requires several databases giving detailed information about airports, navigation aids, instrument landing approaches, FAA aviation routes, and aircraft performance specifications. Programs to manage these databases provide for adding, deleting, and changing the contents of the database as airports add new runways and modify existing ones, as new aviation routes and navigation aids are built, and as new aircraft are brought to the market. To generate a flight plan, you must write a sophisticated program that calculates the best route between two airports taking into account wind, available navigation aids, required minimum altitudes, aircraft fuel requirements and altitude limitations, and so on.

Such an application might need two or three header files to describe the contents of data bases, a common library of functions (for example, to calculate the distance between two points given latitude and longitude, using the principles of spherical geometry), and three or four main application programs. If later program changes modify one of the header files, you will need to rebuild most of the application. If you change one of the library functions (for example, to correct a programming error), you must rebuild the source file containing the function and relink all the executable programs that use the function. Ideally, you only need to recompile the source file containing the changed function, and you could relink the executable programs from existing object modules.

The make command provides a way to permanently record the procedure for building an application and, even better, when you change one or more components, provides a way to rebuild just those portions of the application that depend on the changed components.

To perform its task, the make command requires you to write a script, called a *makefile,* that describes each component of the application and describes the relationship between them. The makefile describes not only the header files and source files of the application, but also the object libraries, object modules, and the executable programs of the application.

To write a makefile, you start by identifying each object that is built from source components. Some objects, such as executable programs, might be built from intermediate components such as object files and libraries. For each such generated object, you must identify the components from which the object is generated and then give the list of operating system commands needed to build the object. When the makefile contains dependency rules for every generated object and the command lists used to generate each object, the makefile is complete.

Chapter 15, "Automating Compilation with make," describes how to write a makefile and use the make command to build an application from a makefile.

Source Code Control System

The Source Code Control System, usually abbreviated SCCS, is a collection of commands that enables you to safely update the source files of an application without losing track of the original code.

Most programmers, myself included, have had the experience of losing the source code to an application. When you begin an ambitious project to add significant enhancements to an existing program, you reasonably assume that you will have the time and skills needed to complete the project. Suppose, however, that something interrupts your work after you have made many changes to the source code and that months pass before you even have the opportunity to return to the project. By then you may have forgotten much of the project details, and the original project may no longer even be wanted. You certainly can't return the source code to its original state, and you may not have time or permission to complete the project. The source code in its current condition is unusable, and can neither be used to rebuild the original product or to build the new product. The source code has been lost.

To be sure, you can always save backup copies of the source code before beginning the new project, and careful programmers may do so as a matter of course. But the technique of saving backup copies is almost useless if you have to do maintenance work on the old application before you can finish the new enhancements. The makefile, if it exists, looks for the original source file names, not their backup names. In any event, a commercial software product may exist in several different release levels in customer locations, and you may be called upon to maintain all active release levels.

SCCS solves these problems by maintaining the source code in a special form that incorporates several different images of the source file in one physical file. Normally the several images correspond to the chronological development history of the file, with each successive *change level* corresponding to a working version of the product at one point in time.

The commands in the SCCS package provide for converting a standard text file into an SCCS file, for extracting the current or any earlier version of the file, for adding a new change level to the SCCS file, for identifying the differences between two change levels of the file, and many other services.

The make command includes support for building applications from SCCS source files instead of standard text files so that you can take advantage of both make and SCCS in your development projects. Chapter 16, "SCCS—Source Code Control System," discusses all the SCCS commands and shows you how to use SCCS effectively for complex development projects.

Automatic Parser Generators

Many UNIX commands are complex programs that have a command language of their own quite distinct from any other programming language. The make command is an excellent example with its makefile syntax. sdb executes subcommands you type to control the execution of the program being tested. The ed, sed, and vi editors accept a command language of sorts; the shells sh, csh, and ksh process a sophisticated command language.

If you want to provide a command language for user interaction with your programs, or develop utilities to process program source files, you must tackle the complexities of scanning tokens of the language and parsing the tokens to "understand" the input statements. These tasks are certainly complex, but they are also well understood. Methods for efficiently scanning and parsing computer languages were developed long ago.

Despite the fact that algorithms for scanning and parsing text such as computer programming languages has long been available, most computer systems do not include tools for doing so. UNIX is unique in offering such tools to expedite your program development project.

The lex command accepts a text describing the tokens of a language, and generates an automatic scanner program in C source code to recognize the tokens. The text uses a language similar to the regular-expression notation used by the grep command. You can use the generated code as a stand-alone program, or you can link the code with your program so you can process the tokens (identifiers, numbers, special symbols) any way you wish.

The yacc command is even more powerful than lex. Like lex, yacc takes as its input a text you write describing the syntax of your new language. As output, yacc writes a complete C function that can parse your syntax and invoke routines you write whenever it recognizes a syntactic structure.

Most often you want to combine lex and yacc so they work together, using the lex-generated scanner to identify individual tokens and the yacc-generated routine to parse the tokens. In fact, yacc is not well suited to recognizing low-level tokens such as names or literal numbers in the input. It works best when its input consists of sequences of predigested tokens such as "if", "(", "identifier", ">", "127", and ")", whereas lex works best at recognizing a token from individual characters such as an identifier or a reserved word such as for or return.

Traditional data processing tasks do not require input in the form of a language. More sophisticated processing, however, may be difficult to describe in any other way. Suppose you want to build a program to format documents on a laser printer, or automatically generate X Window widgets from a description of the screen's appearance. You might accomplish these tasks by providing the user with a language to describe the document or screen format. In any situation where you want to process free-form text, consider using lex and yacc to simplify your programming task.

C Beautifier

The cb utility (its name is an abbreviation for *C Beautifier*) processes a C source file, adjusting tabulation, brackets, and spacing to achieve a consistent style of indentation.

You will probably develop your own style of writing C source code, which you will no doubt feel best formats C statements for clarity and readability with a minimum of effort. The more accustomed you become to your own programming style, the more difficult you will find it to read and interpret other programmers' code, and the more strongly inclined you will be to reformat an old program when you undertake its maintenance or enhancement.

When you work alone, your peculiarities of style do not affect anyone but yourself. When you work within a group, however, peculiarities of style may become an impediment to smooth cooperation between members of the programming team. No one likes to have coding standards imposed on them, but standards are difficult to avoid in a team effort, especially within a corporation that is by nature inclined toward standards, regulations, consistency, and conformance.

The C beautifier may be an acceptable solution when a programming group needs to have a standard style. No one may particularly like the style rendered by cb, but at least it is readily produced and requires no debates to describe. The sample code found in most books on the C programming language, including this one, adopt the style rendered by cb; perhaps preferred by no one, but it's also objectionable to relatively few people.

To cast C source code into a standard style, pass the source file to cb, and store its output in a new file. cb automatically adjusts the placement of braces, brackets, operators, and indentation to conform to the programming style of Kernighan and Ritchie in their early C programming book, *The C Programming Language.*

C Flow Analyzer

The cflow utility is often of value when you must undertake the maintenance of an existing body of source code. When you provide a group of related source files to cflow, the utility produces a stylized listing showing only the function definitions and function calls. Using the listing, you can gain an overall picture of the structure and caller-callee relationships between functions in a complex program.

C Cross-Reference Generator

The C compiler by itself produces no printed documentation of the source programs it compiles. You might find it helpful to use the cxref utility to generate a cross-reference of symbols to analyze during the program development or maintenance process, and to store permanently with the program at the end of the project.

You can use the utility to cross-reference a single source file, showing the line numbers where a symbol is defined and all the places where it's used, or to cross-reference a multifile program where the definition and use of symbols may occur in different files. As with most other programming languages, the cross-reference cites line numbers where symbols are defined and used.

Another C Program Debugger

The `ctrace` utility provides a somewhat different type of debugging facility than the `sdb` command. Whereas `sdb` provides interactive monitoring and inspection of a program while it is in execution, the `ctrace` utility operates on the source-code level, adding statements to your source code that generate an automatic display of function entry and exit, each instruction executed, and the value of each variable when set or modified. The output from a `ctrace`-instrumented program is automatic and continuous, and also quite voluminous.

Including the `ctrace` utility, there are three principal ways to debug a program in the UNIX environment. The first, using `sdb`, is discussed earlier in this chapter. The second is to add `printf` statements to your program to display helpful information while it is executing. You will probably want to remove the `printf` statements you insert for debugging purposes after you finish testing your program. The technique of adding print statements to display variable values and state information is an old and venerable debugging technique, sometimes called *instrumenting* the program.

The `ctrace` utility automatically instruments a C program to display all statements executed and all variable values set or changed throughout execution. The `ctrace` command provides options whereby you can restrict the instrumentation to just one or a few functions to reduce the volume of trace output.

To use `ctrace`, you enter the `ctrace` command supplying the filename of the source file you want traced. The command writes a modified version of your source file that it augments with print statements. You then compile the output of `ctrace` in the same fashion as you would compile the original source file. When you execute the compiled program, trace output appears on the standard error file. You can view the output directly, or using the redirection feature of the shell, you can store the output in a file and view it later.

UNIX Text Editors

Even more fundamental a tool than the C compiler is the text editor you use to prepare source program files. UNIX provides two principal text editors, ed and vi, which are available in almost any version of UNIX. Because they are so universally available, you are probably well advised to become at least minimally functional with one or the other. Many programmers, however, dislike the user interface of these programs and prefer to use one of the commercially marketed text editors. The most popular commercial text editor for UNIX is probably the emacs editor.

The user interface for the ed editor is very simple. Usable with any terminal, ed displays and edits one line at a time. It is what's often called a "line" editor. Although it is a dreadful experience to edit a large text file with ed, you might find, as I do, that ed is quick and convenient for small changes to an existing source file. If you're familiar with MS-DOS, you can consider ed the UNIX equivalent of the EDLIN utility.

The vi editor is a full-screen editor that requires a terminal with at least an addressable cursor. The vi editor enables you to view an entire screen of text at once, to move the cursor quickly from place to place on the screen, and to overtype existing text with new text. Although many users find vi strange and clumsy, and strongly dislike its user interface, I find that for an experienced user, editing with vi can be faster, more efficient, and more productive than editing with any other tool. I recommend that you make an effort to learn to use the vi editor, even when you have other editors available to you that you like better.

The emacs editor is a full-screen editor like vi, but unlike vi you need to learn almost no command language to use it. Using emacs is essentially a process of positioning the cursor where you want to type and then typing. Because it lacks a command language, emacs is busy with control keys that can be as much a burden to remember as a command language. Unlike a command language, however, the number of control key commands available to you is limited by the number of control keys available on your terminal.

Chapter 12, "Using the vi Editor," provides an introduction to the vi editor.

File Utilities

UNIX provides a number of general-purpose commands for processing text files that you may find useful in your programming tasks. You may have occasion to use one or more of these programs to examine or manipulate source program text, but more often you will find them useful when generating and examining files of test data.

The diff utility compares two files and generates an output file showing which lines need to be added to, deleted from, or changed in the first file to yield the second. Use diff not only to determine whether two files are the same, but also to determine how they differ. The diff utility is often used to compare two versions of a source program. The bdiff utility (*big diff*) can process much larger files than diff, but produces a less precise output. The sdiff utility shows the two files in a side-by-side listing and identifies differences with a mark in the center column.

Use grep to locate lines containing a pattern in one or several files. The pattern may be a fixed character string or a regular expression describing a class of character strings. The related utilities fgrep and egrep perform string searches using slightly different algorithms and types of search patterns.

Use cmp to compare two files. If the files differ, cmp reports the line and byte offset within the files where the first unequal character comparison occurs.

Use od to display the contents of a text or binary file in character, octal, or hex format.

The sed utility provides a means to select lines from a text file, or to apply an edit operation to all or selected lines in a text file. Unlike conventional text editors, the sed utility does not store the input file in an internal buffer and can therefore process files of arbitrary size.

Use pg, more, or page to browse a file or group of files. Unlike text editors that store the file to be processed in an internal memory buffer, these utilities can display files of arbitrary size.

Use split and csplit to divide a large file into a set of smaller files. Split divides a file into segments containing equal numbers of lines, whereas csplit (*context split*) divides a file into sections using a variety of criteria.

The sort command sorts files on one or several fields, using alphanumeric or numeric ordering, into ascending or descending sequence.

The comm command is another file comparison utility that identifies lines that appear only in the first file, only in the second file, or that appear in both files. The two files to compare must be in sorted sequence.

The uniq command identifies duplicate lines in the same or different files.

The join command combines two files into a third output file. For lines that contain the same key field, the output file contains one line with the fields of both input lines. join discards lines that do not match.

Subsystems

UNIX is a multiuser, multitasking system. By *multitasking* I mean that the UNIX operating system can execute several programs at once. Typically, the programs don't really execute simultaneously; rather, when one program is waiting for an external event such as terminal input to complete, the system switches its attention to another program. By keeping track of the programs that are in execution and the status each program was left in, the operating system can switch the computer from one program to the next to avoid sitting idle.

A program in some stage of execution is called a *task*. It is important to distinguish instances of the execution of a program because several different users could be executing the same program at once, but with different data. Even though the program they are executing is fundamentally the same, the tasks are different because each instance of the program may be using different input files and producing distinct output.

Most tasks in a UNIX environment are interactive; a specific, identifiable user starts them, (by entering a command, for example), therefore each one can be associated with a specific user and terminal. Some tasks, however, may be working on behalf of the system as a whole and are not associated with any specific user or terminal. These free-running almost invisible tasks are called *daemons* and they provide important services to the system's users.

Print Spooler

A typical daemon present in almost every UNIX system is the print spooler. This daemon, called *lp*, starts when the system is first turned on and remains active until the system is shut down. The lp daemon owns one or more printers, and its job is to accept print requests from users and to schedule the printing on the first printer that becomes available that can handle the request.

As is typical with most daemons, the subsystem consists of two programs. One, the lp daemon, can occur only once in the system because its job is to manage a single resource that the user community must share. The user invokes the other program, `lp`, to submit work to the daemon—usually a file to print.

To users familiar primarily with the DOS environment, the UNIX print spooler seems a little unfamiliar and perhaps threatening. Accustomed to using the printer freely, DOS users expect to specify a printer by its address to their application programs, and expect to arrange a direct connection between the application and the printer.

In the UNIX environment, the system administrator does not generally allow users to write output directly to the physical printer. Rather, you must *pipe* the output to the print spooler (the lp daemon).

You usually arrange this pipe using facilities of the shell. For example, the following command submits the output of the `cflow` command to the print spooler for later printing:

```
cflow *.c ¦ lp
```

If you wish to print a number of text files, you should probably use the `pr` command to format the files for a pleasing appearance on the printed page. The `pr` command inserts page breaks at the appropriate points, and prints the page number at the top of each printed page. If you tell `pr` to print more than one file, it inserts a page break between each file so you can easily locate the listing within the printout.

The following command prints all the C programs in the current directory:

```
pr -f -l56 *.c ¦ lp -dstock
```

The options of the `pr` command modify the way `pr` formats the files on the page. The `-f` option tells `pr` to use the printer's form feed control to skip to new pages. Without this option, pr inserts blank lines at the end of each page to force the printer to advance to the top of the next page. The -156 option tells pr to print only 56 lines per page, perhaps because the printer is a laser device and cannot print near the top and bottom of the paper.

The options of the lp command tell the print spooler how to dispatch the print request. In this case, the -d option specifies the *destination* for the print files. The system administrator presumably has designated one of the physical printers or a class of similar printers to have the destination name stock, which might represent wide green-bar paper. The meaning of destination codes varies from one UNIX system to another. You'll have to discover the destination codes appropriate for your own system, perhaps by asking another user or the system administrator. If you don't specify a destination, the system uses a default destination.

The print spooling system is potentially quite complex. Most UNIX installations don't use all the features available. Because each installation must tailor the print spooler to the kind and number of printers available as well as to the kinds of paper forms and printing requirements that it must support, you must consult with local personnel to determine the specific characteristics of the print spooler you'll use.

Batch Job Scheduler

Using a UNIX terminal is much like using a PC workstation. The machine usually appears as if it is dedicated to you, and you can freely use all the facilities of the operating system. Because of the immediacy of contact between the user and the machine, most work in the UNIX environment is done in the same fashion as in the PC environment: you invoke a computer program to do the work and wait for it to finish before going on.

Sometimes you have work to do that you don't need to do immediately; it can be held and executed overnight when the interactive load on the system is much less. UNIX supports this kind of delayed or scheduled execution with the at and batch commands. The batch command submits a command or list of commands to execute as soon as possible. The system administrator may allow batch work to execute at once, or may hold it until later in the day. The at command requires that you specify a date and time when the work should be done. The work is held in the system until that time, and then executes.

The `crontab` command operates somewhat differently than `at` and `batch`, because with `at` and `batch` once a unit of work executes it is removed from the system, whereas the `crontab` command specifies work to be done at cyclical intervals. The system continues to execute the commands in a `crontab` file every time the system clock matches the commands' execution schedule.

You might use the `at` or `batch` commands to perform compiles or long-running production work when you don't need the work right away. The output returns to you or goes to a system printer when it finishes.

Most often, system administrators use the `crontab` command to schedule work that needs to be done at regular intervals. For example, the `crontab` facility is often used to schedule the clearing out of the system `/tmp` directory once each morning, and to invoke `uucp` communications to other computer systems several times a day.

The `at`, `batch`, and `crontab` commands all work by accepting a command list as you would type the commands at your terminal; they then pass the command list through a pipe to the cron daemon. The cron daemon in turn saves the command lists in a system directory, and watches the system clock for the times when work is due to be performed. At the correct time, or as soon thereafter as possible, the cron daemon logs on a session for the user who submitted the work and passes the command list to the shell for execution. The cron daemon automatically mails output from the session back to the user, unless you have made other arrangements using the shell's redirection facility.

X Window System

Development work on the UNIX X Window System has been ongoing since at least 1985. The X protocol and basic libraries are now up to Release 5, and numerous toolkits are available, among them OSF/Motif and AT&T's Open Look, to facilitate program development within the complex X environment.

The X Window System is designed to support graphical user interfaces replete with menu bars, pop-up windows, buttons, and sliders and scroll bars, in much the same manner as the Microsoft Windows software. X can only work with graphics terminals. The older character-based terminals so commonly found with UNIX systems do not support the pixel drawing methods used by X and so cannot be used with X.

The Microsoft Windows product supports an environment consisting of one computer dedicated to the Windows software and one video graphics display. The display device has no address as such because there can be only one such device per system and its identity is implicit.

The X Window System, on the other hand, was designed from the start to be a terminal-oriented product that supports multiple graphics terminals per computer, and multiple computers per system. The X Window System presumes a networked environment called a *client/server* system, where *clients* are application programs residing on one or more computers in the network, and the *server* is a free-running task associated with a specific graphics display device.

The X server is often implemented as a UNIX daemon and charged with the task of operating the graphics terminals attached to the computer. The X server, however, can also be implemented in the display itself, offloading the computation-intensive video operations from the main computer. In such a strategy, each terminal has its own X server.

When you write programs for X, you must constantly be aware of the address of the terminal your program is using. The address identifies the X server owning the terminal, and the terminal itself when the X server owns multiple devices. The X server and its corresponding terminal may be attached to the same computer where your X application program is executing, but it may also be attached to a remote computer system accessed through telephone lines.

All transactions between the application program and the X server must travel through a telecommunications network in a language called the *X protocol*. This protocol, together with the *tcp/ip* networking software, provides the message transport mechanism that allows the application program and the terminal to be on different computer systems. When the application program and the terminal are located on the same computer system, the X protocol is still used to pass commands and data between the application and the X server, but the networking services of tcp/ip are simulated because no external telecommunications are needed.

The X Window System supports a program interface radically different from that of Microsoft Windows. You cannot port a program written for Windows to the X Window System in any straightforward manner. You must usually rewrite it from scratch. Despite the internal complexities of X, however, the programming interface of X is generally easy to use, primarily because of how it handles memory management issues.

An application program using X executes in much the same manner as any other UNIX program; it occupies its own virtual memory area, at least one megabyte in size, and can freely use the standard memory allocation functions. An X application program is therefore usually unaware of memory space limitations, and can directly access graphical objects such as tables and lists without the need to translate handles. X application programs are free to concentrate on application and graphical display issues without concern for memory management complications.

If you are interested in developing graphical application programs for the X Window System, you need to consult books such those in the Xlib Programming series by Adrian Nye, as well as books describing one of the Motif or Open Look toolkits.

Writing Programs for UNIX

For very small programs, the development strategy is straightforward:

1. Enter the C program source statements into a file named `prog.c`. The C compiler requires source file names to end with the suffix `.c`.

2. If you wish, check the program for syntax errors and suspicious statements with the `lint` utility:

    ```
    lint -u prog.c
    ```

3. Compile the program with the `cc` command:

    ```
    cc -g prog.c -o prog
    ```

4. Test the program. If you find errors, correct the source text using your favorite editor. Then repeat the `lint` and `cc` steps until you are satisfied that the program is error-free.

5. When the program is ready for production usage, compile the program again, this time omitting the debug information generated by option `-g` but requesting optimization of the machine code with option `-O`:

    ```
    cc -O prog.c -o prog
    ```

285

6. Finally, install the program in the executables directory where the program's users can access it. You probably need the assistance of your superuser for this step, because directories such as /usr/bin and /usr/local/bin are usually protected against modification by general users. If you have the necessary permission, you can install the program with the following commands:

```
mv prog /usr/bin
chmod 655 /usr/bin/prog
```

For more complex programs, the development process can be much more involved. You may want to consider all the following possibilities before you begin.

- If the program is complex, you may want to divide it into several source files. One source file might contain the main function and global data declarations, another might contain custom input/output routines, a third might contain utility functions such as memory allocation and error message writers, and a fourth might contain application-specific functions. A goal you might strive for is to keep the size of an individual source file under 1,000 lines of code. Larger modules are more awkward to edit and less easily grasped by new programmers.

- If the application requires more than one executable program, you definitely want to create a separate source file for each program. Functions that may be used by more than one executable program should be stored in separate source files, compiled to object form, and collected into an object library.

- Whenever you divide your application into two or more source files, you want to consider establishing a header file to contain definitions and declarations they share. The principle in deciding what to put into header files is that you should not define or declare anything more than once, especially structure templates; multiple declarations can be a source of errors and inconsistencies.

- Any application containing several source files and involving object libraries cries out for administration with the make command. Construct a makefile early in the project that can build the product as it exists at any point in time. As new parts are added to the system, extend the makefile. Always build test modules using the make command to ensure that the makefile is current, complete, and accurate.

● If the application is important and will be in use for any length of time, it will likely undergo maintenance and enhancement over the months and years to come. If you use SCCS to administrate your source files from the very beginning, you will have better control over your product's configuration. If you don't use SCCS from the beginning of your project, abandon all hope of using it later. The cost in time and effort to identify the real source, and to discover the relationships between the parts, will be too great.

● Use directories to organize and structure all the parts of your product. Set aside one directory to contain anything and everything involved in making and testing the product. You should name one subdirectory `bin`; it should contain all executable programs. You should name another `include`; it should contain all header files. If you use object libraries, create a subdirectory named `lib` to contain the source files for function packages. If the application contains multiple executable programs, create a separate subdirectory for each program to contain the source files exclusive to that program. Store the makefile for the product, along with any documentation, notes, and README files you might have in the top level directory.

● Observe and use the UNIX conventions for file names: *.c* for C language source files, *.l* for `lex` source files, *.y* for `yacc` source files, *.sh* for shell scripts, *.o* for object files, *.a* for object libraries, and no suffix for executable files.

In designing your application, you must weigh the advantages and disadvantages of using stream I/O versus low-level I/O. Use stream I/O whenever possible. More programmers are familiar with the `fopen` set of input/output functions, and the stream I/O package has been optimized for best efficiency.

Although you might think it wasteful, data files are often stored in text format rather than in binary format in UNIX. This is because UNIX incorporates many utilities for manipulating text files. You can well compensate the loss in performance you might experience by the freedom you gain in being able to search, extract, edit, and process your text-form data files using standard UNIX commands without any custom programming. Also consider that data files in text form are easily exchanged between computers and operating systems of differing word size and character set, whereas binary files must be converted.

UNIX presents many opportunities for designing advanced, flexible applications. Its support for daemon tasks, named pipes, and interprocess communications make it feasible for you to undertake multiuser applications that support sharing of common system resources such as a database. On the other hand, UNIX terminals differ greatly in their capabilities. The predictability you might expect in terminal features is not present, and as soon as you depart from the Teletype model of input/output you are confronted by a great many choices and difficulties. UNIX offers tools to help in this area such as Curses and the X Window System, but the choices are never easy to make.

Programming for UNIX is always a challenge to your technical skill and ingenuity, and an opportunity to learn and create.

Summary

This chapter presents an overview of the UNIX operating system, as seen from the programmer's perspective. Because the C programming language is popular in both the UNIX and the DOS environments, this chapter compares UNIX and DOS for the benefit of those who are familiar with one of the systems but not both.

The features of UNIX that differ most markedly from DOS include the following:

- A single memory model with 32-bit pointers; near and far qualifiers are not available.

- 32-bit integers; int means long int.

- A seamless file system; drive prefixes (A:) are not required.

- File access permissions to grant or deny read, write, or execute permission to other users.

- Filenames of up to 14 (sometimes 255) characters, formed with any ASCII characters but the NUL and the backslash.

- Pathnames of up to 2,048 characters.

- The slash character (/) as a pathname delimiter.

- Use of the newline character to delimit lines in a text file; eliminates significance of the b mode letter with `fopen`.

- Omission of the `stdprn` and `stdaux` standard devices.

- Omission of the `findfirst` and `findnext` low-level functions.

- Inaccessibility of BIOS calls and low-level memory areas.

- A variety of terminal equipment attachable to UNIX.

- A dissimilar shell command language.

- Dissimilar programming tools.

The UNIX programming environment offers many tools as standard components of the UNIX operating system. These tools include the C compiler itself, a separate syntax checker (`lint`), an interactive debugger (`sdb`), an execution profiler (`prof`), a library maintenance tool (`ar`), an automatic program builder (`make`), a version control system (SCCS), automatic parser generators `lex` and `yacc`, a number of source program analyzers (`cflow`, `cxref`, and `ctrace`), and a choice of text editors.

Although some or all of these tools may be available for the DOS environment from independent software vendors, the UNIX tools are standardized and, if present at all, have the same form in all UNIX implementations.

The UNIX terminal interface is generic and flexible; it allows attachment of a wide variety of terminal equipment to the system, ranging from inexpensive monochrome text displays to advanced high-resolution color graphics terminals. Such diversity presents a challenge to programmers porting applications from other environments where terminal characteristics may be more predictable. UNIX offers the curses function library and the X Window System as bases for writing terminal-independent code; both tools differ radically, however, from their counterparts in other system environments.

12

Using the *vi* Editor

The vi command invokes the visual text editor for UNIX. The UNIX environment also includes a text editor called ed that is similar to the DOS EDLIN editor, but just as most programmers consider EDLIN inadequate for editing program source files, so too do they rarely use ed for that purpose.

The vi command is actually an alias for the ex text editor, but entering vi invokes ex in *visual* mode. If you enter the ex command, you start the same text editor as the vi command, except that the ex command uses a Teletype (line-oriented) editing interface similar to that of the ed utility, whereas the vi command starts the editor in a visual or full-screen mode suitable for display terminals.

Most terminals used with UNIX today are display terminals rather than the older Teletype-style terminals that were once prevalent, so you'll probably use the vi command almost exclusively and rarely if ever use the ex command. Nonetheless, the ex command (and the ex mode of vi) has its uses. For example, once in a great while you may need to work with a Teletype-style terminal; the visual mode of ex (and hence the vi command) is not supported with Teletype-style terminals. Also, a number of editing commands are available only in the ex mode; you must learn some of the ex commands to fully utilize the capabilities of the editor.

I should warn you at the outset that, if you've ever used a full-screen editor with a display terminal before, you will probably find the vi user interface to be unusual, awkward, and at least initially confusing. Many people never overcome this initial feeling and develop a permanent aversion to the vi editor. This is unfortunate, because the vi interface probably offers greater speed and power than most other editors. As with most things, your speed and proficiency with vi will increase as you learn more commands; in the beginning, editing with vi may go rather slowly for you.

If you have more than one text editor available to you, it might be helpful to switch from vi to one of the other editors whenever you become frustrated or impatient. Gradually, if you persist in trying to work with vi, looking up one or two new vi editing commands with each session, you'll build up fluency to the point where you can use vi for a complete editing session. Only when you can use vi as fluently as other editors can you make an informed judgment as to which editor provides you the greatest ease and efficiency.

Invoking the Editor

The vi and ex commands both have the same format:

```
vi [- ¦ -s] [-l] [-L] [-R] [-r [file]] [-t tag]
   [-v] [-V] [-x] [-C] [+cmd ¦ -c cmd] file...

ex [- ¦ -s] [-l] [-L] [-R] [-r [file]] [-t tag]
   [-v] [-V] [-x] [-C] [+cmd ¦ -c cmd] file...
```

In its simplest form, the command vi *filename* invokes the editor for file *filename*, creating a new file if the file does not already exist. You don't often need the supported options, but they provide features you'll find very handy on occasion. The options are summarized in Table 12.1.

Table 12.1. vi command-line options.

Option	Usage
-	Use the - option when you want to submit editor commands from standard input, such as from a pipe. When you submit commands from standard input, the editor works in "batch" mode; that is, it is not interactive. The editor displays all information and text messages, but does not display the file itself nor the commands you submit to it. The standard input file must contain all necessary editing commands, including the w command to save the edited result, and the q command to quit the editor. The - option is used most often from within a shell script to edit a file using a predetermined set of commands.
-s	The -s option is an alias for - and means the same thing.
-l	The -l option invokes the *lisp* editing option. Specifying -l on the command line is equivalent to entering the command set lisp from within the editor.
-L	The -L option lists the files that were preserved for you when editing was aborted by a system crash. You can recover the preserved files by invoking the editor with the -r option.
-R	The -R option invokes the editor in read-only mode; you can view files, but you cannot change them. Specifying -R on the command line is equivalent to issuing the command set readonly from within the editor.
-r	Use the -r option to retrieve the preserved image of a *file* that was saved for you when the system crashed. From the moment you first make a change to a file until you save it,

continues

293

Table 12.1. continued

Option	Usage
	the editor maintains an image of the modified file in a temporary disk area; if the editor is terminated for any reason, the image is still available in the temporary disk area and can be used to restart the interrupted session. The recovery feature is always enabled; you do not have to do anything special to take advantage of it.
-t	The -t option retrieves the file containing the *tag* and positions to the line where the *tag* occurs. When you use the -t option, you do not normally specify any other filenames on the command line, because the *tag* implies a file. If you specify other filenames, they are edited in addition to the file *tag* implies.
-v	The -v option invokes the ex editor in visual mode. This option is implied by the vi command; entering vi on the command line is equivalent to entering ex -v.
-V	Use the -V option ("verbose") to cause the editor to display all initialization commands on the standard error file. The editor reads initialization commands from the .exrc file in your current directory or your home directory, and from the environment variable EXINIT. Use the -V option most often when you are debugging an editor initialization file and unsure of the commands the editor actually sees.
-x	Use the -x option to edit a file previously stored in encrypted form, or to edit a text file and convert it to encrypted form. If the file was previously encrypted, the -ex option enables you to retrieve and edit the file; if the file is in clear form, the editor remembers the password you enter and stores the file in encrypted form when you exit the editor. You are prompted for the encryption password after you enter the ex or vi command but before editing begins. (For more information about the encryption facility, see the section titled "Encryption.")

Option	Usage
-C	The -C option is like the -x option, except the editor does not attempt to guess whether the file is in encrypted form. When you specify the -C option, the file to edit must be previously encrypted.
+cmd	Use the +cmd option to specify a single command for the editor to execute before accepting any commands from standard input (if the -s option is specified) or from the terminal. This option is useful for quickly positioning a file at a particular line. For example, the command vi +98 file.c positions the editor at line number 98 in file.c.
-c	The -c option is equivalent to the +cmd option; it is provided for compatibility with the UNIX command syntax standard. You should use it in preference to the +cmd form that is obsolete and may eventually be dropped.
file	Normally you list one or more filenames after the ex or vi command name and any options; these are the files that are retrieved for editing. You can switch between the files using the e and n editor commands; the editor remembers your position when you switch to another file, and restores you to that position when you switch back to it. Of course, you can use shell wildcards to specify the list of filenames you want to edit—vi *.c, for example. There is no upper limit to the number of filenames you can specify on the command line. Notice, however, that the visual editor vi does not support split screens, so you can see only one of the files at a time. If you specify a command option that implies the file to edit, such as the -t tag option, you don't need to type the filename at the end of the command line.

The "Editor Features" section later in this chapter discusses many of the features mentioned in the command-line option descriptions.

Edit Modes

The vi editor is always in one of three modes: command mode, edit mode, or input mode. (The edit and input modes are unique to the visual (vi) editor; the ex editor uses only the command mode.) Modes affect the interpretation of a key press, and require that you be conscious of the mode the editor is in at all times. The editor uses modes because a modal approach to keyboard interpretation increases the flexibility of the keyboard and simplifies the editor commands.

When you first start the editor, the top of the file displays on-screen, the cursor is at the top left position, and the editor is in edit mode. In edit mode, the keys of your keyboard each represent an editor command; pressing one does not enter the corresponding character into your file, but instead causes the editor to take an editing action. For example, the *x* key deletes the character under the cursor; the *h* key moves the cursor left one position; and the . key repeats the last edit command you executed. The shift and control keys matter in edit mode because they change the command a key performs: *Shift-a* generates the A command, which you use to add text to the end of the line, whereas the *a* key by itself adds text after the character under the cursor.

In input mode, every character you type is entered into the text of your file following the current cursor position. Many edit commands put you in input mode, often after performing a preliminary action. For example, the A command moves the cursor to the end of the line, and then enters input mode; together the actions enable you to add text to the end of the line. The o command inserts a new, empty line following the line where your cursor is positioned, moves the cursor to the start of the new line, and then enters input mode; the actions enable you to add a new line into the file.

Once you enter input mode, you remain in input mode until you press the Escape key (sometimes labeled Esc on the keyboard). Pressing Escape returns the editor to edit mode. Until then, every character you type is inserted into the file. Even the Enter key adds a character to the file: it generates a "newline" character that ends the current line and starts another. When in input mode, you can add as many lines of text as you wish by pressing Enter at the end of each line and continuing to type. The insertion of text does not end until you press Escape. Even control keys such as the Insert key (Ins) or the cursor movement keys generate codes that can and will be inserted into the text of your file when in input mode.

The editor enters command mode when you type the : command. (You must be in edit mode to type the : command; if you are in input mode, pressing : inserts a colon into your file.) To provide a visual cue that you are in command mode, the editor moves the cursor to the bottom line of the screen, displays a colon in the first position of the line, and waits for you to type a command. When you press Enter, the editor executes the command, clears the bottom line of the screen, returns the cursor to its original position in the file, and resumes edit mode.

If you set the showmode option on, the editor displays a short message at the bottom right of the screen showing the current edit mode. Whenever the editor is in edit mode, the message is blank. In input mode, the message indicates APPEND MODE, INSERT MODE, or OPEN MODE according to the type of command that put you in input mode. The message indicates REPLACE 1 CHAR or REPLACE MODE whenever you are overtyping text. (To find out how to set the showmode option on, see the set editor command.)

To learn to use the vi editor, you need to do the following:

● Understand the distinction between edit and input modes

● Learn a basic set of the visual commands

● Learn some of the ex commands

● Set up a profile for your vi preferences

The following sections explain the editor commands and options, and show you how to set up a vi profile.

Visual Commands

Visual commands are the one- or two-letter commands you enter while in edit mode. Often a visual command consists of a single key press, and the effect of the command is immediately visible. Some commands permit modifiers such as a repeat count, so sometimes a complete visual command may consist of several keystrokes. The editor does not display the command as you type; it merely accumulates the characters in memory until it knows what to do. You may find it awkward at first to enter commands when you can't see what you're typing, but as you gain speed and confidence your discomfort will gradually pass. Unfortunately for beginners, the vi editor user interface was designed for experienced users and can be difficult to get used to.

Cursor Movement Commands

Visual commands fall naturally into groups according to their function. The most basic command group, and the group you'll use most often, is the cursor movement commands. The cursor commands are as follows:

h   Moves the cursor left one character
j   Moves the cursor up one line
k   Moves the cursor down one line
l   Moves the cursor right one character

Usually you can also use the cursor movement keys if your keyboard has them; they are usually marked with an arrow pointing up, down, left, or right. Because all keyboards do not offer cursor movement keys, the vi editor does not require that you use them, and always accepts the one-letter cursor movement commands. In fact, cursor movement keys are really supported by defining vi macros that equate the code the key generates to the equivalent cursor movement command. Such macros are usually part of the default vi profile that comes with your UNIX system.

You are perfectly free to use the cursor movement keys if your keyboard has them and your vi profile (either your own or the default system profile) contains macros to define them, but you may often prefer to use the single-letter cursor movement commands. The h, j, k, and l keys are easy to reach on the keyboard, and therefore afford touch typists the ability to move the cursor without removing their fingers from the "home" position. I've been using the vi editor almost daily for several years, and find that I almost never use the cursor movement keys. The h, j, k, and l commands enable much greater editing speed than do the cursor movement keys.

You can prefix each of the cursor movement commands with a repeat count. For example, the command 8l moves the cursor eight characters to the right, and 3j moves the cursor down three lines.

The h (left) and l (right) commands do not move the cursor beyond the ends of the line; they can move the cursor only left or right within the current line. The k (up) and j (down) commands, however, are not limited to the lines displayed on the screen; if you attempt to move up from the top of the screen, or down from the bottom of the screen, the editor scrolls the display up or down one line as necessary. If you use a large repeat count—for example, 100j to move down one hundred lines—the editor displays the page of text containing the line, with the new current line in the center of the screen.

Extended Cursor Movement Commands

Because you have to move the cursor often while editing a file, the editor provides many additional commands to speed up the process. Using these commands, you can often move to exactly the position you want (or near to it) with only a couple of keystrokes. These extended cursor movement commands are listed in Table 12.2. The notation [r] in front of a command indicates that you can type a number (one or more digits) in front of the command to repeat the command's operation that many times.

Table 12.2. Extended cursor movement commands.

Command	Description
[n] +	Moves down one (n) line
CR	Enter (Return) key—same as +
[n] -	Moves up one line
[n] ^h	Moves left one (n) character
[n] sp	Moves right one (n) character
0	Moves to the first character of the line
[r] _	Moves to the first nonwhitespace character of the line
[r] ^	Same as _
$	Moves to the last character of the line
[n] ¦	Moves to column number n
[n] H	Moves to the top line of the screen (to the nth line from the top)

continues

Table 12.2. continued

Command	Description
M	Moves to the middle line of the screen
[*n*] L	Moves to the last line of the screen (to the *n*th line from the bottom)
[*n*] G	Moves to the last (*n*th) line of the file
[*r*] w	Moves forward to the next word
[*r*] b	Moves backward one word
[*r*] W	Moves forward one blank-delimited word
[*r*] B	Moves backward one blank-delimited word
[*r*] e	Moves forward to the end of the current word
[*r*] E	Moves to the end of the current blank-delimited word
[*r*] f*c*	Moves forward to the next *c* in the current line
[*r*] F*c*	Moves backward to the previous *c* in the current line
[*r*] t*c*	Moves forward to just before the next *c*
[*r*] T*c*	Moves backward to just before the preceding *c*
[*r*] ;	Repeats the last f, F, t, or T command
[*r*] ,	Repeats the last f, F, t, or T command in the reverse direction
[*r*] (	Moves backward one sentence
[*r*])	Moves forward one sentence
[*r*] {	Moves backward one paragraph
[*r*] }	Moves forward one paragraph
[*r*] [[	Moves backward one function
[*r*]]]	Moves forward one function

The + and - commands move up and down one line. Unlike the j and k commands, both + and - position to the first nonwhitespace character of the line; j and k move up and down but leave the cursor in the same column. You can specify a repeat count in front of the command (for example 3+ or 3-) to move up or down multiple lines.

The Backspace key (if your keyboard has one) moves the cursor left when in edit mode; it does not change text. (The command is shown as ^h (Control-h) because most terminals generate the Control-h sequence (ASCII 08) for the Backspace key.) Similarly, the spacebar moves the cursor to the right one position without inserting or changing text. These commands are provided for convenience and are exactly equivalent to the h (left) and l (right) commands.

The 0 (zero) and _ (underscore) commands jump to the first position of the line from anywhere on the current line. The _ command ignores any leading whitespace and positions to the first nonwhitespace character of the line. You might find yourself using _ more often than 0 when editing program files with a lot of indentation. Notice that you cannot use a repeat count in front of the 0 command; the combination 30 would look like a repeat count of 30 and would apply to the command you type *after* the 0, probably giving you an unexpected and confusing result. A repeat count in front of _ works the same as 3+, moving down three lines.

The ^ (caret) command is equivalent to _. It is provided as an alias because some keyboards switch the position of the ^ and _ characters.

The H (*home*), M (*middle*), and L (*last*) commands provide a quick way to move around the screen. They all position to the first nonwhitespace character of the line, like the _ command. The H command moves to the top line on the screen, the M command moves to the middle line of the screen, and the L command moves to the last line of the screen. A number in front of H positions to the *n*th line from the top of the screen; a number in front of L positions to the *n*th line from the bottom of the screen. For example, use 3H to move to the beginning of the third screen line. A repeat count in front of M is meaningless, and the editor ignores it.

The G (*goto*) command by itself moves to the last line of the file. The command *n*G moves to line *n* of the file; for example, 1G moves to the first line in the file.

The ¦ command moves the cursor to a specified column of the current line. You specify the column number like a repeat count; for example, 30¦ moves the cursor to column 30. If the column number lies beyond the end of the line, the cursor moves to the last character of the line.

The w and W commands differ in that the w command considers any nonalphanumeric character to be a word delimiter, whereas the W command considers only whitespace characters (the blank, tab, and newline) as word delimiters. If the cursor is on an alphanumeric character, the w command moves forward to the next nonalphanumeric character; if on a nonalphanumeric character, it moves forward to the next alphanumeric character. For convenience, the w command treats whitespace specially; the command skips over whitespace until it finds the next nonwhitespace character, enabling you to move from word to word in a sentence.

Suppose the cursor is under the s of so-called in the following line of text:

```
the so-called potentate of Istanbul
```

Pressing w moves the cursor forward to the dash, but pressing W moves the cursor forward to the p in potentate. Pressing w twice, or typing the command 2w, moves the cursor forward to the c in called. Pressing w three times (or typing the command 3w) moves forward to the p in potentate. The editor thus considers so-called to contain three words. The w command will move from the p in potentate to the o in of in one step, however, because it skips over whitespace delimiters.

The f, F, t, and T commands are single-character search commands; the lowercase commands search forward in the current line, whereas the uppercase commands search backward. The commands search for whatever character you type after the command, and always ignore the character currently under the cursor. The f and F commands move to the character searched, whereas the t and T commands move to the character just before it. In other words, t moves forward to the character just to the left of the searched character, and T moves backward to the character just to the right of the searched character.

The t and T commands may seem a little peculiar, and in fact they are not often used by themselves. They are very handy, however, when you use them in conjunction with the c (change) command, because they enable you to specify a range of characters up to but not including some character.

Use the semicolon (;) to repeat the last f, F, t, or T command; this saves you having to type the two-character search again. The comma (,) command is like ; but repeats the previous search in the opposite direction. For example, if you enter ft to find the next *t* in the current line, pressing , moves the cursor backwards to the previous *t*.

The e and E commands are handy for moving forward to the end of a word, either punctuated (e) or blank-delimited (E). There are no corresponding commands for moving backward; you have to combine the b and e (or B and E) commands to achieve such an effect.

The editor provides a number of commands for moving the cursor over large chunks of text. The (and) commands move backward or forward one sentence, the { and } commands move backward or forward between paragraphs, and the [[and]] commands move backward and forward between the functions of a C source program.

To the editor, a sentence is any text following a period and two blanks. Notice that *two* blanks must follow a period; if only one blank intervenes between a period and the start of a sentence, the editor does not recognize a sentence break and moves right past it. The two-blanks convention is a holdover from when most text files written in the UNIX environment were used with the nroff and troff text formatters; now that these text formatters are obsolete, the convention is somewhat like a fossil from the older days of UNIX.

A paragraph is any text following an empty line. Thus you can easily skip back and forth between blocks of text separated by a single blank line using the { and } commands.

The editor recognizes a curly brace ({) at the beginning of a line as the start of a C function. Use the [[command to move backward to the start of the current function, and]] to move forward to the start of the next function. For these commands to work consistently, you must format your C program source files so that the opening brace of a function occurs at the beginning of a line, and that other braces in the function are indented. Function skipping does not use the closing brace (}) at the end of a function, although it normally appears at the beginning of the line also.

You can use a repeat count in front of any of the extended cursor-movement commands except 0, M, and $.

Scrolling Commands

The visual editor provides a number of commands that move the entire screen, scrolling text upward or downward as you page forward or backward through the file. The scrolling commands are:

[r] ^f	Pages forward
[r] ^b	Pages backward
[r] ^y	Scrolls up one line
[r] ^e	Scrolls down one line
[r] ^d	Scrolls down one-half page
[r] ^u	Scrolls up one-half page
zCR	Scrolls current line to top
z.	Scrolls current line to middle
z-	Scrolls current line to bottom

The ^f (Control-f) key combination advances to the next page (screenful) of text. The last line of the screen becomes the top line of the new screen so you can visually relate the new page to the previous one. The net result is that the screen advances *n*–1 lines (where *n* is the number of lines in the display). A repeat count in front of the ^f command has the same effect as pressing the ^f key combination that number of times.

The ^b (Control-b) key combination pages backward toward the beginning of the file; it is the logical inverse of the ^f command. Like the ^f command, the ^b command retains one line of the previous screen for orientation; for ^b, the top line of the screen becomes the bottom line of the new screen.

Most terminal keyboards include page-up and page-down control keys, but the control codes the paging keys generate vary from terminal to terminal. Your editor profile (or the default editor profile) usually contains macros to equate the control codes the paging keys generate to the ^f and ^b commands, enabling you to use the keyboard paging keys instead of the control-key combinations. If the paging keys on your keyboard don't seem to work, issue the :map command to check the list of active macros; the npage and ppage macros should specify the control codes your keyboard generates. (See the map command in the section titled "Map Keys" for instructions on defining macros.)

The ^u and ^d commands enable you to move upward or downward in the file by half a screen. Half-screen paging enables you to keep some of the context in view, making it easier for you to keep your place as you scroll forward and back through the file. There are no hardware equivalents for the half-screen paging commands, although you can use the map command to assign the ^u and ^d commands to any keys you find convenient.

The ^y command moves the page of text down one line, exposing a new line at the top of the screen; the ^e command similarly scrolls the text up, exposing a new line at the bottom. You can use a repeat count to specify a multiline scroll. Subsequent ^y and ^e commands without a repeat count then scroll that number of lines until you change the default by specifying a different repeat count. This feature affords you the comfort of the half-page scrolling commands, but gives you control over the number of lines you scroll.

Inserting Text

To insert text into a file, you must first issue a command that switches the editor from edit mode to input mode. Some commands perform a preliminary action before switching to input mode; others just unlock the keyboard and let you type text into the file. You must signal when you finish entering text by pressing the Escape key (often labeled *Escape* or *Esc* on the keyboard).

Some terminals have keys that generate a code sequence beginning with Escape, such as the program function keys. If you press such a key while in input mode, the editor first leaves input mode and then tries to interpret the remaining characters that follow the escape as visual commands. This usually results in a series of beeps as the editor rejects them. Keys that generate control codes beginning with Escape can cause unpredictable damage to your files; you should avoid pressing them unless you know what effect the key causes.

When you create a new file by invoking the editor with a filename that doesn't exist, the editor still begins in edit mode. You can use any of several commands such as a, i, I, or o to begin entering text. Of course, commands that change or delete text won't work because the file initially contains no text.

The following commands enable you to insert new text:

[*r*]	a	Adds text after the cursor
[*r*]	i	Adds text before the cursor (insert)
	o	Adds lines underneath the current line (open)

[r] A	Adds text to the end of the current line
[r] I	Adds text at the beginning of the line
O	Adds lines above the current line

The a command inserts text following the cursor position, whereas the i command inserts text in front of the cursor. The two commands are very similar, and in most situations you can use either one to insert text into the middle of a line. To add text at the front of a line, use i or I; to add text to the end of a line, use a or A. You should adopt either a or i as your standard input command so you can position the cursor and start typing without thinking about which command to use.

If you press the Enter key while typing text, the editor inserts a newline code into the text but leaves you in input mode. The net effect is that you can insert multiple lines with one a or i command.

If the autoindent option is turned on, pressing Enter also generates whitespace at the start of the next line so the text you enter lines up with the text of the previous line. The autoindent option is very useful when editing C program files, because it automatically maintains the current indent. You can use the ^d (Control-d) command while in input mode to lessen the indent by the width of a tab.

The a and i commands enable you to specify a repeat count. If you type a number (one or more digits) in front of the command, when you press Escape the text you type is inserted that number of times. This is a handy way to enter many repetitions of a single character or a group of characters. For example, to input a line of asterisks, you can use the command sequence o<esc>80a*<esc>. The o command inserts an empty line below the current line; the next escape ends input mode, leaving the line empty. The 80a* command then appends the single character * 80 times, giving you a line of asterisks.

You can also use a repeat count with the A and I commands, inserting the same text multiple times at the beginning or end of the line.

The o command inserts a new, empty line below the current line before it switches to input mode, whereas the O command inserts an empty line above the current line. Actually, the o and O commands are not strictly necessary because you can achieve the same affect using A to append text to an existing line, beginning your input with a carriage return.

You cannot use edit commands while in input mode. If you make a typing mistake and need to change the text you entered, you must first press Escape to return to edit mode, and then use edit commands to delete or change the text. The editor provides a minimal set of commands that are usable in input mode; these are summarized here:

`^d`	Backtabs once
`0^d`	Backtabs to the start of the line
`^v`	Literal
`^w`	Deletes last word
`^h`	Backspaces one character
`kill`	Erases the current line

When you use `autoindent`, the `^d` (Control-d) key cancels one level of indent unless you are already at the left margin. To back out to the left margin quickly, use `0^d` (zero followed by Control-d); the `0` appears on the line, but then disappears when you press `^d`.

Use the literal command `^v` to enter a command code as data in your file. For example, to enter an escape character as data (without leaving input mode), press `^v^[` (Control-v followed by Control-[); to enter the `^d` code, press `^v^d`. Interestingly, you can use the `^v` command to find out the code sequence any keyboard key generates: first enter input mode in any file, and then press `^v` followed by the control key. On my terminal, pressing the F1 key generates the characters `^[OP` (where `^[` represents the ASCII escape character), and pressing Backspace generates `^h`.

Use the `^w` command to delete the current blank-delimited word of text. The editor does not blank out the word; the cursor backspaces to the beginning of the word, but you can still see the word to the right of the cursor. If you press Escape, the word disappears. If you resume typing, you type over the word. The editor leaves the word displayed in case you change your mind and want to re-type it, but the word has been internally deleted from the end of the line. Notice that because you are in input mode and cannot move around with the cursor movement commands or keys, the `^w` command can only delete the last word you typed, similar to how the Backspace key only deletes the last character you typed.

You can use the Backspace key in input mode to backspace over the last character you typed, if your terminal generates the ASCII code `^h` (Control-h) for the Backspace key; otherwise you have to type Control-h explicitly to perform the backspace operation.

The `kill` key is whatever key has been specified as such with the `stty` command, either explicitly in your login profile or by system default. By default the `kill` code is the @ character, but most users change the kill code to something else (often using the control code ^u as the `kill` character).

Pressing the `kill` key backspaces to the start of the line. The line remains displayed, but the line has been truncated. If you press Escape, the text disappears; if you resume typing, you type over the displayed characters. Please notice that you do not have to delete leftover characters if you type a shorter text over the original; only the text you type after pressing `kill` appears in the final line.

Deleting Text

The `vi` editor provides the following commands for deleting text:

[r] d *target*	Deletes text from cursor to <*target*>
[r] dd	Deletes the current line
D	Deletes to end of line
[r] x	Deletes one character
[r] X	Deletes characters preceding cursor

The `d` command is the basic delete operation in `vi`. To perform a deletion, position the cursor on the first character to delete, press `d`, and then enter a cursor movement command. The delete command deletes all the text extending from the cursor up to the character where the cursor would have moved.

Because the amount of text deleted by `d` is variable, it does the work of a great many delete commands. For example, `dw` deletes the word under the cursor up to the next nonalphanumeric character; `dW` deletes the word under the cursor up to and including the next whitespace character; and `d0` deletes text from the cursor backward to the beginning of the line. Indeed, the editor has no difficulty deleting in either a forward or backward direction according to the direction the cursor would move, so you can use combinations like `dFc` to delete backward to the preceding *c* in the current line. When deleting backward, the characters deleted exclude the character immediately underneath the cursor.

When you perform a deletion, the cursor doesn't move; the text skipped by the cursor movement command is deleted instead. Thus, `dw` deletes up to but not including the next nonalphanumeric character, except that it also deletes any blanks following the word if the word is delimited by blanks. The reason for this complication is that the w command by itself is complicated: it moves to the next delimiter, but if the delimiter is whitespace, it also skips the whitespace characters.

The d command can delete large amounts of text. For example, the command dG deletes text starting with the character under the cursor up to the end of the file; d) deletes up to the start of the next sentence, and dj deletes the remainder of the current line and the first part of the next line up to the column where the cursor is located.

If the cursor movement is line oriented, the d command deletes lines instead of characters. For example, dG deletes the entire current line through the last line of the file; dH deletes the current line through the first line of the screen. In general, when you use the delete command with any cursor movement command that moves to the first character of a line, such as +, -, j, k, H, M, or L, the entire current line is deleted, not just characters following the cursor.

If you use a repeat count in front of the delete command, the editor attempts to execute the command that many times; 2dW thus attempts to delete two blank-delimited words. Notice that the repetitions might eventually fail; dte deletes from the cursor up to (but not including) the next *e* in the line, but 2dte might succeed only once if only one *e* occurs to the right of the cursor in the current line. If one of the repetitions fails, the editor beeps and then abandons all further repetitions.

The dd command is a special abbreviation meaning to delete the current line; there is no cursor movement command d, so no confusion with the d<target> form can occur. The dd command deletes the entire current line regardless of the cursor's position in the line. A repeat count (for example, 3dd) means to delete the current line and the two lines that follow it.

The D command deletes from the cursor through the end of the line; after its execution, the last character of the line is the character that immediately precedes the cursor. The cursor moves left one position to the new end of line.

The x command deletes the one character underneath the cursor and shifts the remainder of the line left one position. If you want to delete a specific number of characters, use the repeat count to say how many characters to delete: 18x deletes 18 characters, or the rest of the line, whichever is less. Notice that the x command does not delete the invisible end-of-line character as does the d command.

The X command works like x, deleting one character, but in the reverse direction; it deletes the character preceding the cursor. The cursor moves left so that it remains on the same character after the command as before.

Changing Text

The visual commands you use to change existing text are listed here:

[r] c target	Changes text up to target
[r] cc	Changes the current line
[r] C	Changes text to end of line
[n] r	Replaces one (n) character(s)
[r] R	Overtypes text
[n] s	Changes one (n) character(s)
[r] S	Changes the entire current line
[r] J	Joins consecutive lines
[r] < target	Shifts lines left
[n] <<	Shifts one (n) line(s) left
[r] > target	Shifts lines right
[n] >>	Shifts one (n) line(s) right
[r] ~	Inverts case of current character

The c command is the basic command for changing text. The amount of text the c command affects is variable, and is controlled by a cursor movement command that you specify following the c command. Use the cursor movement command you specify as target to identify the range of text to change; it does not cause any cursor movement to occur. The cursor movement command can select text in either a forward or backward direction; if backward, the range of text to change excludes the character immediately underneath the cursor.

The change command operates by first marking out or deleting the text that you selected for change. If the selected text lies completely within the current line, the editor visually highlights the amount of text you selected by changing the last character of the range to a dollar sign ($). If the change affects more than one physical line, the editor deletes the selected text.

The change command then enters input mode. You can type any amount of text to replace the changed text, from nothing at all up to multiple lines of text. The change operation ends when you press the Escape key. If you enter no replacement text, the change is equivalent to deleting the text, because the se-lected text is always deleted (internally if not visibly) before entering input mode.

When you use w or W as the target command, change works somewhat differ-ently than deletion. Where the delete operation also deletes the whitespace fol-lowing the word, the change command only selects the characters of the word itself for replacement; the whitespace following the word remains unaffected. For this reason, cW is always equivalent to cE and cw is always equivalent to ce.

The cc command selects the entire current line for change regardless of where the cursor is positioned in the line. If you specify a repeat count, that many lines are selected for change. For example, 2cc changes two lines: the current line and the line following it.

The C command changes text from the cursor through the end of the current line. It is equivalent to c$ and is provided merely for the sake of convenience.

The r command replaces one character with any single character you type next. Unlike the c command, r does not enter input mode; it therefore provides a quicker way to change one character than c because you don't have to press the Escape key to end the change operation. If you specify a repeat count, that num-ber of characters changes to whatever single character you type next. For example, 3r. changes the character underneath the cursor, and the two characters follow-ing it, to three consecutive periods. If the line is not long enough to permit all repetitions, the editor rejects the entire command.

The R command puts you in replace mode. You can type as much text as you wish over the characters already present on the current line, and if you continue typing, the current line extends to accommodate however much text you type. If you press the Enter key, the editor opens a new line underneath the current one and you can continue typing. Because the editor does not wrap automatically to the next line, and pressing Enter adds a new line, you cannot run onto the line following the current line while in replace mode.

If you type over a tab character while in replace mode, the editor does not retain the tab; the tab is replaced by whatever character you typed over it. As a result, the replace command is awkward to use in a file containing columns of information separated by tabs; if you try to replace a three-character word with a four-character word, you destroy the tab separating the columns and find your-self typing over the text in the next column. In such cases, the cw (change word) command enables you to replace a shorter word with a longer word while leav-ing the tab undisturbed.

The s command (suppose that the s stands for *substitute*) is equivalent to cl; it changes one character. If you specify a repeat count, that number of characters is selected for change. Unlike r, the s command puts you in input mode, enabling you to replace one or more characters with an unlimited amount of text. As always, you must press the Escape key to terminate input mode before you can enter another edit command. The s command is supported as an abbreviation for cl.

The S command selects the entire current line for replacement, erases the line, positions the cursor at the left side of the screen, and leaves you in input mode. It enables you to replace the entire line regardless of the position of your cursor in the line. The S command is logically equivalent to the combination 0cc.

The J command joins the current line and the following line into a single line of text. Although joining two lines together entails nothing more than deleting the newline character that separates the two lines, the editor tries to join lines in a more intelligent manner. Usually, the editor inserts a blank character between the two lines, but if the first character of the second line is a closing parenthesis, the editor joins them flush. If the last character of the first line is a period, the editor inserts two blanks. To my knowledge, the complete set of heuristics for joining lines has never been cataloged; if you don't like the result, just edit it.

You can use a repeat count with J to specify the number of lines to join. A repeat count of 2 means to join two lines, the current and the next; this is the default anyway, so J and 2J are equivalent commands. When you specify a repeat count, you must remember to include the current line in the count.

The < and << commands shift text left by the number of spaces specified by the editor shiftwidth option, and the > and >> commands shift text to the right. A shift is performed by adding or deleting whitespace at the front of the line. The editor takes into account blanks and tabs already present at the front of the line, and converts the new whitespace and the existing whitespace into the minimum number of tabs and spaces that yield the proper indentation.

You can change the amount by which the editor shifts text left or right using the command :set sw=*n* or :set shiftwidth=*n*. The default shift width is eight characters, which is the normal equivalent of one tab. (The colon in front of set means that set is an ex command; it is actually treated as an operator by vi that switches you into ex command mode. For more information, see the "ex Commands" section later in this chapter.)

Both the < and > commands require a target (a cursor movement command) to specify the amount of text to shift. The shift operations cannot operate on parts of a line, so the target you specify must be a line-oriented cursor motion such as j or k. The command >2j, for example, shifts three lines to the right: the current line (always implied), and the line to which 2j would move. If you specify a horizontal motion as *target*, the editor beeps at you and ignores the entire shift command.

The << command shifts just the current line left, and the >> command similarly shifts just the current line to the right. If you specify a repeat count, the editor takes it as the number of lines including the current line to shift.

The left shift commands < and << do not delete nonwhitespace characters at the front of the line. If the shiftwidth value causes nonwhitespace characters to be deleted on one or more lines, those lines are then shifted only by the amount of leading whitespace they each have, leaving the lines flush at the left margin. This means you can use left shifts without fear of losing text; it also means that you can't use left shifts to delete text at the front of the lines. To delete text, you have to use one of the delete commands or the ex substitute command.

The ~ command, like r, operates on only one character: the character under the cursor. If the character is a lowercase letter, it changes to uppercase; if it is an uppercase letter, it changes to lowercase. Nonalphabetic characters do not change. You can use a repeat count to invert the case of any number of adjacent characters on the same line.

Searching Text

Earlier sections introduced you to the primitive searching commands f, F, t, and T, all of which search for a single character in the current line. The editor also provides commands to search forward or backward in the file for any occurrence of a string or a string pattern. The commands for string and pattern searches are as follows:

/*text*/	Searches forward for the string or pattern
?*text*?	Searches backward for the string or pattern
n	Repeats the last / or ? command
N	Repeats the last / or ? command reversed

The / command initiates a search for a string or pattern, beginning at the current cursor position and proceeding forward toward the end of the file. The ? command searches from the character preceding the cursor toward the beginning of the file.

The string or pattern to be found is the sequence of characters between successive / or ? characters. For example, the command /help/ searches forward in the file for the next occurrence of the word help. You can omit the ending / or ?, in which case the search text extends through the end of the command.

To include a / character in the search text of a / command (or ? in a ? command), you must quote the character with a backslash. For example, /he/she is an invalid command, but /he\/she searches for the next occurrence of he/she in the file. The slash is not special in the ? command, and the question mark is not special in the / command; /? locates the next question mark, and ?/ locates the previous slash.

Because the backslash character (\) normally serves the quoting function in a search text, you must also quote the backslash if you want to include it in the search text. The command /a\\b searches for the next occurrence of a\b.

The editor option wrapscan determines what happens when the editor comes to the end of the file when searching for a text. If wrapscan is on, the search wraps to the top of the file and continues until reaching the point where the search started. For a backward search, reaching the top of the file causes the editor to continue searching backward from the end of the file until reaching the starting position. If wrapscan is off, the search stops at the end of the file (top of file for ?). You can set the wrapscan option on with the command :set wrapscan or :set ws (where ws is an abbreviation for wrapscan), and off with the command :set nowrapscan or :set nows.

When the editor cannot find a search text, the cursor does not move. If it finds the search text, however, the editor scrolls forward (or backward) to the screen of text containing the match, positions the line containing the text in the middle of the screen, and places the cursor over the first character of the search text in the line. If it finds the search text on the currently displayed screen, the cursor jumps to the text without scrolling.

The editor option magic profoundly effects string searches. If nomagic is set, the editor interprets literally the characters you write in the search text, except for the /, ?, and \ characters mentioned previously. If magic is set, however, the editor interprets the search text as a regular expression and searches for the pattern it describes.

A regular expression uses some characters as wildcards to indicate a group of strings that the editor should treat equally. When you search for a pattern using a regular expression, any string that matches the pattern stops the search. The special characters you use to form a regular expression are as follows:

.	Matches any character
*	Repeats any number of the preceding *re*
^	Matches the beginning of the line
$	Matches the end of the line
[abc]	Matches the character *a*, *b*, or *c*
[b-e]	Matches any character in the range *b–e*
[^b-e]	Matches any character not in the range *b–e*

When the magic option is set, you must quote any of the characters ., *, ^, $, [, or] with a backslash to use them as part of the search text. Unquoted, they have a special meaning. For example, the search pattern /*\/ searches forward for the next occurrence of */ in the file.

The . symbol matches any character. The search text /t.e matches the, but also matches tie, tje, txe, tHe, and t´e. Incidentally, /t.e also matches the string t.e because the period certainly fits the description "any character." For this reason, people unfamiliar with regular expressions are often confused by the vi search commands, noting that sometimes the command works and other times it does not.

You must use the * symbol in conjunction with some other character or regular expression; it means "any number of occurrences of." For example, the pattern .* means "any sequence of characters," a* means "any number of *a*'s," and ** means "any number of asterisks." An asterisk at the beginning of a search pattern is taken as a literal asterisk, because it has no preceding character on which to operate. Thus, /* locates the next asterisk, but /a* locates a string of as of any length. Notice that "any number" includes zero occurrences; the pattern /ab*c matches abc, abbc, abbbc, and also ac.

The ^ character matches the start of the line, which is distinct from the first character of the line. The pattern /^a only finds the letter a when it occurs at the beginning of a line. A pattern such as /a^c makes no sense because no character can come before the start of the line.

The $ symbol matches the end of a line. The end of the line is distinct from the last character of the line. The pattern /hello$ searches for the word hello, but matches only when the word occurs at the end of the line. Search patterns such as /ab$c make no sense because no text can follow the end of a line.

A pair of brackets ([...]) is a regular expression to match one single character in the text. The contents of the brackets tell the editor which characters can satisfy the search. An expression of the form [xyz] matches the next x, y, or z occurring in the file. You can include the [character anywhere in the list, but to include] in the list of characters you must write] immediately after the opening bracket: []abc] searches for the next occurrence of any one of the four characters], a, b, or c.

For convenience, the editor recognizes the sequence b-e as meaning all the characters from b to e inclusive. Thus the search pattern /[a-z] searches for the next lowercase letter, /[A-Z] searches for the next uppercase letter, and /[a-zA-Z0-9] searches for the next alphanumeric character.

It is sometimes more convenient to specify the characters you want the search to ignore; the notation for this is [^...]. The pattern /[^a-z] means "to find any character that is not a lowercase letter," and /[^a-zA-Z] means "to find any character that is not a letter."

Any character other than these special symbols stands for itself. Thus the pattern /([a-z]*, searches for a lowercase word in a list enclosed in parentheses; the (and , symbols must exactly match the text.

You can combine these symbols in complex ways to define very generic searches. For example, the command /^[a-zA-Z_][a-zA-Z0-9_](searches a function definition at the beginning of a line; a line beginning with main(satisfies the search, as does a line beginning with Crash_and_Burn(.

To repeat a search, use the n command. The N command also repeats the previous search, but in the reverse direction.

Using Marks

It's probably natural to think of text editing as a process somewhat like paging through a book, where you begin at the front and work steadily toward the back.

In reality, because documents and program source files tend to contain many interrelated parts, editing can entail a lot of jumping around as you check a previous statement or change one part to agree with another.

The vi editor supports quick movements from one part of a file to another, and back, using *marks*. A mark is a lowercase letter you associate with a position in the file; you can think of it as a register containing a pointer to one character somewhere in the file. You can save a position in one of the 26 mark registers using the mark (m) command, and later jump back to the same position using the special movement commands ´ (apostrophe) and ` (backquote).

The complete list of commands associated with marking is as follows:

m*x*	Marks the current location with letter *x*
´*x*	Jumps to the line marked *x*
`*x*	Jumps to the character marked *x*
´´	Jumps back to start of line
``	Jumps back to character within line

To associate a mark with your current cursor location, press m followed by one of the 26 lowercase letters. The letter you select becomes associated with your current position in the file. To mark a spot somewhere else in the file, you first must move there using the paging, scrolling, and cursor movement commands, and then set the mark.

To move to a mark, press ` followed by the letter you used to mark the location. The ` command moves to the exact character in the line where you set the mark. The ´ command is similar, but always positions you to the first nonwhitespace character of the line containing the mark. With most keyboard arrangements it's easier to type the apostrophe than the backquote, so you'll probably want to use ´ most often.

For your convenience, the editor supports an automatic form of marking you can use to quickly return to your place after jumping elsewhere in the file. Any command that moves you to an arbitrary position in the file (as opposed to relative cursor movement such as the j command or the scrolling commands) saves your current position. Commands that perform automatic marking include the / and ? search commands, the G command, and the jump commands ´ and ` themselves. To return to your previous position after any of these commands, use ´´ or ``; the `` command returns you to the same line and character within the line, whereas the ´´ command returns you to the start of the line.

Using Buffers

Many editors provide commands to move and copy portions of text from one place to another in a file. Depending on the amount of text you want to manipulate, whether you want to move it or copy it, and where you want to put it, an editor could offer dozens of commands to meet your needs. The vi editor uses a different approach that enables you to achieve the effect of moving, copying, or duplicating text without making you remember a lot of commands.

The vi strategy provides you with a number of text *buffers*. A buffer is a storage area that you can identify by name and use as a place to store or retrieve text. There are 26 named buffers corresponding to the lowercase letters *a* through *z*. In addition, the editor uses nine special buffers identified by the digits *1* through *9* to save text you delete; you can retrieve text from the numbered buffers, but you can't specify a numbered buffer to receive text.

The following list describes the visual commands that support buffering:

"x	Selects buffer x
y target	Yanks text from cursor to target
[n] yy	Yanks one (n) line(s) of text
[n] Y	Yanks the current line (n lines)
p	Inserts buffer text below (after) cursor
P	Inserts buffer text above (before) cursor

You use the *yank* commands (y, yy, and Y) to copy text from your file into a buffer. Just as you do with the c (change) and d (delete) commands, you write a target after the y command to specify the amount of text to copy. The target can be any cursor movement command, enabling you to copy as little as one character or as much as the complete text of your file into the buffer.

The yy command selects the current line for yanking. If you specify a repeat count, that many lines are yanked. The count includes the current line. The Y command is an abbreviation for yy.

The *put* commands (p and P) are the mirror image of yank, copying text from a buffer into your file. The text remains in the buffer after the put, so you can copy the buffer's contents into your file any number of times. If the buffer contains only complete lines of text, then P and p store the text above or below the current line. If the buffer contains a fragment of a line, P and p store the text before or after the cursor in the current line. You cannot specify a repeat count with the put commands.

The " symbol followed by a single lowercase letter is a special flag to vi that designates a buffer. If you place it in front of any of the yank commands, it tells vi into which buffer you want to place the text; in front of the put commands, it tells vi from which buffer to retrieve text; and in front of a delete command, it tells vi where to save the deleted text.

When you specify a numbered buffer (for example, "1) with the put commands, you are retrieving one of the pieces of text that you previously deleted. Buffer 1 contains the most recent text you deleted, buffer 2 contains the text you deleted before that, and so on. Every time you delete text with the d, dd, D, x, or X commands, the deleted text is stored in buffer 1, the previous contents of buffer 1 move to buffer 2, and so on, as if the numbered buffers were a push-down stack.

If you don't supply a buffer specifier in front of the yank and put commands, they use a default buffer that is essentially the same as buffer 1. Each time you use the default buffer, yank discards its previous contents. If you yank some text into the default buffer and then delete some text, the text you yank is replaced with the deleted text. You need to be careful to use text in the default buffer as soon as possible to avoid losing it.

You can use the buffering commands to copy, move, and duplicate text. To copy text, use one of the yank commands to copy the text into a buffer, move to the location where you want to insert the text, and then use p or P to insert the text at the new location. To move text, just delete the text, move to the new location, and use put to insert the deleted text. To duplicate, yank text and then put it any number of times without moving.

A handy sequence of commands you might want to remember is the sequence xp. This sequence uses the default buffer to exchange the order of two characters. If you type the as teh, place the cursor over e and type the commands xp. x deletes the e, the cursor moves to the h, then p inserts the deleted e after the h.

The *mark* command is often helpful when copying or moving several lines of text. For example, you can mark the first line of the range, move to the last line, yank to the marked line, then move to another location and insert the text. The commands might look like this: ma5j"xy´amc"xp. (Because the end of a vi command is usually implicit, a series of visual commands looks like a long word when you write it out.) The first command (ma) marks the current line with a. The second command (5j) moves down five lines. The third command ("xy´a) copies six lines beginning with the current line and preceding upward to the line marked a into the buffer named x. The next command (mc) jumps to another file location marked c, which would have been marked earlier in the edit session. Finally, the command "xp inserts the contents of buffer x after the new cursor location at mark c.

The yank command is generally indifferent to whether you yank the text with a forward or backward cursor movement; the text is stored in the buffer in its proper order in either case. Because of this, you can mark a range of text at either its starting or ending position, and then move to the opposite end of the range and yank it or delete it without having to mark both ends. Of course, you can mark both ends if you wish. For example, if your cursor is currently at the first line of a range, the commands ma5jmb´ay´b mark the current line as a, move down five lines, mark that line with b, jump back to the top line (with the command ´a), and then yank the text through the line marked b. A quicker way to do the same thing using the default buffer is the command sequence ma5jy´a.

As is discussed later, in the section titled "Edit File," you can edit two or more files with the *edit* command (edit is an ex command). The contents of the named buffers remain unchanged when you switch between two files. This enables you to grab some text from one file, bring up another, and then insert the text into the second file with the p or P command. To use this feature, you need to yank or delete text into one of the 26 letter buffers; the default buffer is discarded when you edit a new file.

Filter Lines

The ! command filters one or more lines of text through a shell command. The command format is as follows:

! *target*	Filters lines from cursor to *target*
[*n*] !!	Filters current line (*n* lines)

You specify the lines to filter using a *target*—a cursor movement command specifying the last line of the range. You can only use full-line movements to specify the text processed by !; the command does not work on a portion of a line.

After you enter the ! command, the editor opens an input window on the last line of the screen into which you can type any shell command. The editor invokes the shell as a subprocess and passes your command to the shell. The lines in the range are made available to the command on standard input. The output of the command replaces the text from the current line through *target*.

The ! command can be very powerful, and also a little dangerous. If the shell command you invoke does not write anything to its standard output file, the lines you specify are deleted and replaced with nothing. But if you choose an appropriate UNIX command (one that processes the standard input file and writes its results to the standard output file), you can achieve some pretty dramatic results with just a few key strokes.

For example, if you are editing a data file with information arranged in columns, you can sort selected lines of the file without leaving the editor. The command !G invokes a filter on lines from the cursor through the end of the file; when the editor clears the last line of the screen, it displays the ! character as a prompt. You then type sort and press Enter to see the lines replaced in sorted sequence.

The command !! works like ! except that you specify the lines to edit using a repeat count; that number of lines including the current line are submitted to the shell command. If you specify no repeat count, only the current line is passed to the shell command.

Find Matching Bracket

The % command is one of the handiest of all commands to the C programmer. When you place the cursor over one of the (, {, or [characters in your file and type %, the cursor jumps ahead to the next matching closed bracket on the same nesting level. If the editor cannot find a matching bracket on the same nesting level, it sounds a beep to announce its failure; this probably indicates you mismatched brackets in the file. The editor searches all the way to the end of the file to find the matching bracket.

If you place the cursor on one of the), }, or] symbols and press %, the editor searches backward for the corresponding open bracket on the same nesting level. If you repeatedly press %, the cursor jumps back and forth between the two matching brackets.

Enter *ex* Command

The ex command mode provides a number of commands that have no equivalent in visual mode. To execute an ex command from within visual mode, you must first press :. The editor clears the last line of the screen, displays a : prompt character, and allows you to enter any ex command. The command executes when you press Enter.

While typing the ex command, you can use the input editing commands to correct your typing errors. Your kill character (set by the stty UNIX command) clears the line; ^W backspaces one word; and ^H backspaces one character. If you backspace over the : prompt, the editor abandons ex command mode and returns you to your former position in the file.

For more information about ex commands, see the "ex Commands" section later in this chapter.

Repeat Last Substitute Command

The ex command mode provides a *substitute* command (called s) you can use to replace strings throughout your file. For information about the substitute command, see the "ex Commands" section later in this chapter.

The & visual command enables you to repeat the previous substitute command without having to return to ex command mode. Notice, however, that any address range you specify with the command is ignored. The & command repeats the substitution one time on the current line.

Repeat Last Command

Use the . command to repeat the last visual command you executed that changed text. The . command does not repeat a cursor movement, paging, or scrolling command. You can perform any cursor movement, paging, or scrolling commands you wish without affecting the editor's memory of the last text-changing command.

@—Execute Macro

According to the conventional definition, a *macro* is a stored sequence of commands and operations that you can invoke with a short keystroke or command. The vi editor supports keystroke macros via the map command of ex, and named macros using the so command of ex. In visual mode, only the @ command provides macro capability.

The @ provides a convenient way to prepare a sequence of visual commands using the editor itself and to execute them. The idea is straightforward: type any command sequence you like as one or more lines of text; yank or delete the lines into one of the 26 letter buffers; then type @x, where *x* is the buffer letter to execute the commands. This technique does not support permanent macros, although if you are willing to devote several of your text buffers you can maintain and use multiple macros during an edit session.

You must type the command sequence exactly as you enter it in the vi edit mode. For example, press the Enter key only where you would press the Enter key during command input. This means that you cannot normally write one vi command per line, because commands are not normally separated by a return. If you do not want the command sequence to end with a return, you must store the command sequence in the buffer as a text fragment rather than as a line.

Executing a macro with the @ command does not affect the editor's notion of the last text-editing command. Therefore, pressing . does not repeat the macro or any of the commands in the macro.

As an example of a situation where you might want to use the @ command, suppose a file you are editing contains several calls to a function called parse, as in the following case:

```
if ((words = parse(line,white,table,12)) > 0)
```

If you later decide that the parse function does not need the fourth argument (12 in the above sample), you can create a macro to search for calls to parse and delete the fourth argument. First, add the following lines to your file:

```
/parse(
f,;;dt)0
```

When executed, these commands do the following:

- /parse(searches for the word parse followed by an open parenthesis, which should locate only calls to the function. As usual, you have to press the Enter key after the search text, so the macro starts a new line after the search command.

- The command f, skips forward to the next comma.

- The sequence ;; repeats the f command two more times. The cursor should then be positioned on the comma immediately in front of the fourth argument to the call.

- The command dt) deletes text from the comma up to but not including the next closed parenthesis.

- The command 0 moves the cursor to the beginning of the line. This is necessary because the macro ends with a Enter key operation, moving the cursor down one line. The 0 command leaves the cursor at the beginning of the next line, just in case the next line contains another call to the parse function.

Yank the text into buffer a with the command "adj. The lines are deleted from your file and stored into buffer a. The macro contains the following commands: /, f, ;, ;, d, and 0. It also contains two Enter key operations: one after the / command, and another after the 0 command. The first ends the / command; the second causes the cursor to move down to the next line after executing 0. The combination of 0 followed by Enter positions the cursor at the start of the next line after executing the macro.

To use the macro, type @a over and over again. Each time, your cursor should jump to the next parse function call.

You can use ex commands in a macro in the same manner you use them from visual mode: preface the command with : and end the command with a newline. You may sometimes need to embed special keys in your macro, such as the Enter key or the Escape key. To do so, use the ^v input editing command to "escape" the special key.

Writing macros can be confusing, because the vi editor normally behaves as if the newline character that ends each line of text does not exist. In writing macros, however, you must be aware of every keystroke in the macro, including the newline character at the end of each line. The newline character has the same effect as the j command, causing the cursor to move down one line in the same column. To avoid a newline character at the end of the macro, you must yank or delete the macro into a text buffer as a line fragment; if you yank or delete with line-oriented commands, the macro ends with a newline.

^G—Display File Info

Use the ^G command (hold down the Control key and press G) to display information about your file. The editor clears the bottom line of the screen and prints a line similar to this:

```
"chap12.txt" [Modified] line 212 of 429 --49%--
```

This information shows you the name of the file you are currently editing (chap12.txt), whether or not you need to save the file, which line your cursor is on (line 212), how many lines there are in the file (of 429), and what fraction of the file is in front of your cursor.

The bracketed notations can include [Not edited], meaning that you created a new file and that the file does not as yet exist on disk; and [Modified], meaning that you changed the file and probably should save it.

The idea behind the percentage figure is that you probably looked at the text in your file up to your current cursor location, but may not have seen lines beyond the bottom of the current screen. Interpreted that way, the percentage is that amount of the file that you have already looked at. Actually, the number is the result of dividing your current line number by the total number of lines in the file.

^L—Redraw the Screen

The ^L command, which you enter by holding down the Control key as you press the L key, blanks the screen and then rewrites it. The command is useful when some program other than vi writes to your screen, such as when the operator uses the wall command to send a warning message to all users.

You may sometimes find that the editor loses track of the screen contents and that commands don't seem to work right; moving the cursor right exposes text you hadn't seen before, or when inserting a line other text seems to appear in its place. This kind of confusion usually results when the editor has an incorrect impression of the number of lines on your display screen; either more or less than the physical size of the screen. You can check the editor's screen size with the command :set window; it displays a response such as window=23 on the bottom line. If your physical screen size is different, use the :set window=nn command to tell the editor your real screen size. Better yet, quit the editor, log out, and start over again. Continuing to work with the editor when it has a mistaken impression of your terminal's characteristics is dangerous and can result in corruption of any file you edit.

Q—Exit Visual Mode

The Q command exits from visual mode and puts you into the basic ex command mode. In ex command mode, the editor prompts you with the : character for each command. You cannot use visual commands in ex mode, but ex mode works with any kind of terminal.

To return to visual mode, type vi and press Enter when the editor prompts you with :. You can also issue the x command to save your work and exit, or the q command to discard any changes and exit. Once out of the editor, you can always start over by entering the vi command to invoke the editor in visual mode.

u and U—Undo

The u command restores text changed by your last edit to its original condition. Cursor movement, paging, and scrolling operations do not affect the undo buffer and cannot themselves be undone; however, the ′′ and `` commands provide a similar kind of facility to return to your current location in the file after a command that moves you elsewhere (see "Extended Cursor Movement Commands" earlier in this chapter).

If you use the u command twice in a row, the previous text change is removed and then restored. You can repeatedly press u to compare the before-and-after appearance of a text edit. (In effect, typing u after u undoes the undo!) A limitation of the undo command is that the editor does not provide an undo stack; you can only undo the last text edit. However, the editor can undo an edit operation of any size, even one that affects every line in your file. If, for example, you execute an s (ex-mode substitute) command on several hundred lines and do not like the result, you can undo the substitution, restoring every line changed to its original condition, with one u command.

You can use the U command to undo all changes to the current line of text, provided you did not move your cursor to another line after making the changes. The undo buffer for the U command clears every time you move to a new line. Pressing U multiple times has the same effect as pressing it once; that is, U does not undo U. However, pressing u after U does undo the U command, restoring the line to its edited form.

ZZ—Save and Exit

The ZZ command saves your edited file to disk and exits from the editor, returning you to the shell. The ZZ command is equivalent to the x command of ex mode. The ZZ command is the only way provided to exit from the editor using a visual command; to exit without saving changes you must use the q or q! command of ex mode.

ex Commands

When you invoke the editor using the ex shell command, or switch to ex mode from visual mode, you do not have access to the visual commands discussed earlier in this chapter. The ex commands are similar to those of the ed editor, but ex has more commands and provides more capability than the ed editor. The ex commands are accessible from visual mode by pressing the : key; the editor clears the last line of the screen, displays the ex prompt symbol (always :), and allows you to enter one ex command.

This section does not present all the ex commands; for a complete discussion you should refer to the documentation accompanying your version of the UNIX operating system. The commands this section discusses include all those that are useful from within visual mode, or that are commonly used in the preparation of editor profile scripts.

About Addresses

Many ex commands have an *address* in front of the command. The address is always optional. If you don't supply one, the command applies just to the current line. An address can select one line of the file, or can specify a range of lines in the form *address,address* to which the command applies. When you specify a range, the command executes its function on every line in the range.

The special symbol % is an abbreviation for the range specification 1,$ and is equivalent to it in every way.

An address can take one of the following forms:

nnn   A line number. The first line in the file is 1. In some contexts you can legally refer to line 0, which is never physically present but logically precedes the first line of the file. For example, the command 0a means to add new lines at the top of the file.

.   A dot refers to the current line. The command .d means to delete the current line, and is equivalent to just d.

$ A dollar sign matches the last line of the file. Often used in the form 1,$ meaning from the first through the last line, or .,$ meaning from the current through the last line.

+n   A relative line number. +1 means the line following the current line; +2 means the line after that.

-n   A relative line number. -1 means the line before the current line; -2 means the line before that.

/pat/   Pattern search. The line referenced is the first line found after the current line that contains a string of characters matching *pat*. For *pat*, enter any valid regular expression. (See the "Searching Text" section earlier in this chapter for a discussion of regular expressions.)

?pat?	Backward pattern search. The line referenced is the one closest to but physically preceding the current line that contains a string of characters matching *pat*. For *pat*, enter any valid regular expression. (See the "Searching Text" section earlier in this chapter for a discussion of regular expressions.)
x+n	Where *x* is any legal address and *n* is an integer, the line referenced is *n* lines after the line *x* references. In the form /pat/+3 it references the third line following the next line that matches *pat*.
x-n	Where *x* is any legal address and *n* is an integer, the line referenced is *n* lines before the line *x* references. Useful in forms such as $-1 to mean the line before the last line of the file.
´x	The line marked *x*. ex commands can reference marks set in visual mode. Use any lowercase letter for *x*.

Because you can modify ex commands with a line address or a range of line addresses, you can execute a command to modify many lines at once. For example, you can use the command .,+3s/this/that/ to change the word this to that in the current and next three lines. Similarly, the command ´a,´bw temp writes lines from mark a to mark b into a file named temp.

cd—Change Directory

```
cd path
```

Use the cd command to change the current directory to *path*. Changing the current directory affects all filename references you make in subsequent commands. The editor provides the cd command so you do not need to end your edit session to change the current directory. Notice, however, that when you leave the editor your current directory reverts to what it was when you invoked the editor.

The editor does not provide a pwd command, but you can use the ! command (discussed in the section titled "Execute") in the form !pwd to check what your current directory is.

d—Delete Lines

```
[address] d
```

Use the d command to delete one or more lines of text. If you do not specify *address*, the command deletes just the current line; otherwise it deletes the line or lines specified by *address*.

Because visual mode provides many ways to delete text, you most often use the ex delete command as an operand of the g (*global*) command. For example, the command .,$g/^$/d deletes all blank lines from the current through the last line of the file.

e—Edit File

```
e filename
e! [filename]
e#
e!#
```

Use the e command to edit another file. (Also see the n and rew commands later in this section.) If the file you are currently editing has been changed, the e command does not let you proceed until you save your current file (but see the following discussion of e!). The new file replaces the current file. If *filename* does not exist, you are given an empty buffer to edit, but the new file is not created on disk until you save the new file.

You can use any valid UNIX pathname as the operand of the e command. For example, e /usr/frank/src/new.c is just as valid as the command e new.c. A relative pathname such as ../win/main.c is interpreted in the customary UNIX fashion relative to the current directory, but notice that you can change the current directory with the ex-mode cd command.

Use e! to edit another file and abandon the current file. Any changes you made to the current file are lost. If you do not specify *filename*, the editor defaults to the current file. Thus, e! by itself means to reedit the current file after discarding any changes you made to it; you get to start over.

Use e# to return to the previous file you were editing. To use e# you must have previously executed (or attempted to execute) a command of the form e *filename*, switching from one file to another. The editor remembers the name and your location within the previous file so you can return to it with the short form e#. If you attempt to edit another file with the command e *filename* and the request is denied—for example, because you did not save your changes to the current file—the name of the file you tried to edit becomes known as #. You do not have to retype the filename; just save your changes and then type e# to reattempt the e *filename* command.

The e!# command combines the e! function with e# and results in abandoning the current file, discarding any changes you may have made and then editing the previous file.

f—File Identification

```
f [filename]
```

Use f with no operands to display information about the current file. The information displayed by this command and the visual ^G command are the same.

If you supply a valid file- or pathname as the operand of f, the specified name becomes the new name of the current file. If you later attempt to save the file with the w or x command, the editor tries to write the file with the new name. Only then may it discover that another file already exists with that name or, for a pathname, that the path is invalid.

If you want to store the current file under a new name but continue to edit it (and later save it) with its old name, see the "Write" section on the w command.

g—Global

[address] g/pattern/ [command]

Use the g (global) command to execute another command on selected lines of the file. The g command searches the lines specified by *address* for strings matching *pattern*, and executes *command* on those lines that contain a matching text. If you omit *address*, it defaults to the entire file (including lines above the current line).

For *pattern*, specify the string that identifies the lines you want to change. If the magic option is on, *pattern* may be a regular expression; otherwise the characters in *pattern* are interpreted literally. (See the "Searching Text" section earlier in this chapter and the "set Options" section later in this chapter for more information about the magic option.)

For *command* you may specify any ex command; visual commands are not allowed. Notice that using an *address* qualifier with the target command makes no sense, because the g command invokes the target command for each line satisfying the search.

The g command is most often used to selectively execute the d (delete) and s (substitute) commands.

n—Next File

---

n

If you listed more than one filename on the ex or vi command line, use n (next) to edit the next file in the list. If you made changes to the current file and not yet saved it, or if you have reached the end of the list, the n command fails; otherwise, the editor clears the screen, loads the new file, and positions you at the top in edit mode. (If you are working in ex mode, you see no changes, but your current line is reset to line 1 of the new file.)

q—Quit

```
q
q!
```

Use q (quit) to exit the editor without saving the current file. If you changed the file and haven't saved it yet, the editor warns you that the file has not been saved and refuses to execute the q command.

Use q! to force the editor to quit even though changes have not been saved. All the changes you made to the current file are lost.

If you listed multiple file names on the ex or vi command line when you invoked the editor, and have not yet edited all the files using the n command, the editor warns you that there are files you have not yet edited. If you repeat the q command, the editor quits anyway, as long as the current file is unmodified or saved. The q! command quits in any case.

r—Read

```
r [filename]
r!shell-command
```

Use the r (read) command to insert the complete text of another file following the current line. If you omit the *filename* operand, it defaults to the name of the current file, thus reading in the original unedited text of the file.

Use the r! form to read and insert the standard output of the shell command you give as *shell-command*. For example, the command r!date inserts a line similar to the following into your file: Mon Oct 5 15:12:31 EDT 1992.

rew—Rewind

```
rew
```

Use rew (rewind) to edit the first file in the list of files named on the ex or vi command line. You usually use the rew command after you step through all the files with n and decide you want to browse or edit the list of files again; it resets the editor's internal file pointer back to the first file.

s—Substitute

```
[address] s/pat/new/ [g[c]] [p]
```

Use the s (substitute) command to change occurrences of a text string to a replacement string.

If you specify an *address*, the command executes only on the line or range of lines satisfying the *address* criteria. Otherwise, the command executes on the current line.

For *pat*, specify the text string to replace. If the editor option magic is in force, *pat* is taken as a regular expression identifying a class of strings to replace; if nomagic is in force, the characters in *pat* are interpreted literally.

For *new*, specify the text to replace each occurrence of *pat* in the selected lines of the file. The *new* text is not interpreted as a regular expression, regardless of the magic option. Therefore, you can use characters special to regular expression notation without backslashing in the *new* string.

If you add a g to the end of the command, the command changes every occurrence of *pat* in the line. By default, the substitute command changes only the first occurrence of *pat* in the line.

If you add a c to the end of the command, you are prompted before each change. The prompt shows the text it will replace, and asks you whether you want to make the change. Reply **y** (yes) to make the change, or **n** (no) to skip the change. Regardless of whether you choose to make or skip the change, the command continues until it cannot find anymore occurrences of *pat* in the lines specified by *address*. You can abort the command at any time by pressing your interrupt key (usually ^C).

If you add a p to the end of the command, the editor prints each line changed by the substitute command.

If you do not add any option characters to the end of the command, you can omit the final / after the *new* character string; the end of the command line then delimits the replacement string.

The substitute command adds two special escape sequences you can use in *pat* to those normally permitted in regular expressions: \(and \). Text matching the regular expression enclosed in these special parentheses is saved internally in a buffer. You can use the saved text in the replacement expression by inserting the escape sequence *n*, where *n* corresponds to the first through ninth \(...\) groups in *pat*.

Suppose that you want to change strings of the form calc(*arg1*,*arg2*) in your file with the expression sqrt(*arg1*)+exp(*arg2*). The pattern contains two variable texts that you want to carry over into the replacement pattern. The substitute command to make this change is the following:

```
s/calc(\([^,]*\),\([^,)]*\))/sqrt(\1)+exp(\2)/
```

The pattern is calc(\([^,]*\),\([^,)]*\)). It contains two \(\) terms: the first is \([^,]*\) and the second is \([^,)]*\). The first saves any character string following calc(up to but not including a comma, because the regular expression [^,]* matches any string of characters except comma. The second saves any character string following the comma up to the next comma or closed parenthesis, because the expression [^,)]* matches any string of characters not containing a comma or right parenthesis.

The replacement text uses \1 to refer to the first buffered text in the search pattern, and \2 to refer to the second buffered text in the search pattern. If your file contains the two lines

```
result = calc(sum,*date);
if (calc(new->begin,tmp->last) > 3)
```

executing the substitute command on each produces the following lines:

```
result = sqrt(sum)+exp(*date);
if (sqrt(new->begin)+exp(tmp->last) > 3)
```

If your file contains a great many calls to the calc function and they all need to change, the substitute pattern performs the change much more quickly than hand editing. For only one or two such changes, it is probably quicker to make the changes by hand than to spend the time figuring out the complicated substitute command.

set—Set Options

```
set
set all
set option
set option=value
set nooption
```

Use the set command to display or change editor options. In either ex or visual mode you can abbreviate set to se. For historical reasons the editor provides a two-character abbreviation for all ex command names.

Entered with no operands, the set command displays the options in force that differ from the default setting; the listing usually fits on one line at the bottom of the screen. The command set all displays the settings of all options. A full option listing is so long that, even though the options are listed in a multicolumn format, the editor must scroll your file lines off the top of the screen to fit the option listing at the bottom. After viewing the options, press Enter to restore the screen.

Some editor options are binary switches; the option is either set or not set. For such options, set option sets the option on, and set nooption sets the option off. Other options require a value (usually a string or a number). To specify an option with a value, use the form *option=value*: for example, `shiftwidth=4` or `directory=/var/tmp`. If you write the option with no value, the editor displays the current value of the option.

You can write any number of options on the same line: for example, `set ai aw ts=4 sw=4 nosm`.

The editor options are listed below. Notice that most options have a two-character abbreviation you can use instead of the long option name.

autoindent (ai)
This option causes the editor to automatically insert whitespace at the start of each new line to align the text with the start of the previous line. You can use the `^D` and `0^D` commands to delete some or all of the automatic whitespace. The default is `noautoindent`.

autoprint (ap)
Use `autoprint` when you want the substitute command to automatically display lines it changes. When you use a substitute to change a range of lines, the command displays only the last line changed. The `autoprint` option is ignored in visual mode because text lines are always displayed. The default is `autoprint`.

autowrite (aw)
The `autowrite` option enables you to use the n command to edit the next file without first saving the current file. If current file has been changed, it is automatically saved before bringing in the next file. The default is `noautowrite`.

directory=*path* (dir)
The `directory` option specifies the directory the editor should use for temporary files. The editor often stores large text chunks in temporary files, such as the text it needs to restore for an `undo` command. If you change this option, the new value does not become effective until you edit another file. The default is `directory=/tmp`.

exrc (ex)
When specified in the `EXINIT` string or the .exrc file of your home directory, the `exrc` option tells the editor to search your current directory for an override .exrc file. Setting this option after you start your ex or vi session is too late to affect editor initialization. The default is `noexrc`.

ignorecase (ic)

Use ignorecase when you want the editor to ignore upper- and lowercase distinctions in searches such as with the /, ?, and s commands. The default is noignorecase.

list

When option list is set, the editor displays nonprintable characters in "caret" notation—a tab prints as ^I, an ASCII 03 as ^C, and an end-of-line mark with $. Setting this option enables you to visually distinguish spaces from tabs and to scan for invisible control codes in your text. Set nolist to return the display to normal. The default is nolist.

magic

Set magic if you want to write regular expressions in the pattern string of the substitute command and in the / and ? visual commands. Set nomagic if you don't know how to use regular expressions and want the editor to interpret your search commands literally. The default is magic.

modelines

If the modelines option is set, the editor checks the first five and last five lines of a file when bringing it into memory. If any of these lines contain a string in the form vi:command: or ex:command:, the editor executes the indicated command before displaying the file. The modelines option is normally specified in the EXINIT string or the .exrc file. If you use the modelines option, you must arrange for the editor commands to be transparent to the program using the file. For example, in a C source program you can enclose the vi:command: text in comments. The default is nomodelines.

number (nu)

Use set number when you want a line number displayed in front of each line of your file; set nonumber turns off the display of line numbers. The line numbers are not part of your file and are not stored with the text when you save the file. You cannot edit the numbers; they are updated automatically as you insert and delete lines. The default is nonumber.

novice

Specify the novice option in the EXINIT string or the .exrc file if you want the editor to use option defaults appropriate to beginning users. The novice option forces the options report=1, nomagic, and showmode. The default is `nonovice` except when you invoke the editor with the `edit` command, an alias of the `vi` command.

optimize (opt)

Specify `optimize` when your terminal supports the insert-line and delete-line functions; the editor then uses these terminal functions to minimize the amount of I/O to the terminal. Usually the editor can correctly infer this option from the `terminfo` description of your terminal; you should specify `optimize` or `nooptimize` only when you experience difficulties with the default setting.

paragraphs=*string* (para)

The `paragraphs` option defines format control words that start paragraphs in a document file you are editing. The editor recognizes a format control word as two characters preceded by a period at the start of a line. The editor uses *string* to support the } and { cursor movement commands when editing a document containing `nroff` or `troff` formatting control words. The default value of `paragraphs` defines commands from the `ms` and `me` formatting packages.

prompt

Use the `noprompt` option to suppress the : prompt in `ex` command mode; suppressing the prompt provides an editing environment more like that of the `ed` command. The `noprompt` option is ignored when in visual mode. The default is `prompt`.

readonly (ro)

Use the `readonly` option to prevent the w and x commands from overwriting an existing file. The option does not prevent you from editing the file, only from saving the edited version over the original file; you can still save the edited version by using the w command to write to a new filename. If you want to save a file you edited and find that you cannot because the `readonly` option is set, you can always turn the option off with `set noreadonly` and then repeat the w or x command. The default is `noreadonly` except when you edit a file for which you do not have write permission, or when you invoke the editor with the `view` command, an alias of the `vi` command.

redraw

Use the `redraw` option when you are working with a dumb terminal; that is, a terminal with minimal capabilities. The editor redraws the screen

Programming for UNIX

when this option is set rather than using terminal editing functions. Normally you need to concern yourself with this option only when the editor does not seem to use your terminal properly. The default is terminal-dependent.

`report=n`

Normally the editor emits an informational message on the bottom line of your screen when you yank, put, delete, or read text into your file. If the number of lines affected is less than that specified by the `report` option, the editor omits the report. Novices like to have a low report value so that they can visually confirm the number of lines that appeared or disappeared from the screen; more experienced users prefer a large report value to keep the screen clear of extraneous messages. The default is `report=5`.

`scroll=n`

The value of `scroll` tells the editor how many lines to scroll up or down for a ^F (half-screen forward) or ^U (half-screen backward) command. Because you can change the number of lines scrolled by using a repeat count in front of the ^F and ^U commands, this option is really useful only in writing an EXINIT initialization string or an .exrc file. The default is one-half the value of the `window` option.

`sections=string`

The `sections` option, like the `paragraphs` option, specifies format control words that define document boundaries. The `string` specifies one- and two-character letter sequences corresponding to the control words appearing in your document file. For a one-character control word, specify two characters, the second of which is a blank. You must mark the end of `string` by a newline or colon. The default specifies control words used by the `ms` and `me` formatting packages.

`shell=command`

Specify for `command` the shell command the editor should use to invoke your preferred shell. The default value is taken from the SHELL environment variable.

`shiftwidth=n` (`sw`)

The value of `shiftwidth` specifies the number of characters left or right to shift a line when you use one of the shift commands >, <, >>, or <<. The

340

default is `shiftwidth=8`. If the value of `shiftwidth` differs from the value of `tabstop` the shift is composed by inserting or deleting a combination of blanks and tab characters.

showmatch (sm)

If `showmatch` is set, the editor momentarily flashes the cursor back to the matching (or { when you type) or } in input mode, enabling you to visually verify whether you inserted the correct number of brackets to close an expression. The default is `noshowmatch`.

showmode (smd)

Use `showmode` when you want the editor to display an indicator at the bottom right of your screen when you are in input or replace mode. When no indicator displays, you are in edit mode. The default is `noshowmode`, except when the `novice` option is set or the editor is invoked with the `edit` command, an alias for the `vi` command.

slowopen (slow)

Use the `slowopen` option to suppress screen updating while you are typing in input mode. The `slowopen` function is helpful on some primitive terminals in preventing garbage displays and distracting cursor motions, but undesirable otherwise. The default is `noslowopen`.

tabstop=n (ts)

Use the `tabstop` option to specify the amount of whitespace the editor should display for each occurrence of a tab character in your text. Changing the value of `tabstop` shrinks or expands the displayed width of your text, but does not affect the number of tabs or blanks present in your file or its appearance when printed with the `cat`, `pr`, or other UNIX commands. The default is `tabstop=8`.

window=n

The value of `window` specifies the number of lines the editor uses on your screen. A low value yields faster screen updates when using a remote terminal connection over a slow communication line. The default value is taken from the *terminfo* entry for your terminal type.

wrapscan (ws)

Set `wrapscan` if you want the editor to continue a text search beyond the end of the file. The `wrapscan` option enables you to locate a string in front of your cursor with a forward search, or following your cursor with a backward search. The default is `wrapscan`.

`wrapmargin=`*n* (`wm`)

Specify a nonzero `wrapmargin` value if you want the editor to automatically terminate the current line and start a new one when you reach the end of the screen line. The editor breaks the line at the whitespace following the last word that fits, which may mean that it needs to erase the partial word you've typed and move it to a new line before you can continue typing. The `wrapmargin` option makes it easier for you to input a long text because you do not need to break the text yourself; you can just keep typing. If the `wrapmargin` value is zero, the editor does not break a line automatically; the line extends indefinitely until you press the Enter key. The default is `wrapmargin=0`.

sh—Shell

```
sh
```

Use the `sh` command to temporarily exit from the editor and return to the shell. While in the shell, you can execute any UNIX commands you like. To return to your interrupted editor session, exit from the shell by typing `^D` (Control-D) or use the `exit` shell command. When you return to the editor, it automatically redisplays the screen of text you were editing.

The editor does not actually exit when you issue the `sh` command; rather, it invokes the shell as a subprocess. If while in the subshell environment you log off or cause a severe error that terminates all processes up to your login shell, you lose any file changes you may have made, so it's a good idea to save your file before using the `sh` command. The editor does not save your file automatically before invoking the shell.

If you forget that you have an edit session running, you might invoke the editor again with another `ex` or `vi` command. The second-level editor session starts up with no special indication that you already have an editor session in progress, but if you attempt to edit the file you were working on, you get the original copy of the file, not the version still being edited. If you have any suspicion that you might be working in a subshell, and that you might already have an editor session running, you can issue the ps UNIX command to list your active processes; a quick glance should confirm whether or not the vi or ex command is among the programs you are currently running.

w—Write

```
[address] w [filename]
[address] w! [filename]
[address] w>> [filename]
```

Use the w (*write*) command to copy the editor's buffer to a disk file. If you omit *filename*, it defaults to the current file. You can specify a fully qualified or relative path in place of *filename*. The write proceeds only if no file already exists with the specified *filename*, or if you are writing the entire editor buffer and omitted the *filename* operand. The data written by the w command replaces the entire contents of the disk file.

The w! command writes to the file designated as *filename* even if the file already exists, unless you don't have write permission for the file. The data written replaces the entire contents of the file.

Use w>> to append lines to the disk file. If the file you name does not already exist, the command fails; otherwise, the selected lines are written at the end of the file after any data it previously contained.

Use *address* to write only selected lines to the file. If you omit the *address* specification, the editor writes the entire current buffer. Here are some typical examples of using the *address* qualifier to write only selected lines:

.w temp writes only the current line to file temp. After execution, the file temp contains just one line. If a file named temp already exists, the command fails and the original contents of temp remain undisturbed.

.,$w!out writes lines from the current line through the end of the file into a disk file called out. If the file already exists, the lines replace its contents.

`.,+4w>>work` writes five lines beginning with the current line to the end of an existing file named `work`.

x—Save and Exit

```
x
```

Use the x command to save the current file and exit from the editor. The x command fails if you made any changes and the current file is unwritable: for example, because you do not have write permission for the file or the `readonly` option is set.

If the command `set` with no operands shows that the `readonly` option is set, you can save the file by first setting the option off with the command `set noreadonly`. If `noreadonly` is already in effect, you probably do not have write permission for the file you edited; use the `w` *filename* command to write your edited text to a new filename.

!—Execute

```
[address] ! command
```

Use the `!` command without an address qualifier to execute one shell command without leaving the editor environment. If you specify an *address* qualifier, the designated lines are passed to the shell command as its standard input file, deleted, and replaced by the standard output of the command.

Without an *address* specifier, the `!` command provides a convenient way to execute one shell command without having to first exit from the editor or interrupt the edit session with the `sh` command. The output from the command, if any, scrolls up from the bottom of your screen, replacing the editor's text display. When the command finishes, the editor prompts you to press the Enter key, thus giving you time to study the command's output. Press Enter to redisplay the editor screen.

If you provide an *address* specifier, the editor invokes the command using redirections, passing the addressed lines to the command on its standard input file and replacing the lines with the command's output. This is equivalent to the ! command of visual mode.

The ex-mode ! command is distinct from the visual ! command in that the visual command always replaces text with the output of the command, whereas the ex-mode command offers two modes of operation depending on whether you provide an *address* value.

You can use the ex-mode r! command to insert the output of a command into your file without replacing any lines.

ab, *unab*—Abbreviations

```
ab
ab abbreviation text
unab abbreviation
```

The abbreviation command ab provides the ability to define one or more abbreviations for long text strings. As you enter new text in input mode, the editor monitors the added text character by character. If at any time the character you enter completes an abbreviation previously defined with the ab command, the editor replaces the entire abbreviation string with the full text of the abbreviation. This function occurs during input mode without any special action on your part other than previously defining the abbreviations.

Use the ab command with no operands to display a list of the currently defined abbreviations.

The unab command removes an abbreviation from the list of defined abbreviations. You must specify the name of the abbreviation to remove.

To define a new abbreviation, enter the ab command and specify the one-word abbreviation as its first operand. The replacement text corresponding to the abbreviation, which must follow on the same command, can contain any number of words. You must separate the abbreviation from the text by at least one space.

The abbreviation facility is active any time you are in input or replace mode, regardless of what command you use to enter the mode. Be aware that characters you type when replacing a word (for example, using the visual command cw) are checked for abbreviations; the abbreviation facility is not limited to full-line input.

The abbreviation facility works only with new text you type. If you later define an abbreviation and the abbreviation already occurs in the file, the existing instances are not replaced. In such a case, you must use the substitute (s) command to replace the abbreviation strings.

map, unmap—Key Mapping

```
map
map string command-list
unmap string
```

Use the map command to define a series of editor commands to execute when you press a terminal key. You identify the terminal key by writing as *string* the sequence of character codes the terminal generates when the key is struck. For *command-list* you can write an arbitrarily long series of visual-mode editor commands; the Enter key terminates the command list if you enter the map command interactively. In an EXINIT string or .exrc file, the newline or : character terminates the command list. To enter special keys such as the Enter key in the command list, you can use the ^v escape key in front of it to prevent the editor from acting on the key.

You can use the special code #n as the *string* operand to refer to one of your terminal's function keys. For a PC-style keyboard, reference the F1 key as #1 in the map command.

Suppose your terminal generates the ASCII DEL code for the Backspace key. The editor does not recognize the key as a backspace command because it generates the wrong character. You can correct this by mapping your key to the ASCII backspace character with the following command:

```
map ^v<key> ^v^h
```

In this example, you press Control-v before pressing your Backspace key (represented by the notation <key>). For the command-list part of the map command, you press Control-v again followed by the Control-h key combination. This tells the editor to treat whatever code your Backspace key generates as the ASCII backspace character. (Notice from the "Extended Cursor Movement Commands" section earlier in this chapter that ^h is one of the cursor movement commands meaning backspace one character.)

Because there are some ordinary keys the visual editor does not already use for commands, you can define some simple one-keystroke commands of your own. For example, the following defines a command for g that repeats the previous substitution command for all occurrences of the pattern text on the current line:

```
map g :sg^v<enter>
```

When you type this command, the ^v (Control-v) key tells the editor to treat the next keystroke as data; when you then press the Enter key, the editor adds the character code generated by the Enter key to the end of the command list. If you display the list of key mappings, you see your g command shown as :sg^M because ^M is the control code for the Enter key.

Editor Profiles

After you become accustomed to using the vi editor, you will probably develop a preference for certain option settings and keystroke mappings. To avoid repeatedly setting these options and defining key mappings every time you edit a file, the editor enables you to define a standard editor environment that sets up automatically when the editor starts.

When the editor begins, it first looks for an environment variable called EXINIT. If the variable is defined, its value is taken as a series of commands that the editor tries to execute. If the string contains several commands, each is separated from the next by a newline character.

The editor next looks for a file named .exrc in your home directory. If it finds such a file, it attempts to execute the commands contained within it. If either the EXINIT string or the .exrc file in your home directory set the exrc option, the editor next looks for another .exrc file in your current directory and executes the commands there.

The result of executing all these commands is cumulative; an option set in the EXINIT string remains set unless overridden by a command in one of the .exrc files. Similarly, the .exrc file in your home directory should specify only the options you always want to use; you can override specific options for special cases by adding an .exrc file in other directories.

The commands you most often use in EXINIT strings and .exrc files are the set and map commands. You do not write a colon in front of these commands; the editor expects them to be ex-mode commands and, unlike visual mode, does not need the : command to tell it to switch to ex mode.

Editor Features

The discussion of editor options mentions several features of the editor. Careful study of the command-line options, settable options, and editor commands may not clearly reveal the intent and operation of these features, so I summarize them here.

Recovery Feature

When you invoke the editor and specify a filename to edit, the editor begins by reading the entire contents of the file into a portion of the computer's memory called an *edit buffer*. Using an edit buffer greatly increases the speed of the editor, but also entails some disadvantages. One of these is that the largest file you can edit is limited by the amount of available memory; to edit a larger file, you must split it into pieces and edit the pieces one at a time. Another disadvantage is that, if the editor is terminated unexpectedly, the entire contents of the edit buffer are lost and all your work since you last saved the file disappear with it.

To avoid such a catastrophe, the editor automatically maintains a copy of the edit buffer in a temporary disk file. If the editor completes its work normally, the editor discards the temporary disk file when it exits. If the editor terminates abruptly, however, such as happens on a system crash, your work is still available in the temporary disk file (if the system crash doesn't also corrupt the file system). To resume the interrupted edit session, invoke the editor with the `-r` option; the editor retrieves the temporary disk file instead of the original text file and reinitializes the edit buffer to its condition just prior to the system crash.

It is usually a good idea to save a restored edit buffer immediately, to avoid any possibility of losing your work. The recovery feature is not infallible, and there are conditions where you cannot recover your unsaved file changes.

If the editor successfully saves your changes before the system goes down, it also leaves a mail message for you noting that it saved a copy of your interrupted edit session; you receive the mail message when you log in next. If you see such a message, follow its instructions as soon as you can; the message tells you to recover the edited file using the `-r` option: for example, `vi -r new.c`.

Generally you should not rely too heavily on the editor's recovery feature; it is safer to periodically save your edited file with the `w` command. That way, if the recovery feature fails to preserve your unsaved file changes, you don't need to re-create them later.

Encryption

Sometimes you may want to create text files that contain sensitive or private information—employee salary data is one kind of information that you don't usually wish to make publicly available. The UNIX operating system provides a number of ways to assist you in preventing unauthorized users from retrieving and viewing such files. For example, you can withdraw read permission for users other than yourself by issuing the command `chmod o-r filename`. However, there is always some user who can circumvent the permissions system and who is still able to view your private files; the system administrator is a prime example—although trusted with management of the UNIX computer system, the system administrator may still not be authorized to inspect employee payroll data.

The vi editor can assist you in some situations by keeping your private text files in an encrypted form while on disk. You can still edit the files, and when you view an encrypted file with the editor you can read it just like any other file. However, if you attempt to display the disk file with any other program, the file appears to contain random binary data that is not only unreadable but even dangerous to display; the random binary codes in the file can render many terminals inoperative until the terminal is reset by turning it off and back on.

The editor enables you to create a new file in encrypted form from the start, or convert an existing text file to encrypted form. You can also remove data encryption from a file so it is once again stored in normal text form.

Normally you use the -x command-line option to create or edit encrypted files. When you specify the -x option on the command line, the editor inspects the file before bringing it into memory. If the file does not exist, the editor clears the edit buffer and makes a note that the file should be written in encrypted form when you save it. If the file does exist, the editor inspects it and tries to guess whether the file is in normal or encrypted form. If normal, the editor reads the file into the edit buffer and once again notes that the file should be written out in encrypted form. If the file appears to have been previously stored in encrypted form, the editor attempts to decrypt the file as it reads the file into memory. Because the editor can make a mistake, confusing a normal for an encrypted file or vice versa, the -x option is losing favor to other methods.

The -C command-line option works much like the -x option, except that when you specify -C, the editor always attempts to decrypt the file as it is read into memory. Because the editor doesn't guess whether or not the file is encrypted, no mistake can occur; it then becomes your responsibility to specify the -C command-line option when the file to edit is in encrypted form, and to omit the option otherwise.

Once you retrieve a file with the editor and have it up on your screen, the x and C commands control the encrypted status of the file. When you enter either of these commands, the editor prompts you with the message Enter key: and waits for you to enter an encryption password. If you type an acceptable password, the status of your file changes to encrypted; the next time you save the file it is written to disk in encrypted form. If you enter nothing, the file status is set to normal, and the file is written in plain text when you save it next.

If you attempt to edit an encrypted file without specifying the -x or -C command-line options, you are unable to read or edit the file. If you specify either of these command-line options, you are prompted for the password you set with the X command for the file; if you enter the wrong password, you are still unable to read or edit the file. If you forget the password for an encrypted file, you lose the file. The risk increases in proportion to the number of encrypted files you have.

Summary

The vi editor is not a simple text editor by any means; its power and flexibility is rivaled only by a few commercial text editors. Yet vi is the "standard" UNIX text editor, available on virtually every UNIX system in the world. Its universal usage is one of the reasons for its importance. Every UNIX programmer should have at least a minimal working knowledge of the vi editor.

The vi editor is a full-screen video terminal application and cannot be used with Teletype-style terminals. An alternative form of the editor, called ex, supports Teletype-style terminals, but does not provide the visual context of a full-screen display and does not support the "visual" commands of the vi editor. The vi editor uses three modes to distinguish the meaning of keyboard input. In edit mode, all characters typed represent editing commands; these commands move the cursor, scroll the display up or down, change and delete text, and load and save files. In input mode, all characters typed represent text data and insert the corresponding character into the current file; you have to use the Escape key to terminate input mode when you want to enter an editing command. In ex command mode, the cursor is confined to the bottom line of the screen, and the text you type is interpreted as an ex command. You enter the ex command mode from edit mode by typing a colon, and you return to edit mode by pressing Enter, which also executes the ex command.

You can create editor profiles (files named *.exrc*) in your home directory and in other working directories to set up the editor options and definitions you normally prefer. An editor profile consists of a series of ex commands, usually set and map. The editor reads and executes the commands in a profile every time you start the editor.

The vi editor offers an automatic recovery feature. The editor stores your file changes in a temporary disk file during your edit session. If the system crashes unexpectedly, vi can usually restart your editing session from the interrupted point using the contents of the temporary disk file. The vi editor does not have an autosave feature; its recovery feature is less intrusive than autosave and successful most of the time.

The vi editor is designed specifically for the experienced user. Its many features save time and keystrokes for those who know the editor well. As a result, the editor makes few concessions to the beginning user. Its unfamiliarly structured commands and working modes are sometimes confusing and intimidating to the beginner; many decide never to use it again after their first frustrated attempts. Patience and diligent study are the two virtues any user must have to become proficient with vi. The benefits you can gain are an ease and facility of text editing that you have to experience to believe.

Compiling Programs with *cc*

In this chapter, you encounter the *C Compilation System,* the principal tool by which you convert C language source code into executable binary files. You learn how to use the cc command, and how to install your compiled programs for execution.

You may wonder what I mean by a compilation *system,* if your previous experience is with the more traditional computer languages. Isn't *system* a little pretentious for something that's just a compiler—another computer program after all? In fact, the cc command, which is the most important command in the compiler set and the only one you're likely to use directly, is not a compiler at all.

The tools in the C compilation system include, at a minimum, a preprocessor, a compiler front-end, an optimizer, an assembler, and a link editor. Which tools you need to run depends on the kind of output you need from the system. The cc command selects the proper tools for the options and files you specify, executes the tools, and coordinates the data flow between them.

Command Syntax

The cc command invokes the C preprocessor, the compiler, the assembler, and the linkage editor. It invokes them in the proper order, repeatedly if necessary, to process the C source files, assembler source files, and object files you name on the command line. You use command-line options to control the type and extent of processing, and to tell the individual tools what kind of handling you require.

You can specify C source files, assembler source files, object files, and object libraries on the cc command line. The cc command identifies the type of a file by the suffix appended to its name. It assumes that files ending in .c are C source files, that files ending in .s are assembler source files, and that files ending in .o are object files. It presumes a file ending in .a is an object library, and it searches the libraries at the proper time for functions that your code calls but does not define.

By using appropriate options, you can stop the processing after the preprocessor step, or after the compile and assembly steps. In the former case, you receive the preprocessor output and can inspect it to see whether the preprocessor generated intermediate source code is consistent with your expectations. If you stop processing after the compile and assembly steps, you receive relocatable object files that you can later combine with other object files to generate an executable file.

With one execution of the cc command you can process any number of source and object files, and you can generate any number of object files. You can build only one executable file or shared library, however, with any single execution of the cc command.

If you execute the cc command with no arguments, it tells you the basic command syntax, as follows:

```
cc [ options ] files
```

The syntax is neither strange nor surprising, nor particularly helpful. To understand the capabilities of the cc command, you must delve into the specific options it supports. The following section lists these options.

The cc command supports many options. Some option letters differ only in case, such as the -g and -G options. As is usual with UNIX, case matters; you must type an option letter in the same case as it is shown.

Some options require a value following the option letter. In such cases you can write the value immediately after the option letter, or you can separate the option from its value with one or more blanks and tabs. You can never omit the value, however. If you do so, cc construes the next option or filename on the command line as the option value.

The cc command is unusual among UNIX commands in that you may intersperse filenames and options on the command line. In some cases you *must* specify an option after the filename it affects. A primary example is the -l*lib* option, which specifies an object library the link editor can search for undefined functions. You must specify the -l option after the names of the files that call functions in the library, because during the compilation process the link editor searches the library at the point where the -l option occurs on the command line.

Command-Line Options

Table 13.1 describes most of the command-line options you can use with cc. The options shown are those supported with System V Release 4 and compatible versions of UNIX. Older systems omit many of these options, and several popular UNIX systems support options not shown here. Consult the vendor's documentation for your system to find out which options are available.

Programming for UNIX

Table 13.1. cc command-line options.

Option	Meaning and Usage
-B	*Binding.* Specify -B static to copy library routines into your executable program. Specify -B dynamic to link your program with the dynamic runtime libraries. The static option makes your program larger, but permits your program to run in environments where the dynamic libraries are not available. The dynamic option makes your executable program much smaller because the program dynamically loads the library functions at execution time from a shared library. Shared libraries permit all active programs to use one copy of a function. The default is -B dynamic, and is usually the preferred option because it reduces both disk space requirements and system memory requirements. You can intersperse this option with filenames to switch between static and dynamic binding for selected object libraries. You may not specify this option unless you also specify or accept the default -dy option.
-C	*Comments.* If specified, the -C option prevents the preprocessor from stripping comments out of your source file. Normally, the preprocessor removes all comments from the text it passes to the compiler front-end. You would most likely use this option only when you are halting the compilation after the preprocessor step with the -E or -P option.
-c	*Compile only.* Supplying the -c option causes the compiler to generate object files from source, and then stop. The preprocessor, compiler, and assembler steps are performed normally, yielding an .o (object) file for each .c (C source) and .s (assembler source)

356

Option	Meaning and Usage
	file listed. Because it enables you to relink from object form after compiling only those source files that changed, compilation to object form is the method of choice for programs that contain many source files.
-D*name[=token]*	*Define.* Use the -D option to define symbols for the preprocessor. For *name*, specify the name of the symbol you want to define. For *token*, specify a numeric value or a simple word to assign as the value of the symbol. If you omit *token*, it defaults to 1. Notice that the compiler automatically defines some symbols for you, in particular the symbol unix to show that you are compiling your program in the UNIX environment.
-dc	*Dynamic.* Specify -dy to generate object and executable files that can dynamically bind library function calls at runtime. If you specify -dn, you cannot specify the -B option, and all functions and external references are resolved by binding the external object into your file. The default is -dy, which also implies -B dynamic unless and until you specify -B static explicitly on the command line.
-E	The -E option causes cc to halt the compilation after the preprocessor step and to write the preprocessor output to standard output. If you specify multiple .c files on the command line, the cc executes the preprocessor for all of them. When you want to execute the preprocessor on your source files to inspect the code it generates, use cc with the -E option instead of invoking the preprocessor directly. Some environments integrate the preprocessor with the other compiler tools.

continues

357

Table 13.1. continued

Option	Meaning and Usage
-G	*Generate.* The -G option directs the link editor to generate a dynamic shared library from your object modules. You can use this option only if you also specify or accept the default -dy option. Although you use a separate command (ar) to create a static object library, you use the cc command with the -G option to create a shared object library. You use the -o option to specify the filename of the shared object library.
-g	*Debug.* Specify the -g option when you want the compiler and link editor to include debugging information in your executable file. The compiler generates debugging information when it creates the .o module, and the link editor either keeps or strips it when it links your executable file. Thus, you need to specify the -g option when creating object files with the -c option, and when you link objects together.
-H	*Headers.* Use the -H option as a debugging or documentation aid. When specified, the preprocessor lists the names of all header files it includes, whether or not a nested #include directive caused the inclusion, and writes the listing to the standard error file.
-I *dir*	*Include directory.* Use the -I option to specify an additional directory where the preprocessor should look for include files. The preprocessor searches directories you name with the -I option before it searches the default directories. Any files in the directory override any files in the default directories with the same name. You can define more than one additional include directory by supplying multiple -I options on the cc command line. The preprocessor searches the directories in the order you list them on the command line.

Option	Meaning and Usage
-L *dir*	*Library directory.* Use the -L option to specify a directory where the link editor should look for object libraries. Object libraries are files named lib*name*.a or lib*name*.so, where *name* is the library name specified with the -l option. To define multiple directories, write the -L option for each directory the link editor searches. The options are cumulative and the link editor searches them in the order listed.

If your compilation needs to search only one specific library, you can list it explicitly as one of the files on the cc command. Such a command might look like this:

```
cc -g main.o tools.o parse.o /home/apps/libuser.a
```

Option	Meaning and Usage
-l *name*	*Library.* The -l option specifies an object library the link editor should search for functions your program calls but does not define. You do not need to specify the standard C library. The cc command always arranges for the link editor to search libc.a or libc.so after it processes all other files and libraries. For *name* you can specify one of the other libraries provided with UNIX such as -lm (the math library) or -lmalloc (extended malloc package), or any libraries in your -L directory.

The link editor forms the filename of the object library by prefixing *name* with lib and adding a suffix appropriate to the type of library, .a for static binding, .so for dynamic binding. Thus -lm searches the library libm.a or libm.so.

You must write the -l option *after* the files that reference objects in the library, because the link editor extracts objects from a library only to satisfy an unresolved reference. Thus the following command

```
cc -lm main.o sub1.o sub2.o
```

continues

359

Table 13.1. continued

Option	Meaning and Usage
	is wrong, whereas the following syntax assures that any reference to functions in the math library is properly resolved:

```
cc main.o sub1.o sub2.o -lm
```

If you know that sub2.o does not use any math functions, the following command also works:

```
cc main.o sub1.o -lm sub2.o
```

Option	Meaning and Usage
-O	*Optimize.* Optimize the generated machine code. The standard UNIX C compilation system does not provide alternative forms of optimization; the default form presumably strives to reduce the execution time of the generated program. Because UNIX programs execute in a virtual memory environment, program size is rarely a significant consideration.
-o *pathname*	*Output.* Use the -o option to supply a name for the executable file generated by the link editor step. If you specify the -c option, the -o option becomes superfluous because the link editor does not produce an executable file. For *pathname*, specify a simple filename, or a relative or absolute pathname. If you do not provide an -o option, the link editor names the executable file a.out by default.

If the file specified by *pathname* exists, the link editor writes the new executable program into the existing file. This ensures that any links defined for *pathname* are not broken.

If the file exists and is executing at the time the link editor needs to write its output, the link editor finds that the file is locked and is unable to write its output, which in turn causes the cc command to fail. Therefore, it can be difficult to relink a frequently

360

Option	Meaning and Usage
	used program. The safest way to do so is to rename the old program with the mv command (which can be done even while the program is executing) before executing the cc command.
-P	*Preprocess only*. The -P option causes cc to halt the compilation after the preprocessor step. The preprocessor writes its output to *filename*.i, where *filename* is the name of one of the C source files listed on the command line. The -P option serves the same purpose as the -E option, but is more appropriate when you list several .c files on the cc command line because -P stores the preprocessor output for each in a separate file.
-p	*Profiling*. Specify the -p option to generate an executable program with support for profiling. Each execution of the program creates or overwrites a file named mon.out in the current directory. Use the prof command to analyze and print the information in the mon.out file.
-Qc	Use -Qy to request the compiler and tools to include identifying information in the generated files, or -Qn to suppress the identification. The added information may be useful in problem determination by enabling you to track the date, time, and manner in which a file was generated. The default is -Qy.
-qc	With the System V Release 4 compiler system you have a choice of profiling methods. Specify -qp to include standard profiling in your executable program, or specify the equivalent -p option. Specify -ql (that's an *l* for *line*, not the digit *1*) to generate line-by-line profiling of your program. You must use the lprof command to analyze and format mon.out files generated by the -ql profiling feature.

continues

Table 13.1. continued

Option	Meaning and Usage
-S	*Source only.* The -S option forces the compiler system to halt processing for each .c file after generating the assembler source file and optimizing the assembler code if requested. For each *name*.c file you list on the command line, the cc command generates a corresponding *name*.s file containing assembler source statements. You can later assemble the .s files if you wish by executing the cc command again. (Notice that cc support for this option does not imply that the C compiler front-end always generates assembler source code, although most compiler systems for UNIX do.)
-U *name*	*Undefine.* Use the -U option to remove a previously specified or default preprocessor symbol. The -U option performs the inverse function of the -D option.
-V	*Version.* The -V option causes each of the compiler tools invoked by the cc command to issue an identification message. cc supports this option primarily for system support and maintenance to allow identification of the version of each tool in use.
-v	*Verbose.* Specify the -v option when you want the compiler to use stricter semantic checking. The -v option causes the compiler to detect many of the same errors and suspicious usages that lint diagnoses.
-W *p,args*	The W option provides a way to specify an option directly for one of the compiler tools invoked by cc. Many of the cc options are duplicates of those supported by the tools it calls. For example, the -o, -L and -l options are taken from the ld command line. For options the cc command does not support,

Option	Meaning and Usage
	you can specify the tool for which you want to specify an option, and the value of the option, with -W.

For *p*, specify the program to which the arguments should be passed, using one of the following codes:

p	preprocessor
0	compiler
2	optimizer
b	basic block analyzer
a	assembler
l	link editor

Use *args* to specify the option, including the initial hyphen. If you would normally write the option as two or more words, separate the words with a comma. For example, to pass the option -o filename to the assembler, write the -W option like this:

-Wa,-o,filename.

Option	Meaning and Usage
-Xc	For *c*, specify a code indicating the language level of the source. Compile programs written to the K&R syntax rules with option -Xt, which causes the compiler to generate code consistent with the older interpretation of the language, such as the promotion rules for integers. Compile programs conforming with the ANSI C standard with option -Xc, which uses the new ANSI standard interpretation. There is also an intermediate convention, invoked with -Xa, which applies the ANSI standard interpretation, but like -Xt, issues warnings where the interpretation of syntax differs between the K&R and ANSI language definitions.

The default is -Xt, meaning that by default, compiled programs behave in a manner consistent with the

continues

363

Table 13.1. continued

Option	Meaning and Usage
	older K&R definition of the language. ANSI constructions such as function prototyping, trigraphs, and the preprocessor # operator are understood and produce the expected result, but integer values are promoted according to the old rules.
	The __STDC__ macro symbol has the value 0 when option -Xt or -Xa is in effect, and 1 when you specify option -Xc.

About Shared Libraries

The preceding explanation of options refers to object code binding, static and dynamic linking, and shared libraries. These concepts are all part of the UNIX shared library support, with which you are probably unfamiliar. In this section I present an explanation of the shared library concept and explain some of its terminology.

Binding refers to how the compiler and link editor resolve library function calls and external data references. Binding is a task performed by the link editor when integrating separately compiled program code into a single executable file.

Static binding means that the compiler and link editor physically copy the object you reference (function or data) from a library into your executable file, increasing its bulk but providing fast, simple access to the object.

Dynamic binding means that the compiler and link editor identify external references and add information describing each external reference to your executable file, but do not retrieve the object. Instead, the operating system or runtime routines must retrieve the object during your program's execution. Dynamic binding provides greater flexibility and maintainability for your programs at the cost of increased execution time.

Relocatable is another technical term from compiler theory. It describes the characteristic of a program file that permits UNIX to load them into an arbitrary location in memory. UNIX executable programs are usually *absolute* binaries, which means that UNIX must load them at runtime into a memory location assigned by the link editor. Object files, on the other hand, are normally *relocatable* binary files because the link editor must be able to combine object files into an executable file in an order that it can't predict when it generates the object file.

The terms *binary* or *binary file,* in general, describe a file whose bytes are not limited to ASCII printable characters. When talking about programs, the term describes a program that has been converted from a source language (such as the C language) into a machine language. The binary file may be either relocatable, in which case it's called an *object* file, or absolute, in which case it's called an *executable* file.

The issue of binding has become important in recent years as program complexity grows. Traditionally, every executable program that calls the `printf` function contains a separate copy of the function as part of its executable file. That means that the system disk contains hundreds of copies of the `printf` function. It also means that if the computer is currently executing a dozen different programs, it probably also contains code for the `printf` function in memory a dozen times.

When library functions are small, the cost of all this redundancy is modest. As more system and application programs are developed for networking with tcp/ip and for the X Window System, however, the size of library functions has increased substantially and the cost of redundancy has grown unbearable. A typical X application program might consist of 20K or 30K of real application code, yet bulk to over 1M in size when the X library routines are linked with it. A library of one hundred X application programs would consume over 100 megabytes of disk space.

Shared libraries are an attempt to eliminate redundant library functions from executable program files, thus reducing both the disk space required to store the programs, and the amount of computer memory required to run the programs.

Every program compiled and linked with dynamic binding contains pointers to the shared library and to the code within the shared library that the program references. When you execute such a program, UNIX initially brings it into memory without the shared routines. Only when UNIX encounters an external reference during execution does the system locate the shared library and load the needed code into memory. If a copy of the shared library exists somewhere in memory, the program uses the copy that has already been loaded. UNIX deletes the shared library from memory when all programs using the library have terminated.

Support for shared libraries has added a considerable amount of complexity to the UNIX kernel and to the link editor. It also adds some amount of overhead to each dynamically linked application program and to the system as a whole. The cost of shared library support, however, is usually justifiable by the savings in disk space requirements and by the overall improvement in system performance that results from the reduced memory demand.

The C compilation system of System V Release 4 supports both static and dynamic binding, and implements dynamic binding as the default. All system-provided commands are linked with dynamic binding, reducing the disk space requirements for the operating system commands. The compiler libraries are provided in both a static and dynamic form so you can choose either binding method for your own program development. The cc command options are arranged to assume dynamic binding by default.

For your information, the static and dynamic libraries are provided in the /usr/lib and /usr/ccs/lib directories. If your system includes the X Window System, a shared library version of the X functions exists in /usr/X/lib. Static libraries have filenames ending in *.a*, while dynamic libraries have filenames ending in *.so*.

There are two main reasons for choosing static binding. The first is that dynamic binding adds somewhat to your program's runtime. You may be able to improve an unacceptable program performance by linking the program with static binding. Cases where the improvement is substantial, however, are unusual, and you should base a decision to use static binding on observation and measurement. The other reason is that you may need to execute your program on UNIX systems that do not support shared libraries. Programs compiled on one UNIX system are often executable on other slightly different versions of UNIX because of efforts by vendors in recent years to enhance compatibility and portability between each others' products.

Compiling Simple Programs

Many of the programs you'll write during your career will be simple little knock-offs, often 500 lines or less. Such programs, with only one source file and no header files or object libraries to consider, are very easy to compile. Sometimes you may even want to throw together a quick experimental program, just to try out something. The defaults for the cc command make experimental programs very easy to generate, and even a production program of the one-file variety is not much more difficult.

The simplest cc command you can write is this:

```
cc prog.c
```

This command invokes the preprocessor, compiles the preprocessed source, assembles the compiler output, and links the resulting object file. The cc command automatically deletes the object file after the link step because the -c option is not specified and only one source file is listed. With two or more source files, the cc command retains the intermediate object files for your convenience.

Because the command also omits the -o option, cc writes the executable file with the filename a.out. If you want to save the program for repeated execution, a.out is not a good name because the name doesn't suggest your program's function and because, being the default name, you could later become confused over which source a.out was built from. On the other hand, if prog.c is a short experimental program you'll run once or twice and then discard, a.out is a perfect name because it will remind you later to delete the file.

To execute your program, just type a.out. If the program works properly, either rename a.out to a more permanent name, or delete both prog.c and a.out if they are just part of an experimental program. If you discover errors in your program, you might want to use the sdb utility (the *symbolic deb*ugger) to locate the errors. Unfortunately, sdb doesn't support symbolic debugging for this program because the cc command does not specify the debugging option. In this case, you want to recompile your program with the following command:

```
cc -g prog.c
```

The -g option tells the compiler to generate debugging information in the object file, and tells the link editor to copy the debugging information into the executable file. The sdb utility (discussed in greater detail in Chapter 17, "sdb: The Symbolic Debugger") requires this debugging information to perform its function. Because your choice of debugging methods is restricted unless you compile with the -g option, you should specify the -g option for all compiles until you have fully debugged your program. To put the program into production, you want to compile it again without the -g option to reduce the size of the executable disk file; the debugging information can easily double or triple the size of the file .

If you dislike the executable filename a.out, or want to give the executable file a more meaningful name from the start, use the -o option to tell the link editor what to name the file. For example, you could compile the source file prog.c and name the executable file prog with the following command:

```
cc -g prog.c -o prog
```

Many programmers like to write the -o option at the end of the command, because, in part, to do so seems more consistent with the cc convention of listing things in the order the link editor should process them. You can list the option anywhere on the command line. The link editor, however, simply stores the option value until it's ready to write the executable file. Therefore you often see the command written like this:

```
cc -g -o prog prog.c
```

You can specify a pathname with the -o option instead of a filename. -o /home/bob/bin/prog is valid and causes the link editor to write the executable file directly into the /home/bob/bin directory, saving you the need to move the executable file there yourself with the mv command.

When you have debugged your program and want to store it for yourself or for others to use, you need to store the executable file in a directory readily accessible to its intended users. If you alone will use the program, the most reasonable place to store the file is in your own bin directory. If you store all programs and shell scripts that you write in the same directory, you can easily update your login profile (named $HOME/.profile in your home directory) to include the directory in your search path. For example, the shell statement PATH=/bin:/usr/bin:$HOME/bin causes the shell to search first the system directory named /bin, and then the system directory named /usr/bin, and finally your own program directory /home/bob/bin (assuming your home directory is named /home/bob) for command names.

You should also normally recompile the program without the -g option (to strip out the debugging information), but with the -O option to optimize the generated machine code for fastest runtime performance. Thus, a program you began testing with the command cc prog.c is finally put into production status by compiling it with the command

```
cc -O -o $HOME/bin/prog prog.c
```

Compiling with Multiple Source Files

Important application systems are often large and complex. In theory, even a very large and very complicated program can be written in one source file, but who would want to deal with a program containing 150,000 lines of code? Such a source file might be too large for your favorite editor to read into memory. It would certainly take a long time to compile, and most people would be unable or unwilling to undertake a maintenance or enhancement project on such a formidable piece of source code.

To deal with very large programs, the technique of *modularization*, or breaking the program into many smaller pieces called modules, was developed. The "divide and conquer" approach has many advantages, not the least of which is that it enables several people to work on the program at once. When the system enters the maintenance stage of its existence, modular programs make it possible for several people to learn a part of the program so that no individual needs to be familiar with all the details of the entire program.

The C compilation system supports modular programming by doing the following:

- Supporting the separate compilation of source files that can then be integrated with a link editor

- Allowing functions used by two or more programs to be collected into an object library, eliminating the need to explicitly list every external function on the cc command line

369

● Supporting header files, which you can use as a common repository for definitions used by two or more source files

The compiler and link editor, as supported by the cc command, facilitate the organization of source and object materials into directories that further clarify the relationship between the parts of an application system.

Suppose you plan to build a new text editing system for the X windowing environment, and that your system will consist of two main programs: xb for browsing text and xe for editing text. Both will use scroll bars, pull-down menus, mouse buttons, and similar on-screen objects, as well as the text window itself. In addition, the xe utility will need many functions for manipulating text using the mouse and keyboard control keys. Because you expect the programs to be rather large, and to share some routines, you decide to use a modular approach in building the programs.

Because the browser and the editor will both need to maintain some internal control structures such as a text buffer, it makes sense to describe the main control structures in a header file, thus ensuring that all source files that reference a structure will use identical descriptions of the structure.

It is also evident that, although the editor will need many more routines than the browser, they will nevertheless share some routines in common, such as those for drawing and manipulating the scroll bar. You decide to put common routines in an object library.

To begin the code development process, the first step is to create a top-level directory that will contain the entire product. You create a special directory called /usr/src/edit that is not associated with any one programmer on the project.

The top-level directory will be partitioned into the following subdirectories:

● bin, a directory to contain executable programs both for the product itself and for any special utilities or shell scripts used in support of the project

● include, containing all the header files (files ending in .h)

● lib, to contain the source files (.c) for common modules, the object files generated from source (.o), and the object library itself (.a)

● xb, containing the source files unique to the browser program

● xe, containing the source files unique to the edit program

With this directory structure, you may choose to update the object library or any member of it, to build the xb program, or to build the xe program.

To rebuild the object library from scratch, use the following commands. (Your system would use different filenames; the names I use here are invented for this example.)

```
cd /usr/src/edit/lib   # enter the development area
cc -g -c -I../include *.c    # compile all source files
ar rv libxe.a *.o       # create object library
```

Notice that the procedure is straightforward. Depending on your current directory, there are several forms of the cd command that may switch you into the /usr/src/edit directory; the cd command shown works regardless of your current directory. The cc command compiles all source files into object form, using the shell wildcard filename *.c to name all source files on the cc command line. Finally, the ar command collects all the object files into an archive named libxe.a. Depending on your preferences, you might want to delete the object files once they are cataloged into the library.

The -I option on the cc command tells the compiler to search the include directory for header files before looking in any of the default (system-provided) directories.

To change just one object file in the library, use the following commands:

```
cd lib
vi scrollbar.c                  # edit the scrollbar routine
cc -g -c -I../include scrollbar.c # recompile one file
ar rv libxe.a scrollbar.o    # replace scrollbar member
```

Before you can build either the xb or xe program, you must first ensure that the object library is current. If in doubt, use the first of the preceding procedures to regenerate the library. Then, to build the xb program, use these commands:

```
cd xb
cc -g -c -I../include *.c
cc -g *.o ../lib/libxe.a -o ../bin/xb
```

The first of the two cc commands compiles source files to object form, and the second links the object files to generate the executable program file. The cc command can perform compiling and linking in one step, but the example uses two steps. In the first command, the -c option prevents the cc command from invoking the link editor. In the second command, the lack of any .c files on the command line causes the cc command to skip the compiler step and directly invoke the link editor.

The benefit of using separate compilation and link steps arises during the debugging and program maintenance activities. If only one of the source files needs to be changed, you can rebuild the entire xb program with only one compilation and a relink, as follows:

```
cd xb
vi xb.c
cc -g -c -I../include xb.c
cc -g *.o ../lib/libxe.a -o ../bin/xb
```

The second cc command relinks the xb program using all the .o files in the directory, but the first cc command only rebuilds one of them, namely xb.o. The others remain valid because the corresponding source has not changed. If you always discard the object files after every build of xb, you must recompile all the source files every time you change any one of them.

The example explicitly names the object library on the second cc command as a file the link editor should search to resolve external references. All routines in the object library that the xb program uses are extracted and combined with the *.o files to form the final executable file.

Because, according to our original description of these programs, they also use the X window routines, the cc command should tell the link editor where to find the X routines. To do so, add the -L option to the cc command for linking, as follows:

```
cc -g -L/usr/X/lib *.o ../lib/libxe.a -lX11 -lXt -o ../bin/xb
```

This form of the command tells the link editor where to find library functions two different ways: by explicitly naming the library in the case of ../lib/ libxe.a, and by telling the link editor what directory to search (the /usr/X/lib directory) for libraries without an explicit pathname (libX11.a and libXt.a).

As you can see, the cc commands begin to grow in complexity as you add include directories, object libraries, and object directories to the product configuration. It is unrealistic to expect programmers to remember these lengthy cc commands every time they need to generate a test version of the product. To simplify the product generation process, you can package these commands into shell scripts, or you can use the UNIX make command. The make command offers some advantages you could not hope to achieve in a simple shell script, yet the make command still enables you to write the cc and ar commands (and any others you might need) any way you wish.

The make command is described in Chapter 15, "Using the make Command."

About the *ar* Command

The ar command is a standard component of the UNIX source-code development package. In olden times the command was present in every configuration; nowadays you may not have the command on your system unless you've also installed the C development package.

The ar command is a general-purpose utility that can create an archive from any group of files. An archive is so named because one of its original uses was to collect a set of related files together (such as the source files of a program) for safe-keeping, in case the current versions should become corrupted or lost. The SCCS tool set provides a superior alternative for managing source code, and the tar and cpio commands are better suited to general-purpose backup; the principal use of the ar command today is in the construction of object libraries for use by the link editor.

An archive, as created by the ar command, is a single file that consists of several normal files concatenated end to end, with a header in front of each to describe the file that follows. An archive intended for use by the link editor is usually called an *object library*, and is augmented with a directory at the end of the archive that lists all the files in the archive and tells where each file starts. Do not confuse an archive directory with a standard UNIX directory; the archive directory is a group of records added to the end of the archive. The archive directory is also sometimes called a *symbol table*.

To generate an object library for use by the link editor, you may need to use up to three commands: ar, lorder, and tsort. The lorder and tsort commands sort the list of object files to add to the directory into a sequence that permits the link editor to retrieve object files from the archive in one pass. To order the object files for one pass retrieval, you must know which other object files any given object file may reference. Thus, although your program might call the sqrt routine, the sqrt routine might call a routine called matherr. Ideally the object library containing sqrt and matherr would store sqrt before matherr. When the link editor later finds the sqrt routine and copies it into your executable program, it discovers that it also needs the matherr routine. If it had already passed the matherr routine, the only way to find it would be to start over from the beginning and search for it.

The lorder command reads one or more object files and produces on standard output a list of the external names the files reference but do not define. The tsort routine in turn sorts a list of names so that all references are forward. For example, if both sqrt and exp generate a reference to matherr, the tsort program produces the list sqrt, exp, matherr.

The common way to use the lorder and tsort commands with ar is as follows:

```
ar rv `lorder *.o | tsort`
```

This rather arcane command uses the shell backquote operator. It results in the shell executing the two commands lorder and tsort, and then substituting their output for the quoted expression. The final ar command executed contains the list of object files generated by tsort: for example, ar rv sqrt.o exp.o matherr.o.

The syntax of the lorder command is

```
lorder filenames
```

If you wish to process only some of the object files in the current directory, you must list them explicitly on the lorder command; otherwise the wildcard expression *.o will list all the object files.

The syntax of the tsort command is

```
tsort
```

The `tsort` command looks for its input on the standard input file and produces its output on the standard output file. Normally the output of `lorder` is piped to `tsort` with a statement like

```
lorder *.o ¦ tsort.
```

The `lorder` and `tsort` commands have virtually no application for any purpose except generating a list of object files in the correct order for inclusion in an object library. The full description of the operation of these commands is rather complicated and serves no purpose as long as you use them in the standard way.

> Having said all this about the `lorder` and `tsort` commands, I must tell you that some of the more modern implementations of the link editor work fine without bothering with `lorder` and `tsort`. These link editors use the symbol table at the end of the archive to extract object files from the archive in random order. If you have a version of ar that creates a symbol table, and a version of `ld` (the link editor command called by `cc`) that uses the symbol table, you can use the simpler command `ar r libx.a *.o` to add object files to the archive. If you don't know, try building your archives without `lorder` and `tsort`; if you get error messages from the link editor about unresolved references, you must use `lorder` and `tsort` to build your object libraries.

The ar command has the following syntax:

```
ar keys archive names
```

For *archive*, specify the filename (or pathname) of the archive (object library) you want the ar command to create or maintain. For *names*, specify the names of the object files you want to add, delete, replace, or extract from the archive. For *keys*, specify one of the following letters identifying the main function ar should perform:

d   Deletes the named members from the archive. The archive is copied and rewritten without the named members.

r   Replaces the named members. For each specified name, add the file to the archive if it is not already present, or replace the like-named member with the file in the current directory.

q   The named members are added to the end of the archive without checking if the member is already present. Duplicate member names could result, but if you are adding a great many members that you know the archive does not already contain, the q option executes much faster than the safer r option.

t   Prints table of contents. The ar command lists all the members contained in *archive*. Without the v qualifier, the ar command just lists the member names. With the v qualifier, the ar command displays the original permissions flags, owner and group id, file size, date created, and name of each member.

x   Extract the named members. Each named member is copied from the archive into a file in the current directory with the same name as the member; that is, it "explodes" the archive into distinct files. If you specify the x option and omit *names*, the ar command extracts all members.

In addition to these primary keys, you may also specify the following qualifiers:

c   *Create*. Causes the ar command to suppress the message announcing that it is creating a new directory. Use the c qualifier with r or—for example, cr or cq. The only effect of this option is to suppress a message to the standard error file; it is *not* required in order to create a new archive.

s   *Symbol table*. Use s with options that do not update the archive to cause its symbol table to be rebuilt. The symbol table, if present, speeds link editor execution.

u   *Update*. Combine with r (ru) to cause ar to replace an archive member only if the corresponding file in the current directory is newer than the member. This option is not meaningful with the other options.

v   *Verbose.* Combine the v letter with any of the primary keys to cause ar to list each member it processes. For example, rv causes ar to generate the message a - *member* for each member added or replaced; xv generates the message x - *member* for each member added or replaced. Used in combination with t, tv causes the ar command to list the members in the directory in a long format.

Notice that the ar command does not comply with modern UNIX conventions regarding options. You do not need to write a - in front of *keys*, although ar does tolerate a dash if present.

Finally, I should reiterate that you use the ar command only to generate *static* object libraries. To build a dynamic object library, you must use the -G option of the cc command—for example, cc -G -dy -I../include *.c -o libxe.so.

Summary

This chapter discusses the commands you use to build programs and object libraries from source code.

The cc command is the front end to the compiler. It invokes the preprocessor, the C compiler, an optional code optimizer, the assembler, and the link editor to build the source files you name on the command line. The cc command can process C source files, assembler source files, object files, and object libraries.

Depending on the options you specify, the cc command can run just the preprocessor on your C source files, emitting the preprocessed text so you can inspect the results of your preprocessor directives. Or it can generate object files, invoking the C compiler for your C source files and the assembler for your assembler source files. Finally, the cc command can invoke the link editor to combine any object files you name on the command line together with object files generated from your source files to produce a single executable program.

For simple programs consisting of just one source file, you customarily use one cc command to preprocess, compile, and link, all in one step. For more complex programs generated from several source files, it is more efficient to first compile source files to object files, and then to link the object files together with a separate cc command.

Ordinarily you do not need to invoke the compiler tools directly. The cpp (preprocessor), as (assembler), and ld (link editor) commands are documented in the UNIX system manuals for those occasions when you need to use the tools in special ways the cc command does not support.

You build conventional (static) object libraries with the ar command; it collects object files you already compiled into a single file in a format required by the link editor. The disadvantage of static linking is that it permanently inserts functions retrieved from a library into your executable program, increasing its physical size and neglecting future maintenance to the library functions.

You build dynamic object libraries with the -G option of the cc command. A dynamic object library is structured more like an executable program file, and can be loaded into memory whenever a running program calls one of the functions it contains. The advantage of dynamic linking is that the external functions you call are not physically inserted into your executable program; the link editor inserts special code to load the external function and transfer control to it only when your program actually calls the external function. This results in smaller executable programs and allows your program to use the most up-to-date version of an external function.

Program building can be enormously complex. Fortunately, most situations are simple and you'll only need to use a few of the cc command options and capabilities. It is probably fair to say that at least 99 out of 100 cc commands executed use only some combination of the -c, -g, -o, -I, and -O plain options. If you familiarize yourself with just these five options, it should be quite some time before you need to look at this chapter again.

Finding Errors with *lint*

The lint command is a syntax checker for the C programming language. Performing more and stricter checks than the C compiler itself, the lint utility diagnoses many faulty or suspicious constructions that the compiler passes without comment. In addition, lint can process multiple source files in a single execution and check them for consistency. It helps you find errors such as defining a function with a certain set of arguments in one source file but calling the function with a different number or type of arguments in another source file.

You can treat any diagnostics the lint program issues as warnings and disregard them entirely. For example, lint usually warns about assigning a pointer value of one type to a pointer variable of another type unless you use a cast. You can add the cast or not as you choose, because the compiler itself almost always generates the correct code, even without the cast. Many messages lint generates are intended only as advice, or to call your attention to peculiar code that is syntactically correct but that probably doesn't mean what you think. For example, a statement such as if (a = b) draws the warning found = where == expected.

The lint utility is a valuable adjunct to the C programming environment. Because you have a separate syntax checker available, the compiler can afford to be lenient in its interpretation of the C syntax rules. This fact was taken into consideration by the compiler designers, and it gives you a certain degree of freedom you would not have otherwise.

You should develop a habit of using lint frequently while developing a program. Every time you add a new function to a source file or change existing code, you can run lint to check your changes. If you wait until you completely finish coding before running lint, you're likely to receive a vast amount of output. If you check your code frequently, however, you can keep the volume down to a more reasonable level. When developing a multifile program, also run lint on the whole set of source files before compiling any.

lint Command and Options

The lint command uses the following syntax:

```
lint [-abchkmnpsuvxyFV] [-I dir] [-lx] [-o lib] [-L libdir] files
```

The lint command supports a great many options, most of which enable you to control the amount and kind of diagnostics you receive. Table 14.1 describes the meaning and usage of each option in detail. The options and definitions sometimes refer to the various *passes* of lint. A pass is one complete reading of a source file. lint usually reads and processes each source file twice: once to diagnose syntax errors within the file, and once to check the file's consistency with other source files.

Table 14.1. `lint` command options.

Option	Meaning and Usage
-a	Suppresses diagnostics about the truncation of long integers.
-b	The `lint` program ordinarily diagnoses break statements that cannot be executed—for example, a break following a return statement inside a switch. This option suppresses diagnostics about such superfluous break statements.
-c	Normally the `lint` program performs a first pass on all .c files, collecting global information into a temporary disk file, then performs a second pass to detect inconsistencies between the .c files. When you use the -c option, `lint` saves global information about each .c file in a file of the same name but with suffix *.ln*, and skips the second pass. Later you can perform the second pass by listing all .ln files on the `lint` command. The -c option of `lint` provides a facility similar to the -c option of the cc command, whereby you can first process each source file individually, then "put them together" with a final run.
-h	Use -h to suppress warnings and advisory messages. The output of `lint` then consists solely of definite syntax errors.
-k	Normally you can use the /*LINTED [message]*/ comment in your source file to eliminate `lint` diagnostics for code you want to accept. By specifying the -k option, `lint` issues a diagnostic giving the *message* text for each such comment. Using -k might generate a more complete diagnostic record for your program if you produce a formal documentation package for your code. (A formal documentation package might consist of a listing of your source program with line numbers, a copy of the `lint` output, and the output from the cxref and cflow utilities.)

continues

381

Table 14.1. continued

Option	Meaning and Usage
-lname	Use the -l option to name a lint library to be searched for function descriptions. (lint libraries are discussed later in this chapter.) You do not need to specify -lc; the lint library for the C standard library is searched automatically. If your program uses math functions, specify -lm to include the math lint library.
-m	Use -m to suppress warnings about global variables that could be declared static.
-n	The -n option prevents lint from using the standard C lint library. This option is rarely used and is appropriate only for linting programs that do not use the standard C function library. By excluding the standard C lint library, you can define functions with the same name as a standard function but with a different number and type of arguments.
-oname	Use option -o to create a single lint library for the functions defined in all the .c files on the lint command, and to specify the filename of the lint library. The filename of the lint library is llib-lname.ln. For name, specify the same name you intend to use later with the -l option. For example, lint -ou geometry.c io.c creates a single lint library called llib-lu.ln containing a description of the functions defined in geometry.c and io.c. You can later reference this lint library with the option -lu.
-p	Option -p causes lint to use the portable C lint library and to use stricter syntax checks on your source file. In particular, this option causes all function and variable names beginning with the same eight characters to be considered equivalent. (Some older C compilers ignore characters beyond the eighth in all names, and beyond the sixth in external names.)

Option	Meaning and Usage
-s	Option -s alters the style of lint output to use one line per message and to omit section headings. This makes the output look more like a compiler diagnostics listing, and you might find the output easier to use than the standard format.
-u	The -u option suppresses warnings about functions and variables that are defined but not used, or used but not defined. These diagnostics are not necessarily errors if another source file references the defined items, or if items declared external are defined in another source file. You should not specify this option for a program complete in one source file, however, because undefined items cause link errors, and unreferenced items are wasteful.
-v	By default, lint issues a warning for each function argument that is not used in that function. The -v option suppresses these diagnostics. Generally, an unreferenced function argument implies that you made some kind of error. The -v option is most often used when generating a lint library.
-x	The -x option suppresses warnings about variables that are defined as external but are never used. Unused external definitions cause .o files to be larger than necessary but do not affect the size or performance of an executable program.
-y	Use -y to process the listed source files as if the /*LINTLIBRARY*/ directive appeared in each file. (For more information, see the discussion of LINTLIBRARY in the following section.)
-F	The lint program normally identifies the source file to which a diagnostic pertains by giving the simple filename of the file. Option -F causes lint to give the full pathname of each file in diagnostic messages.

continues

Table 14.1. continued

Option	Meaning and Usage
-I *dir*	Use the -I option to define additional directories where include files can be found. If you use the -I option on the cc command with your source files, you probably also require it on the lint command because lint, like cc, must first invoke the preprocessor before your program can be analyzed. To define multiple include directories, use a separate -I option for each. The directories are searched in the order you list them, and before the default include directories.
-L *libdir*	Use the -L option to define additional directories containing lint libraries. A lint library provides function prototyping information about functions you call but do not define. The C compilation system provides lint libraries for the standard C functions and the math functions. You may provide additional lint libraries for functions you develop and store in your own object libraries. To define multiple directories to be searched for lint libraries, use a separate -L option for each directory. The directories are searched in the order you list them.
-V	Use the -V option to force lint to write a message giving the official name and release level of the lint program. This option is intended for use by system administration personnel to determine the exact update level of the lint program.

In addition to the aforementioned options that influence lint behavior, you can specify the preprocessor options -D and -U to define or undefine macro symbols, and -Xc, -Xa, or -Xt to specify the language level of the source program. The -g and -0 options are recognized and ignored without comment. (This is helpful in writing *makefiles* for use with the make utility, discussed in Chapter 15, "Automating Compilation with make.")

For *files* you can specify any number of file- or pathnames ending in .c or .ln. Files with any other suffix cause an error message and are ignored. Files with a name ending in .ln are assumed to have been generated in a previous `lint` execution with the `-c` option or to be `lint` libraries. Pass 1 is skipped for these files because they are intended to be used in the global analysis of pass 2.

lint Directives

In addition to specifying command-line options, you can embed certain formal directives in your source file to more precisely control `lint` behavior. All these directives are enclosed in C comments, in the form `/*COMMAND*/`, to protect them from interpretation by the compiler. This enables you to leave the `lint` directives in your source program indefinitely.

Sometimes `lint` complains about the syntax of a statement in your program that, for one reason or another, you are unable or unwilling to change. It can be very annoying to have to inspect, research, and then disregard the same error message in every `lint` run for that source file. To help you avoid this situation, the following `lint` directives eliminate specific diagnostic messages.

`/*ARGSUSEDn*/`
Write this directive in front of a function that can be called with a varying number of arguments. For *n*, specify the minimum number of leading arguments that any valid function call must specify. You may omit arguments beyond *n* in any function call or use a different data type than other calls to the same function without complaint by the `lint` utility. If you omit *n*, `lint` allows the following function to be called with any number and type of arguments (including none).

If you do *not* specify the ARGSUSED directive in front of a function, all calls to the function must use the same number and type of arguments.

`/*CONSTCOND*/`
`/*CONSTANTCOND*/`
`/*CONSTANTCONDITION*/`
The CONSTCOND directive suppresses the normal warning when a constant value is used as the conditional expression of an `if` or `while` statement or the `?:` expression. Place the directive in front of the expression or on the preceding line.

```
/*EMPTY*/
```
Use the EMPTY directive in place of a statement body when you write a null statement for the true clause of if. Normally lint issues a diagnostic if the true clause is the null statement. A valid use of this directive might appear as follows, where a null clause is used to simplify the conditional expression of if:

```
if (index < ARRAYSIZE)
    /*EMPTY*/;
else { /* overstepped the end of the array */
    fprintf(stderr, ...
    exit(8);
}
```

```
/*FALLTHRU*/
/*FALLTHROUGH*/
```
Normally lint issues a diagnostic when a case or default code segment ends without a break statement. The diagnostic is intended to draw your attention to an unusual situation where execution proceeds from the suspect case into the following case. If this is your intent, however, the diagnostic is unwanted. Write this directive after the last statement of the case or default to indicate that the break was intentionally omitted.

If a case or default section ends with a return statement, it is understood as being equivalent to a break. lint, however, does not understand a function call that doesn't return, such as exit or longjmp. Use the NOTREACHED directive following such function calls.

```
/*LINTLIBRARY*/
```
Specify the LINTLIBRARY directive before any function definitions in a source file that contains dummy function definitions for the purpose of creating a lint library. Its effect is equivalent to coding the -x and -v options on the lint command line.

```
/*LINTED [message]*/
```
Use the LINTED directive to suppress any diagnostic that would have been issued for the following line of the source file. (Notice that the directive ignores C statement boundaries and applies only to the physical line immediately following the line where the directive occurs.) You cannot use this directive to suppress a warning about an unused variable or

function definition. If you specify the -k option on the lint command line, the LINTED directive itself causes a diagnostic message even though the following line remains undiagnosed. *message,* if present, appears in the diagnostic produced for the LINTED directive.

The LINTED directive is not available in older versions of the lint command.

One use of the LINTED directive is to suppress the diagnostic generated for statements of the general form while (*p++ = *s++);. This is not only syntactically legal but is also an efficient way to copy a null-terminated string.

/*NOTREACHED*/

Use the NOTREACHED directive to indicate that execution does not proceed past the directive. Often used following an exit or similar function call, the directive can inhibit warnings about no value returned from a function, fall through between switch cases, and the like. Notice that a NOTREACHED directive, if you place it following such function calls, can cause a useful diagnostic that is not otherwise noted, such as "unreachable code." For this reason, it is good style to write the NOTREACHED directive following all such function calls.

/*PRINTFLIKE*n**/

When coded preceding a function definition, lint assumes that calls to the function follow the general style of the printf standard library function. For *n*, specify which argument of the function lint should take as the format string. lint confirms that all calls to the function provide a valid format string for that argument, and that subsequent function arguments agree in number and type with the % symbols appearing in the format string.

lint offers the PRINTFLIKE directive primarily to support checking of your printf, fprintf, vprintf, and vfprintf function calls. The standard lint library uses PRINTFLIKE to describe printf itself as printf-like. However, you can write functions of your own that follow the general usage style of printf and use the PRINTFLIKE directive to enhance lint's error checking. Notice, however, that PRINTFLIKE implies that all % sequences in the format string are identical in meaning to the meaning assumed for printf.

/*PROTOLIB*n**/

When *n* is nonzero, the PROTOLIB directive causes function prototypes to be treated the same as function definitions for purposes of creating a lint library. When *n* is zero, function prototypes are treated normally. The PROTOLIB directive is effective only when preceded by the LINTLIBRARY directive.

/*SCANFLIKE*n**/

The SCANFLIKE directive, when you place it in front of a function definition, causes lint to assume that calls to the function follow the general style of the scanf library function. For *n*, specify the function argument expected to be the format string. lint confirms that calls to the function provide a valid format string and that subsequent arguments agree in type and number with all % sequences appearing in the format string.

/*VARARGS*n**/

The VARARGS directive, when you place it in front of a function definition, causes lint to check only the first *n* arguments in calls to the function. When your function definition uses the ellipsis (...) to indicate the start of a variable argument list, you do not need to use the VARARGS directive.

lint Libraries

The purpose of a lint library is to provide a description of the arguments and return values of a family of related functions. It may also contain a description of external data employed by a function, such as the optarg, optind, and opterr values used with the getopt library function. The C development package for UNIX usually contains a lint library for every object library shipped with the package. Thus there is a standard C lint library to go with the standard C function library, a math lint library to go with the math object library, and so on.

Before the adoption of the ANSI standard for the C programming language and the introduction of function prototyping as an inherent part of the language, lint libraries provided the only means available to verify the usage of a standard library function against the type and number of arguments the function requires. Now, function prototypes stored in header files eliminate much of the original motivation for lint libraries. Nonetheless, the C development package continues to employ lint libraries, in part because not all library functions have a corresponding header file to contain their prototypes.

For the most part, you don't need to concern yourself much with the details of lint libraries. If you use functions in your program from an object library other than the standard C library, you already need to list the library on the cc command. For example, you specify -lm when you use functions from the math package. In such cases you should also list the library on the lint command using the same -lm or -lname option.

In some complex application development projects encompassing a number of related programs, it might be helpful to create an object library containing functions used in two or more of the programs. For each object library, it is desirable to create a corresponding lint library.

Even when you use header files and function prototyping extensively, the C compiler cannot protect you against improper or missing prototypes. A lint library can serve as the master definition of the functions in the project's object libraries, thus ensuring consistency in the definition and usage of functions throughout the application.

Creating *lint* Libraries

There are a number of ways to create a lint library, differing primarily in the way you provide the function definitions to lint. In all cases, though, you actually build the lint library with the following form of the lint command:

```
lint [-y] files -oname
```

If the files containing the function definitions include the LINTLIBRARY directive, you do not need the -y option; otherwise, you can use the -y option to suppress extraneous diagnostics from lint that do not harm the usefulness of the resulting lint library.

The -o option tells lint to use abbreviated processing on the source files; only the function and external variable definitions are of interest. For each function and external variable defined in the source files, lint enters a summary description of the item into an output binary file. The *name* value of the option tells lint what name to give the file.

Perhaps the easiest way to describe the functions and external variables in an object library is to run lint with the -o option on the actual source files you use to build the object library. This approach has two disadvantages, however. First, if the project is being developed simultaneously by a group of programmers, some of the library functions might not be written yet. Second, if you use the library's actual source, you have no check that the function definitions as coded actually match the function definitions you intended.

If you have one or more header files that together contain a function prototype for all or most functions in the object library, you can create the lint library from the header files using a special source file that looks like this:

```
/* LINTLIBRARY */
/* PROTOLIB1 */

#include <assert.h>
#include <ctype.h>
#include <locale.h>
#include <setjmp.h>
#include <signal.h>
#include <stdarg.h>
#include <stdio.h>
#include <stdlib.h>
#include <string.h>
#include <time.h>
#include <float.h>
#include <dirent.h>
```

The preceding is an excerpt from the actual lint library source for the standard C library. The lint directive PROTOLIB tells lint to use function prototypes as function definitions, which is all the magic you need to convert your header files with ANSI standard function prototypes into a lint library. If there are any functions included in your object library for which no header file exists, you can add definitions for these functions at the end of the special file after the last #include statement.

The last method for providing function definitions to lint is the most cumbersome of the three but is practical when all else fails. If you are using a compiler that is not ANSI standard (such as the original K&R definition of the

C language), or if your header files contain function declarations but the declarations are not full prototypes, the header-file method doesn't work, so you must use the following method to create a lint library.

Before the ANSI standard provided other means, lint libraries were always created from hand-coded definition files. Such a file contains only dummy function definitions. A dummy definition is a syntactically correct function definition, but it omits the real body of the function and usually is completely empty (in the case of a function returning void) or contains just a return statement. Listing 14.1 shows what a dummy definitions file looks like.

Listing 14.1. A lint library definitions file.

```
#include <sys/types.h>
#include <sys/stat.h>
#include <time.h>

char    *strchr(char *s, int c) { return s; }
char    *strcpy(char *s1, char *s2) { return s1; }
char    *strcat(char *s1, char *s2) { return s1; }
size_t strlen(char *s) { return 0; }
void    exit(int rc) {}
int     stat(char *path, struct stat *buf) { return 0;}
struct tm *localtime(time_t *t) { return (struct tm *)NULL; }
```

The main disadvantage of using a dummy function definitions file is that it takes extra effort to create it and more effort to maintain it every time you add to or change the functions in the object library.

Using *lint* Libraries

There are two ways to use a lint library. One is to explicitly name the library on the lint command, just as you would a source file:

```
lint -u main.c io.c calc.c /usr/applib/llib-luser.ln
```

If you need to reference more than one lint library, the following alternative has some advantages:

```
lint -u -L/usr/applib main.c io.c calc.c -luser -lx
```

In this case, the -L option tells lint what directories to search for lint libraries. You can list as many -L options as you need to name all the directories where lint libraries can be found. The -lname options indirectly tell lint the filenames of the lint libraries to process. lint in turn searches all the -L directories, as well as the default directory for each -lname you specify. The advantage is that you don't need to know in which specific directory a certain lint library is kept; you only need to know the set of directories where it might be located.

Incremental *lint*ing

Just as the cc command enables you to separately compile the source files of a program into object form and then link the object files together, the lint command enables you to run pass 1 on each source file individually, then run a final global consistency check between all the source files.

The advantage is the same in both cases. When you are maintaining a program having several source files, program changes may affect only one or two of the source files; the others remain unchanged. If you previously compiled all the source files to object form, you need only to recompile the source files you changed and then relink all the object files together. The net result is that you avoid recompiling the unchanged source files. If the application consists of many large and complicated source files, it's conceivable that the savings could amount to many minutes, even hours, of computer time.

The lint process is similar in that it requires two steps. The first performs a complete syntax check on each source file individually, and the second analyzes external references between the source files to check for consistent definition and usage. The first pass of lint creates a temporary file for each source file processed. The temporary file lists only the functions and external variables defined or referenced in the source file. Ordinarily the temporary files are thrown away after lint performs the global analysis. If you specify the -c option on the lint command, however, lint performs only the syntax check and saves the temporary files with the name *filename*.ln.

During the original program development effort, and later during the program maintenance effort, you probably will make changes to only a few of the source files at a time. By saving the `lint` output for all the sources, you can do an entire `lint` run on the application by doing syntax analysis just for the changed files and then reusing the .ln files for the unchanged source to perform a new global consistency check. The net result is the same as if you had run `lint` on all the souce files, but it takes much less time.

To use incremental `lint`ing, you must first run the syntax check on all the new or changed source files, and then run global analysis on all the `lint` files. A terminal session might look like this:

```
lint -u -I../include -c main.c    >main.lp
lint -u -I../include -c decimal.c >decimal.lp
lint -u -I../include -c parse.c   >parse.lp
lint -u -I../include -c exec.c    >exec.lp
lint -u -I../include -c inout.c   >inout.lp
(cat *.lp; lint *.ln) ¦ lp
```

In this example, I saved the `lint` diagnostic listing for each source in a file named *source*.lp. The .lp file contains all the error messages and warnings that pertain to just the one source file. Finally, the `cat` command combines and prints all the error message listings and the summary report.

If you later make a change to the source file parse.c, you can reproduce the `lint` run for the entire program using just the following two statements:

```
lint -u -I../include -c parse.c >parse.lp
(cat *.lp; lint *.ln) ¦ lp
```

Notice that this technique results in saving three disk files for every source: the .c file, the .ln file from `lint`, and the .lp message text file.

Interpreting *lint* Output

The output from `lint` is actually several listings in succession. If you list two or more source files on the `lint` command line, the output contains a section for each of the files. Each section starts with the name of the source file—for example, `getline.c:`—so that you can associate the messages that follow with the source file that caused them. The heading is omitted when you specify only one source file.

The final section of the listing describes inconsistencies between the files. Messages in the final section usually cannot be attributed to any one source file. You as the programmer must decide which of the conflicting usages is correct and either adjust your definition of a function or variable or correct the faulty references to it.

Listings 14.2 and 14.3 show two source files that are intended to be linked together. The first contains the `main` function for the program, and the second contains a function definition used by the `main` routine.

Listing 14.2. First of two source files.

```
#include <stdio.h>

extern char *getline(void);

main(int argc, char *argv[])
{
    int exit_value = 4;
    char *line, *ptr;

    while ( (line = getline()) != NULL) {
        if ( (ptr = strchr(line, '=')) == NULL)
            printf("Invalid format: %3m\n", line);
        fputs(line, stdout);
    }

    return (0);
}
```

Listing 14.3. Second source file.

```
/*
 * getline.c - read a logical line
 */

#include <stdio.h>

static char buf[512];

char *
getline(FILE *s)
{
    unsigned int len = 0;
    int ch;

    while ((ch = getc(s)) != EOF && ch != '\n')
        if (len < sizeof(buf) - 1)
            buf[len++] = ch;

    return ((len == 0 && ch == EOF) ? NULL : buf);
}
```

After entering the source files shown in Listings 14.2 and 14.3 into two files named bad.c and getline.c, I executed lint with the following command:

```
lint bad.c getline.c
```

Listing 14.4 shows the output I obtained.

Listing 14.4. lint output.

```
bad.c:
(13) warning: improper pointer/integer combination: op "="

argument unused in function
    (5) argc in main
    (5) argv in main
```

continues

Listing 14.4. continued

```
set but not used in function
    (10) ptr in main
    (9) exit_value in main

implicitly declared to return int
    (13) strchr
getline.c:

assignment causes implicit narrowing conversion
    (17)

value type used inconsistently
    strchr    llib-lc:string.h(39) char *() :: bad.c(13) int ()

function called with variable number of arguments
    getline   getline.c(11) :: bad.c(12)

function returns value which is always ignored
    printf    fputs

function declared with variable number of arguments
    getline   getline.c(11) :: bad.c(3)

malformed format string
    printf    bad.c (14)
```

The listing begins with the comment bad.c:, indicating that the following messages describe problems found in that file. Messages for file bad.c continue up to the line beginning with getline.c:.

The individual file listing begins with a series of messages describing syntax errors and questionable usage found in the file, with each message showing the line number of the source line that caused the message. Thus, the warning improper integer/pointer combination for file bad.c is addressing line 13 of the file, which contains the following text:

```
if ( (ptr = strchr(line, '=')) == NULL)
```

If you're familiar with the standard C functions, you know that `strchr` returns a pointer of type `char*`. You also can see from Listing 14.2 that `ptr` is declared as `char*`. Because the `lint` message for line 13 clearly is complaining about the assignment, you might understandably wonder why `lint` is complaining about the assignment of a pointer value to a variable of the same type. As you shall see, the answer can be found further down in the listing.

After listing errors by line, `lint` prints a number of category summaries. Each summary describes a general type of problem and lists in a tabular format the lines where the problem occurs. There are many general problem categories; Listing 14.4 shows only some of them. For the bad.c file, `lint` found that there were functions having arguments defined but never referenced, unreferenced variables to which a value was assigned, and functions called but never defined.

In the first category, `lint` points out that two arguments of the `main` function, `argc` and `argv`, are never referenced in the function. This is harmless, and the C compiler would accept the function definition without complaint. However, `lint` wonders if you intended to use the arguments but forgot. You could add code to `main` to remedy the diagnostic. Another possibility is that you defined the arguments, thinking you would need them, but found as you developed the body of `main` that the arguments were unnecessary. If so, you might want to remove the arguments. Actually, you know that `main` is always called with these arguments; it just happens that the argument values are unneeded. Because the definition of `argc` and `argv` is good documentation, a good resolution is to add the `lint` declarative `ARGSUSED` in front of the function, like this:

```
/* ARGSUSED */
main(int argc, char *argv[])
{
```

The `lint` listing next points out that the variables `ptr` and `exit_value` both were assigned a value in the code, but that no reference to the values of these variables occurs anywhere in the function. The value is never used, and perhaps the variables themselves are superfluous. On the other hand, this message describing a "questionable condition" might be caused by missing code. The possible causes are endless, ranging from mistakenly omitting `*/` at the end of a comment, thus hiding an entire group of statements, to simply having forgotten to include some critical processing in the function definition. This category of `lint` diagnostics usually requires you to rethink your original reason for defining the variables, and it might lead you to make considerable changes to the source code.

397

The final problem category for file bad.c, titled `implicitly declared to return int`, heralds an enumeration of functions you called but for which lint can find no definition. The lint program assumes, as does the C compiler, that the function calls are valid references to library functions. The C syntax definition specifies that by default an unknown function will be assumed to return an integer value. The lint diagnostic brings this defaulting action to your attention on the off chance that the assumption is not correct and that you should have included a definition of the function somewhere in your program.

Upon examining the functions listed, you find that the strchr function is one for which lint has no definition. But this shouldn't be; strchr is one of the standard C functions and lint should know about it. Furthermore, you know that strchr returns a value of type char*, not int. The problem seems to be that lint is not finding a definition of the strchr function. But the strchr function is defined in the header file string.h. Checking the list of #include statements at the beginning of file bad.c, you see that the string.h header file is never included.

This explains the reason for the original diagnostic about incompatible pointer types on line 13. Because the string.h header file was omitted, lint had no definition for strchr and presumed by default that it returns int, causing the interpretation of the assignment statement on line 13 to be that of assigning an integer value (as returned by strchr) to the ptr variable. The diagnostic for line 13 will go away when the missing #include for string.h is added at the beginning of the bad.c file.

Turning to the diagnostics section for file getline.c, you find no specific line-number diagnostics. The message `assignment causes implicit narrowing conversion` documents the fact that for the assignment on line 17, a longer value is being assigned to a shorter variable, and loss of data might result. You can ignore this message or cast the longer value to the shorter type to eliminate the lint message:

```
buf[len++] = (char)ch;
```

Because most programmers recognize the need for truncation in this case, and only a byte of zeroes is lost, adding the cast is unnecessarily picky and unaesthetic. Most programmers decide to leave the source line unchanged.

The remainder of the messages in the lint listing are not file-specific; they describe problems noted in reconciling the code in the two source files. Unfortunately, there is no indication in the listing where this transition occurs, so it can be difficult to tell where complaints about getline.c end and where reconciliation messages begin.

The categories of messages shown in Listing 14.4 are typical:

`value type used inconsistently`
This message identifies functions for which the return value type is confused. The detailed messages identify the function whose return value type is in question and show the two conflicting usages of the value. In Listing 14.4, the message shows that `llib-lc` (the `lint` library for standard C functions) expects `strchr` to return a value of type `char*`, but that line 13 of file bad.c expects the return value to be of type `int`. Which is correct? If the function is one of yours, you must decide; if it is a library function, your code is wrong. This diagnostic is the most direct hint in the `lint` listing that the string.h header file is missing.

`function called with variable number of arguments`
The `lint` program attempts to reconcile all function calls with the definition of the function, as to return value type and the number and type of arguments. This message indicates that for the listed functions, not all calls agree on the number of arguments the function takes. If the function is one of yours and it does indeed support a variable argument list, you should add the `lint` declarative VARARGS in front of the function definition. Otherwise, at least one of your function calls passes the incorrect number or type of arguments. Generally you must do something to eliminate this `lint` diagnostic.

`function returns value which is always ignored`
This relatively harmless diagnostic lists functions that are defined to return a value, but for which all function calls disregard the value. If one of your functions appears in this list, you probably should change the function to return `void` because you never have a use for the returned value. If the function is a library function, you can cast the value returned by the function to `(void)`, or you can disregard the `lint` message. Many of the standard library functions return a value that is rarely of any use; `printf` frequently appears listed under this message.

`function returns value which is sometimes ignored`
Although no example of this problem category appears in Listing 14.4, it occasionally appears in your `lint` runs. Why do you sometimes ignore

the value returned by the function, and sometimes use it? Should you add the (void) cast in front of calls that don't use the return value? Your reaction to this diagnostic depends primarily on your C coding style.

`function declared with variable number of arguments`
This diagnostic detects discrepancies between a function prototype and the function's actual definition. It usually indicates an error in the function prototype. Unless you intend for the listed functions to support variable argument lists, you almost certainly will need to take corrective action. For each function listed, lint cites the source lines that define the function in conflicting ways.

`malformed format string`
This diagnostic describes statements that include a function call to one of the family of printf or scanf functions. On inspecting the format string, lint found a % symbol that it didn't understand. Double-check your usage of % symbols against the documentation for the function; you probably made a mistake in writing the format string.

The number and variety of conditions lint can diagnose is extensive; the messages just described are by no means a comprehensive list. They are shown to familiarize you with the reporting style used by lint, especially for messages in the format llib-lc:string.h(39) char *() :: bad.c(13) int (), which might appear rather cryptic.

For many, if not most of the warnings lint produces, no mechanical determination of the problem's cause is possible. You must use your judgment to determine how to correct the problem or whether a source-code correction is even necessary. The advantage in using lint to diagnose your source code is that lint detects many questionable conditions that are not overt errors by any stretch of the imagination, but which lead you to recognize an inconsistency or omission in your source code. The disadvantage, of course, is that you often have to wade through vast amounts of "fluff" (irrelevant and useless diagnostics) to find meaningful problems.

If you run lint frequently on the same source file as you develop and maintain it, you might find it tempting to reduce the number of messages by making formal source-code changes of no real substance. For example, you might add a (void) cast in front of calls to printf. Judicious usage of the lint command-line options can reduce the volume of diagnostic messages. But rarely, if ever, do you get a clean bill of health from `lint`. Reacting to every `lint` diagnostic probably would make your code awkward and stilted. Remember that every unnecessary cast you add to the source causes someone reading your program to pause and wonder why the cast is necessary. Every statement you twist and turn to get around `lint` diagnostics confuses your program's reader. Therefore, you want to respond to real problems `lint` finds for you and disregard the rest of its complaints, difficult as it might be for you to leave a dangling diagnostic unresolved.

Notes

Before you leave the discussion of `lint`, there are a few tips about using it that you might find helpful.

If you find the standard output format awkward or unclear, try using the `-s` option of `lint`. The single-line format, closer in style to a standard compiler diagnostics listing, changes the format of individual diagnostic messages as well as their general style of presentation. You might find that some of the more cryptic messages are easier to understand in the `-s` format.

Often you'll want to switch back and forth between your source file and the `lint` listing as you work problems. A fairly convenient way to do this is to save the `lint` output in a file and to edit both with the `vi` editor. The following is a general style for invoking `lint` that you might find convenient:

```
lint -u prog.c >errs; vi errs
```

As soon as you are in the `vi` editor, you can conveniently scroll forward and backward as you look at messages. To switch to your source code, enter the editor command `:e prog.c`. To bring up your source file at a particular line number, use the command `:e +n prog.c`. To switch back to the error listing, enter the command `:e#`. Of course, if you add or delete lines in your source code, the line numbers in the `lint` listing might become useless; just leave the editor and run `lint` again.

You can even run `lint` from within `vi`. If you are currently viewing the source file you want to lint, enter the command `:!lint %`. The `%` symbol stands for the filename of the file you are currently editing. `vi` automatically changes `%` to the current filename before passing the command to the shell.

401

Finally, note that solid syntax errors such as a missing brace or an improperly paired set of parentheses can throw lint so badly out of synchronization with your source code that further error messages are spurious and meaningless. If you receive a particularly large volume of output from lint and some of the diagnostics indicate error instead of warning, correct just the errors that you can understand and resolve, and then run lint again. You might be surprised by the number of diagnostics that disappear.

Summary

The lint command is a syntax checker for C source programs. The lint command complements the C compiler in two ways: it diagnoses more suspicious and questionable forms of coding than does the compiler, and it is able to check the consistency of declaration and usage between several source files.

Normally you use lint in a very straightforward manner. However, the lint command also supports incremental linting, a process much like separating the compilation and linking steps of program building. Incremental linking is useful with multifile programs because it enables you to avoid repeated linting of source files that haven't changed.

If you build your own object libraries, you can also build a lint library to describe the functions in your object library to lint. Lint libraries enable lint to check your programs for proper and consistent use of the functions and external variables in an object library.

The lint command provides a great many options, most of which help you reduce or eliminate unwanted diagnostics. In addition to using command-line options, you can also embed lint directives (special C-style comments) in your source program to eliminate diagnostics for code you know is OK.

A common complaint about lint is that it produces too many diagnostics. Nevertheless, it is also true that programs you check thoroughly with lint have fewer errors in them when you begin testing.

Automating Compilation with *make*

The make command has long been a standard component of UNIX. Many experienced UNIX programmers consider make a vital part of their program development process. The value of make is so well known that versions of it have been developed for the MS-DOS environment. The problem with make is that it can be devilishly difficult to learn. In this chapter I broach the problem head on, and either help you become a proficient afficionado of the make utility or leave you totally confused; it seems that with make there is no in-between.

The overt purpose of the make utility is to execute a predefined sequence of shell commands whenever one file is older than another. Because the operating system automatically records the date and time of last modification for every file, a time stamp is available and presumably reliable for every file in the system. If one of the files is generated from the contents of the other, their time stamps can serve as a useful hint about their status. In the case of a source file and an object file compiled from it, you can observe that normally the object file should be newer than the source file. If you modify the source file, however, the object file is then the older of the two—a sure-fire indication that you need to recompile the source file.

The make command assumes that the shell commands you provide will re-build the older out-of-date file, restoring the normal relationship of time stamps between the file and its precursors. If you compile a source file, for example, the compiler rewrites the object file and its date is then newer than the source file; the object file is then said to be up to date.

The make command is a very general-purpose program, and makes no assumption that the files it's concerned with are source files, executable program files, or files of any other type or usage. This enables you to use make in a great many situations that have nothing overtly to do with programming. The fact remains that programmers are the most frequent users of make, and they usually use it to build object or executable files from source code.

A concept of vital importance to understanding and using make is that of *dependency*. A file *x* is said to be dependent on another file *y* when any change to *y* necessitates rebuilding or regenerating file *x*. This concept can also be expressed as a derivation: the contents of file *x* are derived from the contents of file *y*. The relationship can also be one to many (file *x* is dependent on files *a*, *b*, and *c*), or many to one (if file *x* changes, files *a*, *b*, and *c* must all be rebuilt).

As an aid to discussion, the dependent file is called a *target* file; the files used as input to the process are called *input* files.

To use make, begin by identifying the files you want to administrate. You must then trace back through the procedure you use to construct the desired files; each secondary file you use in the procedure is a file on which the desired file is dependent either directly or indirectly. Once you determine the identity and relationship of all the files involved, set these down in a master file that make uses to generate the desired files for you. This master file is called a *makefile* and is the principal input you provide to the make command.

The remainder of this chapter explains the syntax and options of the make command, the syntax rules for writing a makefile, and also describes the many features and facilities of the make command. Command-line options play a secondary role in using make effectively; by far the most important part of understanding and using make is learning how to write the makefile.

Command Syntax and Options

The syntax of the make command line is as follows:

```
make     [-f makefile] [-b] [-e] [-i] [-k] [-n] [-p] [-q]
         [-r] [-s] [-t] [-u] [names] [macros]
```

You may notice that all options and arguments are optional. If you organize your program development into directories properly (see Chapter 13, "Compiling Programs with cc," for a discussion of directory organization), you should be able to build your applications by entering the make command with no other options or specifications. The options help with debugging the makefile and limiting the actions of the make command.

Table 15.1 explains the meaning of each option.

Table 15.1. make command options.

Option	Meaning and Usage
-f makefile	Use the -f option to specify the filename or pathname of the makefile you want to use with this execution of make. Notice that you *must* separate the option from the filename with at least one blank; the make command does not follow the standard UNIX convention of allowing an option to be either adjacent to or separated from its value.

continues

405

Table 15.1. continued

Option	Meaning and Usage
	If you omit the -f option, make searches for makefile, Makefile, s.makefile, and s.Makefile in that order, using the first file it finds as the makefile for this execution. If the filename found begins with s., make assumes that the file is in SCCS format and executes an interal get command to retrieve the current version of the file.
-b	Specify the -b option to process old makefiles that use an obsolete syntax.
-e	By default, a macro defined in the makefile overrides an environment variable of the same name. The -e option reverses the default and causes an environment variable to take precedence over a macro of the same name. Using the -e option enables you to code the default value for a macro in the makefile and to override its value with an environment variable when you execute make.
-i	By default, make halts execution if any command returns a nonzero exit value (the UNIX convention by which a command indicates unsuccessful execution). Specifying -i causes make to document a nonzero command exit and then continue processing. Normally you should try to write commands so that a nonzero exit occurs only in the event of erroneous processing, and omit the -i option.
-k	The -k option is an alternative to -i that allows make to abandon the generation of a target file when a command exits with a nonzero exit value but asks make to continue with the generation of other targets not dependent on the abandoned target file. Thus -k tells make to build what it can, but to abandon any command list in which one of the commands fails.

Option	Meaning and Usage
-n	The -n option suppresses the execution but not the printing of commands. The option is useful for checking the commands make would execute without actually executing them, and provides the principal means for debugging makefiles.
	Notice that the no-execute mode set by option -n sometimes leads to spurious failure of the make command. For example, make might not be able to proceed because of a missing directory when normal execution would have created the directory; the no-execute mode prevented creation of the directory and thus caused an otherwise valid makefile to fail.
-p	The -p option causes make to list all built-in macros and implicit rules. Use -p when you want to find out what built-in macros and implicit rules your version of make provides. Notice that option -p does not inhibit normal processing; make still tries to find and execute a makefile in the normal fashion.
	The following command can be used to list make built-in macros and implicit rules without taking any other action:
	`make -pf - 2>/dev/null </dev/null`
-q	Use the -q option when issuing the make command from within a shell script. It causes make to indicate by its exit value whether the target name is up to date; that is, whether make would rebuild the target file if invoked without the -q option. A zero exit value indicates that the target file is up to date; a nonzero value indicates that the target file needs to be rebuilt.
-r	The rarely used -r option prevents make from using any built-in macro definitions or implicit rules. Use this option when make built-in definitions conflict with your

continues

407

Table 15.1. continued

Option	Meaning and Usage
	makefile. Your makefile must include all macro definitions and implicit rules that it requires when you use the -r option.
-s	The -s (*silent*) option tells make to execute commands without printing them. By default, make prints each command to standard output before executing it.
-t	Use -t (*touch*) to update the date and time of each out-of-date target
-u	The -u option tells make to unconditionally rebuild all targets, whether or not they appear up to date.

For *names*, specify the objects you wish make to build. If you specify no names, make attempts to build the target of the first dependency rule in the makefile.

A name in this context is not necessarily a filename. The makefile used determines what names are acceptable; they may be simple filenames, partially or fully qualified pathnames, or arbitrary names representing procedures that can be called up from the makefile. A valid name is any name that appears explicitly as the target of a dependency rule, or for which an applicable implicit rule exists either in the makefile or as a built-in rule. (Refer to the "Introducing the Makefile" section later in this chapter for a discussion of targets, dependency rules, and so on.)

For *macros*, you may list one or more macro definitions of the form *name=value*. You must separate macros from one another, like other command-line options and arguments, by one or more spaces or tabs. If *value* contains any character special to the shell, you need to enclose the macro in quotes. A macro you specify on the make command overrides any macro of the same name appearing in the makefile or any environment variable of the same name. The makefile determines whether a macro you write on the command line has any effect, and what the nature of the effect is. (For a detailed discussion of macros, see the "Writing and Using Macros" section later in this chapter.)

Introducing the Makefile

The makefile is a script you write using a language unique to the make command. Your specifications in the script tell make what files it may be called upon to build, what files to use in the build procedure, and what operating system commands to execute to build the file. In some cases the make command can build a file without any specifications from you; make comes complete with a set of built-in specifications that handle many common program generation steps.

The most fundamental part of any makefile is a set of lines called *dependency rules* that describe the files make is to build. A file that make can build is called a *target* file and is (in most cases) the subject of a dependency rule. A dependency rule also identifies the input files make uses to build a target. The target file is said to be dependent on the input files when any change to one of the input files necessitates regeneration of the target file.

To express these relationships in different terms, consider the context in which make is most often used: to compile an executable program from a set of source files. In this discussion, the executable program is called the target file. The source files ultimately determine the content of the executable program, so the executable file is said to be dependent on the source files. The source files are the primary input the cc command uses to compile the executable program.

In its basic form, a dependency rule is a line that looks like this:

```
target: name1 name2 ...
        command
        command
        ...
```

The name appearing to the left of the colon (:) identifies a file that make will be called upon to build. The names to the right of the colon list the files that it uses in the construction of `target`. If any of the files listed to the right of the colon are newer than `target`, make concludes that `target` is out of date and executes the commands listed beneath the rule. If the target file is newer than any of the input files, make doesn't need to do anything; the target is already up to date.

When make begins execution, it first determines which target files it has been asked to build. This is either the list of targets you explicitly named on the make command line, or the target defined by the first dependency rule in the makefile if the command line specifies no target names.

Having identified a target file it should try to build, make then searches your makefile for a dependency rule for the target. If possible, make selects a dependency rule that lists the target file to the left of the colon. Failing that, make tries to find an implicit rule that will yield the target. If no suitable implicit rule can be found, make uses the .DEFAULT: rule. If there is no .DEFAULT: rule, make gives up and reports that it is unable to build the target. (Implicit rules and the .DEFAULT: rule are fully explained later in this chapter.)

Supposing that make can find a dependency rule in your makefile that applies to the target, make next examines the list of input files to the right of the colon. If the list is empty, there are no input files and make simply checks whether the target file currently exists. Because you did not define any files with respect to which the target can be out of date, make is satisfied by the simple existence of the target; that is, it attempts to build the target only if the target file doesn't exist.

If the dependency rule identifies any input files, make checks that each of the input files exists and is up to date. This means that make has to temporarily set aside its current task of building the target file and take up each one of the input files in turn as a new prerequisite target. The entire process starts over, beginning with a search of the makefile for a dependency rule to build the input file. If necessary, make builds the input from its own set of source files. Only when all the input files exist and are up to date does make go on with the next step for the original target.

When make has brought all the input files up to date, or confirmed that they are already up to date, make next checks the time stamp of each input file against the time stamp of the target file. If any of the input files are newer than the target, make concludes that it must rebuild the target file. However, if the target file is newer than any of the input files, the only possible conclusion is that the target file has already been rebuilt since the last change to an input file; make decides that it does not need to rebuild the target file because it is already up to date, and reports success.

To build the target file when it is out of date, make proceeds by executing each one of the commands listed underneath the dependency rule in turn. It invokes a new copy of the shell for each command, passes the text of the command to the shell, and waits for the shell to complete. If the exit value from the shell is zero, make accepts that the command completed successfully and goes on to execute the next command in the list. If the command sets a nonzero exit value, make reports an error and abandons the generation of the target. For most UNIX commands a nonzero exit value means that the command was unable to perform its intended action. There are some commands, though, that use the exit value for other purposes, such as to return a result value. To help with such cases, make provides a way for you to indicate in the makefile that it should ignore the exit value from a particular command.

The make command repeats the preceding procedure for each target you explicitly name on the make command line.

Part of the magic of make is the recursive way it builds files. Its recursive algorithm enables you to design build procedures that use files generated by other build procedures. In fact, the usual method for building C programs requires just such recursion: first you compile the C source file to obtain an object file, and then you link the object files to generate the executable file. When you describe such a procedure to make, you begin by describing the executable file as dependent on the .o (object) files. The object files in turn are dependent on the .c (source) files.

By describing the executable program as dependent on the object files, you make it possible for make to reuse existing object files for which the corresponding source hasn't changed. The net result is that make recompiles only the source files you change, but still builds the complete program from existing or regenerated object files. If you describe the executable file as being directly dependent on the source files, you require make to recompile all source files every time you change any one of them. That is not a very efficient way to proceed.

The sample makefile shown in Listing 15.1 describes the generation of a single executable file from three C language source files.

Listing 15.1. A simple makefile.

```
# Build paystat: payroll status inquiry

paystat: main.o report.o file.o
    cc main.o report.o file.o -o paystat
```

continues

411

Listing 15.1. continued

```
main.o: main.c
    cc -O -c main.c
report.o: report.c
    cc -O -c report.c
file.o: file.c
    cc -O -c file.c
```

The sample contains four dependency rules: one for the final executable file called paystat, and one for each of the three object files main.o, report.o, and file.o. Each of the dependency rules is followed by a command list that uses the input files to build the target file. The command list in each case consists of just one cc command.

The sample makefile places the dependency rule for paystat first, making paystat the default target if someone happens to enter the make command with no operands. If the paystat rule were listed at the end of the makefile (perhaps the more logical place to put the rule), then the rule main.o: main.c would appear first in the makefile; invoking main with no arguments would cause it to build the main.o object file and then stop, which is hardly a useful procedure. Even if the paystat rule appears at the end, you could still build paystat by entering the command make paystat, overriding the default target by naming the target explicitly on the make command line.

General Syntax

A makefile is comprised of the following types of lines:

> Blank lines
> Comment lines
> Macro definitions
> Dependency rules
> Command lines

Blank lines are legal and have no effect; they can be used anywhere except between the lines of a command list to enhance the clarity, organization, and readability of your makefiles.

A comment line can appear anywhere in a makefile except between the lines of a command list. A comment has the following general form:

```
# comment
```

The comment starts with a hash mark as the first word of the line, and ends at the end of the line.

A macro definition has the following general form:

```
name = text
```

For *name*, write any symbol that is acceptable as a shell variable name. If you're not familiar with the UNIX shells, its rules generally specify that a name must begin with a letter and may be followed by any number of letters, digits, and underscores. Both upper- and lowercase letters are acceptable and are distinguished; the name HOME is considered different from the name home.

Any amount of whitespace (blanks or tabs) may appear around the equal sign. The value of the macro begins with the first nonblank character after the equal sign and extends through the remainder of the line. Shell wildcards and command expressions are *not* resolved before assigning the text as the value of the name.

Because make analyzes and stores all definitions before acting on any of them, you may place a macro definition anywhere before its first use. You cannot define and then change a macro value; all assignments to the macro are processed before any references are expanded. In other words, the effect is the same as if you collected all macro assignments at the beginning of the makefile; the last assignment for a macro name wins and sets the value of the macro for the remainder of the makefile.

You can break any long line into a series of lines by ending all but the last with a backslash (\). The occurrence of a backslash followed immediately by a newline character is deleted, in effect pasting together the line with the line that follows it. Notice, however, that you cannot continue a comment line.

413

Writing Dependency Rules

The formal syntax of a dependency rule is as follows:

```
target [target ...] :[:] [ name ...] [; command] [ commands]
```

A dependency rule must start at the beginning of the line. Lines with leading whitespace are assumed to be commands. The presence or absence of whitespace at the beginning of a line is the only criterion by which make distinguishes dependency rules from shell command lines.

For target, specify any identifier that is valid as a pathname, except you may not use any of these characters in the target name: : (colon), = (equal sign), blank, or tab. Also, do not quote the target name with ' or ".

The rule for forming target names implies that make allows a target file to be located in any directory. For example, a target of /usr/apps/payroll/paystat causes make to check for the existence of a file named paystat in the directory /usr/apps/payroll; you must have adequate permission to read, search, and write to the /usr/apps/payroll directory or else make is unable to process the target. To explicitly build such a target, you must issue the make command in the form make /usr/apps/payroll/paystat because make paystat would fail to find a rule with a target name of paystat. In other words, make interprets target names literally and does not recognize or support any abbreviation of a pathname; you must use the full target name in any reference to the target file. Notice that this is true even if you make /usr/apps/payroll your current directory before issuing the make paystat command.

You can name as many targets as you like on the left side of the dependency rule. If you list multiple targets, the rule is taken to apply to all the targets. However, invoking the rule for one target does not automatically invoke the rule for any of the other targets.

There is a special form of target name consisting of two filename suffixes pasted together—for example, .c.o. Target names of this form are used in writing implicit rules. The "Implicit Rules" section later in this chapter explains implicit rules in detail. Do not try to use a target filename beginning with a period (.).

If other files are needed in the construction of a target, you must list each of them to the right of the colon. You don't need to provide a dependency rule for each *name* unless you also require make to build or update the file; if make can find no applicable rule for *name*, it is sufficient if a file of that name exists. In other words, you must either provide a dependency rule telling make how to build the file, or ensure that the file exists before invoking make.

You may use shell wildcards in forming *name* items. For example, a *name* entry of *.c is equivalent to listing all the files in the current directory with a filename ending in .c. Even wildcard names such as b?d.c or b[abx].c will be recognized and expanded according to the shell syntax for wildcard filenames.

If you provide no *name* entries to the right of the colon, make assumes that the target is up to date provided only that it exists. If the target file does not exist, make executes the commands associated with the dependency rule and proceeds on the assumption that the commands successfully created the file, whether or not the file was actually created. This convention enables you to write dummy rules in which no file with the target name ever exists; invoking make with the dummy target name always forces the execution of the command list. A dummy target may be specified as an input name on another rule.

Normally you write one dependency rule for each target file, identifying all the input files on which the target is dependent and specifying all the commands needed to build the target. When you use a colon as the dependency rule separator, make allows you to provide more than one dependency rule specifying the same target file. However, make requires that only one of the rules provide a command list; all other rules for the target must omit *commands* altogether. If the target is out of date with respect to any of the *name* items on any of the rules, make executes the command list.

When you use the double colon (::), make allows you to list a target on several dependency rules and for each rule to specify a non-null list of commands. You must use the :: separator on all rules for that target, however. When building the target, make processes the rules in the order you list them. If any of the *name* items are nonexistent or out of date for any one of the rules, the commands associated with that rule are executed. If all the input files are up to date, make takes no action for that rule and goes on to the next rule for that target.

The double colon rule format enables you to tailor the executed command set according to the particular input files that are out of date. Most programmers don't use the double colon rule format because implicit rules provide a better format to define unique actions for specific input files; input rules are more flexible than the double colon rule.

You may provide a command on the same line as the dependency rule by following the last *name* with a semicolon, and then writing a command. To list multiple commands, you must use the multiline format. Notice that if you write a semicolon at the end of a dependency rule followed by nothing, you have written a null command list, which is quite different from an omitted command list. A null command list is considered to exist, and affects the : and :: multirule restrictions, whereas a dependency rule with neither a semicolon nor following command lines is considered to be a rule without commands.

Writing Command Lists

When the make command finds that a target file is out of date or doesn't exist, it executes the command list associated with the rule for the target. You may write any commands you wish in the command list. Usually the commands you write have the effect of creating the target file, although for a dummy target the commands may do anything at all.

A command list can be empty. An empty command list causes no action and elicits no special comment from make. Empty command lists are often used when (a) the necessary build action has already been achieved indirectly or as a by-product of some other procedure in your makefile; or (b) you have more than one dependency rule for the target and specified the commands in another rule.

If you need to specify only one command, you can write it on the same line as the dependency rule after a semicolon; otherwise, you must give all commands on separate lines following the dependency rule.

Every command in a command list must begin with a tab character. The command list ends at the next line beginning without a tab character. You cannot use blanks in place of the tab. If you write command lines that look proper in every way except that they do not begin with a tab, make reports odd syntax errors for the improper command lines.

Unfortunately, some text editors (emacs is one example) make it difficult to enter a tab at the beginning of a line: even though you press the Tab key, you may get eight blanks at the beginning of the line instead of a tab character. If you have difficulty entering tabs with your favorite editor, you may have to use ed or vi when working with makefiles. If you suspect that some of your command lines do not begin with a tab, there are several commands you can use to visually check for tabs, including ed, sed, and cat. For example, the command cat -vt makefile shows tab characters as the digraph ^I. If these commands do not show a tab character at the beginning of your command lines, you may be able to change leading blanks to tabs using the col or pr command.

You can prefix a command with either of two special characters to affect the way in which make executes the command.

The - (hyphen) in front of a command causes make to ignore the exit value from the command. Make issues a warning message if the command sets a non-zero exit value, but continues execution as if nothing had happened. By default, make terminates not only the current command list and target, but also its entire execution if a command sets a nonzero exit value. The following command, for example, removes a file if it exists, but has no effect if the file is missing:

```
-rm libu.a
```

The @ (at sign) used as the first character of a command causes make to suppress printing the command; the command is still executed, however. The @ is most often used in front of the echo command so you can log a message without having the echo command itself print.

You can use both special characters at the beginning of a command, in either order, to cause printing of the command to be suppressed and its exit value to be ignored.

Both the - and @ characters are stripped from the line before execution. The special character must be the first character of the command but *not* the first character of the line; commands, as always, must begin with the tab character as the first character of the line.

Writing and Using Macros

Consider a hypothetical set of C source files. Each source file contains the definition of one function or of a closely related group of functions. The source files must be compiled and cataloged in an object library. Your objective is to keep the object library in a subdirectory of your home directory, and use it to simplify the development of new programs in the future.

Your catalog of off-the-shelf functions will be called libu.a. The source files you have written to date include alloc.c, error.c, file.c, and parse.c.

Listing 15.2 shows a makefile you could write to build the object library from source.

Listing 15.2. Building an object library (first attempt).

```
# Makefile to generate an object library libu.a

libu.a: alloc.o error.o file.o parse.o
        ar r libu.a alloc.o error.o file.o parse.o

alloc.o: alloc.c
        cc -O -c alloc.c

error.o: error.c
        cc -O -c error.c

file.o: file.c
        cc -O -c file.c

parse.o: parse.c
        cc -O -c parse.c
```

The first time you execute the makefile, `make` must build all object files and the object library. The output of the `make` command looks like this:

```
$ make
        cc -O -c alloc.c
        cc -O -c error.c
        cc -O -c file.c
        cc -O -c parse.c
        ar r libu.a alloc.o error.o file.o parse.o
```

Eventually you may want to add another function to your object library. In addition to writing and testing the function itself, you'll need to update your makefile to include the function. In addition to the new rule and command you'll have to write, you will also have to modify the libu.a rule and its associated command.

Having to add a new filename to both the dependency rule and the command line is redundant and error prone; you could easily forget to add the filename to one or the other of the lines. It would be nice if `make` provided some way to define the list of filenames just once. The `make` command offers just such a facility: you can write a macro that defines a symbol to represent the list of filenames. Wherever you write the symbol in the makefile, make treats it as if you wrote out the entire list of filenames.

Listing 15.3 shows the original makefile rewritten using a macro to define the list of filenames.

Listing 15.3. Building an object library (second attempt).

```
# Makefile to generate an object library libu.a

LIB = libu.a
OBJ = alloc.o error.o file.o parse.o

$(LIB): $(OBJ)
        ar r $(LIB) $(OBJ)

alloc.o: alloc.c
        cc -O -c alloc.c
```

continues

Listing 15.3. continued

```
error.o: error.c
        cc -O -c error.c

file.o: file.c
        cc -O -c file.c

parse.o: parse.c
        cc -O -c parse.c
```

The rules for defining and using macros are simple. To define a macro, write a line having the general format *name* = *text*. The name of your macro should comply with the general rules for writing shell variable names: it must begin with a letter or underscore, and be followed by zero or more letters, digits, and underscores. There is no specific limit on the length of a macro name. The value of the macro is all the text you write after the equal sign up to the end of the line (excluding any whitespace following the equal sign). Notice that you do not have to enclose the macro value in quotation marks even when it contains embedded whitespace. In fact, any apostrophes or quotation marks you write in the value become part of the macro.

To use the macro, write the expression $(*name*). If your macro name is only one character, you can omit the parentheses. Macro references are recognized on dependency rules, within command lines, and in the text of subsequent macro definitions. Because the make command uses the $ (dollar sign) to introduce a macro reference, you must watch out for dollar signs appearing in the commands you write. If you intend a dollar sign to be part of the command and not the start of a macro symbol, write the dollar sign twice; make always treats the special macro $$ as if its value were one dollar sign.

The macro expression $(*name*:.*x*=.*y*) replaces each occurrence of the suffix .*x* with the new suffix .*y* in the value of *name*. The resulting list of amended filenames is the value of the expression. Assume that a makefile contains the following definition of a list of source files:

```
SRC = alloc.c errors.c file.c parse.c
```

You can define a macro giving the corresponding list of object files using the following macro expression:

```
OBJ = $(SRC:.c=.o)
```

You can use the macro expression $(*name*:.*x*=.*y*) anywhere you can use the basic macro $(*name*).

Macros are a great way of eliminating redundancy in a makefile and increasing its flexibility. You can often achieve the affect of editing many lines by altering the text of a macro definition.

Another advantage you can gain from using macros is that the make command enables you to override a macro definition from the make command line or with an environment variable. This allows you to dynamically customize your makefile, changing key characteristics of its behavior, without actually editing the file. To take advantage of this capability, though, you have to plan for it by using macros in your makefiles.

Even as simple a makefile as that shown in Listing 15.3 provides a feature you can take advantage of in program testing. Because it uses a macro to define the name of the object library, you can use the same makefile to create a test version of your object library with the following command:

```
$ make LIB=libtest.a
        cc -O -c alloc.c
        cc -O -c error.c
        cc -O -c file.c
        cc -O -c parse.c
        ar r libtest.a alloc.o error.o file.o parse.o
ar: creating libtest.a
```

Built-in Macros

The make command automatically defines a number of macros you can use to simplify or improve your makefiles. Although the number of predefined macros is now rather large in the current version of the make utility, the following have been standard for many years and you would be well advised to use them in your own makefiles whenever appropriate:

```
AR = ar
ARFLAGS = -rv
AS = as
ASFLAGS =
CC = cc
CFLAGS = -O
LD = ld
LDFLAGS =
LEX = lex
LFLAGS =
YACC = yacc
YFLAGS =
GET = get
GFLAGS =
MAKE = make
MAKEFLAGS =
```

The CC and CFLAGS macros see particularly frequent use. The CC macro defines the standard name of the C compiler; although its value is commonly cc, you should use the macro $(CC) in preference to cc just in case your makefile ever needs to be used in an environment or situation where the compiler has a different name. The CFLAGS macro defines the standard options for the cc command. You'll probably want to specify a value for the CFLAGS macro at the start of your makefile; doing so enables you to change compiler options throughout the makefile by editing only one line.

Although the default value of CFLAGS is the -O option (which causes the C compiler to generate optimized code), most programmers provide an explicit definition of CFLAGS and specify its value as -g, which causes the compiler to generate debugging support in the object file.

All environment variables are added automatically to the list of predefined macros when make begins execution. You can therefore use any environment variable without also writing a definition of the macro. The HOME environment variable is often particularly useful in forming the pathname of target files; because its value is defined outside the makefile, it automatically points to the home directory of the current user.

By default, a macro you define explicitly in your makefile takes precedence over any environment variable with the same name. The default enables you to invent macro names without needing to be familiar with all the shell environment variables that might be in effect. However, it may be convenient to use the reverse convention, causing an environment variable to override a macro of the same name. To cause environment variables to override macro definitions, specify option -e on the make command line.

In addition to predefined macros, make also provides a number of special macros. The value of a special macro changes according to context as make executes your makefile, so unlike predefined macros the text value of the special macros can't be predicted. The special macros are

$@	Name of the current target file
$(@D)	Directory part of the current target name
$(@F)	Filename part of the current target name
$?	List of input files newer than target
$$	Always the single character $

The $@ macro gives the full name of the current target file. The name is a full pathname only if you name the target file by its full pathname. If you use only a simple filename on the dependency rule, the value of $@ is just the simple filename. Because the value of $@ is the name of the current target file, its value is defined only when the $@ symbol occurs in a command line; its value is undefined in other contexts.

The special forms $(@D) and $(@F) enable you to refer to just a part of the target name. The value of $(@D) is the (possibly null) directory prefix of the name. The value of $(@F) is the filename portion of the target name; it includes the filename suffix, if any. If the target name has no directory prefix, the value of $@ and $(@F) are identical and $(@D) expands to the null string.

You can use the special form $$@ (also $$(@D) and $$(@F)) on the dependency rule itself to refer to the current target. These macros are handy when writing a rule to install a file into another directory. For example, the following rule could install a current version of any of the three system commands mv, cp, or rm in the /usr/bin directory:

```
COMMANDS = $(BIN)/mv $(BIN)/cp $(BIN)/rm
$(COMMANDS): $$(@F)
        cp $(@F) $@
```

The $? macro has as its value the list of all input files from the dependency rule which are newer than the target file. If the target file doesn't exist, $? lists all input files. The names in the value of $? are separated by a blank. The $? macro is defined only within command lines of an explicit rule; you should not use the $? symbol in macro definitions, dependency rules, or implicit rules.

The $$ macro has as its value the single character $. Its purpose is to enable you to write a dollar sign in the dependency rule or a command.

The sample makefile can make good use of the predefined macros, as shown in Listing 15.4.

Listing 15.4. Building an object library (with macros).

```
# Makefile to generate an object library libu.a

CFLAGS = -g

LIB = libu.a
OBJ = alloc.o error.o file.o parse.o

$(LIB): $(OBJ)
        $(AR) $(ARFLAGS) $@ $(OBJ)

alloc.o: alloc.c
        $(CC) $(CFLAGS) -c alloc.c

error.o: error.c
        $(CC) $(CFLAGS) -c error.c

file.o: file.c
        $(CC) $(CFLAGS) -c file.c

parse.o: parse.c
        $(CC) $(CFLAGS) -c parse.c
```

Notice that the makefile in Listing 15.4 uses the CFLAGS macro on all compiler commands. To generate a production version of the object library with optimized code instead of debugging support, use the same makefile but invoke it with the following command:

```
make CFLAGS='-O'
```

If you execute the makefile in Listing 15.4, the output of make will look similar to that of Listing 15.3:

```
$ make
        cc -g -c alloc.c
        cc -g -c error.c
        cc -g -c file.c
        cc -g -c parse.c
        ar r libu.a alloc.o error.o file.o parse.o
ar: creating libu.a
$
```

Implicit Rules

A quick examination of the makefile shown in Listing 15.4 is sufficient to disclose a lot of redundancy. By adding the formal use of macros to the original makefile of Listing 15.2, the similarity between the rules for compiling each of the source files is highlighted and made evident. You might wonder whether there is a way to compress the four rules for compiling source files into one rule. After all, the process of compiling a source file into object code is the same regardless of the names of the respective files. Ideally one procedure should need to be expressed only once.

Implicit rules provide a way to describe a generalized procedure. The idea behind implicit rules is that of a *transformation:* the conversion of a file of one type into an equivalent file of another type. With make, you describe the transformation by giving a rule to change a filename having one suffix into a filename with a different suffix.

The most common such transformation (for C programmers) is the generation of an .o file from a corresponding .c file. You can give the procedure for performing such a transformation with an implicit rule like the following:

```
.c.o:
        cc -g -c $<
```

425

The target name of an implicit rule identifies the kind of transformation the rule performs by giving the suffixes of the input and resultant files. You normally do not list any names to the right of the colon because the target name implies an input file.

Whenever make finds that a file is out of date or nonexistent, and it has no explicit dependency rule for building the file, make looks for an implicit rule that yields the desired file from some other file. For example, if make needs to build a file named alloc.o and has an implicit rule named .c.o, make checks the current directory for the presence of a file named alloc.c. Finding that alloc.c exists, make then executes the implicit rule.

The make command only considers filename suffixes that are defined as eligible for implicit rule handling. You define the possible suffixes of a filename with the .SUFFIXES special target—for example:

```
.SUFFIXES: .o .s .c .l .y
```

The order of suffixes is important. If make can find a *filename*.o file in your current directory, it uses it. Finding no *filename*.o, make uses a *filename*.s file. The make command chooses a .c.o implicit rule only when it can find a *filename*.c file but neither a *filename*.s nor a *filename*.o file.

The make command has a built-in .SUFFIXES list:

.o	Object file
.c	C source file
.c~	SCCS C source file (s.*filename*.c)
.y	YACC source file
.y~	SCCS YACC source file (s.*filename*.y)
.l	LEX source file
.l~	SCCS file (s.*filename*.l)
.s	Assembler source file
.s~	SCCS assembler source file
.sh	Shell script
.sh~	SCCS form of .sh (s.*filename*.sh)
.h	Header file
.h~	SCCS header file (s.*filename*.h)
.f	Fortran source file
.f~	SCCS fortran souce file (s.*filename*.f)

If you include a suffix list in your makefile, your new suffixes are added to the end of the built-in list by default. To replace the built-in suffix list, first write a .SUFFIXES: rule with no values to clear make's internal suffix list:

```
.SUFFIXES:
.SUFFIXES: .o .c .y .l .h .m .x
```

The new suffix list causes make to recognize only the suffixes .o, .c, .y, .l, .h, .m, and .x.

The make command is capable of applying a series of implicit rules in succession to achieve a desired result. For example, make will if necessary use an implicit rule .y.c followed by an implicit rule .c.o to build an object file from a YACC source file. If make has the implicit rule .y.o as well as the two rules .y.c and .c.o, it will use the more direct .y.o rule unless doing so would obsolete a .c file in the current directory.

Because you have to write commands for an implicit rule without knowing the full names of the files involved, make provides some special macros to identify the input and target files. These special macros are defined only within the scope of an implicit rule; if you try to use them in a normal dependency rule, you'll find their value to be the null string.

$*	Stem of the target filename
$<	Input filename
$%	Current target member of an archive

The $* macro gives the common part of the input and target filenames. If an implicit rule is called to build alloc.o from alloc.c, for example, the value of $* is alloc. If the target name has a directory prefix, the value of $* contains the same directory prefix.

The $< macro gives the name of the input file. Using the same example of building alloc.o from alloc.c, the value of $< is alloc.c.

The $% macro is set when the target file is a member of an archive. In such cases, the $* macro gives the name of the archive and $% gives the name of the member.

Built-in Definitions

The make command comes with a great number of implicit rules built in. You can use them when writing your makefile by simply omitting to write the implicit rule yourself. You can also override a built-in implicit rule by providing your own definition of the rule.

Some of the most frequently used built-in rules are .c.o, .c.a, .y.c, .y.o, .l.c, and .l.o. Their definitions are as follows:

```
.y.o:
        $(YACC) $(YFLAGS) $<
        $(CC) $(CFLAGS) -c y.tab.c
        -rm y.tab.c
        mv y.tab.o $@


.y.c:
        $(YACC) $(YFLAGS) $<
        mv y.tab.c $@


.l.o:
        $(LEX) $(LFLAGS) $<
        $(CC) $(CFLAGS) -c lex.yy.c
        -rm lex.yy.c; mv lex.yy.o $@


.l.c:
        $(LEX) $(LFLAGS) $<
        mv lex.yy.c $@


.c.o:
        $(CC) $(CFLAGS) -c $<


.c.a:
        $(CC) $(CFLAGS) -c $<
        $(AR) $(ARFLAGS) $@ $*.o
        -rm -f $*.o


.c:
        $(CC) $(CFLAGS) $< -o $@ $(LDFLAGS)
```

The presence of built-in implicit rules can have a drastic shrinking effect on your makefiles. Because make already knows how to build an object (.o) file from a C source (.c) file using the built-in .c.o implicit rule, you can abbreviate the sample makefile in Listing 15.4 to just what is in Listing 15.5.

Listing 15.5. Building an object library using built-in implicit rules.

```
# Makefile to generate an object library libu.a

CFLAGS = -g

LIB = libu.a
OBJ = alloc.o error.o file.o parse.o

$(LIB): $(OBJ)
        $(AR) $(ARFLAGS) $@ $(OBJ)
```

Believe it or not, executing the makefile in Listing 15.5 produces the same output as before, namely

```
$ make
        cc -g -c alloc.c
        cc -g -c error.c
        cc -g -c file.c
        cc -g -c parse.c
        ar -rv libu.a alloc.o error.o file.o parse.o
ar: creating libu.a
$
```

Of the executed commands, the first four all come from built-in implicit rules that you don't need to write. Only the ar command itself was a command explicitly written in the makefile.

Building Archives with *make*

The sample makefile shown in Listing 15.5 does an adequate job of building an archive, but leaves something to be desired. In particular, as written the rule requires you to keep each .o file in addition to the copy in the archive. If the rule deleted all the .o files after adding them to the archive, the next time you execute make it would find that none of the input files exist and would recompile all the source files, even if none had changed and the archive is really up to date.

The rule for libu.a is deficient because it doesn't specify the right inputs for the archive. Actually, the archive considered as a whole file is up to date if all its members are up to date. The rule should be rewritten to indicate that the precursor files for the archive are actually its members.

To name a member of an archive on a dependency rule, you use the special name format *archive(member)*. The special name format tells make that it should check the time stamp for the archive member as opposed to a regular file.

Rewritten to use member names, the makefile would look like Listing 15.6.

Listing 15.6. Building an object library (using member lists).

```
# Makefile to generate an object library libu.a

CFLAGS = -g

LIB = libu.a
OBJ = $(LIB)(alloc.o) \
      $(LIB)(error.o) \
      $(LIB)(file.o) \
      $(LIB)(parse.o)

$(LIB): $(OBJ)
        $(AR) $(ARFLAGS) $@ $(OBJ)
```

If you execute the revised makefile when only the source files exist, you will see the following commands:

```
$ make
        cc -g -c alloc.o
        ar -rv libu.a alloc.o
        rm -f alloc.o
        cc -g -c error.o
        ar -rv libu.a error.o
        rm -f error.o
        cc -g -c file.o
        ar -rv libu.a file.o
        rm -f file.o
        cc -g -c parse.o
        ar -rv libu.a parse.o
        rm -f parse.o
        ar -rv libu.a libu.a(alloc.o) libu.a(error.o) ...
```

The generated commands differ markedly from those of the makefile in Listing 15.5. More importantly, the final ar command is improper; it would not only be rejected by the ar command, but the parentheses would cause problems with the shell.

What happened here is that make no longer uses the default .c.o built-in implicit rule. Because the input file in each case is .c and the target file is an archive (suffix .a), make is using the built-in implicit rule .c.a used for building archive members. The built-in rule creates the archive member by member, and because of it you no longer need to explicitly write the ar command to add the object files to the archive.

The built-in implicit rule .c.a looks like this:

```
.c.a:
    $(CC) $(CFLAGS) -c $<
    $(AR) $(ARFLAGS) $*.o
    rm -f $*.o
```

In one step, for any out-of-date archive member, the rule compiles the source file, adds the generated .o file to the archive, and removes the now redundant .o file.

Because the .c.a implicit rule does so much for you, you must revise the makefile as shown in Listing 15.7.

Listing 15.7. Building an object library (using implicit rules).

```
# Makefile to generate an object library libu.a

CFLAGS = -g

LIB = libu.a
OBJ = $(LIB)(alloc.o) \
      $(LIB)(error.o) \
      $(LIB)(file.o) \
      $(LIB)(parse.o)

$(LIB): $(OBJ)

alloc.o: alloc.h
rbtree.o: rbtree.h
```

Notice that, in this final form of the makefile, the dependency rule for the archive itself includes no command list. All the work of building or updating the archive is done by the .c.a built-in implicit rule.

Also notice that two additional dependency rules were added to the end of the makefile. These specify additional dependencies for the alloc.o and rbtree.o files, showing that the object file is dependent not only on its source file *name*.c, but also on a header file. By including these two additional rules, the archive member is rebuilt if either the header file or the .c file changes.

There are some additional considerations in the building of archive files. For example, your system might require the use of the lorder and tsort commands to organize the members in the correct sequence for processing by the link editor. When members are added piecemeal by the .c.a built-in implicit rule, you have no control over the order in which they are added to the library. To achieve the correct member ordering, you need to rebuild the archive. The following shows how to rewrite the dependency rule for the archive to reorder its members:

```
$(LIB): $(OBJ)
        $(AR) x $@
        $(AR) rv @@temp.a `lorder *.o ¦ tsort`
        rm -f $@
        mv @@temp.a $@
        rm -f *.o
```

The command list begins by extracting all members from the library. A new temporary archive is then built using the `lorder` and `tsort` commands. The `rm` command removes the unordered archive and the `mv` command renames the temporary archive to the final name. Finally, all the .o files that were extracted are once again removed.

If you like, a slightly more efficient way to build or update the archive is to first recompile all out-of-date source files, and then add all the object files to the archive with one ar command. The ar command executes more efficiently adding all members in one pass than when called individually for each object file. The following modified makefile provides a null implicit rule for `.c.a` in order to defeat the built-in rule:

```
# Makefile to generate an object library libu.a

CFLAGS = -g

LIB = libu.a
OBJ = $(LIB)(alloc.o) \
      $(LIB)(error.o) \
      $(LIB)(file.o) \
      $(LIB)(parse.o)

.c.a:;

$(LIB): $(OBJ)
        $(CC) $(CFLAGS) -c $(?:.o=.c)
        $(AR) $(ARFLAGS) $@ $?
        rm -f $?

alloc.o: alloc.h
rbtree.o: rbtree.h
```

433

The implicit rule for `.c.a` uses the semicolon to mean that a command list exists for the rule but the list is empty. Without the semicolon, make would run into a problem. Noting that the rule has no commands, it would conclude that it has no way to build the missing .o files. The null command list forces make to use `.c.a` even though the rule does nothing. All the work is then done in the dependency rule of the archive itself.

The `$(CC)` command uses the special macro `$?` to identify the object files needing to be rebuilt. The macro expression `$(?:.o=.c)` changes the suffix of each .o file to .c to identify the corresponding source file.

It's worth noting that the special macro `$?` expands an archive member name of the form `archive(member)` by stripping the name to just the member name. This is exactly what we need for the ar and rm commands.

One problem with the "efficient" form of the makefile is that, if rebuilding of the archive fails for any reason such as a syntax error in one of the compiles, none of the archive members are updated. When you invoke make again after fixing the problem, all the source files are recompiled no matter how many were successfully compiled before. This is because the dependency rule depends on archive members, not on .o files.

Special Targets

The make command supports four special targets. The "Implicit Rules" section earlier in this chapter already introduced you to the `.SUFFIXES` special target. The other three special targets are `.IGNORE`, `.PRECIOUS`, and `.DEFAULT`.

The special target `.IGNORE` causes make to note and log but otherwise ignore a nonzero exit value from commands in the makefile. Including this target in your makefile has the same effect as including option `-i` on the make command line. To use the `.IGNORE` special target, include the following line in your makefile:

```
.IGNORE:
```

The special target `.PRECIOUS` specifies a list of targets that make should not delete. By default, if make encounters an abnormal termination condition while building a target, it first removes the target file before exiting. The reason for removing the target is to ensure that the next time you invoke make, presumably after having corrected the failing condition, make begins by repeating the attempt to build the incomplete target. In some cases, such as when the target file is an archive, it is either unnecessary or undesirable to delete the object; in the case of an archive, the absence of a member is sufficient to cause the next make execution to reattempt to build the member.

To use the special .PRECIOUS target, include a line similar to the following in your makefile:

```
.PRECIOUS: libc.a
```

You can, of course, list as many target names as you like.

The .DEFAULT special target defines a rule to use when no other dependency rule or implicit rule applies to a target. If you don't provide a .DEFAULT: rule in your makefile and make is unable to find an applicable rule when it needs to build a target, make issues the general error message "Don't know how to make *filename*". If your makefile includes a .DEFAULT: rule, however, make executes its associated command list.

Admittedly, it can be difficult to conceive of a procedure you might write for the .DEFAULT: rule that would cover any possible type of target file. The .DEFAULT rule is mostly useful when you have a number of different files all of which are built the same way. You could use the .DEFAULT rule to specify a catch-all generation procedure and give explicit dependency rules only for exceptional cases.

Using SCCS Files with *make*

The make command contains built-in support for source files stored in SCCS format. When searching the current directory for a file from which to build the current target, make looks for the SCCS form of the files that is acceptable to it. (If you're not familiar with SCCS files, you may need to defer reading this section until after you read Chapter 16, "SCCS—Source Code Control System.")

Use the .SUFFIXES special target to define filename suffixes to which make is sensitive. In particular, make can select an implicit rule to build a file named *name*.y

if it has an implicit rule of the form .x.y and a file in the current directory named
name.x. A suffix can be two or more letters; it does not have to be a single
character.

SCCS files are distinguished not by a suffix but by a prefix. All SCCS files have
names in the general format s.*name* or s.*name.suffix*. To connote an SCCS filename
in the .SUFFIXES list or in the target name of an implicit rule, you must use the
naming format .*suffix~*, where the tilde (~) is a flag make recognizes to mean the
SCCS filename format.

The built-in implicit rules contain rules to extract a regular file from an SCCS
file, and to generate many types of intermediate files from SCCS source files. In
particular, the rules .h~.h, .y~.y, .l~.l, and .c~.c are defined to use the get
command of SCCS, and the rules .y~.c, .y~.o, .l~.c, .l~.o, and .c~.o are available to compile yacc, lex, and C source files. The text of these built-in rules is
as follows:

```
.h~.h:
        $(GET) $(GFLAGS) $<


.c~.c:
        $(GET) $(GFLAGS) $<


.l~.l:
        $(GET) $(GFLAGS) $<


.y~.y:
        $(GET) $(GFLAGS) $<


.sh~.sh:
        $(GET) $(GFLAGS) $<


.c~.o:
        $(GET) $(GFLAGS) $<
        $(CC) $(CFLAGS) -c $*.c
        -rm -f $*.c


.c~.a:
        $(GET) $(GFLAGS) $<
        $(CC) $(CFLAGS) -c $*.c
```

436

```
        $(AR) $(ARFLAGS) $@ $*.o
        -rm -f $*.[co]


.l~.c:
        $(GET) $(GFLAGS) $<
        $(LEX) $(LFLAGS) $*.l
        mv lex.yy.c $@
        -rm -f $*.l


.l~.o:
        $(GET) $(GFLAGS) $<
        $(LEX) $(LFLAGS) $*.l
        $(CC) $(CFLAGS) -c lex.yy.c
        -rm -f lex.yy.c $*.l
        mv lex.yy.o $@


.y~.c:
        $(GET) $(GFLAGS) $<
        $(YACC) $(YFLAGS) $*.y
        mv y.tab.c $*.c
        -rm -f $*.y


.y~.o:
        $(GET) $(GFLAGS) $<
        $(YACC) $(YFLAGS) $*.y
        $(CC) $(CFLAGS) -c y.tab.c
        -rm -f y.tab.c $*.y
        mv y.tab.o $*.o


.sh~:
        $(GET) $(GFLAGS) $<
        cp $*.sh $*; chmod 0777 $@
        -rm -f $*.sh


.c~:
        $(GET) $(GFLAGS) $<
        $(CC) $(CFLAGS) $*.c -o $@ $(LDFLAGS)
        -rm -f $*.c
```

437

All implicit rules beginning with .x~ include a $(GET) (get) command to retrieve the text of the SCCS file. By default, the GFLAGS macro is the null string, so the get command simply retrieves the most recent version of the file. You might like to specify a GFLAGS macro in your makefiles to add the -s option (*silent*; prevents get from logging the version info of the file retrieved) or other options to influence how the retrieval is done.

When an implicit rule is sufficiently complete that the retrieved SCCS file is no longer needed, the rule deletes the file. Rules like .h~.h and .c~.c do not delete the file, however. An unavoidable fallout of using make with SCCS is that you often have unnecessary and unwanted retrieved files lying about your directories.

You can write your own implicit rules to override the built-in ones or to support new suffixes. For my programs that use the yacc parser generator, I often add the following implicit rule to my makefile:

```
.y~.o:
    $(GET) $(GFLAGS) $<
    $(YACC) $(YFLAGS) -d $*.y
    mv y.tab.c $*.c
    mv y.tab.h $*.h
    $(CC) $(CFLAGS) -c $*.c
    rm -f $*.[yc]
```

The advantage of this implicit rule over the built-in version is that, in most cases, you need the #define statements generated by the -d option for compiling programs that use the parser. The header file containing the token definitions is named parser.h for a yacc parser named parser.c. The implicit rule also deletes the obsolete .c and .y files that are no longer needed after building the object file.

Notice that if you also add the rule .y.o, you run the risk of allowing make to use the chained sequence .y~.y followed by .y.o to compile the yacc file; the chained sequence leaves a *filename*.y file lying around because neither rule can safely delete the file.

About the Touch Option

The make command supports a -t (*touch*) option that modifies the usual behavior of make: upon finding that a target file is out of date with respect to its precursor files and when the -t option is specified, make executes the touch command to adjust the time stamp of the target file so that it appears current.

Using the -t option not only defeats the basic purpose of the make command, but also destroys the only record of obsolete target files. If you use the -t option indiscriminately or accidentally, you will no longer know which object or executable files you need to regenerate from source. The only way to recover the validity of your object and executable files is to delete them all and rebuild everything from source code.

Yet there are situations where using -t makes sense. For example, suppose your application uses a header file that is included by all your source files. Being critical to the successful compilation of any source file, your makefile would probably declare a dependency for all object files on the header. Yet if you make a nonsubstantive change to the header, such as adjusting a comment or removing some superfluous unused definitions, the next time you run make it recompiles everything. To avoid an unnecessary and time-consuming rebuild of the entire application, you can issue the command make -t to force all generated files to be newer than the header file.

Because using make -t is dangerous to the integrity of your compiled applications, I cannot recommend its use in any specific situation. You will generally recognize the rare situation where using the -t option is useful. Remember that, when using it, you should be very sure that your application is already up to date, because after using the -t option it will appear so.

Using Directories with *make*

The make command has a basic predisposition to working with files in the current directory. Most of this predisposition arises from the way implicit rules work, which entails a search of the current directory for files make can use to rebuild an obsolete target. When you divide your development files among a hierarchy of directories as most programmers do, you may need to think carefully about your strategy for building the programs with make.

An approach that works well is to create a makefile for every directory containing buildable source code. When you use SCCS to administrate your source code, even a directory of header files needs to be processed by make to extract the current version of each header file from the corresponding SCCS file. To tie all your directories together and to provide one single makefile that can build the entire application, you can store a *super* makefile in the top-level directory.

The basic outline of a super makefile follows this general scheme:

```
# Generate application from several source directories

all:
    cd include; $(MAKE)
    cd lib; $(MAKE)
    cd prog1; $(MAKE)
    cd prog2; $(MAKE)
```

The idea behind the super makefile is to provide an automated execute procedure for building the application. It switches to each component directory in the proper order and executes the makefile stored in that directory. If no build action is needed in a particular directory, the second-level make has no effect; the super makefile does not itself test nor confirm that the objects in the subordinate directory were properly built.

The make command supports the super makefile by automatically propagating any options you specify on the make command to all secondary make commands issued from the super makefile. The options are propagated by storing them in an environment variable called MAKEFLAGS. When the make command begins, it incorporates the value of the MAKEFLAGS environment variable in its setting of internal options and switches; thus specifying command options in the MAKEFLAGS environment variable has the same effect as specifying them on the make command line. Ordinarily the MAKEFLAGS environment variable is null or unset in your top-level shell; it has a non-null value only in the lower-level shells invoked by your make command, and is discarded when the lower-level shells terminate.

The cd command sets the current directory context in which the second-level make commands execute, thus simplifying your task in writing them by enabling you to treat each directory as if it were the current directory when writing the second-level makefile. If you try to combine all your generation steps into one single makefile, not only do you have to use long pathnames for your source and object files, but the implicit rule mechanism often fails; your attempt results either in an extraordinarily unwieldy and cluttered makefile or in one that doesn't work right.

Summary

This chapter discusses the purpose and usage of the make command, as well as the syntax of makefiles.

The make command itself is a very general-purpose program, in much the same manner as the UNIX shell: it does nothing specific on its own initiative, but only follows your instructions. The makefile—a text file you write using a language syntax unique to the make command—describes one or more files called *targets*. A target file is a file you want the make command to build whenever it is out of date with respect to some other file or group of files. Typical examples of target files include object files, object libraries, and executable program files. Whenever you invoke the make command and name one or more target files, make checks whether each target is newer or older than the files from which it is built; if older, make rebuilds the target by executing a list of commands you provided in the makefile.

When your program can be built using a very simple procedure, there is little point bothering with the make command. For complex applications, however, the build procedure can involve many steps using a variety of UNIX commands that must be executed in an exact sequence. The make command is then of great value, because it enables you to permanently record the procedure, and you know that a computer program will always execute the procedure in the same way without skipping any necessary steps or doing them in the wrong order.

The fact that make uses the time stamps of files to control the build procedure also provides a great benefit: make can automatically skip the building of target files that are already up to date. In an application containing many source files, you might change only one or two on any given occasion. Most of the object files you have from the previous execution of make remain valid; you can reuse them when building the complete application. Only the source files you touched need to be rebuilt. The make command uses your specifications in the makefile to identify the targets made obsolete by your changes, and rebuilds just those targets.

The make command is a surprisingly difficult and complex tool to understand and use, all the more so when you realize that its basic concepts and the syntax of its makefiles are straightforward. The complexity arises from the recursive nature of make, from the sometimes non-intuitive features of its processing algorithm, and from the many special-purpose symbols you can use in the makefile that have limited and highly specific uses.

As with most UNIX tools, your level of comfort will increase with experience, and as you experiment with features in the makefiles you write. As long as you master the basics of dependency rules, implicit rules, suffix naming conventions, and the use of macros, you will have a good foundation on which to build.

Remember that you can always experiment freely with your makefiles. Use the @echo command in your makefiles to show the current value of macros such as $@, $*, and $?. Use the -n option to show the commands make would execute from your makefile without actually executing them. If you seem to be having trouble with the operation of implicit rules, try the -r option to disable built-in macros and implicit rules.

Also, don't forget that you can use the full power of the shell in writing your command lines. Shell looping statements might come in handy in some situations, as in the following example rule:

```
$(LIB): $(OBJECTS)
    for FILE in $?;\
    do;\
      fgrep "#include" $FILE >headers;\
    done
```

Each line of the shell statement ends with a backslash so make will join all the lines together before passing them to the shell. Remember, make normally invokes the shell separately for each line in a command list; the shell rejects an incomplete command, so you must write the for statement as you would type it in one line at the terminal. The semicolons provide the necessary separators between the parts of the command, because you can't use a newline to mark the end of lines.

Remember, simpler is better, and you should generally prefer a build procedure that comes naturally to make over a procedure you have to strain to write. For example, building archives tends to be easier (because of the built-in .c.a rule) when you build the archive a member at a time; the so-called efficient method is disadvantageous if any compiles fail, and involves a peculiar override definition of the .c.a rule that could confuse other programmers.

If you must tackle a complex build job with make and have little or no previous experience, you should develop your makefile in stages, setting yourself reachable goals for each new capability you add to the makefile. Try it out often as you develop it; don't try to write the whole thing before you ever run it.

Remember that make has a reputation as a powerful and beneficial tool. That doesn't mean that everyone likes it or that it couldn't be improved. It does mean that, for good or ill, the complexities of make are grounded in the complexities of the tasks we give it and no better tool is likely to come along soon.

16

SCCS— Source Code Control System

The Source Code Control System (known as *SCCS*) is a tool for the management and control of source program changes. Its purpose is to protect your source program text files from unintentional damage or loss by normal editing and maintenance. The assumption underlying SCCS is that a source program is a valuable asset and that its loss or corruption would incur significant cost in time or dollars to the organization or individual owning the file. Using SCCS adds a burden to the software development process. You agree to support the extra burden for the same reason you buy an insurance policy: the cost is small compared to the potential risk.

The normal process of program maintenance and enhancement is a necessary threat to the integrity of a program. A long series of changes left unfinished can leave the source file in an unusable condition. A series of hasty fixes can gradually disrupt the organization of the program until it becomes so bug-laden that it's worthless, or perhaps you just mistype an rm command, deleting your only copy of the source file.

One way to protect the source file against damage or loss is to back it up regularly. All computer installations (even personal computer users) should back up important files regularly. Backups alone, however, are not enough. If you need to see a version of the source file older than a couple of days or weeks, the odds are that no backup exists with such an old copy of the file.

SCCS complements a regular backup schedule by preserving not just the most recent image of the file, but rather all earlier versions of the source file right back to its original writing. SCCS collects all the versions in one physical file and identifies differences between the versions with special control marks. SCCS does not duplicate text common to successive versions, only differences between versions add to the size of the SCCS file.

Usually an SCCS file is much smaller than you might expect. If you were to store each earlier version as a separate file (or as members of an archive), the size of such a collection would be significantly greater than that of the SCCS file. This means that although SCCS files require more disk space than do regular files, the cost is small compared to the volume of data they contain.

SCCS files are also write-protected. You cannot inadvertently delete them. In fact, you must use special SCCS commands to retrieve a version of an SCCS file or to store a new version into the SCCS file. You never directly touch an SCCS file with an editor.

Because you always manipulate an SCCS file using one of the special SCCS commands, this chapter is primarily about SCCS commands: what they are, how to use them, and advice on how not to misuse them.

SCCS Files

You can identify an SCCS file by its name. All SCCS files have names beginning with *s.*. Normally, when you convert an existing file to SCCS format, you form the SCCS filename by adding the prefix *s.* to the old filename. For example, if you had a file named alloc.c, you would name the SCCS version the file s.alloc.c. The name you choose for an SCCS file is important because when you extract the current (or any earlier) version of an SCCS file, SCCS stores the text in a file with the same name as the SCCS file but without the s. prefix.

The SCCS file naming convention can cause you some problems when trying to convert an existing family of source files to SCCS. The SCCS files should have the same names as the original files, but with the s. prefix added. If some of your files have maximum-length names though, the last two characters are dropped when forming the corresponding SCCS filename. (Many versions of UNIX limit filenames to a maximum length of 14 characters.) Fortunately, SCCS allows you to assign any name you wish to the new SCCS file (as long as it begins with *s.*). Not so fortunately, an extracted text has the root of the new SCCS name for its filename, not the old name. For this reason you should always choose reasonably short names for your source files.

An SCCS file cannot contain lines longer than 2,048 characters. If you try to create an SCCS file from a source text having lines longer than 2,048 characters, or add an update with such lines to an existing SCCS file, SCCS rejects the change.

An SCCS file may not contain text characters other than the normal ASCII graphics, plus spaces, tabs, form feeds, and backspaces. In particular, any text line beginning with the ASCII 01 (1 or ^A) character confuses SCCS and renders the SCCS file unusable. SCCS embeds a number of control characters in your text to mark the start and end of differences between versions, and adds some history and control information in lines marked with control characters.

Associated with each SCCS file is a set of control information and properties. Control information includes such data as the list of version numbers stored in the SCCS file, and a descriptive title you can associate with the file. The properties of an SCCS file influence the way SCCS commands can update an SCCS file. For example, an mr flag ,if set, requires you to supply a *Modification Request* number with each file update; organizations can use the MR number to correlate a file update with the problem reports that caused the update. Another property is the users list, which if specified, causes SCCS commands to restrict update authority to users in the list.

The format of an SCCS file is documented in the set of manuals accompanying your particular UNIX system. The format is published so you can, at least in theory, write your own programs to process SCCS files. The format of SCCS files is free to change in future versions of UNIX, though, so relying on the documented format is dangerous and ill-advised. Then too, there is no guarantee that the documentation is complete or accurate. For these reasons I refrain from describing the SCCS file format in this book.

Although SCCS does a good job of minimizing the size of its files, they do tend to grow ever larger. The size of an SCCS file is affected not only by the extent to which its text is modified over time, but also by the number of different versions stored in the SCCS file. The wrong way to limit the growth of SCCS files is to accumulate many small changes into a single update; SCCS is most helpful to you when you file updates at their natural closing point. The right way to limit file growth is to periodically merge updates into a new baseline (without deleting or destroying any earlier baselines). A *baseline* is a version of the file that represents a known, tested, working program. Intermediate updates between the previous baseline and the last update of a maintenance or development cycle are usually of little importance; merging them into one update saves some disk space. If you want to condense your SCCS files periodically, you'll find some helpful hints and shell scripts in the "Merging Updates"-section later in this chapter.

SCCS Commands

SCCS consists of an entire family of related commands that enable you to manipulate and display information about your SCCS files.

admin—File Administration

```
admin [-n] [-iname] [-rrel] [-tname] [-ffc][-dflag] [-alogin] [-elogin]
      [-mnumbers][-y[comment]] [-z] files
```

The admin command creates SCCS files from regular files and allows you to set or change the control information and properties of an SCCS file. The options you specify on the admin command determine the specific action performed by the command, and are listed in Table 16.1.

As you will see from examining the option definitions, the admin command is really a multipurpose command that can perform any of several different actions on a given execution. Perhaps it would have been better if the original authors had provided each of the basic actions in a separate command, but you can achieve the same effect by writing your own shell scripts to call the admin command indirectly. Using a family of shell scripts helps to prevent the specification of mutually exclusive options on the same admin command, and provides a more mnemonic interface to its facilities. For more on this subject, see the "Encapsulating SCCS Commands" section later in this chapter.

The functions you can perform with admin are: creating a new SCCS file with or without an initial text; setting and removing flags from a set of SCCS files; adding, revising, or removing the description for an SCCS file; checking a set of SCCS files for valid checksums and structure; and forcing a corrupted SCCS file to have a valid checksum.

Table 16.1 describes the options you use to invoke these actions.

Table 16.1. admin command options.

Option	Meaning and Usage
-n	Use the -n option to create a new SCCS file. Do not specify the -d, -e, or -z flags together with -n. If you want to create the SCCS file from an initial text, use option -i to specify the filename of the initial version. If you omit option -i, admin creates an empty SCCS file. You can add text later with the delta command.
-iname	Use -i to create a new SCCS file and to supply an initial text. For *name*, write the filename or pathname of the regular file you want to store as the first delta. The -i option implies the -n option. Do not specify the -d, -e, or -z flags on the same command.
-rrel	Use -r to specify the SID code of the initial delta level when you create a new SCCS file with option -i. If you omit the -r option, the first delta defaults to *1.1*.

continues

449

Table 16.1. continued

Option	Meaning and Usage
-t*name*	Use the -t option to provide a file to SCCS containing a description of the SCCS file. The description file may contain any number of lines, all of which become the descriptive text entry for the SCCS file. If the SCCS file exists, admin replaces its descriptive text with the contents of the description file. If you omit *name*, admin removes the description entry of the SCCS file. If you are creating a new SCCS file with option -n or -i and you also specify the -t option, you may not omit *name*.
-f*fc*	Use the -f option to specify flags for a new SCCS file or to add flag settings to an existing SCCS file. (See option -d to remove an existing flag). The first character after -f must be one of the valid flags. Some flags require a value; the value must immediately follow the flag letter. The valid flag codes are described in Table 16.2. You can specify any number of -f options on one admin command to set multiple flags in one pass of the SCCS file.
-d*flag*	Use the -d option to remove a flag from the SCCS file. You can specify any number of -d options on one admin command to remove several flags in one pass of the SCCS file.
-a*login*	For *login*, specify the login name of one user who you permit to make changes to the SCCS file. Use multiple -a options to add several users with one admin command. For *login*, you may also specify a group-ID to add all the users in the group.
-e*login*	For *login*, specify the login name of one user already included in the list of valid users of the SCCS file. admin removes the named user from the list.
-m*numbers*	Use the -m option to specify a list of Modification Request numbers to be associated with the initial delta of a newly

450

Option	Meaning and Usage
	created SCCS file. You may not specify the -m option unless you also set the v flag for the SCCS file on the same admin command.
-y[comment]	Use -y to enter a comment describing the initial delta of a newly created SCCS file. If you specify the -y flag but omit the comment text, the admin command prompts you for the text. If you omit the -y flag, admin stores a default comment for the initial delta.
-h	When you specify the -h option, the admin command checks the named SCCS files for bad checksums and other logical errors. You should periodically run the command admin -h on your SCCS files to detect unsuspected file damage that might be caused, for example, by abnormal termination of the system while admin is updating a file. You may not specify any other options in combination with the -h option.
-z	Use the -z option to force admin to store a valid checksum in the named SCCS files. Forcing a valid checksum may make the SCCS file appear valid if its control structure remains consistent. You should use the -z flag only for the purpose of recovering text stored in a damaged SCCS file, and you should immediately re-create the SCCS file from the recovered text. You may not specify any other options in combination with the -z option.

Table 16.2 describes the flags you may set for an SCCS file. You set a flag with the -f option and remove it with the -d option. Notice that when setting a flag, you write the -f option, the flag code, and any value required for the flag as a single string. Please remember that admin stores the following codes in the SCCS file and they remain permanently associated with it once set. Do not confuse them with the option keyletters that you specify on SCCS commands.

Table 16.2. SCCS file flags.

Flags	Effect
b	Enables you to use the -b option of the get command to force a branch in the delta tree. Notice that automatic branching can still occur; the b flag only affects the use of the -b option to force branching.
cceil	For ceil, specify the highest release number that admin should create for this SCCS file. The value of ceil must be an integer in the range of 1–9999. If omitted, admin can create release numbers as high as 9999.
ffloor	For floor, specify the lowest release number that admin should create for this SCCS file. The value of floor must be an integer in the range of 1–9999. The default floor is 1.
dSID	For SID, specify the SID code that get should retrieve by default. If you do not specify the d flag, get retrieves the current (last stored) delta by default.
istr	The i flag causes admin to consider a file version having no ID keywords to be a fatal error. Normally admin issues a warning message and continues. An attempt to create an SCCS file, or to add or retrieve a delta that contains no ID keywords when the i flag is set for the SCCS file, causes the file creation or change to be abandoned. You set this flag for an SCCS file when you want to ensure that all deltas in the file specify an ID keyword. For str, specify the exact ID keyword sequence you expect in a new text or any file version submitted to the delta command. The str string is optional; omitting it allows any ID keyword or combination. (For more information about ID keywords, see the get command.)
j	The j flag allows two or more pending updates to the same delta; normally admin warns of concurrent update and rejects the second and later update requests. If you proceed to create multiple simultaneous updates to the

Flags	*Effect*
	same version, you must either store the updates as separate branches of the delta tree or merge the updates into one delta. Merging of independently created but overlapping deltas is a tedious and error-prone manual procedure, which is why you must explicitly set the j flag to get into such a situation. For more information, see the "Deltas and Branches" section later in this chapter.
l*list*	Use *list* to specify a list of releases to which further updates cannot be made. You lock a release to indicate that revision to it is logically nonsensical. For example, the locked release represents code that the company has already shipped to customers and the company policy is that it must distribute subsequent code changes in a new release.

For *list*, specify one or more release numbers. If specifying several numbers, separate each with a comma: 15,17,23. You may also write 1a to lock all releases. Notice that you cannot lock update levels within a release; you can only lock whole releases. |
| n | Use the n flag to force admin to create a null delta when adding a new delta, and the new delta skips one or more release numbers. For example, if the last delta is numbered *5.3* and a programmer then opens an update for Release 8 (using the command get -e -r8), admin automatically creates no-effect deltas numbered *6.1* and *7.1*. The null deltas serve as place holders so you can later create updates for the skipped release numbers. If you do not set the n flag and the delta history skips one or more release levels, you cannot subsequently create an update for those releases.

Specifying the n flag for new SCCS files is generally a good idea. A null delta requires a negligible amount of |

continues

453

Table 16.2. continued

Flags	Effect
	space in the SCCS file. Unfortunately, when you discover that you need the n flag, it is too late to go back and put it in. The discovery often comes as a shock to inexperienced SCCS users who only then realize why they needed it.
qtext	Use the q flag to specify a text string that get will substitute for the %Q% ID keyword; by default the ID keyword %Q% has no value. The q flag enables you to associate an arbitrary string with the SCCS file that you can later query with the %Q% ID keyword. You might use it to specify the program or system of which the source file is a component, to specify a language code for the source file, or for any other purpose you find useful.
mname	Use the m flag to specify an override value that get will substitute for the %M% ID keyword. By default get substitutes the tail of the SCCS filename (the residuum left over after removing the s. prefix). One conceivable reason for using the m flag is when you want to associate a module name with the file that is longer than the operating system limit for filenames.
ttype	Use the t flag to associate a type code with the SCCS file; the get command will substitute the type value for occurrences of the %Y% ID keyword in gotten files. There is no default for the %Y% ID keyword.
v[name]	Specify the v flag to require Modification Request (MR) numbers for each delta. If you do not set the v flag, the delta command will not accept MR numbers. Specify an optional name if you want the delta command to call a program of that name to check programmer-supplied MR numbers for validity.

cdc—Change Delta Comments

```
cdc -rSID [-m[mrlist]] [-y[comment]] files
```

The cdc command enables you to change the descriptive comment associated with a file version. The delta comment is a combination of the MR numbers you specify with the -m option, and the comment text you specify with the -y option on the original delta command. You change the commentary using the corresponding options of the cdc command.

For *files*, you can specify a list of SCCS filenames, a directory name, or the special filename -. All SCCS files in a named directory are processed as if named on the command line. For -, cdc reads the standard input file and takes each line as the name of an SCCS file it will process.

You must specify the delta you want changed using the -r option. For *SID*, write the SID code identifying the delta, such as *3.2.*

Use the -m option to add or delete MR numbers from the list currently defined for the delta. Write an exclamation point (!) in front of the numbers you want to delete. If you specify multiple numbers, separate them with blanks or newline characters. Remember to enclose *mrlist* in quotes to have the shell treat the list as part of the -m option. If you specify the -m option without an *mrlist* value, the existing MR list remains unchanged.

cdc inserts modification request numbers you delete into the comments section of the delta with a note identifying them as deleted MRs. cdc validates modification numbers you add if the v flag is set for the SCCS file, and then adds the MR numbers already defined to the list.

If you omit the -m option and the v flag is set for the SCCS file, cdc will prompt you for the list of MR numbers you want to add or delete. If you enter no numbers and just press the Enter key, the existing MR list remains unchanged. Because you do not see a blank-separated list of numbers entered in response to the prompt by the shell, you should not enclose them in quotes.

You may not specify the -m option on the cdc command for an SCCS file unless you set its v flag.

Use the -y flag to append new comments to the comment text already present for the delta. You cannot delete previously entered comment text. If you omit the -y flag, cdc prompts you to enter comment text.

Notice that for both the -m and -y options, prompting occurs only when the standard input file is a terminal. Therefore, the command cdc -r1.3 -y'additional comment' s.text.c </dev/null adds comment text but leaves the MR list unchanged without soliciting a prompt, because the standard input file is redirected.

delta—Store Text Updates

```
delta [-rSID] [-s] [-n] [-glist] [-mnumbers] [-ycomment] [-p] files
```

The delta command adds a new update to an existing SCCS file, thereby creating a new file version. The update may add, change, or delete lines in the current or any other stored version of the file, but the text of earlier versions remains unaffected by the update. Table 16.3 describes the the option keyletters.

Table 16.3. delta command options.

Option	Usage and Meaning
-glist	Use the -g option to specify a list of deltas to be ignored. Using this option has no affect on the text image stored by delta, but may reduce the number of changes found and added to the SCCS file. For *list*, specify one or more SID codes separated by spaces. You can specify a range of SID numbers using the syntax *SID-SID*. For example, -g3.2-3.5,3.7 ignores the deltas 3.2, 3.3, 3.4, 3.5, and 3.7.

456

Option	Usage and Meaning
-m*numbers*	For *numbers*, specify the modification request (MR) numbers you want to associate with this delta. The SCCS file must include the v flag (see the admin command), otherwise the delta command rejects the -m option. To list several numbers, separate each with blanks or tabs, and enclose the entire option in quotes. If the SCCS file includes the v flag and you do not provide an -m option on the delta command, delta prompts you for the list of numbers.
-p	Use the -p option to print a listing showing the differences between the base file version and the text you supply to delta. The listing has the same format as the output of the diff command.
-r	Specify the SID code of the delta upon which your g-file is based. You only need this option when two or more updates are pending for the same SCCS file; it specifies which of the pending updates your delta request satisfies, and the SID code you specify must be the same as the get command reported.

For example, if you issued the command get -e -r2 to request an update to Release 2, the get command might have identified the base update as 2.5. The source file stored in your directory is then the text of delta 2.5. The get command also reports the next SID code to assign to your new update, such as 2.6. If you or someone else later requests an update to Release 3, the p-file shows two different update requests. When you later issue the delta command, you should specify -r2.6 to indicate that your update satisfies the pending request for an update to Release 2. |
| -s | Causes the delta command to suppress the informational messages it would normally display including the statistical report of the number of lines added, changed, and deleted. |

continues

457

Table 16.3. continued

Option	Usage and Meaning
-n	Use option -n to prevent the delta command from deleting your plain text file after storing the update.
-ycomment	For *comment*, provide a string describing this delta. You may use the -y option without a comment to store the delta without a description. Remember to enclose the entire option in quotes if the *comment* string contains characters special to the shell, including blanks and tabs.
	If you do not provide a -y option, the delta command prompts you for a comment. You can enter several lines of text by ending each line but the last with a backslash.

For *files*, specify one or more SCCS files to update. Each filename you list must begin with *s.* or else SCCS will not believe that it's an SCCS file. For each SCCS filename, the command looks in your current directory for a similarly named file without the s. prefix, called the *g-file*. The delta command also searches for a p. file (the *p-file*) having the same root as the SCCS filename. The p-file tells delta which version of the SCCS file your g-file updates. The command then computes the differences between the base version and your new version and stores the differences as a *delta* in the SCCS file. If all has gone well, the delta command then deletes both your g-file and the p-file.

The delta command repeats this series of actions for each SCCS filename you list. Because the filename of your revised text is based on the filename of the SCCS file, you can list several SCCS files and the delta command will pick out the corresponding updated text from your current directory.

SCCS won't allow you to store a delta with the delta command unless you previously announced your intent to do so by executing a get command with the -e option. The get -e command (commonly called *get for edit*) not only gives you a copy of the source file to edit but also creates the p-file that delta will search for later. Updating an SCCS file is thus a two-stage process: first you open the update with the get -e command, obtaining a copy of the text you'll edit, and then, after making your changes, you file the revised text with the delta command.

The two-stage process is intended to prevent concurrent updating of the same file version by two or more programmers. If you weren't required to announce your intent first, you could both proceed with your file edits oblivious that the other is updating the same file or even the same line of text.

The `delta` command deletes your edited text file from your current directory after incorporating your changes into the SCCS file. The deletion provides a confirmation that the update was successful, and in theory should be harmless because you can always retrieve the revised text from the SCCS file with the `get` command. You may nonetheless be surprised when you discover that the file you have spent hours, days, or weeks editing has just vanished. If you really need to retain the g-file, you can specify the `-n` option on the `delta` command to disable the normal delete step.

SCCS does not allow you to store the update if `delta` determines that the update violates restrictions specified by flags in the SCCS file. For example, if the SCCS file lists any authorized users, you must invoke the `delta` command while logged in under one of the approved user IDs. Or if no p-file exists for the SCCS file or it identifies some other user than you as the user who requested the update, the `delta` command fails. It also fails if modification-request numbers are required for the SCCS file but you specify none on the `delta` command line.

get—Retrieve Text Versions

```
get [-adsn] [-ccutoff] [-ilist] [-rSID] [-wstring][-xlist] [-l[p]] [-b]
    [-e] [-g] [-k] [-m] [-n][-p] [-s] [-t] files
```

The `get` command retrieves versions of an SCCS file. Used in retrieval mode, the `get` command merely extracts a read-only copy of a version already stored in the SCCS file; used in edit mode, the `get` command marks a new update in progress and retrieves a writable copy of a version. You must use the `get` command to request permission to update the SCCS file before you can store the update with the `delta` command.

When you specify the -e option, the get command authorizes you to create a new delta (update level) for the SCCS file. Of central importance to understanding and properly using the get command is a clear grasp of the method get uses to identify the base version to which your delta will apply, and to assign the SID code for your delta. The "Deltas and Branches" section later in this chapter discusses these matters at length.

The meaning of the supported option letters is shown in Table 16.4.

Table 16.4. get command options.

Option	Usage and Meaning
-a	For *dsn*, specify the delta sequence number to retrieve or, if you also specify -e, to update. File versions are usually identified by a SID code, not the internal delta sequence number. Specifying this option causes the -r option to be ignored for purposes of selecting a delta.
-b	Use the -b option in combination with the -e option to force get to assign you a SID code beginning a new branch of the delta tree. For example, if executing get -e would select SID code 2.2 as the basis for your update and assign a SID code of 2.3 to your new delta, the command get -e -b would select the same basis but assign the SID code 2.2.1.1 to your new delta. If other branches exist for the base version, get assigns your new delta an unused branch number, such as 2.2.3.1 if branches 1 and 2 exist for version 2.2.
	You do not need to specify the -b option to create a branch delta in some situations. For example, if you issue the command get -e -r2.2 and delta 2.3 exists, the get command automatically assigns the SID code 2.2.1.1 to your new delta. Omitting the -b option does not prevent the get code from assigning a branch SID code when necessary.
	To use the -b option, the SCCS file must have the b flag set. (See the admin command for details about the b flag.)

Option	Usage and Meaning
-c	For *cutoff*, specify a date and time after which no deltas are to be included in the gotten file. Using this option retrieves the latest version of the file as it existed prior to the specified cutoff date.

You write the date and time as a series of two-digit numbers run together, in the sequence year, month, day, hour, minute, and second. You may omit any trailing values to use the default maximum value. Thus -c921022 specifies a cutoff of 23:59:59 on October 22, 1992. You may also interpose non-numeric characters between the digit pairs to make the number more readable—for example, -c92/10/22,17:00 to specify a cutoff date of 5p.m. on October 22, 1992.

Option	Usage and Meaning
-e	Use option -e to request permission to update the SCCS file. Unless you also specify the -g option, the command writes the text of a file version to your current directory just as it would without the -e option. The difference is that get gives the extracted file write permission so you can edit it, and it creates or updates a p-file to reserve a SID code for the new delta you create.

Use the -r or -a option to specify which version of the SCCS file you intend to update. In addition to retrieving a copy of the version for you, the get command assigns a new SID code for the delta you create. If you specify both the -a and -r options, the -a option is used to extract the base text, and the -r option is used to assign the new SID code.

You should notice both the old SID code and the new SID code that the get command logs. The old SID code confirms which version of the SCCS file was retrieved and stored in your current directory, and to which your new delta applies. The new SID code is the SID code that SCCS has assigned to your delta. You may need to specify the SID code when you later file your updated text with the delta command.

continues

Table 16.4. continued

Option	Usage and Meaning
-g	Use the -g option to suppress the actual extraction and writing of a text file. When used in combination with the -e option it causes the normal allocation of a new SID code but prevents the creation of a basis text in your current directory. When used without the -e option, it enables you to create an l-file (see the -l option) or to check the validity and existence of a SID code without creating a file.
-i	For *list*, specify a set of deltas to include in the creation of the extracted file. SCCS applies the specified deltas even if they would not ordinarily be used. You write the list as a series of SID codes or SID ranges separated by commas. A SID range is written as two SID codes separated by a hyphen. For example, 1.2-1.5,2.6,2.8-3.1 selects all the deltas between 1.2 and 1.5 inclusive, delta 2.6, and all the deltas between 2.8 and 3.1 inclusive.
-k	The -k option suppresses the normal replacement of ID keywords in the retrieved text, and causes the gotten file to be created with write permission. The -k option retrieves a file version in the same manner as the -e option but -k does not create a new delta. If you damage or lose the text file stored by get -e, you can retrieve it again by executing get -rSID -k, where SID is the old SID code that get -e logged.
-l[p]	The -l option causes the get command to write a summary of the deltas included in the retrieved text. By default, the get command writes the summary to an l-file named l.*filename* in your current directory. The -lp option writes the summary to the standard output file instead. You can use the -l option with or without the -e option to see the update history for the text retrieved by get.
-m	The -m option causes each line of the extracted file to be prefixed by the SID code of the version and a tab character.

Option	Usage and Meaning
-n	The -n option causes each line of the extracted file to be prefixed by the value of the %M% ID keyword followed by a tab character. Normally the effect is to precede each line with the filename, but if the m flag is set for the SCCS file (see the admin command), its value is used instead of the filename.
-p	The -p option causes get to write the extracted file to standard output instead of to your current directory. When you specify the -p option, get writes informational messages to the standard error file instead of to standard output as it would normally.
-s	The -s option suppresses the display of informational messages such as the SID code and number of lines in the gotten file. You cannot, however, suppress error messages.
-t	Use the -t option to retrieve the top (most recently created) delta in a given release. For example, the command get -r2 -t retrieves the most recently created delta in Release 2. The most recently created delta may not necessarily have the highest SID code in the release.
-w	For *string*, specify an override definition for the What ID keyword (%W%). You can use ID keywords in forming the value of *string*. For example, get -w´%Z%%M%: %I% %E% %G%´ extends the normal definition of %W% to include the date and time of the last delta as part of the expanded value.
-x	For *list*, specify a set of deltas to exclude from the creation of the extracted file. The specified deltas are ignored even if they are ordinarily used. You write the list as a series of SID codes or SID ranges separated by commas; a SID range is written as two SID codes separated by a hyphen. For example, 1.2-1.5,2.6,2.8-3.1 excludes all the deltas between 1.2 and 1.5 inclusive, delta 2.6, and all the deltas between 2.8 and 3.1 inclusive.

When extracting a file version and neither the -e nor -k options are specified, the get command replaces certain strings called *ID keywords* appearing in the text with a predefined value; the replacement value then appears in the stored file rather than the ID keyword. The get command recognizes and replaces an ID keyword wherever it may appear in the text, including within literal strings and comments, so you should take some care to ensure that your source text contains these character sequences only when and where you intend get to replace them.

The ID keywords recognized by get together with a description of the replacement text are shown in Table 16.5.

Table 16.5. ID keywords.

Keyword	Replacement String
%M%	Module name. Either the filename of the SCCS file with the s. prefix removed, or the value of the m flag if set.
%I%	SID code of the delta. For example: *2.1.4.3*.
%R%	Release portion of the SID code. For example: *2*.
%L%	Level portion of the SID code. For example: *1*.
%B%	Branch number of the SID code. For example: *4*.
%S%	Sequence number of the SID code. For example: *3*.
%D%	Current date in the form YY/MM/DD.
%H%	Current date in the form MM/DD/YY.
%T%	Current time in the form HH:MM:SS.
%E%	Date the delta was created, in the form YY/MM/DD.
%G%	Date the delta was created, in the form MM/DD/YY.
%U%	Time the delta was created, in the form HH:MM:SS.
%Y%	Module type; the value of t flag in the SCCS file.
%F%	SCCS filename.
%P%	Full pathname of the SCCS file.

Keyword	Replacement String
%Q%	Value of the q flag in the SCCS file.
%C%	Current line number.
%Z%	The literal string @(#).
%W%	The *what* string, an abbreviation for %Z%%M%\t%I%.
%A%	An alternate *what* string, equivalent to %Z%%Y% %M% %I%%Z%.

C programmers often embed ID keywords in a character literal to cause them to appear within the generated object module and the executable file. For example, the following statement in a source file

```
static char sccs_id[] = "%W% compiled %H% %T%";
```

allows the what command to produce output similar to the following when invoked for the filename of the object file or executable file produced from the source file:

```
$ what myprog
myprog:
        myprog.c  2.4 compiled 06/28/92 13:57:04
$
```

help—Explain SCCS Commands and Messages

```
help [ command ¦ msgno ] ...
```

The help command displays the command format of other SCCS commands or prints an explanation of an SCCS error message.

Specify either an SCCS command name or an SCCS message number as the command argument. For a command name, help writes a brief summary of the

465

command syntax similar to that shown in the boxes in this chapter. For a message number, help writes a brief paragraph to your terminal explaining the possible causes of the error message and may suggest ways to circumvent the error or correct the error condition.

SCCS error messages usually end with a parenthesized code such as (co1). If you enter help co1 you receive the following response:

```
co1:
"not an SCCS file"
A file that you think is an SCCS file
does not begin with the characters "s.".
```

The probable cause of error message co1 is that you omitted the s. in front of the filename on an SCCS command. You may judge for yourself how helpful the message explanations delivered by the help command are to you.

prs—Print SCCS File Status

```
prs [-dspec] [-rSID] [-e] [-l] [-ccutoff] [-a] files
```

The prs command lists information extracted from an SCCS file. The command offers some report formatting capabilities so you can generate custom reports about the status of your SCCS files. The information you can extract, format, and print includes the text of file versions, but the command's chief purpose is to display information about deltas.

For *files*, you can specify a list of SCCS filenames, a directory name, or the special filename -. prs processes all SCCS files in a named directory as if you named them on the command line. For -, prs reads the standard input file and takes each line as the name of an SCCS file it will process.

The meanings of the command-line options are shown in Table 16.6.

Table 16.6. prs command options.

Option	Usage and Meaning
-a	Use the -a option to format and print data about all deltas, including those that have been removed. By default, deltas that have been removed but that are still listed in the delta table section of the SCCS file are ignored.
-c	For *cutoff*, specify a cutoff date as a series of two-digit numbers in the sequence year, month, day, hour, minute, and second. Omitted trailing components default to the highest allowed value. For example, -c8602 is equivalent to -c860228235959, or 11:59:59 pm on February 28, 1986. You can use any non-numeric separator characters between the digit pairs to improve readability—for example, -c86/02/28.
-d	For *spec*, write a description of the information you want to display for each delta. The *spec* is a string consisting of literal characters, the special characters \t (printed as a tab) and \n (printed as a newline), and any combination of data selector codes having the general format :*id*:. The allowable data selector codes are listed following the options. You need to enclose *spec* in quotes (either ´´ or "") if the string contains characters special to the shell (such as the escape character \) or embedded blanks.
-e	Use the -e option to print all deltas in the named file that have a SID code earlier than the cutoff date specified with the -c option or less than the SID code specified with the -r option.
-l	Use the -l option to print all deltas in the named file that have a SID code later than the cutoff date specified with the -c option or greater than the SID code specified with the -r option.
-r	Use the -r option to specify the SID code of the delta to format and print. By default the last created delta is selected.

If you specify no `-d` option, the `prs` command generates a report like the following for each selected delta:

```
s.db.c:
```

```
D 1.3 92/10/17 22:11:22 jjv 3 2 00097/00053/00927
MRs:
COMMENTS:
Bug fixes for MSDOS compilation
```

To print just the basic delta information for each delta in the file, you could use the command

```
prs -d:Dt: -e s.db.c
```

The output would appear as follows:

```
D 1.3 92/10/17 22:11:22 marsha 3 2
D 1.2 92/10/16 21:57:30 jack 2 1
D 1.1 92/10/10 19:55:47 anne 1 0
```

The data selector codes you can use to create custom report formats are defined in Table 16.7. In many cases, a selector code identifies a datum or set of data to be taken from the delta table or the file text. Some selector codes are actually an abbreviation for a related set of data.

Table 16.7. `prs` data selection codes.

Code	Information Substituted
`:Dt:`	Delta information. Equivalent to the string `":DT: :I: :D: :T: :P: :DS: :DP:"`. Generated lines have the general appearance `D 1.2 92/10/17 22:11:33 jjv 2 1`
`:DL:`	Delta line statistics. Equivalent to `:Li:/:Ld:/:Lu:`
`:Li:`	Number of lines inserted by the delta. For example: *00105*.
`:Ld:`	Number of lines deleted by the delta. For example: *00003*.
`:Lu:`	Number of lines in the base text that were unchanged by the delta. For example: *00365*.

Code	Information Substituted
`:DT:`	Delta type. One of the one-letter codes D indicating a normal delta, or R indicating a removed delta.
`:I:`	SID code of the delta. Equivalent to `:R:.:L:.:B:.:S:`. If the branch and sequence numbers are zero, only the release and level are printed. Example values include *2.1* and *3.5.1.2*.
`:R:`	Release number of the delta. For SID code 3.5.1.2, the value of `:R:` is *3*.
`:L:`	Level number within release. For SID code 3.5.1.2, the value of `:L:` is *5*.
`:B:`	Branch number within level. For SID code 3.5.1.2, the value of `:B:` is *1*.
`:S:`	Sequence number within branch. For SID code 3.5.1.2, the value of `:S:` is *2*.
`:D:`	Date the delta was created. Equivalent to `:Dy:/:Dm:/:Dd:`.
`:Dy:`	Two-digit year the delta was created. For example: *83*.
`:Dm:`	Two-digit month the delta was created. For example: *02*.
`:Dy:`	Two-digit day the delta was created. For example: *31*.
`:T:`	Time the delta was created. Equivalent to `:Th:::Tm:::Ts:`.
`:Th:`	Two-digit hour of the day when the delta was created.
`:Tm:`	Two-digit minute of the time the delta was created.
`:Ts:`	Two-digit second of the time the delta was created.
`:P:`	Login name of the user who created the delta.
`:DS:`	Delta sequence number, with leading zeros removed.
`:DP:`	Predecessor delta sequence number, with leading zeros removed.
`:DI:`	Delta sequence numbers of deltas that were included, excluded, and ignored by the -i and -x options of the get command that created the delta. An abbreviation for the string `:Dn:/:Dx:/:Dg:`.

continues

469

Table 16.7. continued

Code	Information Substituted
:Dn:	List of delta sequence numbers included.
:Dx:	List of delta sequence numbers excluded.
:Dg:	List of delta sequence numbers ignored.
:MR:	Modification Request (MR) numbers specified for the delta with the delta command. The text value of this keyword ends with a newline character.
:C:	Delta comments specified with the -y option of the delta command. The text value of this keyword includes one or more lines, each ending with a newline character.
:UN:	User names authorized to modify the SCCS file. These names are those that have been set with the -a option of the admin command. The text value is a series of lines, each containing one user name.
:FL:	Flag list. The text value is a the list of flags and flag values for the SCCS file, as set by the admin command.
:Y:	Module type flag. The string value is the value of the t flag for the SCCS file.
:MF:	MR validation flag. The string value is yes if the v flag is set for the SCCS file, no otherwise.
:MP:	MR validation program name. The string value is the value of the v flag of the SCCS file, or the null string if the v flag is not set.
:KF:	Keyword flag. The string value is yes if the i flag is set for the SCCS file, no otherwise.
:KV:	Keyword validation string. The string value of :KV: is the str value associated with the i flag of the SCCS file.
:BF:	Branch flag. The string value of :BF: is yes if the b flag is set for the SCCS file, no otherwise.

Code	Information Substituted
:J:	Joint-edit flag. The string yes if the j flag is set for the SCCS file, otherwise no.
:LK:	Locked releases. The string value is a blank-separated list of release numbers that are locked, as set by the l flag for the SCCS file.
:Q:	The string value of the q flag for the SCCS file, or the null string if the q flag is not set.
:M:	Module name of the file. If the m flag is set for the SCCS file, then the value of :M: is the value of the m flag, otherwise it is the filename of the SCCS filename with the s. prefix removed.
:FB:	Floor boundary, the release number specified by the f flag of the SCCS file.
:CB:	Ceiling boundary, the release number specified by the c flag of the SCCS file.
:Ds:	The default SID code as specified by the d flag of the SCCS file.
:ND:	The string yes if the n flag is set for the SCCS file, no otherwise.
:FD:	File description, a possibly null series of lines entered with the -t option of the admin command.
:BD:	Body of the text for this delta.
:GB:	Gotten body for this delta.
:W:	The *what* string for this file, equivalent to :Z::M:\t:I:.
:A:	The alternate *what* string for this file, equivalent to :Z::Y: :M: :I::Z:.
:Z:	The *what* string delimiter: always the text @(#).
:F:	The filename of the SCCS file.
:PN:	The full pathname of the SCCS file.

rmdel—Remove Deltas

```
rmdel -rSID files
```

The rmdel command removes a previously stored delta from all the specified SCCS files. You can remove a file version from an SCCS file only if no other versions are based on the version to be removed. Normally you should use the rmdel command only to remove the last update filed with the delta command; other uses are possible but dangerous to the integrity of the SCCS file.

If one of *files* is the name of a directory, all s-files in the directory are processed. If one of *files* is the special filename –, each line of the standard input is taken as the name of an s-file to process.

sact—Show Activity

```
sact files
```

The sact command lists the SCCS files for which an update is pending, as marked by the get command. The information listed is essentially a copy of the contents of the p-file corresponding to each SCCS file named on the command line.

For *files*, you can specify a list of SCCS filenames, a directory name, or the special filename -. sact processes all SCCS files in a named directory as if you named them on the command line. For -, sact reads the standard input file and takes each line as the name of an SCCS file it will process.

sccsdiff—Show Differences Between Versions

```
sccsdiff -rSID1 -rSID2 [-p] [-sn] files
```

The sccsdiff command displays the difference between any two versions of an SCCS file. The output is similar in appearance and meaning to that generated by the standard diff command.

For *SID1* and *SID2*, specify the SID codes of the file versions you wish to compare. If you list multiple files on the command line, sccsdiff attempts to compare deltas having the same SID code in each of the files, which may or may not be meaningful.

The -p option causes sccsdiff to paginate the extracted text of each delta with the pr command before it compares them.

If the texts of the two deltas are very large, the diff command used internally by sccsdiff may not have enough memory to perform the file comparison. You can use the -sn option to tell sccsdiff to invoke the bdiff utility instead of diff, breaking the delta texts into segments of *n* lines each. Note, however, that bdiff may not find the smallest difference between the two delta texts because it cannot see the entire text at once.

unget—Cancel a Pending Update

```
unget [-rSID] [-s] [-n] files
```

The unget command cancels an update in progress, allowing someone else to request an update for the SCCS file. The defining entry for the update is removed

473

from the p-file, and the p-file is then erased if it becomes empty. The unget command also removes the g-file from the current directory if it can find it. (The g-file is the text file that was created by the get -e command.)

The unget command cancels a previously authorized delta request only when the same user who initiated the delta request issues the command.

The command-line options that you can specify are shown in Table 16.8.

Table 16.8. unget command options.

Option	Usage and Meaning
-r	For *SID*, specify the SID code identifying the delta you wish to cancel. You do not need to specify the -r option unless you have initiated two or more updates for the same SCCS file.
-s	The -s option suppresses the logging of informational messages. You cannot suppress error messages.
-n	Use the -n option to prevent removal of the g-file from your current directory. Notice that although you retain the edited text of the update, you cannot store it with the delta command unless you request another update with the get command.

what—Display SCCS Version Marks

```
what [-s] files
```

The what command displays the version information it can find in the named files. The what command searches each named file for the string @(#), and then prints whatever text follows up to the next quote, slash, newline or null character. In most cases these *what* strings are generated using SCCS ID keywords and therefore identify the change level of the source, object, or executable file generated from an SCCS version.

Use the -s option to stop searching for @(#) strings in a file after finding the first such string.

To get the flavor of the what command you might try the following experiment:

```
$ cd /usr/bin
$ what ls rm awk
```

The output of the what command tells you something about the ls, rm, and awk commands, although the specific text you see depends on your version of UNIX. It also demonstrates that the UNIX system developers use SCCS ID keywords in their code to help identify the version of their products installed in customer locations, a policy you might do well to emulate.

Deltas and Branches

SCCS is, of course, all about changing text files. SCCS refers to a single set of text changes as a *delta*. A delta may incorporate many different individual text alterations. It's not the number or kind of text changes you make but the sequence of events that determines the identity of a delta.

A change begins when you make a delta request with the get -e command. One of the functions of get -e is to provide you with a source file to change; you cannot directly edit the SCCS file, so the get command writes a copy of the text file to your current directory. You can then proceed to edit the text using any text editor you please to form a new, revised text. You may make any number of modifications to the text, adding, changing, and deleting lines as necessary, or even creating a new replacement text from scratch, until the text appears in the form you wish.

The change ends when you store a modified version of the text file with the delta command. The difference between the text given to you by the get command and the text you present to the delta command represents one delta (one increment of modification) to the source file. The `delta` command internally invokes `diff` or `bdiff` (which are also UNIX commands) to identify the specific differences between the starting and ending copies of text. The differences (and only the differences) are inserted into the SCCS file, and together constitute the delta. Later, the `get` command can re-create the text you presented to `delta` by taking an earlier version of the file plus the textual differences, editing the earlier version to reflect those differences, and writing out the result.

An entire copy of the text containing the edits represented by a particular series of deltas is called a *version*. You retrieve versions from the SCCS file using `get`, and store them using `delta`. The version given to you by `get -e` is the *basis* for the new version you create. SCCS carefully records the identity of the base version you used in creating a new delta because the delta itself consists only of changes; the base version provides the text to be changed by the delta to produce the new version.

An SCCS file may contain many different text versions. Because the main point of SCCS is to enable you to retrieve, and possibly to edit, any of the stored versions, SCCS must provide you with a way to refer to a version, whether to retrieve a copy of the version or to request permission to edit it. SCCS uses a series of numbers called an *SCCS ID* (or *SID* for short) to name each version. Programmers often informally refer to the *change level* of a source module; SCCS formalizes this concept and uses the SID code to distinguish individual increments to the change level.

The SID is composed of either two or four sets of digits separated by periods. For example, *2.1* and *32.15* are valid SID codes, as are *1.18.2.4* and *15.17.109.6151*. Each number can have a value ranging from 1 to 9999. The first number is called the *Release* number, the second is called the *Level* number, the third is called the *Branch* number, and the fourth is called the *Sequence* number. Thus the format of a SID is *R.L* or *R.L.B.S*. You'll never see a SID code consisting of one or three number sets.

Because the level, branch, and sequence numbers must always be at least 1, the first delta in a release is R.1, the second R.2, and so on. SID codes having only two sets of numbers are considered to have a branch and sequence number of zero.

The release number corresponds to a major series of changes. If you develop software commercially (or for distribution to corporate branch offices), you could identify each version of the software that you send out by a new release number.

Using such a scheme, you could examine a version of the software actually in use in the field by retrieving one of the deltas 1.1, 2.1, 3.1, and so on.

As it happens, programmers sometimes make errors in the programming process; it's not inconceivable that a fielded version of the software—say change level 2.1—contains an error. Most people are willing to forgive this fallibility, but only insofar as programmers are willing to correct an error once it's found. This basic fact of life leads unerringly to the need to create a revision to change level 2.1, which SCCS enables us to do. The change level of the source file then becomes 2.2.

It is outside the scope of this discussion to address the issue of what you should do with the software after you make a change to it. You might recompile the software using version 2.2 of the problem source file and distribute it only to the user site that experienced the problem, or you might redistribute it to everyone in the hope of staving off future complaints. What is pertinent to note is that, as you continue to make small corrections and improvements to the code, its change level continues to increase through the series 2.3, 2.4, 2.5, and so on.

Many software organizations find that it's just too expensive to redistribute corrected software to all users as the corrections are developed. Rather, at periodic intervals when the number of error corrections and improvements seem to merit such an action, the organization rebuilds all the software, establishes new distribution libraries, and announces to the world at large that a new release of the software is available.

When rebuilding the software for the new distribution, the careful organization establishes a null delta (one containing no actual text changes) at the next higher release number. This action permanently identifies the content of each source file comprising the release, because, by definition, SID code 3.1 will be the same as the highest delta to the source file in Release 2.

After distribution of Release 3 to customers begins, the entire cycle of development and maintenance begins over again until Release 4 becomes necessary and is created in the same manner.

When software is in use at many different user locations, it can be difficult, if not impossible, to maintain every location at the current release level. For software vendors who wish to charge for a new release, the decision to upgrade has to be left to the customer. And when different locations are using different releases of the software, you can rest assured that the programming organization receives problem reports about all the active releases, not just the current one.

The programming organization is forced to adopt a policy about fixing out-of-date releases. One strategy is to correct a problem only if it also appears in the current release, and then to fix it only in the current release. For organizations adopting such a policy, the SCCS locked-releases flag (see the `admin` command) may be useful to ensure that programmers do not attempt to change old releases of the software.

An alternative strategy that is usually more palatable to customers is to agree to make the fix to the obsolete release while assuming responsibility within the programming organization to check whether the correction also pertains to subsequent releases (or at least the current release), and perhaps to correct those releases as well.

Consider the problem, however, that the second strategy causes for a source code management tool such as SCCS. You sit at your terminal and ask it to create a delta to SID code 2.5 of the failing source file. SCCS knows that Release 3 of the source file already exists; it has at least one delta numbered 3.1. Should it call the new version 2.6? And what if 2.6 already exists? The approach taken by SCCS when you attempt to update a version with SID code *R.L* and version *R.L+1* already exists, or if Release *R+1* exists, is to create a branch delta. A branch delta has a four-part number, for example 2.5.1.1. A branch delta is known by its number format to be one that is *not* incorporated in the next higher release. When fixing an old release, it's evident that making a change to 2.5 will not (and certainly should not) alter the contents of change level 3.1.

Two-part numbers are always on the *main branch*, an SCCS term referring to the normal sequence of changes in which each change level serves as the basis for the next. Because of this, you can always be sure that any text change incorporated in a delta with a two-part number (for example, 2.5) also appears in the text of the next sequential two-part number (2.6) unless explicitly altered or removed. Branch deltas, however, are not on the main branch and never affect the contents of subsequent versions on the main branch.

If you ask SCCS to create a delta to version 2.5.1.1, SCCS assigns the number 2.5.1.2 to the new delta. If, however, you ask to make a change to 2.5 and 2.5.1.1 already exists, SCCS creates a new second branch by assigning the number 2.5.2.1 to the delta. The existence of two branches, 2.5.1 and 2.5.2, indicates that version 2.5 serves as the basis for two different variations of the source file. The branches diverge from the same point, but can never join. They cannot join because a version in branch 2.5.1 is never used as the basis for a version in branch 2.5.2: if you ask to change version 2.5.1.2, the next SID code assigned is 2.5.1.3; if you ask to change version 2.5.2.1, the next SID assigned is 2.5.2.2. A series of changes on a branch can be extended only by asking to change a version on that branch, and the new version is always assigned a SID code on the same branch.

If versions 2.5.2.1 and 2.5.2.2 both exist and you ask to change version 2.5.2.1 (using the command get -e -r2.5.2.1), SCCS allocates a new previously unused branch number to the delta—for example, 2.5.3.1. This means that you cannot tell simply by inspecting the numbers in a SID code where the delta is located in the delta tree.

The term *delta tree* refers to the branching structure exhibited by the predecessor-successor relationships between deltas. As you can see from Figure 16.1, the order of succession from one delta to the next can be complex. It is, however, hierarchical, because one SCCS version is always based on one and only one predecessor version.

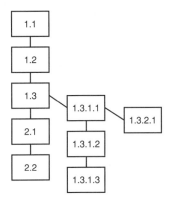

Figure 16.1. The branching structure of a delta tree.

The get command is responsible for assigning a SID code to a new delta when you use the -e option. The number assigned is chosen in part based on the file version you ask to modify, and in part on the position the new delta will occupy in the delta tree of the SCCS file. The only influence you have on the choice is by the SID code of the version you elect as the basis for your change, and whether you use the -b option on the get command. If you specify the -b option and its use is allowed by the presence of the b flag in the SCCS file itself, then SCCS creates a branch delta emanating from your chosen basis; otherwise, it chooses a number according to the rules shown in Table 16.9.

479

Table 16.9. SID code assignment rules used by `get`.

-r Option	Conditions	SID Retrieved	SID Created
None	—	mR.mL	mR.mL+1
None	-b	mR.mL	mR.mL.mB+1.1
-R	R > mR	mR.mL	R.1
-R	R = mR	mR.mL	mR.mL+1
-R	R < mR	R.mL	R.mL.mB+1.1
-R	R < mR[1]	hR.mL	hR.mL.mB+1.1
-R.L	No trunk successor	R.L	R.L+1
-R.L	Trunk successor	R.L	R.L.mB+1.1
-R.L	-b	R.L	R.L.mB+1.1
-R.L.B	No successor	R.L.B.mS	R.L.B.mS+1
-R.L.B	Branch successor	R.L.B.mS	R.L.mB+1.1
-R.L.B	-b	R.L.B.mS	R.L.mB+1.1
-R.L.B.S	No successor	R.L.B.S	R.L.B.mS+1
-R.L.B.S	Branch successor	R.L.B.S	R.L.mB+1.1
-R.L.B.S	-b	R.L.B.S	R.L.mB+1.1

[1]*This rule applies when R is less than mR and no delta exists in Release R. This condition can arise only when release numbers were skipped and the n flag is not set in the SCCS file. The symbol hR means the highest release occurring in the SCCS file less than the specified release.*

The following list explains the abbreviations used in Table 16.9:

mR is the highest release occurring in the SCCS file.
mL is the highest level within the release.
mB is the highest branch number occurring in the release.
mS is the highest sequence occurring in the branch.

Upon inspection of Table 16.9, you may notice that a new branch is always created within the release when (1) you specify the `-b` option on the `get` command; and (2) a successor delta exists on the main branch (*trunk* delta). The latter simply means that you cannot create a new delta on the main branch (two-part number) when the main branch already extends beyond your chosen base delta.

Encapsulating SCCS Commands

The SCCS commands can be awkward to use directly. For example, the admin command performs several different mutually exclusive functions, each of which could in theory be implemented by a separate command. The get command also has two main variants: one for retrieving a copy of a file version, and another for initiating a delta request. Most of the commands support many different option keyletters that can be difficult for the beginning user to remember.

If using SCCS for your important development projects interests you, you may want to minimize the learning curve for staff with no previous SCCS experience, to prevent the use of certain options and features, or to build into the commands some knowledge of your in-house conventions. The judicious use of shell scripts can do much to improve the SCCS user interface depending on your wants and your creativity.

About the Samples

The following sections describe a family of shell scripts that encapsulate the standard SCCS commands and (maybe) make SCCS easier to use. The shell scripts by no means demonstrate all the things you can do to systematize the management of source programs or to automate the program administration process, but they are intended to demonstrate some possibilities.

The sample shells all share some common philosophies about the best way to organize and manage source files. Premier among these philosophies is that of setting aside a special, unique directory to contain the source files of an application family. The sample shells all expect the user to define an environment variable named *SCCS* giving the pathname of the directory for SCCS to use. Once set, all of the shell commands reference that directory exclusively until the user changes the definition of *SCCS*. The following commands show one way to set the value of the *SCCS* environment variable:

```
$ SCCS=/usr/apps/payroll/src
$ export SCCS
$
```

The commands are also designed to enable (in fact, to require) the user to specify filenames without the s. prefix. This means that a user can always refer to a file by the same name, whether it's in his current directory or just a version in an SCCS file.

Finally, you might notice that the shell commands enforce some policies about the use of SCCS files. For example, the `store` shell script always issues the `admin` command with a constant set of flags defined for new SCCS files; the user cannot modify the flags used for creating new files. The sample always sets the `i` flag, enforcing the rule that all text files will contain an ID keyword, and sets the `n` flag to avoid problems during later program maintenance. You might prefer other settings, but the point is that you can easily set and enforce such standards simply by modifying the `admin` command buried inside the `store` shell script.

If you become serious about administrating SCCS files through a family of intermediary shell scripts, you might want to prevent the user from invoking the SCCS commands directly. One possible way of doing so is to move the SCCS commands themselves out of the directory where they're normally located into a special directory with a secret pathname only you know. You then need to modify the shell commands to invoke the SCCS commands with their full pathnames. To complete the arrangements, you remove read permission from the shell commands so no one can find out the pathname where the commands are located by looking at the shell scripts.

Additional issues involving the security and protection of your source-code directories from damage and tampering are discussed in the "An Approach to Source Code Libraries" section in this chapter.

Creating SCCS Files with *store*

Creating new SCCS files is always a clumsy and irritating task, and is perhaps the SCCS function that most benefits from being embedded in a shell script. Not only is it desirable or necessary to encode a number of arcane flag options on the command, but it is impossible to add several new SCCS files, all with an initial source text, with one admin command; you can use the -i option of admin only with one file at a time.

The store command, shown in Listing 16.1, not only enables a user to add several new files with one command, but also requires only one command argument. The reason for this is that the user must write a special, auxiliary file to define the files to add. For each new file, the auxiliary file gives not only its name but also a brief, one-line description. The shell script then automatically arranges to use the -t option of the admin command (a rather tricky option to use) to store the description text with the new SCCS file.

You must name the auxiliary file new. To add any number of new files, the user just enters the command store new. Once you create the new SCCS files, the shell script automatically removes the raw text files that were converted to SCCS form, and then removes the new file. Because the store shell script ensures that every SCCS file has a description text associated with it, it becomes possible to write another shell command (called index) that lists all the SCCS files in the application directory with their descriptions. (The index shell script is presented later in the "Listing the SCCS Directory with index" section.)

The shell script provides the beginnings of support for user security. When initially creating a new SCCS file, the store command uses the -a option of the admin command to authorize only the current user to access the file. That is, initially, only the user who stores a new file can change it. The allow command, described later in the "Managing Access Privileges with allow and deny" section, provides a means to extend change authority to other users.

You also can use the store command to store a new delta to an existing SCCS file. Both functions are combined into the same shell script because doing so enables the user to think of filing text in the SCCS directory as a *store* operation; you either store a new file or a changed one. In either case, you have a raw text file in your current directory to store away in the SCCS directory. To invoke the delta function, list the names of the source files.

483

The delta command issued by the store shell script does not provide any cute or tricky embellishments, and in particular it does not provide easy means for entering the comment text for a delta. You can add support for delta comments if you like; I omitted them because most programmers prefer to write fairly extensive comments in their source files to describe formal change activity. Such comments usually contain much more information than could reasonably be stored in a delta comment.

Listing 16.1. The store command.

```
# store.sh - store a new file or a delta
# %W% - compiled %E% %U%

if [ -z "$SCCS" ]
then
    echo "SCCS: environment not set" >&2
    exit 1
fi
if [ ! -d "$SCCS" ]
then
    echo "$SCCS: not a directory" >&2
    exit 1
fi
if [ $# -eq 0 ]
then
    echo "Usage: $0 files"
    exit 1
fi


if [ $1 = new ]
then # add new files to SCCS library

    while read NAME description
    do
        if [ -f $NAME ]
        then
            echo "$NAME:"
```

```
              echo "$description" >.store
              admin -fi -fn -i$NAME -a$LOGNAME -t.store $SCCS/s.$NAME ¦¦ exit
              rm $NAME
         else
              echo "$NAME: not found" >&2
         fi
    done <new
    rm -f .store new

else # store deltas

    for FILE
    do
         echo "$FILE:"
         delta -y $SCCS/s.$FILE
    done

fi
```

When I tested the store shell script, I used the shell commands themselves as the raw material to build a new SCCS library. Before issuing the first store command, I created a file called new that contained the lines presented in Listing 16.2.

Listing 16.2. A sample new file.

```
activity.sh       List updates in progress
allow.sh          Approve users for file updates
br.sh             View file versions
change.sh         Get file for update
copy.sh           Copy a file version to current directory
deny.sh           Remove user permission for file updates
index.sh          List files in SCCS library
leave.sh          Cancel pending updates
status.sh         Show current file status
store.sh          Add files or deltas to SCCS library
```

I also ensured that I had a text file for each in my current directory, because the store command had no support for creating an initial empty SCCS file. Then the following command was sufficient to create each SCCS file with all the proper flags, user authorizations, descriptive title, and initial text:

```
$ store new
activity.sh:
allow.sh:
br.sh:
change.sh:
copy.sh:
deny.sh:
index.sh:
leave.sh:
status.sh:
store.sh:
$
```

Of course, it is necessary to use the raw store.sh script for its first execution. Once the SCCS directory contains all the files in SCCS format, however, it is both possible and desirable to begin using the make command to install executable copies of the shell scripts from the current SCCS versions. You should store the makefile shown in Listing 16.3 in the SCCS directory with the application SCCS files. To build the executable form of the application, switch to the SCCS directory and enter the make command.

Listing 16.3. A makefile to build the executable shells from the current SCCS version.

```
# create SCCS administration commands in $(BIN) directory

BIN = /usr/bin

PROGS=  $(BIN)/store \
        $(BIN)/allow \
        $(BIN)/deny \
        $(BIN)/index \
        $(BIN)/change \
```

```
                $(BIN)/leave \
                $(BIN)/activity \
                $(BIN)/status \
                $(BIN)/br \
                $(BIN)/copy

.sh~:
                $(GET) $(GFLAGS) -p $< > $*
                chmod 711 $*

all: $(PROGS)

$(PROGS): $$(@F)
                cp $(@F) $@
```

The makefile installs the executable shell scripts in whatever directory you use for public user-written commands. The sample makefile in Listing 16.3 chooses /usr/bin as the standard directory for executable commands, but you may prefer another; if so, just change the value of the BIN macro.

Execution of the make command produces output of the following form:

```
get  -p s.store.sh > store
chmod 711 store
cp store /usr/bin/store
```

The chmod command sets execution permission for the file, enabling you to invoke /usr/bin/store or just store as a command. The permissions 711 also deny read access to users; the more normal 755 permission flags would grant execution permission and read permission to all users.

Listing the SCCS Directory with *index*

After adding some new files to the SCCS directory with the store command, it is natural to want to display the directory's contents. The index command does just that, and provides more useful information than an ls command does, because index not only lists the SCCS files in the directory but also gives a brief description of each file by displaying the description text of the SCCS file as well as the file's name.

Listing 16.4 shows the index.sh shell script. The script uses the prs command as its basis, but also does some additional work to enhance the appearance of the listing. The output of the index command has the same format as is shown in Listing 16.2; the actual information displayed depends on the filenames and descriptions in your own SCCS library.

Listing 16.4. The index command—listing SCCS files.

```
# index.sh - list files in an SCCS directory
# %W% - compiled %E% %U%
#1.1    original writing
#1.2    changed 'ne' to '-ne', cleaned up printout

if [ -z "$SCCS" ]
then
    echo "SCCS: environment not set" >&2
    exit 1
fi
if [ ! -d "$SCCS" ]
then
    echo "$SCCS: not a directory" >&2
    exit 1
fi

prs -d':M:\t:FD:' $SCCS ¦ sed '/^$/d' ¦ sort
```

Other than the mandatory validation of the SCCS environment variable, the shell script contains only one effective command line. The sed command removes blank lines from the prs output caused by the :FD: data selector, and the sort command orders the listing by filename.

The code for index.sh includes some lines that were inserted when making updates to the file. These lines, beginning with #1.1 and #1.2, show a method for annotating a file to describe change activity. By employing appropriate standards for writing change comments, it would be possible to extract a listing of change history from all SCCS files. The sample shell scripts in this chapter do not provide a facility for reporting change history, but would be based on just such an approach.

Managing Access Privileges with *allow* and *deny*

The SCCS admin command provides a basic facility for limiting the set of users authorized to create new deltas for an SCCS file. The store shell script activates the facility by specifying an authorized-user list with only one entry when you initially create an SCCS file. If the admin command was written with no -a option at all, all users could modify the SCCS file. The definition of as few as one authorized user, however, limits access rights to those users whose login names appear in the list.

The allow and deny commands, shown in Listings 16.5 and 16.6, provide the ability to add and remove users from an SCCS file. The commands are based directly on the capabilities of the admin SCCS command, and add no new features to SCCS. Their purpose is rather to simplify the user interface of the admin command: it's much easier to remember the mnemonic command names allow and deny than it is to remember the -a and -e options of the admin command.

The allow and deny commands are perhaps modeled a little too closely on admin. The commands enable you to specify only one user per command, but to list any number of files where the user is to be added or removed. You might prefer to modify the shell scripts to allow the naming of several users on one command.

The commands themselves produce no output, and none of the shell scripts in the sample package display the list of authorized users for an SCCS file. Writing a shell command to display authorized users is just one of the many ways to extend and improve the sample package.

Listing 16.5. The `allow` command—granting access rights to a user.

```
# allow.sh - approve user access to SCCS file
# %W% - compiled %E% %U%

if [ -z "$SCCS" ]
then
    echo "SCCS: environment not set" >&2
    exit 1
fi
if [ ! -d "$SCCS" ]
then
    echo "$SCCS: not a directory" >&2
    exit 1
fi
if [ $# -lt 2 ]
then
    echo "Usage: $0 user files..."
    exit 1
fi

user=$1
shift

for FILE
do
    if [ -f $SCCS/s.$FILE ]
    then
        admin -a$user ${SCCS}/s.$FILE
    fi
done
```

Listing 16.6. The `deny` command—revoking user access rights.

```
# deny.sh - deny user access to SCCS file
# %W% - compiled %E% %U%
```

```
if [ -z "$SCCS" ]
then
    echo "SCCS: environment not set" >&2
    exit 1
fi
if [ ! -d "$SCCS" ]
then
    echo "$SCCS: not a directory" >&2
    exit 1
fi
if [ $# -lt 2 ]
then
    echo "Usage: $0 user files..."
    exit 1
fi

user=$1
shift

for FILE
do
    if [ -f $SCCS/s.$FILE ]
    then
        admin -e$user ${SCCS}/s.$FILE
    fi
done
```

Retrieving File Versions with *br* and *copy*

The previous commands store, index, allow, and deny provide overall management of SCCS files but no content management. You now need some commands
for retrieving, editing, and updating the file versions stored in an SCCS file. Fore-
most among these must be a command to view one of the file versions, often
known as a *browser utility*. There is also some justification for allowing users to

copy a selected file version to a disk file without intent to update it; such a command might form part of a facility for compiling the application.

The br command shown in Listing 16.7 provides the ability to extract and view a specified version of one or more files in the SCCS directory. I chose the command name br (rather than browse) because such a command would probably be used very frequently; a shorter command name saves time.

The br command and shell script tackle a number of thorny problems, one of these being where to store the extracted file temporarily while the user is viewing it. The strategy chosen is to create a working directory in the system /tmp space and to hold extracted files there with their normal filenames. Although the user will often invoke br to view just one file, br enables you to browse any number of files. Using a new directory created for the purpose simplifies the question of where to store the files.

Another consideration is that, to avoid user confusion, the extracted files should have their expected names. Most UNIX commands for displaying text files (among them page, pg, and vi) all show the name of the file they are displaying. If the display utility shows an unexpected or cryptic filename, the user may be uncertain which file he or she is viewing. The only way to ensure that you can safely store a file under a fixed, predetermined filename is to create a new directory for the purpose.

Of course, creating temporary directories in the system /tmp space entails some risk that an occasional cancelled br command will leave trash directories lying around. The br command tries to minimize that possibility by using the trap shell built-in command to attempt to remove the directory before exiting; failing that, the umask shell built-in command ensures that the temporary directory will be completely unprivileged so anyone noticing the trash directory can easily remove it.

It is also desirable for the user to be able to choose the UNIX command used to display files. Several are available and suitable for the purpose, and some (such as emacs) may not even be part of the standard UNIX distribution. The br shell script achieves this by using an environment variable as the display command. If the user does not normally set one of the tested environment variables, br chooses a default. Other UNIX commands, such as mailx, similarly use an environment variable to represent the user's choice of a command for text viewing. It's not unlikely that one of the environments VISUAL, EDITOR, or PAGER already exist in the user's environment. If not, it requires little effort to add the appropriate definition to the user's login profile.

Listing 16.7. The br command—browsing SCCS files.

```
# br.sh - display an SCCS file version with the user's favorite pager
# %W% - compiled %E% %U%


Usage="Usage: $0 [-rSID] [files]"


if [ -z "$SCCS" ]
then
    echo "SCCS: environment not set" >&2
    exit 1
fi
if [ ! -d "$SCCS" ]
then
    echo "$SCCS: not a directory" >&2
    exit 1
fi


while [ $# -gt 0 ]
do
    case "$1" in
    -r[1-9]*)  REL=$1; shift ;;
     -*)  echo "$Usage" >&2 ; exit 1 ;;
      *)  break ;;
    esac
done


# process list of names


edit=${VISUAL:-${EDITOR:-${PAGER:-pg}}}


umask 000
dir=${TMPDIR:-/tmp}/br.$$
trap "cd; /bin/rm -rf $dir; exit" 0 1 2 3 15
mkdir $dir ¦¦ exit
cd $dir
flist=
```

continues

493

Listing 16.7. continued

```
if [ $# -eq 0 ]
then
    get -s $REL $SCCS
else
    for FILE
    do
        get -s $REL $SCCS/s.$FILE
    done
fi

if [ -f * ]
then $edit * </dev/tty >/dev/tty
else echo No files.
fi
```

The copy command, shown in Listing 16.8, provides a basic facility for retrieving the current version of an SCCS file. A more complete implementation might emulate the cp command, allowing a directory to be named on the command line where the files should be stored. As written, the copy command always stores the extracted file in the current directory. Notice the use of the -l option to create an l.*filename* file for each file extracted; the l-file contains a detailed history of the deltas used in the construction of the extracted file and might be of some interest to the user. The disadvantage of option -l is that it creates an excess of possibly useless files in the user's directory; you may want to remove the -l option from the get command.

Listing 16.8. The copy command—extracting the current version.

```
# copy.sh - copy all or selected files from SCCS library
# %W% - compiled %E% %U%

if [ -z "$SCCS" ]
then
    echo "SCCS: environment not set" >&2
    exit 1
```

```
fi
if [ ! -d $SCCS ]
then
    echo "$SCCS: not a directory" >&2
    exit 1
fi

if [ $# -gt 0 ]
then
    for FILE
    do
        echo "$FILE:"
        get -l $SCCS/s.$FILE
    done
else
    get -l $SCCS
fi
```

Making a Delta Request with *change* and *leave*

The change command, shown in Listing 16.9, and the leave command, shown in Listing 16.10, provide the ability to request a delta and to cancel a pending delta. They are the equivalents of the get -e and unget SCCS commands.

The change command adds no special value other than allowing the user to specify an ordinary filename rather than an s. filename on the command line. Perhaps more noteworthy is that, as written, the change command provides no support for requesting a delta to any but the most recent version of an SCCS file. The omission of such a capability is equivalent to a policy against the revision of old releases. If you have or want to use such a policy, you'll want to perpetuate this omission.

If you do wish to allow deltas to old file versions, there are several approaches to consider. The most direct way to add the appropriate support to the change shell script is to add code for an -r command-line option that is then just echoed on the get command. A more subtle approach is to use an environment variable, perhaps called REL, that specifies the release the user is currently working with. All commands in the sample package should then be revised to use the REL environment variable to select a file version. The use of an environment variable means that the user does not have to specify an -r option on every command when working consistently with an older source-code release.

Listing 16.9. The change command—requesting a delta.

```
# change.sh - issue delta request
# %W% - compiled %E% %U%

if [ -z "$SCCS" ]
then
    echo "SCCS: environment not set" >&2
    exit 1
fi
if [ ! -d $SCCS ]
then
    echo "$SCCS: not a directory" >&2
    exit 1
fi
if [ $# -lt 1 ]
then
    echo "Usage: $0 files"
    exit 1
fi

for FILE
do
    get -e $SCCS/s.$FILE
done
```

The leave command's name was chosen to suggest leaving a file untouched for which a user had previously requested a delta. Its purpose is simply to undo the effects of a previous change command.

The `leave` command goes farther than the `unget` SCCS command by saving the user's file before `unget` deletes it. The file is moved to a subdirectory of the user's home directory called `trash`. The reason for saving the file is that the user may have spent many long hours editing the file before deciding to abandon the update. If the user changes his or her mind again, the user can always recover the edits from the `trash` directory.

The approach used by `leave` is somewhat superior to simply using the `-n` option of the `unget` command. Using the `-n` option would result in spurious source copies proliferating through the user's directory hierarchy, whereas gathering them in a trash directory allows the user to review its contents periodically and delete old or obviously unwanted trash.

Listing 16.10. The `leave` command—cancelling a pending delta.

```
# leave.sh - cancel pending updates
# %W% - compiled %E% %U%

if [ -z "$SCCS" ]
then
    echo "SCCS: environment not set"
    exit 1
fi
if [ ! -d $SCCS ]
then
    echo "$SCCS: not a directory"
    exit 1
fi

trash=$HOME/trash
if [ ! -d ${trash} ]
then
    mkdir ${trash} || exit
fi
for FILE
do
```

continues

Listing 16.10. continued

```
    cp $FILE ${trash}
    chmod -w ${trash}/$FILE
    unget $SCCS/s.$FILE
    [ -f $FILE ] && rm -f ${trash}/$FILE
done
echo "A copy of your files was saved in ${trash}/ ..."
ls -l ${trash}
```

Creating Status Reports with *activity* and *status*

The activity command shown in Listing 16.11 prints a report showing all the files in the SCCS directory for which update activity currently exists. Unlike the sact command, activity prints nothing for files having no pending delta.

Output from the activity command looks like this:

```
$ activity
leave.sh    george    92/10/27 16:17:09 1.1 -> 1.2
change.sh   marsha    92/10/27 15:25:05 2.8 -> 2.9
$
```

Each line gives the name of the file being updated, the login name of the user who owns the pending delta, the date and time the delta request was granted, and shows the basis SID code and new SID code. The information displayed is the same as that shown by sact but perhaps arranged in a better way.

You might notice that the activity command bypasses the sact command altogether and instead uses the contents of the p-files in the SCCS library directly. Doing so turns out to be simpler than trying to edit and rearrange the output of sact.

Listing 16.11. The `activity` command—showing outstanding delta requests.

```
# activity.sh - show updates in progress
# %W% compiled %E% %U%

if [ -z "$SCCS" ]
then
    echo "SCCS: environment not set" >&2
    exit 1
fi
if [ ! -d "$SCCS" ]
then
    echo "$SCCS: not a directory" >&2
    exit 1
fi

cd $SCCS
if [ -f p.* ]
then
    awk '{printf "%-12s %-8s %s %s %s -> %s\n", \
        substr(FILENAME,3), $3, $4, $5, $1, $2}' p.* | sort +1
else
    echo No updates in progress.
fi
```

The `status` command, for which the shell code is given in Listing 16.12, provides an overview of the update status of each of the files in the SCCS directory. Where a pending delta is outstanding for a file, the output of `status` shows information about the delta. Where no pending delta exists, the output describes the most recent change level of the file. You might find the output of `status` handy when preparing to rebuild your application; it highlights those source files where someone is still working on an update, and indicates for other files how recently they have been updated.

The output of `status` is essentially that of the `prs` command; it looks like this:

```
activity.sh   D 1.3 92/10/27 12:38:05 jjv 3 2
allow.sh      D 1.2 92/10/27 12:38:07 jjv 2 1
change.sh     U 1.3 92/10/27 16:17:10 jjv
```

Listing 16.12. The status command—summarizing the update level of all files.

```
# status.sh - show current file status
# %W% - %E% %U%

prs -d´:M: :Dt:´ $SCCS ¦ sort ¦
    while read NAME info
    do
        if [ -f $SCCS/p.$NAME ]
        then
            awk ´{ printf "%s\tU %s %s %s %s\n", \
                NAME, $2, $4, $5, $3}´ NAME=$NAME $SCCS/p.$NAME
        else
            echo "$NAME\t$info"
        fi
    done
```

An Approach to Source Code Libraries

For a small development project involving only one or two programmers, the logistical problems are few and easily managed. To keep track of your source files, you only need to create a directory and store your files there. For a larger project involving many programmers, dozens or hundreds of source files, and formal distribution of software products to a user community with a commitment to ongoing maintenance, the problems are much greater. Indeed, research in software engineering methods continues to press forward in universities and corporate centers around the world, addressing the same topics with which SCCS attempts to deal.

Data Security and Integrity

Data security and integrity have to do with ensuring that the software you have built continues to exist, that perturbations and corruptions do not damage the source code, its documentation or history, and that the cause and origin of source code changes are clearly identifiable and attributable.

I did not write the preceding paragraph easily. Every word has a reason for being there. For example, a regular program of backups is critical to ensuring the continued existence of source files, as is the use by SCCS of read-only access permissions to prevent accidental erasure of SCCS files. A perturbation would be an ostensibly legitimate, syntactically correct modification to the text of a file which no member of the programming team intentionally made, perhaps caused by an operating system bug that pasted two files together into one file. A corruption could be caused by overwriting a section of the text file with binary garbage, or by a text editor that wrote out the lines of its edit buffer in the wrong order. Similar damage to older versions of an SCCS file, or misrecording of the programmer who filed an update impair the validity of a file.

An important step for any large software development project is establishing a set of directories for housing the developed software. Ideally the directories should not be owned or directly writable by any member of the development team, or by any other user; all modifications and manipulations of the directories and their contents should be performed under programmatic control by programs that enforce management policy.

SCCS permits you to make such a step by providing the means in the guise of SCCS commands to manipulate source files through the intermediation of programs that check authorization and maintain the integrity of the data files. When you create the top-level directory to hold the software product, you assign as its owner a unique login ID to protect the directory and its contents from writing by any other user.

To enable SCCS commands to manipulate objects in the directory, you must use the chmod and chown system commands to set the set-uid permission flag on and to set their user-ID to that of the product directory. This grants the SCCS commands the privilege of writing in the directory but withholds it from other users.

You also use the -a and -e flags (or shell scripts such as the `allow` and `deny` commands) to grant access privileges for a source file only to those programmers who are assigned responsibilities for those source files.

Accomplishment of these aims gives you the knowledge that no user's hand directly touches the source code or other components of the software, and ensures that you know who is manipulating it.

You also insist that all derived components of the product such as executable files or, more particularly, a `bin` subdirectory in the product top-level directory, are built with the `make` command. Using `make` religiously to generate the product from source ensures that you know *how* to generate it at all times and have a *record* of the generation procedure. If you do not have a makefile, you risk losing the product when critical staff leave and take their knowledge of build procedures with them. If you allow hand-made components, you risk having one or more components that pass quality assurance testing but without assurance that you have a controlled copy of the source that generates the components.

You probably need to build shell scripts or even programs to assist with the maintenance and generation of the product libraries, because standard components such as `make` often require a user to have direct write access to the source libraries.

You have an adequate grip on your software libraries when: you feel (justifiably) confident that they will not vanish or be corrupted, and you have adequate recourse should they do so; you can find out who made any particular change and ask him or her why; you have all the source code for your object and distributable materials; and when you know that your ability to build and maintain the product will not be diminished by the loss of any particular member of the staff.

Configuration Control

Perhaps the greatest inadequacy of SCCS is that it administrates each file as if it were an isolated entity unrelated to any other file. In point of fact, this is not the case.

Consider, for example, an assemblage of source files that has undergone several cycles of maintenance and release. The source files exhibit widely varying current change levels. If you stop development at some arbitrary point in time, build the product and send it out, and then resume development, how do you have any idea which change level of a file was shipped? It may not at all be evident at a later time that version 2.14 of one file and version 2.8 of another file are equivalent, having been the distribution change level for those files in Release 2.

A more subtle problem concerns the very identity of source files comprising a release. In its earliest versions, a software product might encompass some 15 source files and no more. As time progresses and new features are added, first one and then another file is added to the product library. Unless you take special pains to prevent it, a latecomer to the product configuration might have a SID level of 2.2 that makes it appear to have been a component of Release 2, when in fact it never appeared in the product until the fifth distribution.

Time causes not only the invention of new modules but the banishment of old ones. It's entirely possible that several source files in your product library are proper components only of old releases long since abandoned, and aren't even included in the generation procedures for the current release.

SCCS provides no ready tool in itself to identify which of a group of source files are in fact components of a given release. This incapacity is not only a threat to the integrity of the software, because it leaves the question of which files *ought* to exist in your product directories, but also threatens your ability to generate the proper product configuration at any given point in time.

The most available tool to control and manage configuration is an SCCS-administered makefile for the product. At least a makefile that is subject to version control has the advantage of being able to build the right components from the right source for any particular version of the makefile.

A version-controlled makefile, however, is not an adequate tool because it cannot produce a simple list of the source and generated components; the files it accesses and generates in any given execution are wholly a matter of circumstance. The makefiles of complicated products are also, usually, complicated themselves, and not at all a simple record from which you'd wish to extract a list of components.

An effective configuration control system interposes a mechanically maintained set of lists between the development team member and the library. Each list identifies the member files of a release and shows which version of a file constitutes the current version for that release. Publication of the release in the form of a full set of distribution materials made available for shipment to end users, or as a member of a package of fixes delivered to one or several users, also is noted.

The tools for full and effective configuration management are not included with SCCS and are not readily constructed from available UNIX commands and facilities. Your alternatives are to settle for little or no configuration control, to use manual methods to administrate configuration tracking, or to build new tools to do the job. The last alternative is a more expensive choice than it seems because there is no generally recognized standard for configuration control and tracking; it therefore becomes an open-ended task of experimentation, refinement, and evolution.

A Practical Approach

A practical approach to the management of source code is still possible with the available tools. It consists, at a minimum, of the following steps:

- Establish a system-level directory to contain each distinct application system you want to manage. Assign a user ID to these directories that no other users share, such as *SCCS*. Deny write permission in these directories to anyone except the owning user ID.

- Subdivide each top-level directory into a structure that suits the application. You may want to have any or all of the following subdirectories:

bin	Contains the executable program components of the application.
include	Contains all header files used in compiling the source.
lib	Contains all source files used to generate the object library or libraries of common subroutines.
man	Contains any manual pages or online documentation files included in the distribution package.
src	Contains the source files for simple executables built from one source file.
	In addition, you may want to set aside a special subdirectory for each executable component with multiple source files. By packaging the source files together you identify their relationship to one another.

● Modify the SCCS commands to have set-uid permission and a user ID matching that of your application libraries. Extend the commands with a package of shell scripts if necessary. These commands become the sole means for adding, changing, and deleting the contents of the application libraries. They therefore become the means for implementing the management policies you want to use with the libraries.

● Assign one individual to have login authority and responsibility for the libraries. This person will have the unenviable job of doing by hand anything that your program tool set cannot do, of periodically running the admin -h command against the libraries and dealing with any problems it reports, and of ensuring that the libraries are backed up periodically and effectively.

● Identify the source components for each application and insert them into the libraries as SCCS controlled files. If you have no source code to start with, so much the better. If you do, remember that the public copy of a file may not be the current copy. As an example, if Joe copied the public file to fix some problems, compiled it to object, mailed the object module to Harriet who tested it and then added it to the distribution package, the current source resides somewhere in Joe's directories. You must be suspicious of every copy of the source file, with whatever date stamp, with any conceivable variation of the file's name, because in an uncontrolled environment the public copy is the least likely of all to be the real current source file.

● Establish a makefile for every release of the application that you need to support. Add the earliest level of the makefile as a new SCCS file, and then add later release levels as deltas to the base file.

● Distribute the product built from the new application library to your end users as soon as possible. If you already have earlier versions in the field, you probably won't be able to maintain them with your new tools. Your objective is to get your end user base onto the controlled system as soon as possible so that problem reports pertain to the source code you actually have.

● Monitor the problems you experience working day-to-day with the system. As time permits, modify the administration policies and enhance the tools to keep pace with your discoveries.

Admittedly, the tasks described above are much too time-consuming and difficult for you to use with casual software. Unfortunately, too much software is treated as casual software when it is actually critical to the day-to-day operations of a company or organization. When software is the actual product your company sells, its proper management should be an issue of concern at the highest levels.

An SCCS Glossary of Terms

A large vocabulary of specialized terms has grown up around SCCS to simplify references to the many types of objects SCCS creates and manipulates. Without some understanding of these terms, you will find most documentation of SCCS to be opaque and confusing. To help you over the rough spots, I offer the following glossary of terms. Most of this terminology is presented earlier in this chapter, and if you have not already done so, you should read the chapter to get the fullest possible definition of these terms.

base version   Also *base text*. A base version is the complete text of one version of an SCCS file to which a particular delta applies. Because a delta is defined to be a set of changes, every delta is associated with a predecessor version of the file to which it applies; the predecessor version is the basis for the delta.

branch   One subtree of the SCCS file. All deltas in the branch proceed from the same precursor file version. Of course, a branch may have many sub-branches. A branch occurs where two or more deltas change the same earlier delta.

checksum   A numeric value computed by SCCS and stored in the SCCS file to detect corruption or damage to the file. SCCS recomputes the checksum every time one of the SCCS commands updates the SCCS file. The checksum of an SCCS file can be made valid using the `-z` option of the `admin` command.

delta   A set of changes to a base text. The first version in an SCCS file is considered to be a delta to a null file (as would be created by `admin -n`). A delta is comprised of instructions to add, change, or delete text by line number, plus the text to be added or to replace the base text. A version of an SCCS file is retrieved by applying a succession of deltas in the same order they were created, beginning with a null text and ending with the delta whose SID code matches that of the version to be retrieved.

g-file   A single delta retrieved by the get command, also called the *gotten* file. The g-file usually has no explicit existence and is either stored under another filename or written to standard output.

gotten file   A version (or delta) as retrieved by the get command from an SCCS file. The gotten file is conceptually identical to the plain text file originally stored with the admin or delta command. See also *g-file*.

ID keyword   A special symbol of the form %X% that you can embed in a source text. When extracted with the get command, the symbols are replaced with information taken from the SCCS file. For example, the keyword %I% is replaced with the SID code identifying the update level of the extracted text.

l-file   Written by the get command when you specify the -1 command-line option. The file contains a summary of all the deltas applied in creating the text file extracted by get. The filename of an l-file is created by changing the prefix *s.* to *l.*.

Modification Request   A number or identification code having an arbitrary format and assigned by the SCCS user which presumably establishes a correlation between a problem report and a source-code correction that solves the problem (also abbreviated *MR*). SCCS does not administrate problem reports, but does provide a means by which you can identify the file update or updates that respond to and fix a problem report. Only software development and maintenance organizations have a use for modification request numbers. If you use SCCS for your own purposes you will probably have no use for MR numbers.

MR number   See *Modification Request*.

SID   Also *SID code*. An abbreviation for *SCCS ID*. The SCCS ID is a two- to four-part number in the form *R.L.B.S* where *R* is the release number, *L* is the change level within release, *B* is a branch number, and *S* is a sequence number. The delta SID codes *4.5*, *4.5.1.2*, *4.5.2.1*, *4.6*, and *5.1* are listed here in increasing order.

update   A colloquial term having the same meaning as *delta*.

version   One complete copy of an SCCS file as it appears after the application of a sequence of deltas; it is equivalent to the plain text of the file you used to create the SCCS file or that you presented to the delta command. Each version is identified by a unique SID code. A version differs from a delta in that a delta consists of a set of changes to a base text, whereas a version is the text resulting from application of the changes.

x-file A temporary file created by the delta command. It contains the original SCCS file while the new delta is being inserted into it. The filename of an x-file is created by changing the prefix *s.* to *x.*.

Summary

SCCS, the Source Code Control System, is a family of UNIX commands that assists you with the maintenance of program source files. SCCS is one example of a version control system—a tool that collects, archives, and makes available to you not only the current but also all previous versions of a source file.

SCCS provides commands to convert a plain text file into an SCCS file (admin), to retrieve a version of an SCCS file or to request to change it (get), to store a new version of the file (delta), to display the list of changes in an SCCS file (prs), to remove a previously stored change (rmdel), to cancel a pending request for change (unget), to compare two versions of an SCCS file (sccsdiff), and to display the pending change requests (sact).

SCCS is simple enough to use that one programmer can make practical use of it for small projects, although its main application is for larger development projects encompassing many source files and several programmers. The user interface to SCCS is clumsy, consisting of several commands having many options. This chapter shows one possible approach to improve the SCCS user interface with shell scripts.

The general problem of source code management is complex, and good solutions to it are not readily available. SCCS addresses a core set of needs but ignores issues such as managing one release of a software product as a unit. Even so, the benefits conferred by SCCS are such as to commend its use to anyone doing serious software development.

The Symbolic Debugger: *sdb*

The second most useful tool for a C programmer—
second only to the C compiler itself—is the symbolic
debugger, or sdb. With it you can set breakpoints, trace
instructions, display and modify data, inspect source
code, monitor hardware register contents, and perform
many other functions essential to effective debugging.

One of the biggest advantages of sdb is that you do
not need to be familiar with the computer's machine
language to use it. You can express interactions with the
debugger entirely in terms of your C program's source
elements, such as line numbers, function names, and
variable names. To use symbolic debugging, however, you
must compile your program with debugging support.

Request the C compiler include debugging support in your object files and executable programs by specifying the -g option on the cc command line. This option causes the C compiler to include in the generated object file a line number table and a description of the assigned memory location and data type of every variable and function. Without the added information, sdb still can perform all its functions, but it is limited to debugging on the machine-language level.

The basic scenario of a debugging session begins with entering the sdb command, where you give the name of the executable program to debug, and optionally the name of a core file and a source directory. The debugger then loads your executable program into memory, but does not begin its execution. At this point the debugger writes a prompt to your terminal and waits for you to enter commands. The start of your debugging session looks like this:

```
$ sdb bin/route - src
Source path: src
no process
*
```

The Source path line documents the directories that sdb searches for source files. The message no process means the loaded program is not currently running; you must use one of the r or R commands to start it before you can use any of the tracing commands.

The rest of this chapter presents the sdb command-line syntax as well as the commands you use to control the debugging session.

Command-Line Syntax

```
sdb [options] binfile [corefile] [path[:path...]]
```

For *binfile*, specify the filename or the pathname of the binary executable file that sdb should load for debugging. If the program was compiled without debugging information, sdb issues the following message to warn you that source-level debugging is not possible:

```
Warning: no -g information in binfile
```

For `corefile`, specify either - to proceed without a core file, or the pathname of a core file. (The term *core* comes from the old days of computing when memory was built of many tiny doughnut-shaped magnets called cores.) A core file is a recording of memory made before the abnormal termination of your program. It is written into the directory that was the current directory at the time of the error, which might not necessarily be the same as the current directory when you started the program. If you provide a core file, `sdb` uses it in place of the initialized and uninitialized data segments of the executable file, thereby making it possible for you to inspect memory contents at the time of termination.

For `path`, specify the pathname of one or more directories where `sdb` can find the source files that were used to compile the executable program. List multiple directory pathnames in the form `path1:path2:...`, using a colon to separate the pathnames. The debugging information in the executable file identifies which parts of the executable file were built from which source files, allowing `sdb` to infer the filename of the source containing a particular section of the program. If all of the source files are in the current directory, or if you have no source files, you can omit the source-directory list.

If you omit the source-directory list and specify the `corefile` argument as -, you can omit the `corefile` argument.

The debugger loads the executable program and the optional `corefile` into memory and then halts before starting program execution. This gives you the opportunity to inspect or change memory contents and to set breakpoints before beginning execution.

The debugger can execute your program one instruction at a time, or continuously until a breakpoint or a specified line is reached, or at normal speed. You specify the size of an *execution unit* by issuing the appropriate debugger command. When the debugger is not executing instructions, it waits for you to enter a command. It signifies that it is waiting for a command by writing an asterisk (*) prompt. You type debugger commands immediately after the prompt character without first pressing the Return key.

To terminate your debugging session and return to the shell, enter the q command at any prompt. If the debugger is working and you want to quit anyway, press ^c (or the INTR character you defined with the stty command) to get the debugger's attention, then type q at the prompt.

Table 17.1 gives the allowable options you can specify on the sdb command.

Table 17.1. sdb command options.

Option	Meaning and Usage
-e	Use machine-level debugging. Any debugging information in the executable program is ignored.
-s*signo*	Use the -s option to prevent trapping of interrupts. Specify the signal that sdb is to ignore by writing one of the valid signal numbers as the value of *signo*. Normally sdb intercepts all signals, writes a message describing the signal it intercepted to your terminal, and waits for you to enter a command. You want to use the -s option when your program uses certain signals, and you want the signals to quietly pass to your program for processing.
-V	Use the -V option to have sdb write its current version identification to the terminal. If the command line contains no other arguments, sdb exits after printing its version information.
-W	Normally sdb writes a warning message when the core file is older than the executable file, or when a source file is newer than the executable file. The -W option suppresses these warnings.
-w	Use option -w when you plan to modify the object file or the core file during your debugging session. Ordinarily sdb inhibits writes to these files to preserve their integrity.

Debugging Commands

As soon as you start sdb, you can control virtually all its operations by commands you type at the terminal. These commands fall into the following main categories:

● *Examining data.* These commands, including /, ?, =, and !, enable you to inspect and change the contents of variables and data areas in your running program.

● *Examining source files.* The e, p, w, and z commands and others enable you to view sections of the currently active source file, search for text, and change the debugger's current position in the source file.

● *Controlling execution.* The r, R, b, B, d, D, s, S, c, C, g, i, I, and other commands provide the ability to set and delete breakpoints, to execute your program one instruction at a time or continuously until a breakpoint is encountered, to change the normal sequence of execution, and to start and stop your program.

● *Miscellaneous.* Other commands provide a means to exit from the debugger (q) or to invoke the shell from within sdb (!).

The following sections describe the sdb debugging commands in alphabetical order.

a—Announce Line or Function

```
[proc:][line]a
```

The a (*announce*) command sets a special breakpoint. If you specify a source line, sdb prints the line number and text of the line every time it is executed. If you specify a function, sdb prints the top line of the stack trace when the function is called. This usually identifies the function and line from which the specified function is called. Specify a function name for *proc* when you want to announce the function, or a line of source code in another (not the current) source file. Specify a line number for *line* to announce line numbers; omit *line* to announce the function named by *proc*.

The a announce command is equivalent to entering the breakpoint command in either the form b l;c to announce a line or b T;c to announce a function.

The following examples show how to use the announce command:

235a   Prints the line number and text of line 235 of the current source file each time it is executed.

findLastChar:16a   Prints 16 and the text of the source line every time it is executed. The particular line 16 to be announced is line 16 of the source file containing the findLastChar function.

findLastChar:a   Prints the top stack frame identifying the currently active function whenever the function findLastChar is entered.

b—Set a Breakpoint

```
[proc:][line]b [commands]
```

Use the b command to set a breakpoint. A *breakpoint* is a line in one of the source files of your program where the debugger should cease execution when execution reaches that line. The debugger terminates the current execution unit whenever it reaches a breakpoint, regardless of the normal range and termination conditions of the execution unit.

For *line*, specify a line number in the current source file. You can discover the line number of a desired C instruction using any of the several debugger commands for viewing source code. If you do not specify a line number, the breakpoint is set at the current line.

Use *proc* to specify the function containing the line number. You need to use *proc* when setting a breakpoint at a line in some source file other than the current source file. You can always qualify the line number with a function (*proc*) name; if the function occurs in the current source file, *proc* has no effect. Specifying a *proc* name always resets the current line to the first executable line of the function.

Use *commands* to list one or more debugger commands to automatically execute when reaching the breakpoint. Write each command as you would type it in response to a debugger prompt, and separate a series of commands with semicolons. The debugger executes the commands upon reaching the breakpoint, and then halts with a prompt in the normal manner. If you want sdb to continue program execution after executing *commands*, add the c command (...;c) to the end of the command list.

B—List Breakpoints

```
B
```

The B command prints a list of all the breakpoints currently set. The listing looks like this:

```
*B
0x80497b4    route.c:834    FindRoute
0x8049efc    route.c:1092   FindGreatCircleRoute
```

The hexadecimal number at the start of each line gives the memory address of the machine instruction where the breakpoint is set. The expression route.c:834 gives the equivalent source-level location in terms of the function (route.c) and the line within the source file (834). If the line is the first executable line of the function, the last field gives the name of the function. Otherwise the last field has the form *name*+0x*offset*, where *name* is the name of the function containing the breakpoint and *offset* is the hexadecimal offset of the machine instruction from the beginning of the function.

If you want to get rid of some of the breakpoints listed, use the d command.

c and *C*—Continuous Execution

```
[line]c [count]
[line]C [count]
```

The c command resumes execution of your program until the next breakpoint or until your program terminates; the c command executes instructions continuously without stopping, unlike the s command, which executes instructions one at a time.

If you specify a *line* number in front of the c command, execution stops when your program reaches that line number. This is equivalent to setting a temporary breakpoint.

Specify an integer *count* value when your program contains breakpoints that stop execution and you want them to be ignored. The c command detects but ignores the specified number of breakpoints; the next breakpoint reached halts execution. Notice that *count* decrements for each occurrence of a breakpoint reached, whether or not it is the same breakpoint.

You can use the optional *count* value to specify the number of breakpoint events you want to ignore after execution resumes. For example, the command c5 restarts your program until the sixth time a breakpoint is encountered. Notice that *count* specifies the number of *occurrences* of a breakpoint to ignore, not the number of *different* breakpoints to ignore. For the example c5, all five of the ignored breakpoint events might be caused by a breakpoint you set at one line number.

If program execution halted because of a signal, issuing the c command resumes execution after discarding the signal; your program does not receive the signal. The C command passes the signal to your program for processing as the first step of resuming execution. In all other respects the C command is identical to the c command.

d—Delete Breakpoints

```
[proc:][line]d
[address]d
d
```

Use the d command to delete breakpoints.

If you know the line number where the breakpoint is set, use a command like 235d to delete the breakpoint at line 235. If there is more than one breakpoint having the same line number, you must qualify the line number with the name of the function—for example, main:235d.

If you enter the d command with no qualifiers, sdb lists all the breakpoints one by one. To delete a breakpoint, respond with y or d after it is listed; a response beginning with any other character keeps the breakpoint.

D—Delete All Breakpoints

```
D
```

The D command deletes all breakpoints.

e—Examine Source File

```
e
e function
e filename
e directory/
```

Enter the e command with no argument to print the name of the current source file.

If you specify a function name, the source file containing the function becomes the current source file and the current line is set to the first executable line of the function.

Specify a filename to bring in the named file and make it the current source file. The current line is set to the first line of the file.

If you specify a directory name (which you must end with a trailing slash so the e command can recognize the name as a directory rather than a filename), the named directory is added to the end of the source directory list. If sdb was previously unable to locate the source file containing a particular function, adding a directory to the source directory list may enable sdb to support full symbolic debugging for the function.

g—Goto Line Number

```
lineg [count]
```

Use the g command to resume normal execution, but starting with the line number you specify as *line* instead of the next sequential instruction. The g command of sdb has the same effect as the goto C statement. You cannot use the g command to go to a line outside the currently active function.

You can use the optional *count* value to specify the number of breakpoint events you want to ignore after execution resumes. For example, the command 235g5 resumes execution starting at line number 235 until the sixth time a breakpoint occurs, your program receives a signal, or your program terminates.

i and *I*—Execute Machine Instructions

```
i [count]
I [count]
```

The i command is just like the s command, except that i executes one machine instruction instead of one line. If your program is currently halted because sdb intercepted a signal, the I command passes the intercepted signal to your program before executing the machine instruction; the i command discards the signal.

Use the *count* value to specify the number of machine instructions to execute. By default, the i and I commands execute one machine instruction. Sdb reports each instruction executed regardless of *count*.

k—Kill

```
k
```

Use the k command to terminate the active user process for the program you are debugging. An active user process is the UNIX operating system's mechanism for keeping track of programs being executed; when the user process is destroyed, the program is no longer known to the operating system. Once killed, you can no longer use execution debugging commands such as c and s, but the program instructions and data still reside in memory and you can still inspect and modify them. Use the r or R command to make the program executable again.

l—Print the Last Executed Line

```
l
```

Use the l command to print the last source line executed in your program. If the last breakpoint report has scrolled off your terminal and you no longer remember your current position in the program, use the l command to find out. The p command is similar but prints the current instead of the last executed line, which source file commands such as w and z can change.

m—Trap Changes to Memory Contents

```
variable$m [count]
address:m [count]
```

The m command resumes program execution until it detects a change to the memory location designated by *variable* or *address*. It then reports the source file and line number of the statement that changed the memory location and halts.

To specify the monitored location by name, type the name of the variable followed by a dollar sign ($). To specify the monitored location by its address, enter a hexadecimal number (for example, 0x80c130b4) followed by a colon (:). The dollar sign or colon tells sdb which kind of specifier you entered, but has no other significance.

Use the *count* value to prevent termination of the m command by breakpoints. The m command ignores up to *count* breakpoint events; the next breakpoint encountered halts execution in the usual way.

Depending on the particular implementation of sdb on your system, the m command may monitor just the single byte at the specified location or the machine word containing the specified location. In no case does the m command attempt to monitor all the bytes contained in the variable. The m command can only detect a reference to the location that changes its value. Modifications that leave the value of the location unchanged are not detected or reported.

In most implementations, the m command is implemented in software by effectively setting a breakpoint at every program line. For this reason, it may take a *very* long time for the m command to halt.

M—Print Address Maps

```
M
```

The M command prints the address maps currently in use by your program. Address maps are only available for a program in execution, and do not exist before you execute the r command, after you execute the k command, or after your program terminates by itself.

The address maps describe which areas of memory are in use and which executable objects occupy the areas. Output of the M command may look similar to the following, depending on the hardware characteristics of your system:

ADDRESS	SIZE	OBJECT NAME
0x08048034	0x0000496a	bin/route
0x0804d9a0	0x00001384	bin/route
00000000	00000000	bin/route
0x80000094	0x0002a220	/usr/lib/libc.so.1
0x8002b000	0x00001ce0	/usr/lib/libc.so.1

In the sample, the object bin/route occupies two memory areas, and the shared object library /usr/lib/libc.so.1 also occupies two. You may reasonably conjecture that for each object, one of the areas contains instructions and the other contains data. You may find the maps helpful in interpreting the address values of pointer variables in your program.

p—Print Current Line

```
p
```

The p command prints the number and text of the current line. Its output is identical to that printed when a breakpoint halts execution. If you forget where your program stopped, use the p command to find out.

q—Quit

```
q
```

Use the q command to exit from the debugger. Your program, if executing, is also automatically terminated and removed from the system.

r—Run a Program

```
[count]r [arg ...]
```

The r command starts execution of your program at its normal entry point, which for C programs is the beginning of the main function.

List command-line arguments after the r command as you would if r were your program's name. You may specify a redirection operator in the normal way, using all forms of redirection supported by the standard shell. Notice that you cannot use shell variables to specify an argument value because sdb has no access to the shell's variable definitions.

If you list no command arguments, sdb begins program execution using the same argument list as the previous r command.

To regain control before execution of the first instruction, set a breakpoint for the main function—main:b—and then issue the r or R command.

R—Run a Program with No Arguments

```
R
```

Use the R command to start program execution with a null or empty argument list. You cannot use r to run a program without arguments because the r command uses the absence of an argument list to mean "start the program with the same arguments as before." To give an empty command line to your program, you must use the R command.

s and *S*—Single Instruction Execution

```
s [count]
S [count]
```

Use the s command to execute one C statement. To execute several statements before stopping, specify the number of statements you want to execute as the *count* value.

The s command follows a function call into the called function; the S command quietly suspends tracing until the called function returns, enabling you to step from one instruction to the next within the same function.

Programming for UNIX

t and *T*—Print the Stack Trace

```
t
T
```

Use the t command to print the list of functions beginning with the currently active function. The output from t looks like this:

```
Route(org=0x804fbe8,dst=0x804fbbc)      [route.c:771]
main(argc=4,argv=0x8047d04,0x8047d18)   [route.c:607]
_start()
```

Each line shows the name of the function and displays the argument values that were passed to the function. Pointer values are shown in hexadecimal; integer and string arguments are displayed as an integer or string respectively. The bracketed information identifies the last line executed in the function, giving the name of the source file and the line number of the last executed line.

The T command displays just the top line of the function trace. In other words, it describes the currently active function.

v—Control Amount of *sdb* Output

```
level v
```

The v command controls the amount of terminal output the s, S, and m commands generate.

If you specify the s, S, and m commands without a *level* value, they only print the current function and source filename when either changes. A value of *1* causes the commands to print each source line before executing it. A value of *2* prints each source line and also the corresponding machine instructions the compiler generates.

V—Print Version Information

```
V
```

Use the v command to display the version information of sdb. You would probably want to know the version information when preparing a problem report about sdb for your UNIX vendor.

x and *X*—Print the Current Machine Instruction

```
x
X
```

The x command displays the hardware registers and their contents as well as the current machine instruction. All displays are in hexadecimal. Output of the command *may* look like this, depending on the particular machine you are using:

```
%eax      0x80539cc      %ecx      0x804fbbc      %edx      0x804ded8
%ebx      0x8002bfe4     %esp      0x8047c40      %ebp      0x8047c60
%esi           0         %edi      0x805a02c      %eip      0x80495ee
%eflags        0         %trapno        0x1
FPSW 0xffff0020     FPCW 0xffff137f      FPIP 0x0804b7e2      FPDP 0x08047c30
ST(0) [ EMPTY ] 0x0000 0000 0000 0000 0000 == 0
ST(1) [ EMPTY ] 0x0000 0000 0000 0000 0000 == 0
ST(2) [ EMPTY ] 0x0000 0000 0000 0000 0000 == 0
ST(3) [ EMPTY ] 0x0000 0000 0000 0000 0000 == 0
ST(4) [ EMPTY ] 0x0000 0000 0000 0000 0000 == 0
ST(5) [ EMPTY ] 0xbff3 967f 69ea f2e2 f6c1 == -0.00028705160127046
ST(6) [ EMPTY ] 0x3ff7 fff5 6c80 a3c0 4f88 == 0.0078112392232281
ST(7) [ EMPTY ] 0xc005 90b3 3300 0000 0000 == -72.349998474121
0x80495ee        (RouteATP+6:)       movl    $0x00000001,0xec(%ebp)
```

The x command displays only the current machine instruction, which is the last line the x command displays.

w—Print a Window of Lines

```
[proc:][line]w
```

Use the w command to print the current line and the five lines before and after it. If you also specify a function (proc) and/or line number, the current line is set to that position before printing.

z—Print More Source Lines

```
[proc:][line]z
```

Use the z command to print the current line and the nine lines after it. Used repeatedly, each z command displays the next nine lines of source. If you also specify a function (proc) and/or line number, the current line is set to that location before printing.

/—Print a Variable

```
variable/[format]
```

The / command prints the value of variable using a default format appropriate to the data type of the variable, or using the explicit format you specified.

If *variable* is a pointer, sdb displays the pointer value in hexadecimal unless it points to a string, in which case sdb displays the text of the string it points to. If *variable* is an array, sdb displays all of its elements, one per line, in the format you specify (or the default format, if you specify no format). If *variable* is a structure, sdb displays each of its members in the default format for its data type.

To display the *n*th element of an array, use the command *variable*[*n*]/; *n* must be a decimal, hexadecimal, or octal number. You may also display the object pointed to by a pointer variable using the command *variable*[0]/, because pointers and arrays are equivalent in C.

To display one member of a structure when you have a pointer to the structure, specify the expression *p*->*name* for *variable*, where *p* is the name of the pointer variable and *name* is the member name. You may also use the dot operator to display a member of a structure. For example, struc.name/ displays the value of the name member in structure variable struc. To display all members of a structure, use the expression p->* or p.*.

You can combine the deferencing operators (->, [], and .) in any way the C language allows, including chained applications of the operator. For example, the command p->next->name/ displays the value of member name in the structure pointed to by next pointed to by p.

For *format*, specify the way you want the value of *variable* to display. A format specifier consists of an optional *count*, an optional *size*, and an optional *type*, all strung together as an unbroken sequence of characters. Of course, *format* itself is optional; sdb assumes a default format if you don't specify one.

The *count* portion of a format says how many things you want to display; give a simple decimal number for *count*. The count value applies to the *size* and *type* specifiers following it in the format, not to the default size and type of the variable.

For *size*, specify nothing, b (meaning *byte*), h (meaning *halfword*, or two bytes), or f (meaning *fullword* or four bytes). If you don't specify a size modifier, sdb uses a size appropriate to the *type* part of the format. If you specify neither a size nor a type, sdb defaults to the natural size and type of *variable*.

For *type*, specify nothing or one of the following one-letter codes:

Type	Type of Data
c	Character
d	Signed decimal
u	Unsigned decimal
o	Octal
x	Hexadecimal
f	32-bit single precision floating-point
g	64-bit double precision floating-point
s	Assumes *variable* is a string pointer and prints the data pointed to by *variable* as a string
a	Prints *variable* as a string
p	Pointer to a function
i	Machine instruction with symbolic operand addresses
I	Same as i but prints only numeric operand addresses

The following shows some examples of display commands using an explicit format specifier. In the examples, sp is a four-byte pointer variable.

sp/x	Displays the value of sp as a 32-bit hexadecimal number—for example, 0x32578c
sp/4x	Displays the four fullwords of memory beginning at the location of sp—for example, sp/0x32578c 0x7 0xc08c4531 0
sp/c	Displays the value of sp as characters—for example, sp/´\001´ ´\0´ ´\0´ ´\0´
0xc08c405c/s	Assumes that memory location 0xc08c405c is a string pointer and prints the string pointed to by the value at that location: 0xc08c405c/"this is a string"

/text/—Search for String

```
/regular expression[/]
```

When the / character appears at the start of a line, sdb performs a string search instead of displaying memory contents. The command searches forward from the current line to the end of the current source file for the text string you specify as *regular expression*.

For *regular expression*, you can write a simple text string (such as a function or variable name) or you can write a regular expression to describe the string you want to find. Use the same rules as the ed text editor for forming the regular expression. (If you don't have access to the documentation for the ed command, you can use the string notation described in Chapter 2 of this book, because that notation is very similar to the ed implementation of regular expressions with the one notable exception of the + operator, which isn't supported by ed or sdb.)

?—Examine Code Segment

```
[proc:][line]?[format]
variable:?[format]
```

The ? command formats and displays memory from the code segment of the program; see the / command to format and display variables and data in the data segment.

For optional *proc*, specify the name of a function containing the source line if you mean a line in a source file other than the current one. For *line*, specify an executable line of the source file. For *variable*, give the name of a function or of a variable you declared with the const type qualifier; the object named must be statically allocated in the code segment (ordinarily variables are allocated in the data segment). You must append a colon (:) to a variable name so that sdb can distinguish it from a *proc* name.

Programming for UNIX

For *format*, you can specify a size and type to override the default characteristics of the variable or executable line; you may not specify a *count*, however. The codes for size and type are the same as those for the *format* portion of the / command. The default format is i, meaning that the location is interpreted as a machine instruction.

?text?—Search Backward for String

```
?regular expression[?]
```

The ?text? command performs a backward text search in the current source file, starting at the current line and working backward to the first line of the file. You can omit the final ? because the end of line adequately delimits the end of the regular expression; its use is supported for compatibility with the ed string search operation.

For *regular expression*, write a simple text or a regular expression. The sdb command supports any of the regular expressions the ed command supports; see the documentation for the ed text editor command of UNIX for additional information.

=—Print Address

```
variable=[format]
line=[format]
number=[format]
```

Use the = command to display the address of a variable, the address of the first machine instruction generated for an executable source line, or to convert *number* from one number base to another. See the description of the / command for an explanation of the *format* specifier.

For *variable*, sdb displays the address of the variable. The default format is lx, which means that the address displays as a 32-bit hexadecimal number.

For *line*, sdb displays the address of the first machine instruction corresponding to the source line.

Use *number* and an explicit *format* specifier to convert numbers between the decimal, hexadecimal, and octal representations. For example, the command 0x35=d displays the decimal equivalent of hexadecimal 35; the command 0177=x converts the octal 0177 to hexadecimal.

!—Assign a New Value to a Variable

```
variable!value
```

Use the ! command to assign a new *value* to a specified *variable*. For *variable*, give the name of a variable or data area using the same syntax as you would to display the variable (see the / command for a discussion of the many ways you can designate a data area). For *value*, specify a numeric or character constant, or the name of another variable. You can write numeric constants in decimal, hexadecimal (beginning with 0x), or octal (beginning with 0). A character constant is written ´c; because sdb allows only one literal character c after the initial apostrophe, it does not allow a final apostrophe.

When you specify the name of another variable for *value*, sdb copies its value to the receiving data area. You can use the full syntax of the / command to designate both the sending and receiving data areas. Notice, however, that you cannot legally assign all types of values to *variable*; the assignments that are valid are those that are valid in the C language. In particular, assigning a structure value to a different structure type or to a nonstructure variable is not allowed. The normal conversion and promotion rules apply when assigning a numeric value of one type to a numeric variable of another type (see Chapter 4, "Expressions," for an explanation of those rules).

number—Display a Source Line

```
number
number+
number-
```

If you enter a line number by itself as an sdb command, sdb sets its current line pointer to that line of the current source file and then displays the line. Notice that changing the current line position in the source file is *not* equivalent to the g command; it only affects other sdb commands that display source lines.

If you write a + after the line number, sdb advances the current line by the specified number of lines. For example, 10+ skips forward ten lines in the current source file and prints that line.

Writing - after the number causes sdb to back up that many lines in the source file and print the line it finds. For example, if the current line is 50, the command 10- prints line 40. A subsequent z command prints lines 40–49 because the command also changed the current line to 40.

Call a Function

```
function(arg,...)
function(arg,...)/m
```

Enter a function call in the normal C syntax to cause sdb to execute the function as if it was called from your program. Besides any effect executing the function may have, sdb prints the value returned by the function as an integer. Suffix the function call with /*format* to print the return value in another format, where *format* is any of the formats supported by the / command.

You can specify an *arg* as an integer, character, string constant, or the name of a variable known within the currently active function. Numeric and character constants follow the rules of the ! command.

#—Comment

```
#text
```

You can use the *comment* command to enter remarks on the sdb command line. If you have a means of recording and saving terminal input and output (such as an attached hardcopy printer), you may want to annotate your debugging session by inserting appropriate comments about what you are doing, or writing reminders to yourself for later use. sdb itself ignores any command line you enter beginning with #.

!—Execute a Shell Command

```
!command
```

Any line you enter prefixed with ! is passed to the shell for execution. This command differs from the ! command used to set or change the value of a variable because here the ! symbol begins the line.

One way you might be interested in using the ! command is to invoke the vi editor to make program corrections from within your debugging session. Just enter !vi filename at any sdb prompt.

<—*sdb* Input

```
<filename
```

Use the < command to have sdb execute the debugger commands contained in the file *filename*. The file should only contain valid sdb debugging commands and comments.

Summary

The sdb command acts as a supervisor, standing between your program and the computer. Using sdb commands, you can determine when and how your program may execute. You are also able to stop your program at any point to inspect it and, if desired, to change the contents of any of its variables and data areas. By using these capabilities to acquire clues, you can form hypotheses about the reason your program fails and verify the hypotheses with direct observation of program behavior.

Unlike some of the tools available for the MS-DOS environment, sdb does not offer windows with pull-down and pop-up menus and mouse-selectable options and controls. Such tools often make it easier for a beginner to accomplish some useful work with little or no recourse to a manual, but for the experienced user all these gadgets tend to get in the way. Certainly a novice without a manual confronted with an sdb prompt will not know what to do, but when you consider that you'll be a novice for only a small percentage of your career, features that help you during that stage are of little use over the long run. The sdb utility offers short commands that produce useful information with little effort, and that makes every function as easy to access as every other—none are hidden inside nested menus that are hard to reach and hard to get rid of.

The principal commands that you'll use over and over are the r (run a program), / (display variables), b (set breakpoints), and w and z commands (display source lines). If you learn these few commands thoroughly, you'll have studied about 20 percent of sdb, but it will meet 80 percent of your needs (the old 80-20 rule). The stack trace commands t and T are also fairly handy, but definitely lower in priority. Study the a (announce) and m (monitor) commands only when the need arises—you'll use them very infrequently.

Mastering the format specifier of the / command takes a little work, but it pays off big when you can use it effectively to see memory contents in a meaningful and appropriate way. It may be unfortunate that sdb provides no simple dump command to display raw unformated hexadecimal memory areas, but with practice you can get what you need from the format specifier. You'll need to play with it when the opportunity arises to get a feel for how it works.

For what it's worth, I think sdb is easier to use than the pretty menu-driven windows-like debugging tools. I can usually accomplish what I want to with less effort and more quickly in the UNIX environment working with sdb than in the MS-DOS environment working with the typical debugger you find there. I didn't feel that way in the beginning, but I'll never be at the beginning again. If you really feel you need the windows-type interface, keep an eye out for advertisements in the trade journals—there are several software vendors that are starting to market debugging utilities based on the X Window System. Such tools will become more plentiful and more powerful as time goes on. I'm not so sure whether this is progress. I think I'll stick with sdb.

Using the Standard Library Functions

The C programming language is unusual in that it provides no input/output operations or file definition declaratives. This is because the designers of the C language want to avoid incorporating machine-dependent concepts into their compiler. Their strategy is to let the C compiler developers provide a library of functions appropriate to each machine environment.

The strategy works well, though not quite as originally envisaged. The UNIX versions of the C standard library incorporate input/output functions so general in design that the functions have proven adaptable to nearly all other hardware environments. The result is that C programmers have available a body of functions for machine interface that are almost machine-independent, and are able to write programs that can compile and execute on a wide variety of hardware with little or no modification.

The committee of the American National Standards Institute (ANSI), which recently adopted a national standard for the C language, included in their standard a description of a group of functions that must be provided with any compiler that claims to conform to the ANSI C standard. The functions they adopted have been in use for many years and are already familiar to most experienced C programmers.

The standard function library includes functions for reading and writing files, renaming and removing files, manipulating strings, allocating and managing dynamically allocated memory, and a great many more. This chapter describes the most essential functions in the package. You will probably use all these functions heavily in your C programming projects and come to know them as initimately as any other part of the C language.

File Operations

Although UNIX incorporates a more fundamental file concept than that of the *stream*, the stream file is suitable for most purposes and usually more efficient to use than the underlying operating system services. The stream I/O package is designed to operate most efficiently when you process a file sequentially—beginning at the front and working your way progressively toward the end of the file.

The stream functions associate a *buffer* with a stream file when you open it. The buffer holds data that has been read until you request it, or collects data you've written until the buffer is full. The buffer allows the stream functions to read and write large blocks of data rather than the many small pieces your program may require; this results in fewer operating system requests to read or write the file, and greatly increases your program's performance.

The stream I/O package is optimized for sequential file processing, but does not restrict your program to sequential processing. You can use certain of the functions to skip around in a file, reading and writing data according to your needs.

fopen—Open Stream File

```
FILE *fopen(const char *filename, const char *mode);
```

The fopen function opens a file for input, output, or updating. The identity and state of the file is summarized in an I/O block called a FILE structure; its address returns to your program as the return value of the fopen function. You must use the returned pointer in all subsequent operations on the file, so you generally need to save the return value in a variable of type FILE *. If the file cannot be opened—for example, because it doesn't exist—the fopen function returns a NULL pointer and the reason for the error is noted in the errno global variable.

For *filename*, you may specify any string designating a file in a form acceptable to the operating system. For UNIX, the filename can be a simple filename or a full or relative pathname; filenames and relative pathnames are resolved with respect to the current directory in the usual UNIX fashion.

For *mode*, you specify a literal character string or string pointer. The string specifies one or two characters indicating the manner in which you intend to access the file. The acceptable mode strings are these:

r   Use the mode "r" to open the file for reading. The file must already exist; the error "file not found" occurs if the file cannot be found. The file position is set to the first byte of the file.

w   Use the mode "w" to open a file for writing. The file is created if it does not exist; otherwise, an existing file is truncated to zero length so that it only contains what your program subsequently writes into the file. Mode "w" does not physically delete an existing file; any links to the file remain undisturbed. The file position is set to the first byte of the file.

a   Use mode "a" to open a file for appending data to its end. The file is created if it does not exist; otherwise an existing file is opened for output and its contents remain undisturbed. The file position is set to the location immediately following the end of the file.

r+   Use mode "r+" to open an existing file for update. The file is initially opened for input with the file position set to the first byte of the file. The file must already exist; it is not created, and inability to find the file causes fopen to fail. You can write to the file after reading EOF (the end-of-file indication), or at any time by calling the fseek function; you don't need to close the file to switch between read and write modes.

w+   Use mode "w+" to open a work file. The file is initially opened for output with the file position set at offset zero. The file is created if it does not already exist; otherwise, it is truncated to zero length so that it contains only the data you subsequently write to it. You can switch between reading and writing at any time by calling the fseek function; after fseek, either a read or a write is permitted, but subsequent accesses must be of the same type until you call fseek again.

a+   Use mode "a+" when you need to read data in the file, but also wish to add new data to the end of the file. The file is initially set for reading the first byte. You can switch between reading and writing at any time by calling the fseek function. Notice that writing is always forced to occur at the end of the file despite any positioning that may be established by reading or with the fseek function. A write operation always resets the current file position to the location immediately following the last byte in the file.

You can accomplish switching to output mode with the fflush, fsetpos, and rewind function calls in addition to fseek; for additional details, see the UNIX documentation for your system.

The fopen function does not allocate the stream buffer for the file; its allocation is deferred until the first function call that actually reads or writes data. You can influence the size of the stream buffer, control the buffering mode, or provide your own buffer by calling the setbuf or setvbuf functions after fopen but before reading or writing data; for additional details, see the UNIX documentation for your system.

The stream file opened by fopen uses one of the available file descriptors. The maximum number of file descriptors available to your program is (usually) indicated by the value of the _NFILE preprocessor symbol in the /usr/include/stdio.h header file. If you plan to use many files concurrently in your program, you may need to consider the system limit on the number of simultaneously open files.

You should include the stdio.h header file in any source file that calls the fopen function or any of the stream file functions. The header defines the stdin, stdout, and stderr symbols as stream files so you can use the stream I/O functions to read and write the standard files. It also contains prototype declarations for all the stream file functions.

C programs often use a statement like the following to open a stream file:

```
FILE *input;

if ((input = fopen("data","r")) == NULL) {
    perror("data");  /* report open failure */
    exit(8);         /* terminate */
}
```

freopen—Reopen a Stream File

```
FILE *freopen(const char *filename, const char *mode,
              FILE *stream);
```

The freopen function first closes the stream file pointed to by *stream*, and then attempts to open it again for the specified *filename* and with the specified access *mode*. For *stream*, provide the FILE pointer of a file already open. The *filename* and *mode* strings have the same meaning as for the fopen function.

If the file designated by *filename* can be opened, the same value of *stream* you provided in the function call is returned as the value of the function. If the open fails, the function returns NULL and the stream I/O block pointed to by *stream* is closed and deleted; you must not attempt to reference the memory area pointed to by *stream* and must not pass it as a file pointer to other stream functions.

541

The value of the freopen function lies mainly in its ability to reassign the file from which stdin reads, or to reassign the file to which stdout or stderr writes. If your program requires only one input file, you can design your program to use stdin as the default input source and to use a file named on the command-line if the user provides a name; use the freopen call to reassign standard input to the user's named file, thus allowing the remainder of your program to read from stdin in either case.

You may also wish to use freopen to bypass the overhead of reallocating memory for a stream file I/O block and buffer, as fclose followed by fopen would do.

fdopen—Attach Stream to File Descriptor

```
int fdopen(int fd, const char *mode);
```

Use fdopen to associate a stream file with the file descriptor of a previously opened file. The fdopen function does not physically open the file; it creates a FILE structure and arranges for stream buffering. You are responsible for specifying a file access mode that is consistent with the way the file designated by fd was actually opened.

You can use fdopen to convert a file descriptor you received from the low-level open system call to a stream file, or to associate a stream file with a file descriptor opened by the shell using its redirection operator. You might use the open system call to open a file in a way not supported by fopen; once opened, the fdopen function enables you to convert the low-level file descriptor to a fully functional stream file. By way of example, the following code uses open to open a file for input, but unlike fopen the open call can create an input file when it doesn't exist. Once opened, the fdopen call converts the file to a stream file.

```
#include <stdio.h>
#include <fcntl.h>
```

```
char *fname;
FILE *stream;
int fd;

if ((fd = open(fname, O_RDONLY | O_CREAT, 777)) < 0) {
    perror(fname); /* open failed */
    exit (1);
}
stream = fdopen(fd, "r"); /* convert to an input stream */
```

fclose—Close a Stream File

```
int fclose(FILE *stream);
```

Call the fclose function to indicate that you no longer need to access the file represented by *stream*. If you wrote data to the file, the current contents of the stream buffer are written out if they were not previously written. In any case, the FILE structure and the associated stream buffer are destroyed, freeing the dynamic memory they occupied.

For *stream*, provide a pointer to a FILE structure previously returned by an fopen, freopen, or fdopen function call.

Because data you write to the file is collected in a stream buffer rather than being directly written to the file, previous output function calls may appear to successfully write data to the file when in fact they perform no file data transfer. The return value of fclose indicates whether any data remaining in the buffer could be successfully written out; a zero value indicates success, a nonzero value indicates failure. For small files containing fewer bytes than the size of a stream buffer, the fclose function may be the only function call that actually attempts to write data to the file. It is therefore very important that you test the return value of fclose if you want to detect and report output errors.

Features of the standard function library automatically linked with your program ensure that any files remaining open when your program exits normally are properly closed. If your program is terminated abruptly by the operating system, however, unwritten data remaining in a stream buffer will not be written to the file, causing the loss of some or all of your program's output.

The basic skeleton of calls for all programs doing I/O with the stream functions looks like this:

```
{
    FILE *file;
    char *fname;

    if ((file = fopen(fname, "r")) == NULL) {
     perror(fname);
     exit(1);
    }
    ...
    fclose(file);
    return;
}
```

perror—Write System Error Message

```
void perror(const char *prefix);
```

The perror function formats and prints a message text to the standard error file. The message text consists of a predefined string corresponding to the current value of the errno global variable, prefixed by the string value of *prefix*. The purpose of the perror function is to log an error message describing a system-defined error. The string you provide for *prefix* should help the user associate the error with some object known to him such as a file or a command-line argument.

The output of perror is a line to the standard error (stderr) file having the format

prefix: file not found

feof—Test for End-of-File

```
int feof(FILE *stream);
```

The feof function tests the stream I/O block pointed to by *stream* to determine whether an end-of-file condition was previously detected. The function returns a zero value (false) to indicate no EOF condition, or 1 (true) to indicate the presence of an EOF condition.

Once detected, an end-of-file condition is noted and preserved in the stream I/O block. Functions that read or write to the file do not proceed when the EOF indication is set; you must clear the indication with clearerr before further reads and writes to the file are possible.

The feof call is usually implemented as a macro; writing an expression for *stream* that has side effects may yield unexpected results.

ferror—Test for File I/O Error

```
int ferror(FILE *stream);
```

The ferror function tests the stream I/O block pointed to by *stream* to determine whether an error condition other than end-of-file was previously detected. The function returns 0 (false) to indicate no error condition, or 1 (true) to indicate the presence of an error condition.

Once detected, an error condition is noted and preserved in the stream I/O block. Functions that read or write to the file do not proceed when the error indication is set; you must clear the indication with clearerr before further reads and writes to the file are possible.

The ferror call is usually implemented as a macro; writing an expression for *stream* that has side effects may yield unexpected results.

clearerr—Clear Error Flags

```
void clearerr(FILE *stream);
```

Use the clearerr function to reset the EOF and file error indicators in the stream I/O block. Clearing the indicators does not remove the external condition that caused the end-of-file or error, but does allow read and write requests to proceed. If the external condition persists, subsequent read or write requests may reactivate the indicators.

The clearerr call is usually implemented as a macro; writing an expression for stream that has side effects may yield unexpected results.

getchar—Read Byte from *stdin*

```
int getchar(void);
```

The getchar macro reads the next character from the standard input (stdin) stream file. It is equivalent to getc(stdin).

getc, *fgetc*—Read One Byte

```
int getc(FILE *stream);
int fgetc(FILE *stream);
```

Use getc to read the next character from the stream file designated by *stream*. The value of *stream* should be a pointer to a FILE structure previously returned by an fopen, freopen, or fdopen function call.

Successive calls to getc return characters of the stream file one after another. If the file is a normal text file, each line of text ends with a newline (\n) character. Upon reaching the end-of-file, the next call to getc after reading the last character returns the symbolic value EOF; EOF is defined in the stdio.h header file.

The current position in the input file, and hence the next character getc reads, is changed by the rewind, fseek, fsetpos, and ungetc functions.

The getc call is usually implemented as a macro; writing an expression for *stream* that has side effects may yield unexpected results. The fgetc call is a function, not a macro, and is equivalent to getc in all other respects.

gets, *fgets*—Read String

```
char *gets(char *buf);
char *fgets(char *buf, size_t length, FILE *stream);
```

Both gets and fgets read the next line of text into the character array pointed to by *buf*. The gets function reads from the standard input (stdin) file, and fgets reads from the file pointed to by *stream*. Reading begins at the current file position, which may not necessarily be the beginning of a physical line, and ends after reading a newline character from the input file. The gets function discards the newline character, whereas fgets stores the newline character in the buffer. Both functions then store a null character (\0) to form a conventional string.

Both functions return a NULL value when the end-of-file is encountered and no characters have been read; otherwise, they return a pointer to the first stored character (namely *buf*). If reading of text is terminated by an end-of-file condition rather than by a newline character, a NULL value isn't returned until you try to read the next line.

Use the gets function with caution (if at all) because it does not observe any limitation on the length of the input line; a line of text longer than the character array pointed to by *buf* results in storing data beyond the end of the character array. This can possibly destroy data that follows it or a portion of the stack, and lead to unpredictable and catastrophic program behavior.

The fgets function stops reading text after reading and storing a newline character when the end-of-file is encountered, or when *length*–1 characters are read and stored. If the input file may contain lines longer than *length*–1 characters, you must be prepared to process incomplete line segments.

putchar—Write Byte to *stdout*

```
int putchar(int c);
```

Use putchar to write one byte to the standard output (stdout) file. The byte written is the least significant eight bits of the integer value of c. The byte is normally written at the end of the file, but if you previously changed the current file position with rewind, fseek, or fsetpos, the byte is written at the next output location.

If successful, putchar returns the value of c; otherwise, putchar returns the value EOF (–1).

The putchar call is usually implemented as a macro; writing an expression for c that has side effects may yield unexpected results. It is equivalent to the call putc(c,stdout).

putc, fputc—Write One Byte

```
int putc(int c, FILE *stream);
int fputc(int c, FILE *stream);
```

Use putc (fputc\) to write one byte to the stream file pointed to by *stream*. The value you specify for *stream* must be a pointer to a FILE structure returned by a previous `fopen`, `freopen`, or `fdopen` call. The byte written is the least significant eight bits of the integer value of `c`. The byte is normally written at the end of the file, but if you previously changed the current file position with `rewind`, `fseek`, or `fsetpos`, the byte is written at the next output location.

If successful, `putc` (`fputc`) returns the value of `c`; otherwise, it returns the value `EOF` (−1).

The `putc` call is usually implemented as a macro; writing an expression for `c` that has side effects may yield unexpected results. Use `fputc` when you cannot use the macro `putc`; `fputc` is a function equivalent to the `putc` macro in all other respects.

puts, fputs—Write String

```
int puts(const char *s);
int fputs(const char *s, FILE *stream);
```

The `puts` function writes the string `s` to the standard output file, followed by a newline character. The `fputs` function writes the string `s` to the stream file pointed to by `stream`, which must be a pointer to a `FILE` structure returned from a previous `fopen`, `freopen`, or `fdopen` call. Notice that `fputs` does *not* write a newline character after the string; you must include any newline characters needed in the string pointed to by `s`.

Both `puts` and `fputs` return the number of characters written, if successful, or `EOF` (−1) if an error occurred.

fread—Read Block

```
size_t fread(const void *s, size_t size, size_t nelems,
          FILE * stream);
```

Use fread to read a fixed number of bytes from the stream file pointed to by *stream*. For *stream*, specify a pointer to a FILE structure returned from a previous fopen, freopen, or fdopen call. For *size*, specify the size in bytes of one unit of data to be read, and for *nelems*, specify the number of units to read. The total number of bytes read is the product of *size* and *nelems*. Bytes are stored into successive positions of the memory area pointed to by s.

You can use the fread function to read an arbitrary number of characters by specifying a size of 1 and the number of characters to read as the value of *nelems*. You may also use fread to read one or more fixed-size structures or elements of an array; specify the size of each structure or the size of an array element as *size*, and the number of structures or elements to read as the value of *nelems*.

The return value from fread is the number of *size*-byte blocks of data read: either the value of *nelems* if all the data was read successfully, or an unsigned integer value less than *nelems* if the number of *size*-byte blocks read was less than *nelems*. An incomplete block is not counted. For example, if you specify a block size of 16 bytes and a count of eight blocks, but only 120 bytes can be read, the return value is 7, meaning that only seven full-sized blocks could be read. When *size* is 1, the return value is equivalent to the number of bytes read.

When the end-of-file is encountered, the return value from fread is the number of full blocks stored, or zero if no data was stored.

fwrite—Write Block

```
size_t fwrite(const void *s, size_t size, size_t nelems,
              FILE * stream);
```

Use fwrite to write a fixed number of bytes to the stream file pointed to by *stream*. For *stream*, specify a pointer to a FILE structure returned from a previous fopen, freopen, or fdopen call. For *size*, specify the size in bytes of one unit of data to be written, and for *nelems*, specify the number of units to write. The total number of bytes written is the product of *size* and *nelems*. Bytes are taken from successive positions of the memory area pointed to by s. Successive blocks of data must each be of size *size* and physically adjacent in memory, as are the elements of an array.

You can use the fwrite function to write an arbitrary number of characters by specifying a size of 1 and the number of characters to write as the value of *nelems*. You may also use fwrite to write one or more elements of an array or fixed-size structures; specify the size of an array element or the size of each structure as *size*, and the number of elements or structures to write as the value of *nelems*.

The return value from fwrite is the number of *size*-byte blocks of data written: either the value of *nelems* if all the data was written successfully, or an unsigned integer value less than *nelems* if the number of *size*-byte blocks written was less than *nelems*. An incomplete block is not counted. For example, if you specify a block size of 16 bytes and a count of eight blocks, but only 120 bytes can be written, the return value is 7, meaning that only seven full-sized blocks were written. When *size* is 1, the return value is equivalent to the number of bytes written.

printf—Write Formatted Text

```
int printf(const char *format, arg1, arg2, ...);
```

Use printf to write the character string pointed to by *format* to the standard output (stdout) file. The return value from printf is the number of characters written. If the string pointed to by *format* contains one or more sequences of characters beginning with % (the percent sign), each sequence is replaced with the formatted value of one of the arguments of *printf*. The first sequence is replaced with the formatted value of *arg1*, the second with the formatted value of *arg2*, and so on.

A sequence of characters beginning with % defines a substitution format. A substitution format string has the general syntax %*[flags][width][.precision]type*.

In general, *flags* specifies special formatting procedures for the output string. *width* specifies the number of character positions within which the formatted value is to be justified. *precision* specifies an upper limit on the amount of formatted

551

data to be output. *type* is a one-character code describing the type of the source argument (*arg*) as well as the type of formatting to be done.

You can write both the *width* and the *precision* values as *, indicating that the width or precision does not appear in the format string. Instead, the next `printf` argument specifies the *width* or *precision* value; the argument should be of type int. As a trivial example, the call `printf("%*.*d",12,5,i)` prints the value of i in a field 12 characters wide and with a precision of five digits. Notice that the actual value to print appears as the third argument following the format string because the first two arguments are required to specify the field width and precision.

The acceptable *type* codes are as follows:

%
Writes one percent sign (%). This format code provides the only means to print a percent sign with the `printf` function.

c
Writes the ASCII character corresponding to the integer value of the corresponding `printf` argument. For example, if the format is %c and the value of the corresponding argument is 97, the single character a prints in place of the format string %c.

d, i
Writes the value of the corresponding `printf` argument as a signed decimal number. The digit characters are right-justified in a field *width* characters wide and padded on the left with blanks; the *precision* specifies the minimum number of digits to print. If no *width* or *precision* is specified, the full number prints with no leading zeros or blank padding and occupies just the number of character positions needed. For example, the format string %d and an argument value of 37 prints the characters 37. The format string %5.4d, on the other hand, prints b0037 (the b represents a blank) for the same value. The i type code has the same effect as d.

e, E
Writes the value of the corresponding `printf` argument as a floating-point number. The argument must be of type double or long double; if long double, specify a type code of Le or LE. The output consists of a possible leading minus sign, followed by a mantissa of one integer and six fractional digits (or *precision* fractional digits if a precision is specified), and an exponent in the form e±dd. The type code E prints an exponent of E±ddd. The

552

number of exponent digits printed is at least two, but can be more. If a precision of 0 is specified together with the # flag character, the decimal point does not print.

f   Writes the value of the corresponding printf argument as a fixed-point fractional number with a possible leading minus sign. The argument must be of type double or long double; if long double, specify a type code of Lf. The number of fractional digits printed is equal to the *precision* specified, or six in the absence of a *precision*. If a *precision* of zero and the flag character # are both specified, only the integer digits of the number are printed with no trailing decimal point.

g, G   Writes the value of the corresponding printf argument in either the e (E) or the f format depending on the size of the value and the *precision* specified. The number prints in scientific notation (e or E) if its exponent is less than –4 or greater than or equal to the *precision*; otherwise, format f is used. The *precision* specifies the number of fractional digits to appear in either format; a *precision* of 0 is taken as 1. A decimal point appears in the printed result only if followed by nonzero fractional digits. The argument must be of type double or long double; if long double, specify a type code of Lg or LG.

o   Prints the value of the corresponding printf argument as an unsigned octal number. The *precision* specifies the minimum number of digits to print. A special flag of # forces the printed result to start with a 0 character.

p   Prints the value of the corresponding printf argument as a pointer value; the actual format is dependent on the machine and the library implementation. The purpose of the p type code is to permit displaying the value of a pointer in a portable fashion and without prior knowledge of the size and characteristics of a pointer value.

s   Prints the string pointed to by the corresponding printf argument, which must be of type char*. A *precision* specifies the maximum number of leading characters of the string to be printed, and you can use it to print just a leading portion of a string, or to print strings not terminated with a null character.

If you specify a *width*, the string is right-justified and padded on the left with blanks to the specified length, unless you also specify the - flag.

u Prints the value of the corresponding `printf` argument as an unsigned decimal number. The *precision* specifies the minimum number of digits to print.

x, X Prints the value of the corresponding `printf` argument as an unsigned hexadecimal number. The x format prints the characters abcdef for the hexadecimal digits greater than 9; the X format prints the characters ABCDEF. The *precision* specifies the minimum number of hexadecimal digits (not bytes) to print. The special flag # causes the printed result to start with the characters 0x or 0X.

The following *flag* codes can appear immediately following the % character; the meaning of some flag characters depends on the *type* code and may be further described in the preceding list.

· Left justifies the result in a field of *width* characters. If you do not specify a *width*, the - flag has no effect.

+ Forces the result of a signed numeric conversion to begin with + when the value is positive. Ordinarily a leading sign prints only for negative values.

space Reserves a position in the printed result for a sign character. In other words, it prints a sign character of *space* for positive values and a sign character of – for negative values.

For type codes o, x, and X, prefixes the converted number with a special radix identifier. For type codes e, E, f, g, and G, forces a decimal point to appear in the printed result. For type codes g and G, also forces a zero decimal fraction to print.

0 For the integer and floating point conversions, forces the printed number to be padded on the left with leading zeros to the width specified by *width*. Ignored when a *precision* is also specified.

You must write the letter l (lowercase L) in front of an integer type code when the corresponding argument is of type `long int`. You can write the letter h in front of an integer type code when the corresponding argument is of type `short int`.

The compiler automatically promotes arguments of type `float` to `double`; indicate floating-point arguments of type `long double` by writing the letter `L` in front of the `f`, `e`, `E`, `g`, or `G` type code. The `l`, `h`, and `L` prefixes are meaningless in front of the `c`, `p`, and `s` type codes.

fprintf—Print Formatted String

```
int fprintf(FILE *stream, const char *format, ...);
```

Use `fprintf` to write the string pointed by `format` to file `stream`. The `fprintf` function is identical to the `printf` function, except that `fprintf` writes its output to a specified stream file, whereas `printf` writes to the standard output file.

The return value from `fprintf` is the number of characters written, or the value `EOF` if an error occurs during output.

sprintf—Print Formatted String to a Buffer

```
int sprintf(char *buf, const char *format, ...);
```

Use `sprintf` to substitute the value of arguments following the `format` argument into the string pointed to by `format`, and to store the resulting string in the character array pointed to by `buf`. The `sprintf` function adds a null character to the end of the stored text to form a conventional string.

The `sprintf` function is identical to `printf` except that the formatted result is stored in a buffer instead of being written to the standard output file. For `buf`, you must provide a character array large enough to contain the formatted string and the trailing null character; `sprintf` does not check for overflow and overwrites data following the buffer if it is too short.

The return value from sprintf is the number of characters stored in *buf*, excluding the trailing null character.

vprintf, vfprintf, vsprintf—Print Using Variable Argument Lists

```
int vprintf(const char *format, va_list args);
int vfprintf(FILE *stream, const char *format, va_list args);
int vsprintf(char *buf, const char *format, va_list args);
```

The vprintf function is equivalent to printf, vfprintf is equivalent to fprintf, and vsprintf is equivalent to sprintf, except that these functions accept a variable argument list instead of a conventional argument list.

You can use these functions to write your own text formatting routines using variable argument lists. For example, the following sample routine generates an error message from a format string and arguments supplied by the caller, and then terminates the program:

```
#include <stdio.h>
#include <stdarg.h>
#PRINTFLIKE1*/
void crash(int rc, char *format, ...)
{
    va_list args;

    fprintf(stderr, "myprog: ");        /* identify program */
    va_start(args,format);              /* initialize varargs */
    vfprintf(stderr, format, args);     /* format caller's message */
    va_end(args);                       /* end varargs */
    fputc('\n', stderr);                /* terminate caller's message */
```

```
    exit(rc);
    /*NOTREACHED*/
}
```

For more information about variable argument lists, see the UNIX documentation entry for *varargs* and the macros va_start, va_end, va_arg, and va_list.

scanf—Read Formatted Input

```
int scanf(const char *format, arg1, arg2, ...);
```

Use scanf to read character data from the standard input file, to convert the character data into an internal format, and to store the converted values into variables. The amount of data read, the number and type of conversions performed, and the number and type of arguments following *format*, are determined by special character sequences beginning with % in the format string.

The input stream is generally assumed to consist of a sequence of values separated by whitespace (blanks, tabs, and newline characters). The scanf function extracts the character strings between whitespace, converts each string to an internal value of the type described by the next % conversion specification in the format string, and stores the converted values in the successive arguments following *format*. To store a value, scanf requires a pointer to the variable, not the value of the variable; therefore, in most cases, you should write the arguments *arg1*, *arg2*, and so on, in the form &*variable*. Array names do not need to be prefixed with the address operator (&) because, according to C convention, an array name is a pointer to the first element of the array.

Each format specifier has the general format %*[*]*[width]type*. An asterisk, if present, signifies that scanf should scan the value described but not store it; no argument should be provided in the scanf function call for such values. A *width* value, if present, specifies the maximum number of data characters scanf should read and store.

The possible format specifiers are presented in the following list. For the integer conversions d, i, o, u, and x, write the letter l in front of the conversion type code to signify conversion to a long int; similarly, use the letter h to signify conversion to a short int. For the floating-point conversions e, f, and g, the letter l in front of the code signifies conversion to double, and L signifies conversion to a long double variable.

%   Expect a literal percent character in the input stream at this point. The character, if present, is ignored and the conversion continues. If a percent sign is not the next character, conversion halts.

d, i   Expect a signed decimal number. The number is converted to a binary signed integer value and stored at the location pointed to by the next argument. The argument should be of type int*. The conversion type i is equivalent to d.

u   Expect a signed or unsigned decimal number. The number is converted to a binary integer value and stored at the location pointed to by the next argument. The argument should be a pointer to an unsigned integer variable.

o   Expect an unsigned octal number. The input should consist only of octal digits (0–7); the digits are converted to a binary integer and stored at the location pointed to by the next argument. The argument should be a pointer to a signed or unsigned integer variable.

x   Expect an unsigned hexadecimal number. The input should consist of a sequence of the digits 0–9 and the letters a–f or A–F. The digits are converted to a binary integer and stored at the location pointed to by the next argument. The argument should be a pointer to a signed or unsigned integer variable.

e, f, g   Expect a floating-point number. The input may consist of any reasonable numeric format including a plain integer (ddd), a number with fractional digits (dd.ddd), or a mantissa and exponent (d.ddde±99). You can prefix the number with a leading sign character, either + or -. You may write an exponent with e or E, and may include or omit a sign. The corresponding argument is assumed to be a pointer to a float variable.

s   Expect a string. The string is copied to the character array pointed to by the next argument (which should be of type char* or char[]) up to the next whitespace character. A null character is appended to the stored characters.

c   Expect a sequence of characters. By default, one character is read and stored at the location pointed to by the corresponding argument. Specify a width value—for example, %5c—to read and store a fixed number of characters.

[Expect a sequence of characters comprised of a specified character set. Specify this conversion in the form %[abc] or %[a-c], where the characters enclosed in brackets are the characters expected in the input stream. Two characters separated by a dash define the range of characters included between them. To include a dash in the character set, write it immediately after the opening bracket ([-) or immediately before the closing bracket (-]). An opening bracket can be included in the character set by writing it anywhere; you must write a closing bracket immediately after the opening bracket for it to be taken as one of the characters in the set. For example, %[]abc] defines a set of four characters including the closing bracket. If a caret (^) immediately follows the opening bracket, the expected characters consist of any character *not* listed.

By default, one character is read and stored. To read and store multiple characters, specify a width value—for example, %5[a-z] to read and store five lowercase letters.

The return value from scanf indicates the number of values it was able to store. You can store less than the expected number of values if scanf finds a conflict between a format specifier and the actual input data—for example, when the format specifier is %d but the next input character is neither whitespace nor a digit. When a conflict occurs, scanf halts, returns the number of values converted and stored, and leaves the input stream positioned at the offending character.

If scanf finds the end-of-file before storing any values, it returns EOF. It also returns EOF if an error occurred reading the input stream. Use the feof and ferror macros to distinguish between the two meanings of EOF.

fscanf, sscanf—Read and Convert Text Data

```
int fscanf(FILE *stream, const char *format, ...);
int sscanf(char *buf, const char *format, ...);
```

The fscanf function is equivalent to scanf, except that fscanf reads from the file pointed to by *stream* rather than the standard input file.

The sscanf function is equivalent to scanf, except that sscanf scans and converts text in the character array pointed to by *buf*.

fseek—Set File Position

```
int fseek(FILE *stream, long offset, int mode);
```

Use the fseek function to change the current position of the file pointed to by *stream*.

The *mode* value specifies an integer code indicating the starting point with respect to which positioning is performed. The stdio.h header file defines the following symbolic modes:

SEEK_SET   The value of *offset* specifies the actual location within the file as a byte offset relative to 0.

SEEK_CUR   The value of *offset* specifies a number of bytes to add (if positive) or subtract (if negative) from the current file position; the sum of the current file position and the specified relative byte offset becomes the new file position.

SEEK_EOF   The value of *offset* specifies a number of bytes to be added to the end-of-file position. An *offset* value of 0 addresses the location immediately following the last byte of the file; a negative value addresses bytes backward from the end of file position. Normally you would not use a positive value of *offset* together with a mode of SEEK_EOF.

The fseek function resets any error and EOF indications for the file, and reestablishes orientation such that, for an update file, (mode "r+", "w+", or "a+"), the next data transfer request can be either a read or a write.

Notice that fseek permits positioning to locations beyond the end of the file. A subsequent write leaves a gap in the file where no data is written. This is entirely legal on UNIX systems; a later attempt to read any part of the gap returns zeros (null characters).

The fseek function returns –1 if it is unable to perform the requested seek operation; otherwise, it returns 0. A seek operation is expressly forbidden when the file is opened to a terminal device or to a pipe.

rewind—Reposition to the Start of a File

```
void rewind(FILE *stream);
```

Use rewind to position to the first byte of a file. The rewind call is equivalent in all respects to the call fseek(stream, 0L, SEEK_SET). See the fseek function for more information.

ftell—Return the Current File Position

```
long ftell(FILE *stream);
```

561

The ftell function returns the current file position as an offset from the beginning of the file. In other words, if the value returned by ftell is subsequently used in the call fseek(stream, ftellpos, SEEK_SET), the file position is restored to its current value.

Dynamic Memory Management

The UNIX system provides a flexible facility for dynamically allocating blocks of memory. The functions malloc, realloc, calloc, and free comprise the memory management package.

malloc—Allocate a Block of Memory

```
void *malloc(size_t size);
```

The malloc function attempts to allocate a block of memory at least *size* bytes long. If successful, the address of the block is returned as the value of the function; if unsuccessful, malloc returns a NULL pointer. Generally, you must cast the pointer returned by malloc to a pointer of the desired type, for example:

```
buffer = (char *)malloc(2048);
```

The pointer returned by malloc designates a memory area properly aligned for any use; its size is a multiple of the smallest unit that provides proper alignment for any type of data item. The allocated area is not cleared before being returned to you; if you require any particular initialization of the area, you must initialize it after the call to malloc.

You should never rely on `malloc` to allocate the requested storage. Instead, you should use a statement like the following to allocate memory:

```
struct employee *ptr;

if ((ptr = malloc(sizeof(*ptr)) == NULL) {
    fprintf(stderr, "not enough memory\n");
    exit(3);
}
```

realloc—Reallocate a Previously Allocated Block

```
void *realloc(void *ptr, size_t size);
```

The `realloc` function attempts to reallocate the area pointed to by *ptr* to a size of at least *size* bytes. If possible, the area is reallocated by extending it to the requested size. If it cannot be extended, the current area is released and a new area allocated; the contents of the previous memory block are copied to the new area up to the length of the previous block.

If `realloc` is successful, the address of the reallocated area is returned as the function's value. If `realloc` is unsuccessful it returns a NULL pointer. Notice that if `realloc` fails, the area you attempted to reallocate is released; references to the area are no longer valid and any data in the area is lost.

If you provide a *ptr* value to `realloc` that you did not previously obtain from `malloc`, `calloc`, or `realloc`, the result is unpredictable. In particular, the free memory chains used by the `malloc` package to locate blocks of memory may be destroyed, and future calls to `malloc`, `realloc`, or `calloc` may return invalid pointers or cause abnormal termination of your program.

calloc—Allocate and Initialize an Array

```
void *calloc(size_t size, size_t nelems);
```

The calloc function attempts to allocate an area large enough to contain *nelems* elements each of size *size*. If successful, calloc clears the entire area to binary zeros and returns a pointer to the first byte of the area. If unsuccessful, calloc returns a NULL pointer.

Generally, you must cast the pointer returned by calloc to a pointer of the desired type. For example:

```
short *table;

table = (short *)calloc(sizeof(short), 100);
```

free—Release a Previously Allocated Block

```
void free(void *ptr);
```

Use free to return an area of memory previously allocated with malloc, calloc, or realloc to the pool of available memory. For *ptr*, you must provide a pointer value that you previously received from one of the allocation functions. If you provide an improper value, the memory chains may become damaged, leading to future failure of the allocation functions and possible abnormal termination of your program. In particular, the NULL pointer is never a valid value for *ptr*.

Summary

This section introduces some of the most frequently used functions of the C standard function library; there are many more.

The numerous functions in the standard I/O package are designed to meet the needs of most programs; they are not suitable for all applications, and in fact are particularly unsuitable for programs that process the data in a file in random order. Because the functions are simple to use and optimized for efficient performance, you should become comfortable with them and use them whenever possible.

The `malloc` family of storage management functions provides the basic tools for allocating tables, structures, chained lists, and many other important data structures. The most common mistakes programmers make with these functions is failing to properly initialize a memory area returned by `malloc`, and ignoring a NULL return value. Whenever you cannot predict the amount of data your program will be called upon to process, and you require an arbitrary, possibly large number of structures or table elements, you should consider the use of dynamic storage allocation to manage your data. Because UNIX typically provides a very large amount of *heap* or uncommitted free memory for each active program, the flexibility and adaptability you gain from the use of dynamic memory management is considerable.

PART

III

Reference

Syntax of the C Language

The syntax of executable C statements is so straight-forward as to hardly require formal description. The complexity of the language derives from the richness of expression syntax and the recursive power of the declaration statement. Because of the unusual complexity of declarations and expressions, I cannot describe C syntax in any simple way.

The following "Syntax Description" section describes C syntax using a method of recursive definitions. Just as English grammar can be described using abstractions such as nouns, verbs, prepositional phrases, and conditional clauses, the following definition of C uses abstract *classes* to represent valid constructions, and *tokens* to designate the actual characters and symbols you type into your program.

The definitions proceed from the most general to the most specific. The first definition, that of a *source-file*, describes the largest syntactic object in the C language. From that first definition the entire remaining syntax description unfolds as you encounter more detailed language structures and their descriptions.

A class name ending in *s* such as *external-defs* or *declarations* is a special abbreviation meaning one or more repetitions of the object; in the source program, each repetition is separated from the next by whitespace (blanks, tabs, newlines, and comments). For example, *declarations* means repetitions of a *declaration*. The definition of declaration shows that a declaration ends with a semicolon. When you write several declarations in a row, you need no special separators between them other than whitespace.

A class name ending in *-list* indicates repetitions of the base class name separated by commas. For example, a *declaration* consists of a *type* followed by a *variable-list*. The definition of *variable* shows that a *variable* can be just a *declarator*; a *declarator* can be just a *named-object*, and a *named-object* can be just an *identifier*. Thus one example of a valid declaration is `int x, y, z;` where `int` is the *type* and `x, y, z` forms a *variable-list*.

Some class names are used but never defined. The class *identifier* means any valid name that is not also a reserved word. The class *typedef-name* means an identifier you declare with the `typedef` statement; a typedef name looks just like any other identifier and cannot be distinguished syntactically—the C compiler must use special tricks to identify usages of typedef names in a source program.

The entries for the names of syntactic classes are displayed in **boldface**. Within the definitions, the names of literal words and symbols appear in a `computer typeface`; a syntactic class name appears in ***bold italics*** when it is a required element of a larger structure; and a syntactic class name appears in *regular italics* when it is optional.

Other than identifiers and typedef names, which are really tokens that you invent, all other symbols in your program are predefined character sequences that have a special meaning in the C language. Examples of tokens are `auto`, `if`, and the operator `&&`. The syntax definitions show tokens in a **`bold computer typeface`** when the token is a required element, and in a `regular computer typeface` when the token is optional.

Syntactic elements (class names and tokens) written across the line define a sequence; you must write the elements in the sequence shown. A vertically stacked series of lines in a definition represents a set of choices; you can form valid instances of the class using any one of the lines as a model.

Finally, notice that a syntax definition can and usually does describe statement forms that, while syntactically valid, are meaningless and not allowed by the compiler. For example, the syntax description allows you to define a function as having storage class auto, but the C compiler does not accept such a declaration. Syntax description cannot take meaning into account; they deal only with the form of statements. There are additional restrictions and limitations on valid usage that you'll find in the main body of this book.

Syntax Description

Source-file:
    external-defs

External-def:
    function-definition
    declaration

Function-definition:
    type **declarator** *declarations* **block**

Declaration:
    type *variable-list* ;

Type:
    class **qualified-type**

Class:
    `auto`
    `register`
    `static`
    `extern`
    `typedef`

Qualified-type:
    `const` *basic-type*
    `volatile` *basic-type*
    basic-type

Basic-type:
> void
> *signed-numeric-type*
> *structure*
> *union*
> *enumeration*
> *typedef-name*

Signed-numeric-type:
> signed *numeric-type*
> unsigned *numeric-type*
> *numeric-type*

Numeric-type:
> char
> int
> short
> long
> short int
> long int
> float
> double
> long double

Structure:
> struct *identifier*
> struct *identifier* { *members* }

Union:
> union *identifier*
> union *identifier* { *members* }

Enumeration:
> enum *identifier*
> enum *identifier* { *enumerator-list* }

Enumerator:
> *identifier*
> *identifier* = *constant-exp*

Variable:
    declarator
    declarator = initializer

Initializer:
    assignment-exp
    { initializer-list }
    { initializer-list , }

Declarator:
    pointers **named-object**

Pointer:
    `*`
    `* const`
    `* volatile`

Named-object:
    identifier
    (declarator)
    named-object [*constant-exp*]
    named-object (*arglist*)
    named-object (*identifier-list*)

Arglist:
    parameter-decls
    parameter-decls , ...

Parameter-decl:
    type declarator
    type abstract-declarator

Abstract-declarator:
    pointers
    pointers **unnamed-object**

Unnamed-object:
    (abstract-declarator)
    unnamed-object [*constant-exp*]
    unnamed-object (*arglist*)

Member:
>*qualified-type struct-declarator-list* ;

Struct-declarator:
>*declarator*
>*declarator* : *constant-exp*

Typename:
>*qualified-type* abstract-declarator

Block:
>{ *declarations statements* }

Statement:
>*label* **statement**
>**block**
>*executable-statement*

Executable-statement:
>`if` (*exp*) *statement*
>`if` (*exp*) *statement* `else` *statement*
>`switch` (*exp*) *statement*
>`while` (*exp*) *statement*
>`do` *statement* `while` (*exp*) ;
>`for` (*exp* ; *exp* ; *exp*) *statement*
>`goto` *identifier* ;
>`break` ;
>`continue` ;
>`return` *exp* ;

Exp:
>*assignment-exp*
>*exp* , *assignment-exp*

Assignment-exp:
>*conditional-exp*
>*unary-exp aop assignment-exp*

Aop:
>`=`
>`*=`
>`/=`

%=

+=

-=

<<=

>>=

&=

^=

¦=

Conditional-exp:

logical-exp

logical-exp **?** *exp* **:** *conditional-exp*

Constant-exp:

conditional-exp

Logical-exp:

relational-exp

logical-exp **¦¦** *logical-exp*

logical-exp **&&** *logical-exp*

logical-exp **&** *logical-exp*

logical-exp **¦** *logical-exp*

logical-exp **^** *logical-exp*

Relational-exp:

shift-exp

relational-exp **==** *relational-exp*

relational-exp **!=** *relational-exp*

relational-exp **<** *relational-exp*

relational-exp **>** *relational-exp*

relational-exp **<=** *relational-exp*

relational-exp **>=** *relational-exp*

Shift-exp:

arithmetic-exp

shift-exp **<<** *arithmetic-exp*

shift-exp **>>** *arithmetic-exp*

Arithmetic-exp:

unary-exp

arithmetic-exp **+** *arithmetic-exp*

arithmetic-exp - arithmetic-exp
        arithmetic-exp * arithmetic-exp
        arithmetic-exp / arithmetic-exp
        arithmetic-exp % arithmetic-exp

Unary-exp:

    postfix-exp
    (*typename*) *unary-exp*
    & *uexp*
    * *uexp*
    + *uexp*
    - *uexp*
    ~ *uexp*
    ! *uexp*
    ++ *uexp*
    -- *uexp*
    sizeof *uexp*
    sizeof (*typename*)

Postfix-exp:

    primary-exp
    postfix-exp [*exp*]
    postfix-exp (*argument-list*)
    postfix-exp . *identifier*
    postfix-exp -> *identifier*
    postfix-exp ++
    postfix-exp --

Primary-exp:

    identifier
    constant
    string
    (*exp*)

Argument:

    assignment-x-exp

Constant:

    integer-constant
    character-constant
    floating-constant
    enumeration-constant

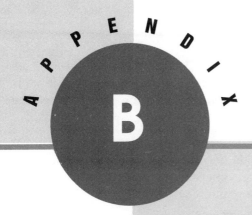
Operator Priorities

Appendix A, "Syntax of the C Language," describes the parts of an expression in detail. At a more general level, every C expression consists of terms and operators; the operators act on the terms of the expression to yield new calculated values. When an expression contains more than one operator, the sequence in which the operators act can be governed explicitly with parentheses or allowed to act in a default order determined by the compiler. The C language associates a *priority* with each operator. In the absence of parentheses, the operator with greater priority acts before the operator with lesser priority.

Table B.1 describes the expression operators in order of decreasing priority; operators listed earlier in the table take precedence over operators that follow. Grouping parentheses are not shown in the table; the parentheses operators shown are those of function invocation. Parentheses used for grouping cause the expression contained within them to be treated as a unit: The expression within the parentheses is evaluated entirely before using the value in any neighboring operations outside the parentheses.

Operators listed on the same line have equal priority. Neighboring operators having the same priority are evaluated in the order specified in the *Associativity* column. In particular, notice that adjacent unary operators and successive assignments are evaluated starting with the rightmost subexpression.

Please notice that the C compiler does not guarantee the order in which it computes subexpressions of an expression. Although an expression enclosed in parentheses is evaluated as a unit, its evaluation may occur earlier than necessary and the result saved until used. Subexpressions having side effects may yield an unpredictable result if the side affect can change the value of any of the terms of the expression. If you require a specific order of evaluation because of side effects, you may need to divide the expression into several statements.

Table B.1. Operator priorities.

Priority	Operator	Name or Function	Associativity
1	( )	Function call	Left to right
1	[ ]	Array subscript	
1	->	Pointer dereference	
1	.	Structure member	
2	!	Logical NOT	Right to left
2	~	Complement	
2	++	Increment	
2	- -	Decrement	
2	+	Plus sign	
2	-	Minus sign	
2	*	Pointer dereference	
2	&	Address of lvalue	

Priority	Operator	Name or Function	Associativity
2	`(type)`	Cast	
2	`sizeof`	Size of lvalue	
3	`*`	Multiplication	Left to right
3	`/`	Division	
3	`%`	Modulus (remainder)	
4	`+`	Addition	Left to right
4	`-`	Subtraction	
5	`<<`	Left shift	Left to right
5	`>>`	Right shift	
6	`<`	Less than	Left to right
6	`>`	Greater than	
6	`<=`	Less than or equal	
6	`>=`	Greater than or equal	
7	`==`	Equal to	Left to right
7	`!=`	Not equal	
8	`&`	Bitwise AND	Left to right
9	`^`	Bitwise Exclusive OR	Left to right
10	`¦`	Bitwise Inclusive OR	Left to right
11	`&&`	Logical AND	Left to right
12	`¦¦`	Logical OR	Left to right
13	`?:`	Conditional	Right to left
14	`=`	Assignment	Right to left
14	`+=`	Add	
14	`-=`	Subtract	
14	`*=`	Multiply	

continues

579

Table B.1. continued

Priority	Operator	Name or Function	Associativity
14	/=	Divide	
14	%=	Modulus	
14	&=	AND	
14	^=	Exclusive OR	
14	¦=	Inclusive OR	
14	<<=	Shift left	
14	>>=	Shift right	
15	,	Comma	Left to right

Preprocessor Syntax

The preprocessor syntax is far less sophisticated than that of the C language proper, and it is possible to describe it in a much more visual manner than C.

In the syntax description, *identifier* is any name beginning with a letter or underscore and followed by zero or more letters, digits, and underscores.

The ANSI C preprocessor treats the source file as a sequence of *tokens*. You may also write a token sequence as part of some preprocessor directives. A *token* is a blank-delimited sequence of alphanumeric characters, a special character, or a sequence of special characters defined by the C language: `while` is a token, as are the arbitrary words `unix` and `basket`, and the operator `&&`.

A quoted string is *not* a token and you may not use it as part of a token sequence. Some preprocessor directives (notably `#include`) accept a string as a value. Cases where the syntax allows a string value are clearly indicated in the syntax description, and you may not use strings in any other ways.

The `if` and `elif` directives accept a constant expression. The preprocessor uses the C definition of a constant expression, and you may use any of the C operators except `sizeof`, cast, or the postfix operators (), [], ->, or . (dot) to form a constant expression. Notice, however, that a constant expression may use as terms only literal integers and symbols defined by the `define` directive; the preprocessor cannot evaluate variables.

You may follow the `if`, `ifdef`, `ifndef`, `elif`, and `else` directives by one or more lines of text. Preprocessor directive lines may appear among the text lines, and are processed if the text section is processed; otherwise, they are ignored. The effect enables the use of nested `if-else-endif` structures.

Your C compiler system may support directives in addition to those specified by the ANSI C standard shown here. The standard calls for the preprocessor to ignore directives it does not recognize, as an aid to porting C code to other computer systems. If you use nonstandard directives in your code, the directives may perform other than the expected function or cause fatal compilation errors when the code is processed on different systems.

Syntax Description

Directives:

```
# define identifier tokens
# define identifier( identifier , ... , identifier ) tokens

# error tokens

# if constant-exp
# ifdef identifier
# ifndef identifier
text
# elif constant-exp
text
# else
```

```
text
# endif

# include <filename>
# include "filename"
# include tokens

# line number "filename"
# line number

# pragma tokens

# undef identifier
```

Operators:

`defined(identifier)`

> Used as a term in a conditional expression, it has the value 1 (true) if *identifier* was defined by the `define` directive or by the `-D` option of the `cc` command; otherwise, the value is 0 (false). After `undef`, an identifier appears to be undefined.

`#arg`

> In a macro definition, *#arg* generates `"value"` where *value* is the value of the macro argument *arg*.

`arg1 ## arg2`

> In a macro definition, this generates *value1value2* where *value1* and *value2* are the values of the macro arguments *arg1* and *arg2*.

Predefined Macros

The ANSI C standard specifies that the C preprocessor will automatically define several *identifier* symbols before processing the source file. You may use these symbols without defining them. A specific preprocessor implementation may or may not permit you to `undef` and redefine them.

__LINE__   The line number of the line in which this macro appears, as a decimal number: 10

__FILE__   The filename of the source file in which this macro appears, as a string: "user.h"

__DATE__   The current date indicated by the operating system, as a string: "Jan 01 1992"

__TIME__   The current time indicated by the operating system, as a string: "04:59:59"

__STDC__   The constant 1 if the compiler conforms to all ANSI C specifications *and rejects all nonconforming code*; 0 otherwise. The UNIX compiler may indicate a value of 1 for the __STDC__ macro only when the cc command line specifies certain options.

APPENDIX

D

Standard Function Library

UNIX Header Files

The C compiler system for UNIX provides at least the following header files in the /usr/include directory. Additional header files may be present depending on the installed features and the specific version of UNIX in use.

a.out.h	filehdr.h	malloc.h	scnhdr.h	tar.h
agent.h	float.h	math.h	search.h	term.h
aouthdr.h	ftw.h	memory.h	setjmp.h	termio.h
ar.h	grp.h	mnttab.h	sgtty.h	termios.h
assert.h	ieeefp.h	mon.h	shadow.h	time.h
core.h	langinfo.h	nan.h	siginfo.h	ulimit.h
cpio.h	ldfcn.h	nl_types.h	signal.h	unctrl.h
crypt.h	libelf.h	nlist.h	stand.h	unistd.h
ctype.h	libgen.h	prof.h	std.h	ustat.h
curses.h	libgenIO.h	pw.h	stdarg.h	utime.h
dirent.h	libw.h	pwd.h	stddef.h	utmp.h
dlfcn.h	limits.h	regexp.h	stdio.h	utmpx.h
elf.h	linenum.h	regexpr.h	stdlib.h	values.h
errno.h	link.h	reloc.h	string.h	varargs.h
fatal.h	locale.h	rje.h	stropts.h	wait.h
fcntl.h	maillock.h	sac.h	syms.h	windows.h

The following is a list of header files available in the directory /usr/include/sys. Many of these header files are automatically included by a header file of the same name in the /usr/include directory.

acct.h	fcntl.h	shm.h	stat.h	uadmin.h
ascii.h	ioctl.h	sigaction.h	termio.h	ulimit.h
dir.h	priocntl.h	siginfo.h	time.h	unistd.h
dirent.h	sem.h	signal.h	types.h	utsname.h
errno.h	sema.h	socket.h		

UNIX Standard Function Library

The C compiler system of System V Release 4 includes the following functions in the standard C library and the math library. Additional functions are present in the standard libraries depending on the installed features and the specific version of UNIX you are using. Other features such as networking or the X Window System provide additional function libraries.

The functions are listed in alphabetical order by name. Where possible a function prototype is given for each function so you can compare the arguments expected by a UNIX function to the function definition you may be familiar with in another environment.

The existence of a UNIX function having the same name, return value, and arguments as a function in another environment (such as MS-DOS) does not guarantee that the two functions will operate in equivalent fashion. However, because the UNIX standard function library has served as a model for the implementation of C in non-UNIX environments, equivalence of function prototypes can be safely construed as evidence of equivalent function.

Non-UNIX environments sometimes provide several variants of a function to accomodate different memory addressing schemes. The UNIX function library does not incorporate such variants because UNIX offers only one very large address array to each active program; it is equivalent in most respects to the MS-DOS Large or Huge memory models. In particular, you will find that UNIX offers no `farmalloc` function. C programs developed in a non-UNIX environment should convert `farmalloc` and similar function calls to the standard `malloc` family of functions.

```
void     __assert(const char *, const char *, int);
int      __filbuf(FILE *);
int      __flsbuf(int, FILE *);
void     _exit(int);
int      _tolower(int);
int      _toupper(int);
long     a64l(const char *);
void     abort(void);
int      abs(int);
int      access(const char *, int);
int      acct(const char *);
double   acos(double);
float    acosf(float);
double   acosh(double);
int      advance(const char *string, const char *expbuf);
unsigned alarm(unsigned);
int      ascftime(char *, const char *, const struct tm *);
char*    asctime(const struct tm *);
double   asin(double);
```

```
float   asinf(float);
double  asinh(double);
double  atan(double);
double  atan2(double, double);
float   atan2f(float, float);
float   atanf(float);
double  atanh(double);
int     atexit(void (*)(void));
double  atof(const char *);
int     atoi(const char *);
long    atol(const char *);
char*   basename(char *);
char*   bgets(char *, size_t, FILE *, char *);
int     brk(void *);
void*   bsearch(const void *, const void *, size_t, size_t,
                int (*)(const void *, const void *));
size_t  bufsplit(char *, size_t, char *);
void*   calloc(size_t, size_t);
double  cbrt(double);
double  ceil(double);
float   ceilf(float);
int     cftime(char *, char *, const time_t *);
int     chdir(const char *);
int     chown(const char *, uid_t, gid_t);
int     chroot(const char *);
void    clearerr(FILE *);
clock_t clock(void);
int     close(int);
int     closedir(DIR *);
char*   compile(const char *instring, char *expbuf, char *endbuf);
char*   copylist(const char *, off_t *);
double  copysign(double, double);
double  cos(double);
float   cosf(float);
double  cosh(double);
float   coshf(float);
int     creat(const char *, mode_t);
char*   crypt(const char *, const char *);
```

```
int     crypt_close(int *);
char*   ctermid(char *);
char*   ctime (const time_t *);
char*   cuserid(char *);
char*   des_crypt(const char *, const char *);
void    des_encrypt(char *, int);
void    des_setkey(const char *);
double  difftime(time_t, time_t);
char*   dirname(char *);
div_t   div(int, int);
int     dlclose(void *);
char*   dlerror(void);
void*   dlopen(char *, int);
void*   dlsym(void *, char *);
double  drand48(void);
int     dup(int);
int     dup2(int, int);
int     eaccess(const char *, int);
char*   ecvt(double, int, int *, int *);
void    encrypt(char *, int);
void    endgrent(void);
void    endpwent(void);
void    endutent(void);
void    endutxent(void);
double  erand48(unsigned short *);
double  erf(double);
double  erfc(double);
int     execl(const char *, const char *, ...);
int     execle(const char *, const char *, ...);
int     execlp(const char *, const char *, ...);
int     execv(const char *, char *const *);
int     execve(const char *, char *const *, char *const *);
int     execvp(const char *, char *const *);
void    exit(int);
double  exp(double);
float   expf(float);
double  fabs(double);
float   fabsf(float);
```

```
int        fattach(int, const char *);
int        fchdir(int);
int        fchown(int,uid_t, gid_t);
int        fclose(FILE *);
int        fcntl(int, int, ...);
char*      fcvt(double, int, int *, int *);
int        fdetach(const char *);
FILE*      fdopen(int, const char *);
int        feof(FILE *);
int        ferror(FILE *);
int        fflush(FILE *);
int        ffs(const int);
int        fgetc(FILE *);
struct group * fgetgrent(FILE *);
int        fgetpos(FILE *, fpos_t *);
struct passwd * fgetpwent(FILE *);
char*      fgets(char *, int, FILE *);
int        fileno(FILE *);
int        finite(double);
double     floor(double);
float      floorf(float);
double     fmod(double, double);
float      fmodf(float, float);
FILE*      fopen(const char *, const char *);
pid_t      fork(void);
long       fpathconf(int, int);
fpclass_t  fpclass(double);
fp_except  fpgetmask(void);
fp_rnd     fpgetround(void);
fp_except  fpgetsticky(void);
int        fprintf(FILE *, const char *, ...);
fp_except  fpsetmask(fp_except);
fp_rnd     fpsetround(fp_rnd);
fp_except  fpsetsticky(fp_except);
int        fputc(int, FILE *);
int        fputs(const char *, FILE *);
size_t     fread(void *, size_t, size_t, FILE *);
void       free(void *);
```

```
FILE*   freopen(const char *, const char *, FILE *);
double  frexp(double, int *);
int     fscanf(FILE *, const char *, ...);
int     fseek(FILE *, long, int);
int     fsetpos(FILE *, const fpos_t *);
int     fsync(int);
long    ftell(FILE *);
int     ftruncate(int, off_t);
int     ftw(const char *, int (*)(const char *, const struct stat *,
            int), int);
size_t  fwrite(const void *, size_t, size_t, FILE *);
double  gamma(double);
char*   gcvt(double, int, char *);
int     getc(FILE *);
int     getchar(void);
char*   getcwd(char *, int);
struct tm * getdate(const char *);
gid_t   getegid(void);
char*   getenv(const char *);
uid_t   geteuid(void);
gid_t   getgid(void);
struct group * getgrent(void);
struct group * getgrgid(gid_t);
struct group * getgrnam(const char *);
int     getgroups(int, gid_t *);
char*   getlogin(void);
int     getmsg(int, struct strbuf *, struct strbuf *, int *);
int     getopt(int, char *const *, const char *);
char*   getpass(const char *);
pid_t   getpgid(pid_t);
pid_t   getpgrp(void);
pid_t   getpid(void);
int     getpmsg(int, struct strbuf *, struct strbuf *, int *, int *);
pid_t   getppid(void);
int     getpw(int, char *);
struct passwd * getpwent(void);
struct passwd * getpwnam(const char *);
struct passwd * getpwuid(uid_t);
```

```
char*   gets(char *);
pid_t   getsid(pid_t);
struct spwd * getspent(void), *fgetspent(FILE *), *getspnam(const char *);
int     getsubopt(char **, char *const *, char **);
uid_t   getuid(void);
struct utmp * getutent(void);
struct utmp * getutid(const struct utmp *);
struct utmp * getutline(const struct utmp *);
void    getutmp(const struct utmpx *, struct utmp *);
void    getutmpx(const struct utmp *, struct utmpx *);
struct utmpx * getutxent(void);
struct utmpx * getutxid(const struct utmpx *);
struct utmpx * getutxline(const struct utmpx *);
int     getw(FILE *);
int     gmatch(const char *, const char *);
struct tm * gmtime(const time_t *);
int     gsignal(int);
double  hypot(double, double);
int     initgroups(const char *, gid_t);
int     ioctl(int, int, ...);
int     isalnum(int);
int     isalpha(int);
int     isascii(int);
int     isatty(int);
int     iscntrl(int);
int     isdigit(int);
int     isencrypt(const char *, size_t);
int     isgraph(int);
int     islower(int);
int     isnan(double);
int     isnand(double);
int     isnanf(float);
int     isprint(int);
int     ispunct(int);
int     isspace(int);
int     isupper(int);
int     isxdigit(int);
```

```
double   j0(double);
double   j1(double);
double   jn(int, double);
long     jrand48(unsigned short *);
int      kill(pid_t, int);
void     l3tol(long *, const char *, int);
char*    l64a(long);
long     labs(long);
int      lchown(const char *, uid_t, gid_t);
void     lcong48(unsigned short *);
int      ldaclose(LDFILE *);
int      ldahread(LDFILE *, ARCHDR *);
LDFILE*  ldaopen(const char *, LDFILE *);
int      ldclose(LDFILE *);
double   ldexp(double, int);
int      ldfhread(LDFILE *, FILHDR *);
char*    ldgetname(LDFILE *, const SYMENT *);
ldiv_t   ldiv(long, long);
int      ldlinit(LDFILE *, long);
int      ldlitem(LDFILE *, unsigned int, LINENO *);
int      ldlread(LDFILE *, long, unsigned int, LINENO *);
int      ldlseek(LDFILE *, unsigned int);
int      ldnlseek(LDFILE *, const char *);
int      ldnrseek(LDFILE *, const char *);
int      ldnshread(LDFILE *, const char *, SCNHDR *);
int      ldnsseek(LDFILE *, const char *);
int      ldohseek(LDFILE *);
LDFILE*  ldopen(const char *, LDFILE *);
int      ldrseek(LDFILE *, unsigned int);
int      ldshread(LDFILE *, unsigned int, SCNHDR *);
int      ldsseek(LDFILE *, unsigned int);
long     ldtbindex(LDFILE *);
int      ldtbread(LDFILE *, long, SYMENT *);
int      ldtbseek(LDFILE *);
double   lgamma(double);
int      link(const char *, const char *);
struct lconv * localeconv(void);
struct tm * localtime(const time_t *);
```

593

```
int     lockf(int, int, long);
double  log(double);
double  log10(double);
float   log10f(float);
double  logb(double);
float   logf(float);
char*   logname(void);
void    longjmp(jmp_buf, int);
long    lrand48(void);
off_t   lseek(int, off_t, int);
void    ltol3(char *, const long *, int);
int     maillock(char *user, int retrycnt);
int     mailunlock(void);
struct utmpx * makeutx(const struct utmpx *);
void*   malloc(size_t);
int     matherr(struct exception *);
int     mblen(const char *, size_t);
size_t  mbstowcs(wchar_t *, const char *, size_t);
int     mbtowc(wchar_t *, const char *, size_t);
void*   memalign(size_t, size_t);
void*   memccpy(void *, const void *, int, size_t);
void*   memchr(const void *, int, size_t);
int     memcmp(const void *, const void *, size_t);
void*   memcpy(void *, const void *, size_t);
void*   memmove(void *, const void *, size_t);
void*   memset(void *, int, size_t);
int     mincore(caddr_t, size_t, char *);
int     mkdirp(const char *, mode_t);
char*   mktemp(char *);
time_t  mktime(struct tm *);
double  modf(double, double *);
float   modff(float, float *);
struct utmpx * modutx(const struct utmpx *);
long    mrand48(void);
double  nextafter(double, double);
int     nftw(const char *, int (*)(const char *,
            const struct stat *, int, struct FTW *), int, int);
int     nice(int);
```

```
long     nrand48(unsigned short *);
int      open(const char *, int, ...);
DIR*     opendir(const char *);
int      p2close(FILE *[2]);
int      p2open(const char *, FILE *[2]);
long     pathconf(const char *, int);
char*    pathfind(const char *, const char *, const char *);
int      pause(void);
int      pclose(FILE *);
void     perror(const char *);
int      pipe(int *);
FILE*    popen(const char *, const char *);
double   pow(double, double);
float    powf(float, float);
int      printf(const char *, ...);
void     profil(unsigned short *, unsigned int, unsigned int,
                unsigned int);
void     psiginfo(siginfo_t *, char *);
int      ptrace(int, pid_t, int, int);
int      putc(int, FILE *);
int      putchar(int);
int      putenv(char *);
int      putmsg(int, const struct strbuf *,
                const struct strbuf *, int);
int      putpmsg(int, const struct strbuf *, const struct strbuf *,
                 int, int);
int      putpwent(const struct passwd *, FILE *);
int      puts(const char *);
int      putspent(const struct spwd *, FILE *), lckpwdf(void),
                  ulckpwdf(void);
struct utmp * pututline(const struct utmp *);
struct utmpx * pututxline(const struct utmpx *);
int      putw(int, FILE *);
void     qsort(void *, size_t, size_t, int (*)
                (const void *, const void *));
int      raise(int);
int      rand(void);
int      read(int, void *, unsigned);
```

```
struct dirent * readdir(DIR *);
int     readlink(const char *, void *, int);
void*   realloc(void *, size_t);
char*   realpath(char *, char *);
char*   regcmp(const char *, ...);
char*   regex(const char *, const char *, ...);
double  remainder(double, double);
int     remove(const char *);
int     rename(const char *, const char *);
void    rewind(FILE *);
void    rewinddir(DIR *);
double  rint(double);
int     rmdir(const char *);
int     rmdirp(char *, char *);
int     run_crypt(long, char *, unsigned, int *);
int     run_setkey(int *, const char *);
void*   sbrk(int);
double  scalb(double, double);
int     scanf(const char *, ...);
unsigned short * seed48(unsigned short *);
void    seekdir(DIR *, long);
void    setbuf(FILE *, char *);
int     setgid(gid_t);
void    setgrent(void);
int     setgroups(int, const gid_t *);
int     setjmp(jmp_buf);
void    setkey(const char *);
char*   setlocale(int, const char *);
int     setpgid(pid_t, pid_t);
pid_t   setpgrp(void);
void    setpwent(void);
pid_t   setsid(void);
void    setspent(void), endspent(void);
int     setuid(uid_t);
void    setutent(void);
void    setutxent(void);
int     setvbuf(FILE *, char *, int, size_t);
long    sgetl(const char *);
```

```
int      sigaction(int, const struct sigaction *, struct sigaction *);
int      sigaddset(sigset_t *, int);
int      sigaltstack(const stack_t *, stack_t *);
int      sigdelset(sigset_t *, int);
int      sigemptyset(sigset_t *);
int      sigfillset(sigset_t *);
int      sighold(int);
int      sigignore(int);
int      sigismember(const sigset_t *, int);
void     siglongjmp(sigjmp_buf, int);
void     (*signal(int, void (*)(int)))(int);
int      sigpause(int);
int      sigpending(sigset_t *);
int      sigprocmask(int, const sigset_t *, sigset_t *);
int      sigrelse(int);
int      sigsend(idtype_t, id_t, int);
int      sigsendset(const procset_t *, int);
void     (*sigset(int, void (*)(int)))(int);
int      sigsetjmp(sigjmp_buf, int);
int      sigsuspend(sigset_t *);
double   sin(double);
float    sinf(float);
double   sinh(double);
float    sinhf(float);
unsigned sleep(unsigned);
int      sprintf(char *, const char *, ...);
void     sputl(long, char *);
double   sqrt(double);
float    sqrtf(float);
void     srand(unsigned int);
void     srand48(long);
int      sscanf(const char *, const char *, ...);
int      (*ssignal(int, int (*)(int)))(int);
int      step(const char *string, const char *expbuf);
int      stime(const time_t *);
char*    strcadd(char *, const char *);
char*    strcat(char *, const char *);
char*    strccpy(char *, const char *);
```

```
char*       strchr(const char *, int);
int         strcmp(const char *, const char *);
int         strcoll(const char *, const char *);
char*       strcpy(char *, const char *);
size_t      strcspn(const char *, const char *);
char*       strdup(const char *);
char*       streadd(char *, const char *, const char *);
char*       strecpy(char *, const char *, const char *);
char*       strerror(int);
int         strfind(const char *, const char *);
size_t      strftime(char *, size_t, const char *, const struct tm *);
size_t      strlen(const char *);
char*       strncat(char *, const char *, size_t);
int         strncmp(const char *, const char *, size_t);
char*       strncpy(char *, const char *, size_t);
char*       strpbrk(const char *, const char *);
char*       strrchr(const char *, int);
char*       strrspn(const char *, const char *);
size_t      strspn(const char *, const char *);
char*       strstr(const char *, const char *);
double      strtod(const char *, char **);
char*       strtok(char *, const char *);
long        strtol(const char *, char **, int);
unsigned long int strtoul(const char *, char **, int);
char*       strtrns(const char *, const char *, const char *, char *);
size_t      strxfrm(char *, const char *, size_t);
void        swab(const char *, char *, int);
int         symlink(const char *, const char *);
void        sync(void);
long        sysconf(int);
int         system(const char *);
double      tan(double);
float       tanf(float);
double      tanh(double);
float       tanhf(float);
pid_t       tcgetpgrp(int);
int         tcsetpgrp(int, pid_t);
long        telldir(DIR *);
```

```
char*    tempnam(const char *, const char *);
time_t   time(time_t *);
FILE*    tmpfile(void);
char*    tmpnam(char *);
int      toascii(int);
int      tolower(int);
int      toupper(int);
int      truncate(const char *, off_t);
char*    ttyname(int);
int      ttyslot(void);
void     tzset(void);
long     ulimit(int, ...);
int      ungetc(int, FILE *);
int      unlink(const char *);
int      unordered(double, double);
void     updwtmp(const char *, struct utmp *);
void     updwtmpx(const char *, struct utmpx *);
int      ustat(dev_t, struct ustat *);
int      utime(const char *, const struct utimbuf *);
int      utmpname(const char *);
int      utmpxname(const char *);
void     va_end(va_list);
void*    valloc(size_t);
pid_t    vfork(void);
int      vfprintf(FILE *, const char *, void *);
int      vprintf(const char *, void *);
int      vsprintf(char *, const char *, void *);
pid_t    wait(int *);
int      waitid(idtype_t, id_t, siginfo_t *, int);
pid_t    waitpid(pid_t, int *, int);
size_t   wcstombs(char *, const wchar_t *, size_t);
int      wctomb(char *, wchar_t);
int      write(int, const void *, unsigned);
double   y0(double);
double   y1(double);
double   yn(int, double);
```

ANSI Defined Functions

To facilitate the transport of C programs between differing hardware and operating-system configurations, the ANSI standard defines a selected group of functions that any ANSI C conforming compiler must provide. The standard also specifies header files to use with the functions. To ensure maximum portability between differing computer systems, you should, wherever possible, restrict your use of system-provided header files and functions to the set in the following list.

The ANSI standard set of header files includes the following:

```
<assert.h>
<ctype.h>
<errno.h>
<float.h>
<limits.h>
<locale.h>
<math.h>
<setjmp.h>
<signal.h>
<stdarg.h>
<stddef.h>
<stdio.h>
<stdlib.h>
<string.h>
<time.h>
```

Functions for input and output include the following:

```
FILE *fopen(const char *filename, const char *mode);
FILE *freopen(const char *filename, const char *mode, FILE *stream);
int   fflush(FILE *stream);
int   fclose(FILE *stream);
int   remove(const char *filename);
int   rename(const char *oldname, const char *newname);
FILE *tmpfile(void);
char *tmpnam(char s[]);
int   setvbuf(FILE *stream, char *buf, int mode, size_t size);
void  setbuf(FILE *stream, char *buf);
```

A family of input/output functions assists with the conversion of machine formatted binary data to and from an external printed format. These functions are as follows:

```
int    fprintf(FILE *stream, const char *format, ...);
int    printf(const char *format, ...);
int    sprintf(char *buf, const char *format, ...);
int    vprintf(const char *format, va_list arg);
int    vfprintf(FILE *stream, const char *format, va_list arg);
int    vsprintf(char *buf, const char *format, va_list arg);
int    fscanf(FILE *stream, const char *format, ...);
int    scanf(const char *format, ...);
int    sscanf(char *string, const char *format, ...);
```

The following functions read and write one character or one string at a time:

```
int    fgetc(FILE *stream);
char *fgets(char *s, int n, FILE *stream);
int    fputc(int c, FILE *stream);
int    fputs(const char *s, FILE *stream);
int    getc(FILE *stream);
int    getchar(void);
char *gets(char *s);
int    putc(int c, FILE *stream);
int    putchar(int c);
int    puts(const char *s);
int    ungetc(int c, FILE *stream);
```

The direct input and output functions read or write a block of data of fixed specified size:

```
size_t fread(void *ptr, size_t size, size_t count, FILE *stream);
size_t fwrite(void *ptr, size_t size, size_t count, FILE *stream);
```

A number of functions control the current position within a stream file. The functions in the following list are generally usable only with disk files. In UNIX, file positions form a continuous series of adjacent locations permitting straightforward access to any part of a file. Other operating systems may impose restrictions on the use of file positioning functions.

```
int    fseek(FILE *stream, long offset, int origin);
long   ftell(FILE *stream);
```

601

```
void   rewind(FILE *stream);
int    fgetpos(FILE *stream, fpos_t *ptr);
int    fsetpos(FILE *stream, const fpos_t *ptr);
```

A number of functions (which may be implemented as preprocessor macros) examine or manipulate the FILE structure directly, to detect or reset error conditions, or to provide information about the stream file. These functions are as follows:

```
void   clearerr(FILE *stream);
int    feof(FILE *stream);
int    ferror(FILE *stream);
void   perror(const char *msg);
```

The functions defined in the ctype.h header file perform classification tests on an individual character. They operate in a manner intended to be insensitive to the characteristics of the particular character set of the machine, and you should use them whenever you cannot assume the ASCII character. All these functions accept an integer character and return a logical *true* or *false* value. They are as follows:

```
int    isalnum(int c);
int    isalpha(int c);
int    iscntrl(int c);
int    isdigit(int c);
int    isgraph(int c);
int    islower(int c);
int    isprint(int c);
int    ispunct(int c);
int    isspace(int c);
int    isupper(int c);
int    isxdigit(int c);
int    tolower(int c);
int    toupper(int c);
```

The string-handling functions defined in the string.h header file assist with examining and manipulating strings. They are:

```
char * strcpy(char *s, const char *t);
char * strncpy(char *s, const char *t, size_t n);
char * strcat(char *s, const char *t);
```

```
char * strncat(char *s, const char *t, size_t n);
int    strcmp(const char *s, const char *t);
int    strncmp(const char *s, const char *t);
char * strchr(const char *s, int c);
char * strrchr(const char *s, int c);
size_t strspn(const char *s, const char *t);
size_t strcspn(const char *s, const char *t);
char * strpbrk(const char *s, const char *t);
char * strstr(const char *s, const char *t);
size_t strlen(const char *s);
char * strerror(int n);
char * strtok(char *s, const char *t);
```

The following additional functions defined in memory.h examine or manipulate character arrays of fixed specified size and are useful when the character is not delimited by a trailing null character.

```
void *memcpy(void *s, const void *t, size_t n);
void *memmove(void *s, const void *t, size_t n);
int   memcmp(const void *s, const void *t, size_t n);
void *memchr(const void *s, int c, size_t n);
void *memset(void *s, int c, size_t n);
```

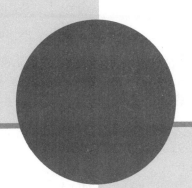

Index

Symbols

A

Programming for UNIX

F

M

N

O

Q

R

Programming for UNIX

T

U